The Legend Returns
and Dies Harder
Another Day

The Legend Returns and Dies Harder Another Day

Essays on Film Series

Edited by JENNIFER FORREST

McFarland & Company, Inc., Publishers
Jefferson, North Carolina, and London

LIBRARY OF CONGRESS CATALOGUING-IN-PUBLICATION DATA

    The legend returns and dies harder another day : essays on film series / edited by Jennifer Forrest.
    p.   cm.
    Includes bibliographical references and index.

    ISBN 978-0-7864-3943-0
    softcover : 50# alkaline paper ∞

    1. Film series — History and criticism.   I. Forrest, Jennifer, 1958–
PN1995.9.S34L44   2008
791.43'75 — dc22   2008026991

British Library cataloguing data are available

©2008 Jennifer Forrest. All rights reserved

No part of this book may be reproduced or transmitted in any form or by any means, electronic or mechanical, including photocopying or recording, or by any information storage and retrieval system, without permission in writing from the publisher.

Cover photograph ©2008 Shutterstock

Manufactured in the United States of America

McFarland & Company, Inc., Publishers
  Box 611, Jefferson, North Carolina 28640
  www.mcfarlandpub.com

Table of Contents

Introduction   1

1. The Poetics of Film Series
   JENNIFER FORREST   21

Early Cinema

2. The Intertextuality of Early Cinema: A Prologue to *Fantômas*, Film and Novel
   TOM GUNNING   39

Classic Hollywood Cinema

3. Tarzan in Novel and Film
   MICHAEL HARNEY   57

4. Narcissistic Doubling and the Question of Identification in Film Series: The Case of Nancy Drew
   CAROLE MARTIN   81

5. The Trouble with Maisie: Insubordination and the Empowered Woman Series
   JENNIFER FORREST   105

The New Hollywood

6. The James Bond Films
   JAMES CHAPMAN   130

7. Who's Your Daddy? Politics and Paternity in the Star Wars Saga
   SUSAN ARONSTEIN *and* ROBERT TORRY   158

Europe

8. The Transfiguration of Old Fritz: *Münchhausen* and the Fridericus Series
   THOMAS L. COOKSEY ... 178

9. Caroline and Angélique: Seductresses of the French Screen
   PIERRE SIVAN ... 197

Japan, Hong Kong, and India

10. Through the Years with Godzilla and Tora-San: Film Series in Postwar Japan
    WILLIAM M. TSUTSUI ... 210

11. Serial Brotherhood: The Better Tomorrow Films and Some *Wuxia* and Western Cousins
    KENNETH E. HALL ... 241

12. The Allegorical Imagination in Hindi Film Series
    RASHMI DORAISWAMY ... 263

About the Contributors ... 293
Index ... 297

Introduction

This collection examines a selection of film series representative of three periods in American film history (silent cinema, Classic Hollywood cinema, and the post–Classic Hollywood or New Hollywood era), and of non–American national cinemas (France, Germany, Hong Kong, Japan, and India). *The Film Encyclopedia* situates film series solely within the context of Classic Hollywood studio modes of production: the B-unit series production model became the one adopted for the production of television series. Accordingly, *The Film Encyclopedia* does not discuss silent film series, and it identifies those coming after the 1950s dismantling of the Hollywood studio system as "not truly series in the original sense of the term," since they were not planned as series, but rather were issued as sequels. The industry, however, does recognize them as series. As David A. Cook notes, "By 1974, sequels and series, the very fodder of B-film production during the studio era, loomed as a major strategy for risk reduction among the majors, who have since devoted approximately 10 percent of their rosters to these categories. (Combined with reissues, in fact, sequels and series accounted for 17.6 percent of all Hollywood releases from 1974 to 1978)" (4).[1] Contrary to the studio era, however, the series productions of the New Hollywood benefit from substantial budgets. In addition, while *The Film Encyclopedia* does not mention foreign series production, a glance at the "series" section of James L. Limbacher's *Haven't I Seen You Somewhere Before? Remakes, Sequels, and Series in Motion Pictures and Television, 1896–1978* reveals an astonishing number of series produced by other major national cinemas, evidence that any vibrant foreign commercial cinema needs, if not necessarily to adopt and adapt the model established by Hollywood, then to create a production practice that will satisfy the demands of exhibition and industry viability. This book has the objective of offering a definition, both looser (the inclusion of silent, New Hollywood, and foreign series) and more restrictive (distinguishing film series from the bundle of other "recycled" scripts), of the industry practice of producing film series, and of situating film series analysis within the greater framework of popular cinema studies.

Hollywood's "Recycling Mania"

"Here's where we keep the numbers for our sequels. I can't wait for Shrek 19!"[2]

Every year film and cultural critics decry what they perceive as the increased use by Hollywood studios of what is derisively called today the "recycled" script, a practice that refers to everything from genre films adhering to tried and often true formulas, remakes, sequels, series, and spin-offs. While a look at recent releases in movie theaters seems to confirm their conclusions, in fact, these critics grossly overestimate contemporary Hollywood's production of "recycled" material: it doesn't come even remotely close to reaching the level of "recycling" during the classic studio era. Although written in 1987, the statistics cited in Thomas Simonet's "Conglomerates and Content: Remakes, Sequels, and Series in the New Hollywood" continue to be applicable to current studio practices: any post–Classic Hollywood era's studio's annual film production will always be substantially lower than that of the Classic Hollywood studios, which had to produce literally hundreds of films a year to feed the "maw of exhibition" created by their theater holdings.[3]

In the late 1980s and throughout the 1990s, the *bête noire* of newspaper, magazine, and trade paper film critics was the remake, in particular the Hollywood remake of French films. Whether the result of coincidence, or in direct response to such critiques, or whether the reflection of the increasing inclusion in film studies programs of popular film and popular film practices, academic presses in the last ten years have published the first serious works by film scholars on the remake: Carolyn A. Durham's *Double Takes: Culture and Gender in French Films and Their American Remakes* (1998), Andrew Horton and Stuart McDougal's edition, *Play It Again Sam: Retakes on Remakes* (1998). Lucy Mazdon's *Encore Hollywood: Remaking French Cinema* (2000), my *Dead Ringers: The Remake in Theory and Practice* (2002), co-edited with Leonard R. Koos, and Constantine Verevis's *Film Remakes* (2006).[4] While remakes continue to preoccupy film critics, their presence has been eclipsed to a great extent in recent years by sequels and series. In a December 2002 *New York Times* article Michiko Kakutani bemoaned the marked presence of "recycled" films in those weekly, quarterly, and end of the year lists of top-grossing films. "A year ago," she points out, "half of the Top 10 grossing films were sequels" (1+). Not surprisingly, in her end of the year assessment of 2002's contribution to the arts (film, music, television, theater, etc.), she concludes that it was a year in which the "The Idea Was Not To Have One":

> It was a year that witnessed the 20th installment of the James Bond franchise, the 10th "Star Trek" movie, the eighth "Halloween" sequel, the fourth Jack Ryan/Tom Clancy film, the fourth movie featuring Hannibal the Cannibal, the third Austin Powers picture, the second of a projected seven Harry Potter movies, and the 1,234,567th Cinderella story starring the starlet du jour [1].

While she included a pseudo-genre, and later in the article, remakes and adaptations from other media in her list of pre-tested materials, her primary target was film sequels and series (although she treats them all as one and the same practice).[5] The James Bond, Star Trek, and Austin Powers movies are clearly film series, namely a group of films related by recurring core characters and in which each entry is an independent episode, or "sequel" to the previous movie. Featuring less continuity than the former series, the Jack Ryan/Tom Clancy films (character and novelist, respectively) are a series as well, with Alec Baldwin being the first to portray Jack Ryan in *The Hunt for Red October* (John McTiernan, 1990), with Harrison Ford taking over the role in *Patriot Games* (Phillip Noyce, 1992) and *Clear and Present Danger* (Phillip Noyce, 1994), and with Ben Affleck as the latest incarnation of Jack Ryan in *The Sum of All Fears* (Phil Alden Robinson, 2002).[6] The Hannibal Lecter films are a true series as well with *The Silence of the Lambs* (Jonathan Demme, 1991), *Hannibal* (Ridley Scott, 2001), and *Hannibal Rising* (Peter Webber, 2007) as adaptations of Thomas Harris's novels of the same name; however, *Red Dragon* (Brett Ratner, 2002), another adaptation, overlaps with another "recycling" practice in that it was a remake of Michael Mann's lower budget *Manhunter* from 1986. The Halloween films are technically a series: like many post–Classic era series, there is the semblance of a continuing story (each "sequel" offers Dr. Loomis pursuing the evil Michael Myers) which functions primarily to justify a new, and basically independent, horror adventure that does not depend on a knowledge of the earlier entries (series). The Lord of the Rings trilogy that Kakutani mentions later in the article, however, possesses a distinctive serial quality in that each entry but the final one ends with the story unresolved.[7] Among the remakes, Kakutani cites elsewhere in the article John McTiernan's *Rollerball* (2002), the remake of Norman Jewison's 1975 film of the same name, *The Four Feathers* (Shekhar Kapur, 2002), the remake of Zoltan Korda's 1939 film of the same name, and *Mr. Deeds* (Steven Brill, 2002), the remake of Frank Capra's *Mr. Deeds Goes to Town* (1936).[8] Her reference to Cinderella tales suggests both a subgenre of the woman's film and the remake, since Kakutani finds that *Maid in Manhattan* (Wayne Wang,

2002) reworks (or "rips off," to use her term) material found in *Working Girl* (Mike Nichols, 1988) and *Pretty Woman* (Garry Marshall, 1990). Finally, among the material originating from other media, she lists *Jackass: The Movie* (Jeff Tremaine, 2002), *Scooby-Doo* (Raja Gosnell, 2002), and *Spider-Man* (Sam Raimi, 2002), which come from television and comic books respectively.[9]

Regardless of Kakutani's inclusion of genre films and remakes in her list of reprehensible film production practices, it is clear that series and sequels are the new target of newspaper film criticism. Five months after her article, there was another *New York Times* article, one proposing to explain "Why Hollywood Loves to Repeat Itself." In it, Laura M. Holson states that between May and August of 2003, studios were planning on issuing "16 sequels, prequels or franchise installments" (36).[10] "That's more than twice the number that appeared in 2002," states Paul Dergarabedian, president of Exhibitor Relations (Holson 36). Previews of 2004's films promised more of the same. Commenting on Hollywood's repetition syndrome, Kakutani contends that

> Reality shows, like the fast-food franchising of movie characters and television shows, are just another symptom of Hollywood's current deficit of ideas: its ham-handed efforts to fill an ever deepening vacuum of ideas with cheap, lowest-common-denominator spectacles and low-risk, easy-to-merchandise sequels [1+].

While the terms "recycling mania" and "franchising" reflect Kakutani's privileging of originality (a post–Romantic requirement for artistic expression in all mediums) and her membership in the class of tastemakers, her position *vis-à-vis* the bulk of Hollywood productions, however, is more complex. In this essay, she also dismisses *Possession* (Neil LaBute, 2002) and *White Oleander* (Peter Kosminsky, 2002) for being adaptations from novels (a category into which the Lord of the Rings trilogy, the Jack Ryan, the Hannibal Lecter, and the Harry Potter films also fall), a stance that elucidates more clearly her classification system: only a screenplay with no prior literary source is original, and ideally, that in which the director is also the screenwriter (i.e., an *auteur*).[11] While Kakutani's inclusion of adaptations within the category of "recycled" material serves most to distinguish between the *pre-tested* materials behind the bulk of Hollywood film production (materials coming from a variety of related and non-related mediums: best-selling novels and popular comic books, radio programs, television series, and, in the case of remakes, series, sequels, and serials, Ur-films, etc.) and *original* work, regardless of the medium, it does not offer, however, a useful distinction between and explanation of the reuse of material/formulas within the medium of film itself.

Jeannette Catsoulis's more recent *New York Times* essay, "Sequels: Stay Fresh or Die Hard," comes on the heels of a group of 2007 summer series entries that include *The Bourne Ultimatum* (Paul Greengrass), *Harry Potter and the Order of the Phoenix* (David Yates), *Live Free or Die Hard* (Len Wiseman), *Spider-Man 3* (Sam Raimi), and *Ocean's Thirteen* (Steven Soderbergh). While Catsoulis finds that the first three of these films, "Though hardly artistic milestones, ... were smart, entertaining and — most important — keenly attuned to the expectations of their audiences," she doesn't make matters any clearer regarding the distinction between sequels and series (17). Those qualities that typify the series, as in *Ocean's Thirteen*'s "interchangeable crimes, locations and dames" represent the types of "sequels" of which she disapproves. Praiseworthy qualities are those that fulfill the "essential challenge of a sequel: creating a hero who evolves without abandoning his nature" (17). In other words, a sequel is good when it behaves most like a sequel, and bad when it behaves most like a series.

Defining Film Series Against Other Formulaic Films

Series, sequels, remakes, genre films, and adaptations (of source novels/texts) do indeed follow proven formulas. In terms of the New Hollywood era, as David A. Cook notes, "With so much riding on each film, blockbuster production sought to ensure profitability by relying on what had worked with audiences in the past" (27). In order to define a film series, it is important to understand not only how they differ from, but also what they share with, other formula-driven formats.

One major division emerges in a consideration of audience. The audience for true sequels and adaptations of critically acclaimed novels and works of literature, for example, generally belongs to the more educated classes: while the producers of remakes seek the greatest possible returns on their investments by attracting the largest possible audience (i.e., people who have *and* who haven't seen the original), an important subsection of the audience for them belongs to the group that appreciates adaptations of literary works (readaptations of Jane Austen novels like *Pride and Prejudice* and *Emma*)[12] and/or the group that finds more than entertainment value in watching movies. While newspaper, magazine, and trade paper critics generally find distasteful the practice of remaking films of recognized artistic quality (e.g., William Friedkin's 1977 *Sorcerer*, a remake of Henri-Georges Clouzot's critically acclaimed 1953 *Le Salaire de la peur*/*The Wages of Fear*; Jeremiah S. Chechik's 1996 remake of Clouzot's 1955 *Les Diaboliques*/*Diabolique*), they do, however begrudgingly, bestow praise on those remakes that rise above their source film by virtue of the "upscaling" of the director, the actors, and the production values.¹³ Steven Soderbergh, a director who enjoys *auteur* status, for example, has received critical acclaim for his remakes: *Traffic* (2000 — an upscaling of a British television mini-series), *Ocean's Eleven* (2001 — an upscaling of the 1960 Lewis Milestone film of the same name), and *Solaris* (2002 — a disavowed homage to Andrei Tarkovsky's film of the same name).¹⁴

The accepted wisdom is that genre films, series, and sequels are destined for less discriminating consumers, non-generic films for more refined audiences.¹⁵ Genre creations, whether in art or literature, have, since the classical period, been associated with degrees of conformity to a set of rules governing particular genres. Classical literature is generic. The Romantic period, however, rejected classical aesthetics — one that "directs us to view the world in like manner"— in favor of originality and the transgression of rules (Shiff 169). Since then, it is "'popular culture,' mass culture, that is generic, ruled as it is by market pressures to differentiate to a limited degree in order to cater to various sectors of consumers and to repeat commercially successful patterns, ingredients, and formulas" (Neale 177). Film scholars like Rick Altman and Mark Jancovich have noted that genre films are not advertised in such a way that they exclude the spectators that are not patrons of genre films, or of a particular genre. On the contrary, they contend, that advertisements for films aim to "suggest" genres rather than "announcing" them, as a way to appeal to a wide range of audiences (Jancovich 35). For example, *The Silence of the Lambs* (an adaptation) "was clearly presented as a film that offered all the pleasures of a horror film, thus appealing to those who identified with the genre, while simultaneously reassuring others that it would not display any of the features that were often associated with the genre by those who disidentified with it: a lack of quality or a surfeit of misogyny" (Jancovich 36). The film was decidedly an upscaling of the previous adaptation, *Manhunter*, which possessed lower production values and clear generic markers (crime/horror). A sign of the success of both the film's upgraded status (expensive production, top-tier production team, the presence of top box-office actors, etc.) and its toning down and blurring of generic markers, it enjoyed both critical and financial success, as well as received Oscars for best actor, actress, director, adapted screenplay, and film of 1991.¹⁶

While series and sequels have a lot in common with genre films, not all genre films belong to film series. Every genre film, series, and sequel presents the same general format, similar historical period and place, and similar themes, characters, and actions/adventures as other films to which they are related with one important difference: where the genre film's formula presents similar character types, films in a series or a sequel always present the very same principal characters.

Series films share qualities associated with sequels, but they normally address different audiences. A series installment and a sequel share the same principal characters operating in the same historical and regional context with similar themes and actions as their preceding films do. Film series generally offer a modicum of serial continuity in subsequent installments by following, as for example, Nick and Nora Charles (the Thin Man series) through the birth and childhood of their son, with all the lifestyle modifications that such an event entails, but each entry is not, for all that, merely a sequel. The main focus of each entry is not continuing their story in a truly linear fashion, but offering a new crime detection adventure for the duo. The sequel takes place in a semblance of real time; the series ostensibly belongs to an eternal present. In contradistinction to the series, the sequel picks up the thread of its characters' lives, sometimes where the previous film left off (as in Michael Curtiz's *Four Wives* [1939], the sequel to his *Four Daughters* [1938]), and sometimes years later (as in Richard Linklater's *Before Sunset* [2004], which catches up with its protagonists nine years after their first encounter, a time framework that happens to correspond neatly in real time with the year of the film *Before Sunrise* [1995]). In the case of the Andy Hardy series, *You're Only Young Once* (Seitz, 1937), starring Mickey Rooney, while often described as a sequel to *A Family Affair* (Seitz, 1937) was instead the official entry to the series. The true sequel as a cinematic term referring to a particular format, therefore, is the second, and generally the last, film featuring a continuing story with the same basic characters.

For her article on series and sequels, Holson interviewed industry executives who admitted that resorting to ready-made material reflects the rise in the cost of production and marketing of films: studios "are passing on risky projects they might have jumped at two years ago." It stands to reason, therefore, that they are all "betting on sequels" (36). Neither Holson nor the industry executives make a distinction between sequels and series, using "sequel" as a general term that identifies any production that follows on the tail of a successful earlier release, whether that means through a film that picks up on a story where a previous film left off (the "true" sequel) or new adventures for recurring characters (the "true" series). Holson breaks down the "sequels" into two categories. In the first category go the Lord of the Rings and Matrix types of films, both of which are identified elsewhere as trilogies, and the latter of which is equally called a "series," despite the continuous storyline. In the second category go the movies that are created "after a movie becomes a hit — this summer's examples include 'Barbershop 2,' 'X2: X-Men United' and "2 Fast 2 Furious,'" namely films that could potentially form part of series. Despite the number "2" attached to these films, this practice generally refers today, not to the sequel, but to the film series.[17]

Within the category of film series, the term couldn't be used in more broad a fashion to describe a variety of groupings of films. Depending on what period of American film history is under discussion, the term refers to quite different industry practices: as noted earlier, in its most narrow usage film historians generally point to B-unit film production during the Classic Hollywood era, especially in terms of the team effort.[18] The term has been bestowed on films sharing a similar title, theme, actors, or any combination of the three. From the Classic Hollywood, one can cite the Busby Berkeley Gold Diggers films, which shared, however, only the repeated title from one installment to another, Berkeley's lavish musical/dance production numbers, as well as the theme or subgenre of the backstage musical. From the same era, Fred Astaire and Ginger Rogers performed in a "series" of films that shared neither titles nor characters. Performance artist Matthew Barney's experimental *Cremaster* films (1995–2002) have been called a series, but are related only by their title. The characters in Polish director Krzysztof Kieslowski's *Three Colors* films, *Bleu/Blue* (1993), *Blanc/White* (1994), and *Rouge/Red* (1994) appear together only in the final news report sequence of the last film: no relation exists between these characters nor between each film's story other than the republican ideals of liberty (blue), equality (white), and fraternity (red) as symbolized in the French flag.[19] These groups of films do not qualify as series. The Jesse Stone films starring Tom Selleck, however, while made for a different medium (television), clearly fall into the classification proposed by this volume.[20]

There is a problematic category of series that blurs the lines separating genre, film series, adaptation, and remake: those films based on a source text that has attained folk-epic status within a particular culture, such as the Dracula and Frankenstein movies, the first based on the 1897 eponymous novel by Bram Stoker, the second on *Frankenstein, or the Modern Prometheus* by Mary Wollstonecraft Shelley (1818). While a few of the films within the grouping of Dracula and Frankenstein films are indeed remakes (readaptations), the majority of the films in each series are not, as in the Dracula, Frankenstein, and Mummy series from the 1930s (Universal Studios) and those from the late 1950s to the early 1970s (Hammer Films). Those that are remakes are specifically readaptations that return to the source text, and treat that source text with a certain reverence, as in Francis Ford Coppola's *Bram Stoker's Dracula* (1992). As Thomas Leitch notes, "The goal of the readaptation, like that of the literary translation, is fidelity (however defined) to the original text, which it undertakes to translate as scrupulously as possible (presumably more scrupulously than earlier versions) into the film medium" (44). The Universal and Hammer Dracula and Frankenstein series films, however, are faithful only to the core characters.

While the Dracula and Frankenstein series all began in one original source text, there are a great many series, especially those from the Classic Hollywood era, that draw almost exclusively upon popular novel series, as in the Perry Mason series (from Erle Stanley Gardner's novels). In France, as well, the 1950s Lemmy Caution movies starring American expatriate Eddie Constantine were based on the hard-boiled novels by Britain's Peter Cheyney.[21] There are series that have little to do with their source text after the initial entry in the series, as in The Thin Man movies based on *The Thin Man* (1934) by Dashiell Hammett, or the Ma and Pa Kettle series, spun off from the immensely popular film, *The Egg and I* (Chester Erskine, 1947), itself adapted from Betty MacDonald's 1945 best-selling autobiography. Finally, there are film series which do not feature the same characters, only the same performers and titles, for example, the Bob Hope and Bing Crosby "Road to..." and Marx Brothers movies, Bombay cinema's Khiladi films, as well as the film series featuring a performer whose name is also that of the lead character, as in Mexico's Cantinflas movies from the 1940s through the 1960s.[22] These latter movies fit easily within the rubric of "true" film series, since their characters—as in the case of the Marx Brothers, with Groucho and his cigar and large greasepaint moustache, silent Harpo and his top hat, red wig, trench coat, and horn, Chico and his Pinocchio cap and Italian accent—are fixed like those of the stock characters of the *commedia dell'arte*, such that varying character names are essentially superfluous.

While there is indeed a need for a study of "series" and the mediums in which they operate in a general sense of the word, the aim of this anthology adheres to the technical definition of a "group of films, each complete on its own but sharing a common cast of main characters with continuing traits and a similar situation format that despite plot variations remains true to a basic premise and develops according to an expected formula" (Katz 1242).

Although much recent scholarly criticism has been devoted to genre films, adaptations, and, as stated earlier, remakes, series and sequels, however, have excited precious little interest outside of filmographies.[23] Among the filmographers of Hollywood cinema, Michael R. Pitts and James Robert Parish have practically cornered the market in reference guides, not only for film series, but for genre pictures as well (westerns, detective films, science fiction, etc.), testimony to how strongly film series resemble genres in their exploitation of a given formula.[24] A film series can even become its own subgenre: a good example of the overlapping of genre and series is the Charlie Chan detective series, which began in the mid–1920s as silent features and continued through the late 1940s. With fifty-three films in the series, it fairly qualifies as a subgenre of the detective drama in its own right, with its own peculiar conventions that must be invoked in some fashion. An impressive example from the post-studio era is the James Bond series, which has lasted over five decades and twenty-one films with practically the same basic production philosophy and team to ensure thematic and narrative continuity. It, too, fairly qualifies as its own subgenre of the espionage film, itself a subgenre of thrillers.

B Movies and Blockbusters

The essays in this book represent a variety of genres — action, adventure, comedy, detective, family, historical, martial arts, mystery, romance, sci-fi, and thriller — spanning the entire history of world cinema. They equally offer a broad selection of critical approaches — historical, political, cultural studies, genre studies, gender theory, etc.— as well as examinations of other national film series (Germany, France, Hong Kong, India, Japan — the last four cinemas either rivaling or following close behind the United States in annual film production, and often entering into a vigorous dialogue with their American influences). One of the most productive and intertextual of the international cinemas is in Hong Kong, where film series are perhaps as prevalent as they are in the United States.

The book opens with "The Poetics of Film Series," which offers an analysis of the series form in general, and of film series in particular, as a point of departure for the discussions of the specific series in the following chapters. The essay examines four facets of the form: *mise-en-abyme*, or the ways in which film series internally address or reflect their form, or both; *reception*: a reinterpretation of the role of the "reader" of series "texts" in comparison to the "reader" of quality "texts" as defined by the semiotician, Umberto Eco; *seriality/seriesicity*: a revision of the historical place and function of the series form, (a) *vis-à-vis* serial forms, and (b) with respect to varying types and degrees of media technologies; and *authorship*: an exploration of questions of authorship vs. audience in series forms.

The section "Early Cinema" contains Tom Gunning's "The Intertextuality of Early Cinema: A Prologue to *Fantômas*, Film and Novel." While films had been adapted from literary works before 1907, they made reference to, rather than reproduced the narratives of these works, banking on audience familiarity rather than reproducing their complex narratives: the pre–1907 cinema did not have the technical capacity to render them on the screen. After 1907, in imitation of the successful adaptations of the French *films d'art* that catered to more refined audiences, film companies equally adapted popular fiction in order to attract the masses. In 1913, Louis Feuillade brought the popular Fantômas novel series to the screen. This actor-centered series, as well as other series from the period (the Nick Carter, Nat Pinkerton, and Nick Winter series, for example), contributed enormously to bringing actors out of the anonymity of early cinema and into what was becoming the star system.

The section "Classic Hollywood Cinema" contains three essays exploring, adaptation from a popular literature series to screen; gender identification and the series format; and the class dynamics of the empowered woman series. Michael Harney's "Tarzan in Novel and Film" discusses the archetypal figure of Tarzan in the novels and in the cinema. First appearing in a story by Edgar Rice Burroughs in 1912, Tarzan has figured in more than forty films, of which only a few have been based on any of Burroughs' subsequent Tarzan novels. Harney situates both the literary and cinematic incarnations of Tarzan within the tradition of the medieval chivalric romance. Tarzan, as a modernized knight errant, prefigures the twentieth-century superhero. Adapting Tarzan to the screen entailed modifications, dictated by concrete market considerations such as audience demographics and accommodating industry censors, as well as cultural factors. The superiority of the Tarzan of the novels plays out through a privileging of the white Western male over non-white populations. Logically, such a hierarchy subordinates the novels' women as well. The cinematic Tarzan, however, is complemented by the equal partner he has found in Jane, a dynamic representative of an egalitarian mode that extends to Tarzan's relations with non-white populations. Harney argues, however, that despite the many differences between the Tarzan of the novels and of the movies, the two media share the same iconic agenda.

Carole Martin's "Narcissistic Doubling and the Question of Identification in Film Series: The Case of Nancy Drew" explores the different ways in which spectators identify with the principle characters of Classic Hollywood B-film series versus A-class pictures. Drawing initially upon reader-response critiques, which consider gender an essential element in the way readers interact with texts, in the larger sense of the word, and feminist criticism, especially feminist film criticism, which conceptualizes the female spectator as identifying with male protagonists, Martin offers film scholar Raymond Bellour's interpretation of these identification processes as being based rather on the relation of "narcissistic doubling." This model, which describes Classical Hollywood cinema, applies solely, she contends, to A movie production, but does not apply, however, to B movies. Taking the Nancy Drew series from the late 1930s as representative, not only of B production, but of a certain type of production (film series), the author suggests that the series' repetitive sequencing (the open-ended structure of the form) and framing of a single character works against the way in which narcissistic doubling "naturalizes" cross-gender identification in A-class films like *The Big Sleep* (Howard Hawks, 1946).

My essay, "The Trouble with Maisie: Insubordination and the Empowered Woman Series" examines a series within the group of empowered woman films of the 1930s and 1940s. I argue against the standard feminist stance that Classic Hollywood cinema's privileging of patriarchy deprives women both as characters and as spectators of agency: series films featuring female leads work against subordination. While each individual film within these series seemingly strives to return these women to their traditional feminine spaces, it is in reviewing each empowered woman series as a whole, here the Maisie series, that it becomes clear that the final scenes' reintegration of the heroine into society is, in the overall context of the series, indicative of her insubordination.

The section "The New Hollywood" features two chapters representative of post–Classic Hollywood series: James Bond and Star Wars. James Chapman's "The James Bond Films" addresses the surprising longevity of a series whose source texts' Cold War context seemingly doomed the effort to a short existence. Chapman argues that the three basic narrative modes that have been identified by critics as informing the novels (the sexist, the imperialist, and the phallic) have been reconfigured over the course of the film series's history, reflecting a continual accommodation by its producers of political-cultural changes in popular culture. This deliberate adaptation to change is seen both in the consistently strong box-office performance of the films in the domestic and the international markets, the latter which, unexpectedly, outperforms the former.[25]

Susan Aronstein and Robert Torry's "'Who's Your Daddy?': Politics and Paternity in the Star Wars Saga" examines one of the most popular series in the cinema of the New Hollywood: the Star Wars films. However much co-opted by Reaganites, the authors argue that the original trilogy left post–Vietnam audiences with a basic hope in democratic ideals (hence the re-titling of the first film as *A New Hope* [George Lucas, 1977]). While the films' underlying theme concerned Luke's quest for his father, the authors argue that the films represented a political appeal, not to fathers, but to grandfathers, namely to the ideals championed during World War II. The addition of three prequels to the original three films privileges the narrative over the chronological order of production, as witnessed by the new titles and the affixing of numbers. The authors contend, however, that it is through a study of the films in the order of chronological production that one perceives a distinct post–9/11 pessimism indicative of the failure of the first three films' millennial promise of a return to the ideals of the grandfathers.

The next section offers two essays about two important European producers of film: Germany and France. Thomas L. Cooksey's "The Transfiguration of Old Fritz: *Münchhausen* and the Fridericus Series" takes as its point of departure recent studies of the Nazi-era's production of *Münchhausen* (Josef von Baky, 1943). These critical assessments are split between identifying the film either as embodying Nazi ideology or as resisting all ideology. Cooksey proposes an alternate reading that identifies the film as a logical extension of, and therefore ideologically consistent with, the Nazi propaganda machine's agenda of linking the *Führer* with the historical figure of Frederick the Great (as portrayed in the Fridericus series) through the retroactive association of the literary figure of Münchhausen with the filmically *faux* Frederick, of the historical with the fantastic. The production of the *Münchhausen* of 1943 was necessitated by the failure to convincingly rewrite the historically problematic Frederick, and by extension German greatness.

Pierre Sivan's "Caroline and Angélique: Seductresses of the French Screen" examines two series from the 1950s and 1960s. French producers developed the Caroline and Angélique series in an effort to compete on their own turf with the Hollywood cinema: the lavish costume drama/adventure film. For the Caroline films, two American films served as powerful references: *Forever Amber* (Otto Preminger, 1947) and *Gone with the Wind* (Victor Fleming, 1939), the latter of which was leading at the French box-office in 1950. The enormously successful novels on which the Caroline films were based, as well, modeled themselves according to the tried-and-true formulas of American bestsellers. The films offered French audiences familiar historical periods: for Caroline, the events of the Great Revolution; for Angélique, the seventeenth-century court of Louis XIV. The political visions of the two series could not have differed more: the Caroline films adopted an anti-revolutionary stance, drawing obvious parallels between the revolutionaries and the Nazis of the German Occupation, a period still fresh in many memories; the Angélique films, however, conformed to the democratic and republican credo of the Revolution.

The final section of this volume presents studies of series from Japan, Hong Kong, and India. William Tsutsui's "Through the Years with Godzilla and Tora-san: Film Series in Postwar Japan," surveys two of Japan's most popular postwar film series and the fundamental historical, cultural, and economic factors that shaped their development: the Godzilla films (28 films in 50 years), which have enjoyed a huge international following, and the sentimental Tora-san series (48 films in almost 30 years), whose success is almost entirely domestic. While the two series share neither similar genres nor similar production values (Godzilla movies benefited from higher budgets than the more low-tech Tora-san movies), they do reflect how the Japanese film industry recognized that film series, in general, were essential to its economic health and viability, and how that health and viability point to the industry's ability to continually adapt to fluctuating market conditions, shifting audience demographics, and changes in the cultural climate.

Kenneth E. Hall's "Serial Brotherhood: The Better Tomorrow Films and Some *Wuxia* and Western Cousins" studies the popular Hong Kong Better Tomorrow series. Family and kinship relations, in both the literal and figurative senses of the terms, figure prominently in the three films in the series, in which biological ties and triad loyalty intersect. The triad battle components of the films serve to continue the "heroic bloodshed" tradition belonging to both the East and the West. The family and kinship components, Hall argues, contain as well the thematic structure of prodigality, it, too, common to Eastern and Western traditions. Hall explores these affinities in contrasting the Better Tomorrow films with Hollywood's Zorro and Godfather movies, the former the most recent installments of which owe an enormous debt to Hong Kong cinematic martial arts choreography, and the latter, which have had a great influence on the triad film.

Finally, Rashmi Doraiswamy's "The Allegorical Imagination in Hindi Film Series" is probably the first attempt to define film series in Hindi cinema, especially that of post-colonial India. Although the discussion situates Hindi series firmly within the context of postcoloniality and the ensuing fashioning of different narratives and personae, the great similarities between Hollywood and Hindi series production are striking: the interdependence of series and genre; series as the production of creative teams; the importance of the perceived fit between actor and role; the targeting of popular audiences; and the popular status of these series, even in their movement from B to A productions. But as Doraiswamy notes, Hindi cinema ultimately both references and works against the models offered by Hollywood: difference emerges through the way its series contribute to the construction of national identity through allegory. She isolates four series that represent the three historical stages in the evolution of a Indian national allegory: two series sharing the same character and two series sharing the same title, charting national allegory, first, in the 1950s (a nation in the making), second, in the 1970s (the transitional period of a nation in unrest), and third, from the 1980s to the present (decentralization and a fragmented national imaginary).

* * *

This collection should serve to open the dialogue on film series within the greater discipline of popular film studies, first, by offering an expanded definition of, but not the final word on, the term — one that incorporates pre- and post–Classic Hollywood series, as well as those produced by foreign cinemas — and second, by examining the practice of film series as defined from a variety of critical perspectives. Unfortunately, there exist far too many film series nationally and internationally than any one book can treat critically, so understandably those represented in this volume are but a very small sample. In addition, not all the films discussed are as yet or ever will be readily available on DVD. There are, however, scholarly works on individual series (e.g., James Chapman's *Licence to Thrill: A Cultural History of the James Bond Films* [2000]). There are monographs that include discussions of film series production within the larger context of a particular historical period and locale (e.g., Richard Abel's *The Ciné Goes to Town: French Cinema, 1896–1914* [1994]) or of popular cinema (e.g., David Bordwell's *Planet Hong Kong: Popular Cinema and the Art of Entertainment* [2000]). This is the first scholarly treatment devoted entirely to film series alone, and, it ideally responds to this gap by including film series within the expanding focus of film studies programs to include serious critical studies of popular film.

Notes

1. According to Thomas Simonet's statistics, in 1940, 100 or 20.87 percent out of total 479 films produced in the major studios were sequels and series (4 and 96 respectively). The average for the entire 1940s was 20.48 percent. Simonet's table for the 1970s does not corroborate the numbers given by Cook: the average for the entire 1970s was 5.93 percent (41 out of a total 691 films being sequels [24] and series [17]) (158).

2. Comedy sketch by Jerry Seinfeld in the NBC promotion for DreamWorks Animation's 2007 film *Bee Movie* (Steve Hickner and Simon J. Smith). Seinfeld shows the viewer what goes on behind the scenes, opening a variety of doors that lead to such oddities blatantly foreign to a production team: the rooms storing the color red, the color yellow, "where men try on shoes," a Czechoslovakian gymnast, etc. The numbers for sequels are kept in what appears to be a utility closet, with #9 and #2 held up by knives.

3. The "maw of exhibition" is the term used by Tino Balio in his chapter "Feeding the Maw of Exhibition" in his edited volume *Grand Design: Hollywood as a Modern Business Enterprise, 1930–1939* (Berkeley: University of California Press, 1993) 73–107. When considering Classic Hollywood earnings, it is customary to think almost solely in terms of film production. The studios counted heavily, however, on controlling national theater exhibition and thereby secure maximum returns from their holdings. As Tino Balio notes, these returns could be significant, since, "Although these chains consisted only of around 20 percent of the theaters in the country, they contained nearly 80 percent of the first-run houses and the most profitable subsequent-run houses" (7).

4. There have been reference works on remakes going back as far as the 1970s: Michael B. Druxman's *Make It Again, Sam: A Survey of Movie Remakes* (1975), James L. Limbacher's *Haven't I Seen You Somewhere Before? Remakes, Sequels, and Series in Motion Pictures and Television, 1896–1978*, Robert A. and Gwendolyn Wright Nowlan's *Cinema Sequels and Remakes, 1903–1987* (1989), and Doris Milberg's *Repeat Performances: A Guide to Hollywood Movie Remakes* (1990). In terms of critical treatments of the practice, the French film journal *CinémAction* tackled the subject as early as 1989 in its special issue devoted to *Le*

Remake et l'adaptation. Ten years later, the French film journal *Positif* revisited the remake in May and June special issues.

5. A glance at many recent articles in newspapers and magazines shows the same preoccupation in general with "recycled" material, but the main focus of virtually all of them is the release of sequels and series.

6. Harrison Ford has had the unique good fortune to figure in three film series or sequels and never find himself identified solely as Han Solo, Indiana Jones, or Jack Ryan. Then again, these series and sequels are A-productions. William Powell had similar luck in the 1930s and 1940s, playing detective Philo Vance three times and Nick Charles (The Thin Man series) six times. Once again, his autonomy from the character may be due in no small measure to the films' classification as A-pictures and to his status as a lead actor. During the Classic Hollywood era, however, most series were B-unit productions featuring primarily character actors, not top stars.

7. *The Film Encyclopedia* defines a serial as a "multi-episode film, usually an action-adventure melodrama, presented in theaters one chapter at a time in weekly installments over a period of several months. Each chapter typically ends in a cliff-hanger, a moment of suspense and uncertainty that leaves the audience eager for resolution that does not come until the next chapter" (1242). While this technical definition locates serials historically as phenomena of the silent film and Classic Hollywood film eras, the Lord of the Rings films clearly possess serial elements: several episodes presented in regular installments (the first film was released in 2001, the second in 2002, and the third in 2003), with all but the last episode leaving the spectator in suspense until the next film.

8. *Mr. Deeds Goes to Town* was also a short-lived television series (1969–70) with Monte Markham starring as Longfellow Deeds.

9. The feature-length Scooby-Doo and the Spider-Man movies — two installments for the first, three for the latter — reflect the relatively smooth transfer of series from one medium into another.

10. "Franchise" is the word *du jour* used both to describe blockbuster series and to mark them as purely commercial enterprises. The Wikipedia encyclopedia offers this definition: "A media franchise is an intellectual property involving the characters, setting, and trademarks of an original work of media (usually a work of fiction), such as a film, a work of literature, a television program, or a video game. Generally, a whole series is made in that particular medium, along with merchandising and endorsements. Multiple sequels are often planned well in advance and, in the case of motion pictures, actors and directors often sign multi-film deals to ensure their participation" (<http://en.wikipedia.org/wiki/Media_franchise>).

11. She links the formulaic with Hollywood and originality with art-house films, particularly foreign films: "Movies by Pedro Almodóvar (*Talk to Her*), Zacharias Kunuk (*The Fast Runner*) and Alfonso Cuarón (*Y Tu Mamá También*) reminded us that original, new work is still being done — at least by foreign directors" (Kakutani 1+). Other newspaper and magazine critics are less exacting, citing original scripts as anything not coming from a pre-tested material (television, comic books, best-selling novels, etc.).

12. Classic Hollywood studios rarely remade prestige productions. As Tino Balio notes of production practices at Warner Bros., "Having once acquired an expensive property, it seems reasonable that a studio would want to reuse it often. After all, it had great name value and would provide a cheap and easy way to replicate success. But the studio seldom recycled expensive properties (e.g. *Green Pastures*) because they were by definition easily recognizable by many people and therefore were likely to make audiences feel cheated if reused" (100). The audiences that would feel "cheated" with such remakes would be those protective of their cultural capital. When Warners did reuse properties, they remade those belonging to B movies, whose audience is deemed to be less discriminating.

13. The term "upscaling" is used by Bordwell and Thompson to describe how

post–Classic Hollywood studios "enhanced production values" (391). They produced fewer films, yet counted on those fewer films to guarantee equally strong returns. "Even minor genres benefited from efforts to turn B scripts into A pictures" (391). This is evident today in film series like the Spider-Man films, which feature major actors and actresses (Tobey Maguire and Kirsten Dunst) and elaborate production and set design using the latest technology.

14. While invoking the memory of the original film, Soderbergh "disavows" his debt to it by claiming that his work revisits Stanislaw Lem's 1972 source novel for Tarkovsky's film, passing it off as a readaptation rather than as a "true" remake. For a discussion of disavowal and the remake, see Thomas Leitch: 37–62.

15. In "Typologie du roman policier," Tzvetan Todorov notes of the novel since Romanticism that a great work of literature is deemed to be one that "establishes the existence of two genres, the reality of two norms: that of the genre it transgresses, which dominated in preceding literature; and that of the genre that it creates" (56: my translation). An author coming from the Romantic tradition, therefore, denies the influence of any predecessor, instead offering his work as instances of a new genre: the genre in his style. The same is true in cinema.

16. The use of Jonathan Demme as the director for *Silence of the Lambs* represented an upscaling because Michael Mann's credits at this stage, while impressive, were primarily in television. A reassessment of Mann's range would come about, of course, with his critically acclaimed 1992 film *The Last of the Mohicans*.

17. *French Connection II* (John Frankenheimer, 1975) and *Bridget Jones: The Edge of Reason*, also known as *Bridget Jones's Diary II*, (Beeban Kidron, 2004) are true sequels in that they continue the stories of the originals. A blurring of the distinction between sequel and series appears in the Krrish films from India: although the action/adventure film *Koi ... Mil Gaya 2: Krrish/There's No One Like You* (Rakesh Roshan, 2006) is a true sequel to *Koi ... Mil Gaya/I Found Someone* (2003), *Krrish 2*, a series entry, is scheduled for release in 2009. The Lethal Weapon films, however, are a true series, even though each new release was announced with the numbers associated with sequels, thereby confusing the two practices. Each film's adventures are unrelated, however, to those of the previous films. In *Lethal Weapon* (Richard Donner, 1987) Martin Riggs/Mel Gibson and Roger Murtaugh/Danny Glover take down a drug baron. In *Lethal Weapon 2* (Richard Donner 1989), the bad guys are South African smugglers. In *Lethal Weapon 3* (Richard Donner, 1992), the duo dismantles an arms racket. And in *Lethal Weapon 4* (Richard Donner, 1998), Riggs and Murtaugh take on Chinese Triads. Of interest are developments in the Indiana Jones series, which did not resort to numbers for each new installment: it used the main character's name in association with a new adventure. The efficacy of the series's nostalgic appeal to B-movie series *and* serials from the Classic Hollywood era, in particular swashbuckler/western/adventure series, most assuredly necessitated the use of the name of the principle character in each new installment in the series.

18. Interestingly, the team spirit that was the hallmark of B-movie series production in the studio era is replicated in many respects in the post-studio era, in which certain names are associated with certain series. For example, Richard Donner is the director of all the Lethal Weapon films. Like the Superman and Indiana Jones series, the Lethal Weapon series kept basically the same core collaborative team (writers, stars, etc.) that had initiated the formula.

19. Similarly, the low-budget Apocalypse films carry the numbers indicative of series practices beginning in the last half of the twentieth century, but *Apocalypse: Caught in the Eye of the Storm* (Peter Gerretsen, 1998), *Apocalypse II: Revelation* (André van Heerden, 1999), *Apocalypse III: Tribulation* (André van Heerden, 2000), and *Apocalypse IV: Judgment* (André van Heerden, 2001) share only the development of themes from the Bible.

20. Film series are a rarity on television.

21. There were seven films in this B series that began in 1953, with the last and eighth being an uncharacteristic entry: Jean-Luc Godard's New Wave homage to the series, which had no source in a Cheyney novel: *Alphaville, une étrange aventure de Lemmy Caution/Alphaville* (1965). Bernard Borderie, who adapted and directed five of the Lemmy Caution entries, was also the writer/adapter and director of the Angélique series discussed by Pierre Sivan in this anthology. Eddie Constantine also appeared on West German, Austrian, and French television as Lemmy Caution in the 1980s.

22. The majority of the prolific Cantinflas movies were directed by Miguel M. Delgado.

23. No list of the studies on genre and adaptation can be exhaustive, but within the general category of film genre, a short list of often cited works includes Stephen Neale's *Genre and Hollywood* (2000), Barry Keith Grant's *Film Genre Reader* (1986), *Film Genre Reader II* (1995), and *Film Genre Reader III* (2003), Rick Altman's *Film/Genre* (1999), and Thomas Schatz's *Hollywood Genres: Formulas, Filmmaking, and the Studio System* (1981). Within particular film genres, a short list includes Rick Altman's *The American Film Musical* (1987), John Cawelti's *The Six Gun Mystique* (1984), and Marcia Landy's editions *Imitations of Life: A Reader on Film and Melodrama* (1991) and *The Historical Film: History and Memory in Media* (2001). For studies on the adaptation of fictional works, a short list includes Thomas M. Leitch's *Film Adaptation and its Discontents: From "Gone with the Wind" to "The Passion of the Christ"* (2007), Michel Serceau's *L'adaptation cinématographique des textes littéraires: théories et lectures* (1999), and Stuart Y. McDougal's *Made into Movies: From Literature to Film* (1985). There are also myriad studies on the adaptation of particular authors' novels, for example, Linda Troost and Sayre Greenfield's *Jane Austen in Hollywood* (2001).

24. A short list of filmographies include James Robert Parish's *The Great Movie Series* (1971), Bernard A. Drew's *Motion Picture Series and Sequels: A Reference Guide* (1990), James L. Limbacher's *Haven't I Seen You Somewhere Before? Remakes, Sequels, and Series in Motion Pictures and Television, 1896–1978* (1979). Among filmographies devoted to specific series within a genre, there are Ken Hanke's *A Critical Guide to Horror Film Series* (New York: Garland, 1991), Michael R. Pitts's *Famous Movie Detectives* (Metuchen, N.J.: Scarecrow, 1979) and *Famous Movie Detectives II* (Metuchen, N.J.: Scarecrow, 1991), and Kim R. Holston and Tom Winchester's *Science Fiction, Fantasy and Horror Film Sequels, Series and Remakes: An Illustrated Filmography, With Plot Synopses and Critical Commentary* (1997).

25. David Bordwell and Kristin Thompson isolate the Bond films as "probably the most profitable series in the history of cinema" (395).

Works Cited

Bordwell, David, and Kristin Thompson. *Film History: An Introduction*. New York: McGraw-Hill, 1994.

Catsoulis, Jeannette. "Sequels: Stay Fresh or Die Hard." *New York Times* 26 August 2007: 17.

Cook, David. A. *Lost Illusions: American Cinema in the Shadow of Watergate and Vietnam, 1970–1979*. New York: Scribners, 2000. Vol. 9 of *History of the American Cinema*. 10 vols.

Grant, Barry Keith, ed. *Film Genre Reader II*. Austin: University of Texas Press, 1995.

Holson, Laura M. "Why Hollywood Loves to Repeat Itself." *New York Times* 11 May 2003, sec. 2: 36.

Jancovich, Mark. "The Meaning of Mystery: Genre, Marketing and the Universal Sherlock Holmes Series of the 1940s." *Film International* 17 (2005): 34–45.

Kakutani, Michiko. "The Idea Was Not To Have One." *New York Times* 29 December 2002, sec. 2: 1+.

Katz, Ephraim. *The Film Encyclopedia*. 3rd edition. New York: HarperPerennial, 1998.

Leitch, Thomas. "Twice-Told Tales: Disavowal and the Rhetoric of the Remake." *Dead Ringers: The Remake in Theory and Practice*. Ed. Jennifer Forrest and Leonard R. Koos. Albany: SUNY Press, 2002: 37–62.

Neale, Steve. "Questions of Genre." Grant 159–183.

Shiff, Richard. "Phototropism (Figuring the Proper). *Retaining the Original: Multiple Originals, Copies, and Reproductions*. Ed. Kathleen Preciado. Washington: National Gallery of Art, 1989: 161–79.

Simonet, Thomas. "Conglomerates and Content: Remakes, Sequels, and Series in the New Hollywood." *Current Research in Film: Audiences, Economics, and Law*. Vol. 3. Ed. Bruce A. Austin. Norwood, N.J.: Ablex, 1987: 154–162.

Todorov, Tzvetan. "Typologie du roman policier." *Poétique de la prose*. Paris: Editions du Seuil, 1971: 55–65.

1

The Poetics of Film Series

Jennifer Forrest

STEVE MCBRIDE: You don't mean that you're actually gonna try to run for mayor?
TORCHY BLANE: Well, I certainly am. And what's more, I'm gonna win.
STEVE MCBRIDE: Oh, go on, can't you take a joke? You can't do that.
TORCHY BLANE: Why not?
STEVE MCBRIDE: Because you're gonna marry me.
TORCHY BLANE: If there's any law that says a mayor can't get married, we'll have it changed.
STEVE MCBRIDE: Ah, what kind of a nincompoop do you think I'll be, married to a mayor? What do you want me to do, stay home and peel the potatoes while you run the city?
TORCHY BLANE: Oh, you won't have to do that. I'll be getting a very good salary. We'll hire a cook.
STEVE MCBRIDE: Listen, if we hire a cook, I'm gonna pay for it with my own dough. And what's more, you're gonna stay home where you belong, and take care of my babies, MY BABIES!
TORCHY BLANE: Now, you listen to me, Steve Mc.... Babies, oh, Steve, thousands of them!
STEVE MCBRIDE: Huh?
TORCHY BLANE: Why the city's full of them, Steve! What a slogan! A vote for Torchy Blane is a vote for your baby! Why, you've given me my platform, Steve! That's it! We'll clean up the city! We'll make it a fit place to raise babies in!
— *Torchy Runs for Mayor* (Raymond McCarey, 1939)

The Torchy Blane film series belongs to the group of empowered woman films from the 1930s and early 1940s. Torchy is blonde, beautiful, brainy, and brash, and eternally bound for the altar with police lieutenant Steve McBride. In nine films produced in rapid succession over four years, Torchy Blane, the female reporter for the *Star*, for one reason or another, never quite makes it to City Hall to obtain a marriage license, not, as would be supposed, because her policeman boyfriend continually gets cold feet, but because, when given a choice between a justice of the peace and a new scoop, Torchy usually opts for the latter.¹ In short, Torchy is a master of displacement: she defers not only the day of her wedding, but often does so by playing with words or images, transferring meaning from one contextual usage to another. In the above exchange, she (along with the ensuing film frames) deflects the physical babies that Steve wants her to have onto billboards representing babies in a mayoral campaign. On another occasion, when Steve refers to having children, she imagines her cozy domicile filled with little mass-produced typewriters (she does, after all, claim to have ink for blood).²

The practice of deliberately shifting from the denotative to the connotative use of words and images postpones more than just Torchy's wedding; it is the practice that defines the entire Torchy Blane series. Some series films announce extradiegetically the deferment of the closure that characterizes them, as in the closing credits of the second James Bond film, *From Russia with Love* (Terence Young, 1963): "The End ... Not Quite the End. James Bond will return in the next Ian Fleming thriller, *Goldfinger*," a technique that teases the viewer similar to the serial proper's cliffhanger (Chapman 138, in volume). Other film series, like Fantômas and Maisie, work under the recurring diegetic predicament of their main characters being broke and in desperate need of money and/or a job. The Torchy Blane movies skirt narrative closure structurally through the perpetual putting off of the one thing that could end the series: a wedding and the removal of Torchy to the domestic sphere. While each episode opens with a crime and leads to the comforting solution of that crime and the reestablishment of law and order at film's end, the inevitable delaying of the wedding throughout the entire series denies the viewer the "reassuring" narrative closure that typifies the genre(s) to which the series belongs, as well as the series's own peculiar formulaic structure.³ Indeed, the viewer and the film producer desire anything but the series's narrative closure, the former, because of the particular pleasure that series offer, the latter, because of the cost-effectiveness and low-financing risk of the series format.

Open-endedness is at the very heart of the series format, whether in film, literature, radio, television, or comics. Series also have no beginnings and no true ends. Yes, technically there are production releases that determine a beginning of a series, but, if we take the purest form of the series, each entry can be appreciated without consideration for the order of production. This absence of true diegetic chronology springs not only from the films' open-endedness, but from their suspension in time as well. As regards the Superman comic book series, for example, Umberto Eco notes that, outside the time associated with the evolution of one episode, the notion of time as a "law that leads from life to death" does not exist, for otherwise Superman would age and ultimately die (113–14). Most successful series do contain, however, a certain degree of serial continuity, as in the evolving personal life of Martin Riggs (Mel Gibson) in the Lethal Weapon films.

This is not the open-endedness that attracts highbrow audiences to art films, of course, however much both film series and art films encourage the viewer to interact in some fashion with the medium. Art films will often deny the viewer the comforting resolution associated with genre films. Series films permit generic closure (on the level of individual entries), but ultimately deny resolution (on the level of the series as a whole), because the idea is for the series to continue indefinitely. Art films present what they claim are unique stories that deny that they have any generic underpinnings. Series films flaunt their formulaic nature, banking on the viewer's wish for more adventures featuring the same characters. The significant trait serving to distinguish between these two forms of open-endedness is that, whereas art films promote a distinction based on their singularity, on their willful unlikeness to any other film, series films boast their singular replicability: each new entry promises to be both the same and different.

Social-Cultural Perspectives on the Series Form

Given the popularity of series, it is clear that certain audiences actively seek the kind of pleasure that such repetition and peculiar brand of open-endedness can offer. This pleasure has been explained as an instance of the Freudian concept of repetition compulsion: a child attempts to master separation anxiety from his mother by repeatedly playing at separation from his toys. According to Irène Krymko-Bleton, the adult reader who finds a series of novels — and by extension a film series — to which he can become attached, experiences, "The return to the reassuring world of repetition and moderated, controlled, and foreseeable variations that permit him to get reinvigorated in a protected corner of his childhood" (43).[4] Umberto Eco in *The Role of the Reader* locates the appeal of series in their ability to counter the disruptions of the contemporary world with the escape of comforting sameness and repetition (121). The meaning produced by each installment is always one and the same: the world of crisis can be restored to order. In this, the series seems to share traits with genres, which, according to the common wisdom, make order out of disorder. Both repetition compulsion and escape from the troubles of modern society can adequately serve as partial explanations for the success of an early cinema series like Louis Feuillade's Fantômas: each entry would ostensibly have helped the viewer to come to terms with the lawlessness that plagued France in the first decade of the twentieth century, while also communicating a sense that law would eventually triumph over disorder.[5] But repetition compulsion and escapism do not explain the massive appeal of a literary series figure like Sherlock Holmes, a drug addict who lives on the margins of society, or like Fantômas, who is just as thrilling a character as Detective Juve, and who is equally as masterful in the art of disguise, of film series characters like Ma and Pa Kettle, who are ill-adapted to modern conveniences and urban ways, of Tora-san, who is ill-equipped for assuming a responsible role in Japanese society, of Isma'il Yasin, who is "always up against orders and commands, and as sort of Egyptian Jerry Lewis, ... can never seem to get these straight," or Torchy Blane, who continually refuses to assume her traditional female role as wife and mother (Malkmus 84).

A private detective who works outside of the legitimate, often inept, forces of the law (Sherlock Holmes), a criminal whose disguises and savoir-faire permit him to circulate in sophisticated society so as to undermine it from within (Fantômas), a couple of yokels who wallow in dirt and disorder (Ma and Pa Kettle), a middle-age good-for-nothing (Tora-san), a woman of marriageable and childbearing age who skirts her social destiny as wife and mother (Torchy Blane), these are characters that contradict Eco's explanation of the reassuring repetition of the series format. On the contrary, given the social position of these series heroes and heroines, it can be surmised that in many ways the series aficionado seeks disruptions to, and subversions of, the status quo. The open-endedness of the unauthorly series is both a familiar and comforting place to which to return (genre) *and* the site of a certain resistance and insubordination. The genre(s) to which a series belongs, in tandem with the series's episodic nature — both guaranteeing the restoration of law and order at each film's end — serve to deflect attention away from the will to resistance inherent in the form's very repetition. An important component of the appeal of characters and the series to which they belong lies in how they offer and prolong a mode of resistance and insubordination for dominated groups, who continue to be the targeted audience of such fare.

The targeted audience for film series is often identified as the mass audience, composed of the entertainment-seeking lower and (lower-) middle classes, the upper-middle and upper classes possessing "higher" expectations associated with art. For Martin Esslin, who found in the series form an example of the "folk epic," series "represent a common meeting-ground of the imagination of a people or civilisation where its preoccupations and interests are focussed." Folk art, because it springs from the "collective subconscious of simple people (including, of course, the vulgar and uneducated entrepreneurs who promote it) will inevitably be mostly crude, vulgar, repetitive, unoriginal, poorly characterized and sentimental" (195). Esslin was concerned in 1975 with the advances in, and the exploitation of, media technology. He feared that the "vulgar" products of the neurotic subconscious of the United States (particularly its television series) would have a deleterious effect on other cultures with competing or entirely antithetical "collective subconscious" myths. Esslin's disapproving eye looking down from the pedestal of dominant culture, however, judges series in terms of that culture's standards of good taste, a stance whose purpose is precisely to police, if not exclude, the unrefined expressions of "simple" people. One senses in Esslin's ambivalence to the series that there is less a discomfort with the perceived imperialistic uses made of series than with the hybrid and unregulated nature of the form. It is doubtful that he had the same reservations regarding the exportation of prestige films, works that reflect a particular culture's greater aesthetic discrimination, its higher moral aspirations, and the distinctive voices of its finest creative representatives.[6] Indeed, in speaking in the same breath of both the "collective unconscious," an all-desiring id unconstrained by a proscripting superego, and the "vulgar and uneducated entrepreneurs" whose sole purpose is stereotypically the exploitation of unsuspecting consumers, Esslin references on the one hand the modern equivalent of the medieval fair described by Mikhail Bakhtin in *Rabelais and His World*, in which undifferentiated, communal expression operates in a marginal space outside authorized zones (where there is neither authority nor author), and, on the other hand, the post–Romantic ideal of keeping pure art distinct from base commerce.

In *The Role of the Reader*, his semiotic study devoted to determining precisely the role of the reader, Umberto Eco reveals a similar ambivalence toward literary series production and reception. Eco's purpose was to distinguish between different types of texts for which there would be necessarily different kinds of readers and reading strategies.[7] He proposed a basic binary opposition between "open" and "closed" texts, to which correspond respectively worldly and naive readers. Paradoxically, series texts (Superman comics, Ian Fleming's James Bond novels) are "closed" texts that are "open to any possible 'aberrant' decoding" (aberrant because not intended by the author), in other words, to any interpretation, counter-interpretation, or use (Eco 8). Eco notes regarding what he calls "closed" texts that, "These texts are potentially speaking to everyone.... It is enough for these texts to be interpreted by readers referring to other conventions or oriented by other presuppositions, and the result is incredibly disappointing (or exciting — it depends on the point of view)" (8). John Fiske offers an example of unrestricted interpretation with "Young urban Aborigines in Australia watching old Westerns on Saturday-morning television [who] ally themselves with the Indians, cheer them on as they attack the wagon train or homestead, killing the white men and carrying off the white women" (25). While this particular reading was either unintended or unanticipated by the producers of the Westerns, the assumption is that these viewers did not have enough authorial directives or obstacles to prevent such antithetical interpretations.

But is this really a case of unintended random interpretation? Especially in terms of transnational interaction, does this mean that most transcultural contact with American film products necessarily results in unrestricted interpretation and subsequent subversion of its product (as in the instance offered by John Fiske and in the way described by Esslin and Eco)? David Bordwell has noted regarding popular Hong Kong cinema — a cinema that has produced innumerable series (the Better Tomorrow, Once Upon a Time in China, and the One-Armed Swordsman series, to name a few) — that "popular cinema ... is deliberately designed to cross cultural borders," first, because "there are more commonalities than differences in human cultures" (in this sense, to echo Eco, these films are indeed "potentially speaking to everyone" in every culture), and second, because different cultures do not exist in cultural vacuums: "when they come into contact, borrowing is inevitable" (xi). Conventions belonging to, and techniques exploited by, one culture can be appropriated and often transformed by another culture. In this sense, the collective unconscious and the conscious are both at play. But Bordwell's conviction about the greater commonalities in cross-cultural film reception may be supported by comparisons that have been made to particular Hollywood film series. On the one hand, as critics within a particular national context or theoretical stance often contend, citing the similarities between one culture's films and Hollywood movies can be indicative of the derivative quality of these films *vis-à-vis* Hollywood productions: the amount of borrowing can eclipse a particular culture's potential artistic contribution to its own national cinema. On the other hand, instances of series like Algeria's Inspector Tahar and his faithful sidekick, which elicit references to the Hope-Crosby Road to ... movies, and Egypt's Isma'il Yasin, which bring to mind Jerry Lewis films, while they can represent valid indictments of Hollywood's dominance, may also reflect essentially stock social types existing in all cultures (Malkmus 84–85). While today non–American cinemas that aspire to critical recognition define themselves as working against an imperialistic and homogenizing Hollywood narrative paradigm, seeking to create movies that reflect specific cultural conditions and moments, those national cinemas with the means and market for large-scale production will make commercial films, of which many will adopt the series format.

While Eco seems less disturbed by the results that the reading of "closed" texts can produce ("disappointing" or "exciting"), he is dismissive of the potentially disorderly or random nature of those readings, precisely because of the small degree of authorial control involved. On the one hand, Eco's naive reader (whose culture may not be the same that produced Superman or James Bond) will not necessarily be the victim of colonization, as evidenced with Fiskes's example of Aborigines viewing American Westerns, since the texts lend themselves to multiple interpretations by "other conventions" or "other presuppositions." On the other hand, Eco himself as a casual reader of easily and rapidly "consumed" (and, hence, disposable) texts feels somewhat conflicted in that least bibliophilic of pleasures. One need only cite Eco's impeccable intellectual credentials (well-published and respected scholar and critic) to comfortably dismiss the potential cultural value of such low texts. The pleasure is as fleeting as the memory of the text (a paperback abandoned in an airplane seat or casually passed on to a friend with equally mixed tastes, a film viewed once, never to be visited again once it has been "consumed," etc.) that provided that pleasure, and easily explained as one of those nasty little habits that we, people of significant cultural capital, all harbor but acknowledge with reluctance.

Indeed, rather than function as an impartial examination of readers and reading strategies, Eco's analysis of the difference between a reader's role in "closed" and "open" texts ends by reaffirming the distinction of the high from the low, the tasteful from the vulgar, the artistic from the commercial, the original from the formulaic. The reader/spectator for the "closed" text seeks entertainment. The reader/spectator for the "open" text, however, seeks art, or that value which increases with the passage of time, encourages repeated readings/viewings, and which boasts transcendent qualities wholly freed from the bonds of time.[8] But Eco's guilty pleasure also possesses a component in which neat categories like high and low, and in particular, art and commerce, are upset. In referring to "closed" texts, Eco continually uses terms related to the verb "to consume" ("closed" texts are to be consumed quickly by the reader and discarded, "closed" tales do not "consume" themselves), a term that, while used primarily to emphasize the ephemeral nature of such texts, equally situates the series in an uncomfortable co-mingling of art and commerce, the same mixture that troubled Esslin. Eco and Esslin both associate "closed" texts with industrial-capitalist technologies, mass society, and the culture of consumerism. While it may be argued that Eco's description of "closed" texts refers to all formulaic texts in the context of commercial exploitation, whether as a singular instance of a genre or as a series, it is clear that the series (indicated by the two chapters he devotes to Superman comics and to Ian Fleming's Bond novels), by its very ability to spawn seemingly innumerable episodes, represents a greater degree of the formulaic. Add to that the absence of an author.

Historical Perspectives on the Series Form

Roger Hagedorn's theory regarding serial forms (the series proper, the serial proper, and the serial), while not offering an explanation for the pleasure such forms seem to give, does identify the consumer of them as belonging to a mass audience. While seriality as a literary and performance form has easily been around since the medieval period, its exploitation, he contends, only became significant with the development of large-scale publication, in particular with the serialized novel in newspapers in the early nineteenth century.[9] Serial forms, he argues, serve to "*promote the medium in which they appear,*" primarily in the way that they generate "product loyalty," not only to a particular product but to the producer's other products as well (5, emphasis in the original).[10] Newspaper publishers were able to lower the price of their newspapers and demonstrably increase their subscriptions simply by introducing the serialized novel as a standard feature. In general, he argues, those who have sought to establish a consumer for a new medium (e.g., film, radio, comics, television), have made specific use of serial forms: "One reason for this commercial success is that the serial cultivates a dependable group of consumers who are then available and predisposed to consume other types of texts provided by the medium in question" (12).

While on one level this argument is convincing, the development of the serialized novel in newspapers, however, presupposed the emergence of both large-scale publication *and* the entry of a new, larger, increasingly literate segment of the population into the consumer pool, along with the subsequent inclusion of the latter in considerations of the former's potential markets. While the medium's new technology (large-scale publication) had the potential to increase readership, that potential could only be actualized once the reading public for both newspapers and the serialized novel was in place.

In this instance, Hagedorn is referring essentially to a widened elite reading public, one for whom aesthetic considerations were increasingly important, and not to a mass readership. He offers Emile Girardin's *La Presse* and its serial publication of Honoré de Balzac's *La Vieille Fille* in 1836 as the first step in the movement towards increasing production volume, and thereby expanding readership.[11] In France, that new market was the bourgeoisie, who, under Napoleon, benefited from the establishment of public secondary schools and universities devoted in principle to education for all. As for the popular classes, however, primary education did not become free and obligatory until 1881–1882. In the United States and Great Britain as well, free and compulsory primary school education did not come about until the last half of the nineteenth century. The media for a true mass reading public did not realize its full potential until the second half of the nineteenth-century, in England with the "penny dreadfuls," in the United States with the "dime novel," and in France with the corresponding "roman-feuilleton."[12] Hagedorn notes that for the publishing industry, "the newspaper serial reduced financial risk by placing a novel in a large and less capital-intensive public forum, where it could demonstrate its commercial appeal and generate reader recognition — which explains why virtually every work of fiction written at the time appeared in serialized form before being published in book format" (6). It would be erroneous, however, to make the association between the newspaper serialization of novels like Charles Dickens *Pickwick Papers*, whose readers belonged to the middle class, and the publication of Nick Carter or Jesse James stories, whose readers belonged primarily to the popular classes. Serialized novels by authors like George Eliot and Balzac were coopted for high culture and have figured ever since as part of the cultural capital of the dominant classes. The stories published in dime novels and penny dreadfuls, however, whose content was generally deemed of little literary quality, and whose readers generally were esteemed to possess little cultural capital, were rarely appropriated for high culture.

In the nineteenth century, possessing the means to produce in great quantity necessitated rethinking notions of consumer markets. For all that, capitalism did not and does not represent one market, rather many markets representing different social groups (gender, ethnicity, age, levels of education, and so on) and classes (working class, middle class, and so on). A medium like film must cater to many different markets, the largest one of which is evidently the popular audience, and in order to compress the number of markets which they need to consider at any one time and with any one product, producers will often ambiguously suggest markers indicative of various genres so as not to alienate large groups unreceptive to a certain film type. In order to appeal to audiences with greater cultural aspirations, producers will upscale "low" material with higher production values, bigger actors, attention to the details of character psychology (as in New Hollywood series). The margin for crossing over between popular and prestige audiences, however, is limited: the latter encourages aesthetic distance, the former some form of participation. During the Classic Hollywood period, this distance was physical, as first-run movie theaters did not generally show series films, at least, not in urban centers, and rarely attached to the bottom half of bills. Because the popular audience, which favors genre and film series, is proportionally larger than the audience for prestige fare, it stands to reason that the production of works catering to that audience will be proportionally greater. Big commercial operations depend on this audience for viability, which in turn makes possible the ability to cater to smaller, elite audiences as well. It is common knowledge, for example, that B-unit films, of which series outnumbered all "recycled" productions (remakes, sequels, etc.), were the breadwinners for major and minor studios during the Classic Hollywood period, allowing them not only to remain solvent and provide steady work for their contract actors, but providing the means by which the major studios, at least, could offer the better-crafted and more costly productions that brought them prestige.

Hagedorn's contention that the series form flourished (and continues to flourish) as a result of modern media technologies turns on his privileging of serial over series forms, with the latter merely representing a secondary instance of seriality. In this he echoes Esslin who cited the *Iliad* and the *Odyssey* as examples of early series's forms. By reversing the order of focus, an entirely different historical and critical configuration presents itself. While not offering a specific term to differentiate between serial and series, Tudor Oltean does identify the "series" as the dominant category when referring to seriality: "A series requires a different story which is concluded in each episode, while the serial is provided with continuous storylines — normally more than one — that continue each episode.... Series and serial are thus two different types of series" (14). His approach, as well, however, situates the exploitation of the form firmly in the post-industrial period. Martin Priestman offers perhaps the best solution to the terminological quandary: "The series as such is the form which repeats, theoretically *ad infinitum*, the same kind of action in roughly the same narrative space or time-slot, featuring at least one character continuously throughout. Its particular qualities deserve a more accurate name than 'seriality': 'seriesicity,' perhaps" (51).

In identifying the serial as the quintessentially modern form for the promotion and establishment of new medias, Hagedorn's references to pre-industrial instances of seriality as "rudimentary"— citing highbrow literary examples like Honoré d'Urfé's *L'Astrée* and Madame de Sévigny's *Le Grand Cyrus*, in essence, long novels with courtly, not popular, origins — seemingly posit that neither series nor serials could realize their potential as dominant modes of popular entertainment without modern methods of production and distribution (5). In addition, Hagedorn's comment suggests the existence of only one market prior to the emergence of the mass market: the educated and moneyed classes. But there were other earlier uses of the series form, both literary and non-literary, that had the breadth and scope of industrial technologies (without, however, the benefit of their speed of production and distribution), as well as a large consuming public.

As an instance of a literary series, in France from the twelfth to the fourteenth century, a lengthy series of popular parodies of the aristocratic *chansons de geste* (epic poetry) and courtly romances (like the *romans bretons*) were written, with origins most likely in oral tales, and featuring the crafty fox (Renard) in his struggles against the wolf (Ysengrin) (*Le Roman de Renart*).[13] While the *chanson de geste* and the courtly romance were texts characterized by idealized notions of chivalry and the codification of relations between the sexes and among members of a higher social-economic class, the tales in the *Roman de Renart*, satirical in nature, had no such moral concerns and were, therefore, best suited to bringing to life the customs and social conditions of the period during which they were written (aspects for which films series are equally noted).

As an instance of a performance series, the *commedia dell'arte* with its myriad scenarios featuring stock characters like Pantalone, Punchinello, Arlecchino, Pulchinella, and Colombina enjoyed enormous success, primarily with the popular classes, but to varying degrees had bourgeois and aristocratic patrons as well, and this for well over five centuries.[14] Like film series, *commedia dell'arte* performances took a familiar structure (based on the typical traits associated with certain characters and the typical situations in which they would find themselves) and strove to make each one different, usually through the improvisational skills of the comedians. Like film series, which played an important role in creating the star system in the silent years, the *commedia* is credited with establishing the professional actor. And like film actors who are often conflated with their celebrated series roles (Basil Rathbone and Sherlock Holmes, Ann Sothern and Masie, Bela Lugosi and Dracula, etc.) or seek conflation with these roles (Kwan Tak-hing and the legendary Huang Feihong, etc.), in early seventeenth-century France, *farceurs* like Hugues Guéru, Robert Guérin, and Henri Legrand actively exploited the entertainment identities that became inseparable from their stock characters Gaultier-Garguille, Gros-Guillaume, and Turlupin (Fournel 436). The conflation of actor and character was not unwelcome, even with actors who moved back and forth between the fairground stage and officially sanctioned theaters, unlike many of today's film actors who often seek solely the distinctions conferred by prestige productions.

Problems of Authorship

As in series of all kinds, one cannot easily locate a site of authorship in *commedia* pantomime (even when there is clearly an author) primarily because of the generally collaborative, sometimes predatory (in addition to using parody, a form of borrowing, these productions often borrowed significantly from other works), nature of the series form (either as the production of a team of authors and/or performers, or as that of different successive authors).

Like television series, Classic Hollywood film series, and Hong Kong commercial cinema, *commedia* pantomimes involved a good deal of improvisation on the part of all members of a team or troupe, further complicating the search for a definitive written source. As regards popular literature, an example of problematic authorship is the Nancy Drew mystery series, the novels which have been the creation of several authors, all written pseudonymously under the name Carolyn Keene. A complex paternity is also found in the Saint film series from the Classic Hollywood period. RKO had purchased the film rights to several Saint novels by Leslie Charteris. While most of the films were based on Charteris's Saint stories, the fifth film in the series (*The Saint Takes Over* [Jack Hively, 1940]) had no other connection to the source than the two main characters (Simon Templar and Inspector Fernack), a common practice at the time. By the time of the filming of the seventh film in the series, Charteris was fighting with RKO over the liberties taken with both the character and the series, and as a result, "refused to permit the filming of any more of his properties" (Pitts 241).[15] Not to be outmaneuvered by Charteris, the studio started a new series, merely switching to another source text, Michael Arlen's story, "The Gay Falcon," yet all the while retaining the earlier characterization of the Saint. The Falcon was portrayed in the first four films by none other than the actor who had become synonymous with the Saint (George Sanders), and to all intents and purposes, the characterization was more or less a virtual "carbon copy of the Saint" (Pitts 241). Only the first of the sixteen Falcon films was based on Arlen's story, with the third, *The Falcon Takes Over* (Irving Reis, 1941), being an adaptation of Raymond Chandler's *Farewell, My Lovely*.[16]

Once a series character becomes fixed in the popular imagination, the original author often loses a certain degree of control over that character to other authors, if not to the public in general. To take Sherlock Holmes as an example, there are more non–Arthur Conan Doyle–authored stories featuring the master sleuth than ones by Doyle himself. In the 1940s Universal B film series, too, several of the entries, all directed by Roy William Neill, had no source in a novel or story by Arthur Conan Doyle outside of the key characters: *Sherlock Holmes in Washington* (1943), *The Woman in Green* (1945), *Terror by Night* (1946). As scholars of popular culture know, once a character seizes the popular imagination, there is a great temptation on the part of fans to have a say in the development of a character and/or to participate in some fashion with the series. This is sometimes the result of a series having been terminated, as in the first television *Star Trek* series, whose fans — perhaps the first truly large-scale underground fan organization — invented in an unfettered environment of creativity myriad unauthorized products, from novels, to stories, to games, to paraphernalia, until the *Star Trek* copyright holders got wind of this activity and jumped in to claim sole rights to the exploitation of the money-making potential of the enterprise.[17]

In our post-romantic era in which the original work of art is deemed fixed and inalterable, the tendency is to dismiss the seemingly authorless (because "anyone" can write an episode) products of the series format as ultimately frivolous and disposable. The tendency to invent new adventures for characters belonging to popular literature or film, particularly ones in series, is far greater than it is for those belonging to works that have been sacralized, not because of obstacles presented by copyright law, but because there exists greater respect for and more intense policing of original works. A case in point is legal wrangling recently involving a character who is felt to belong exclusively to her author and to high art. Italian author Pia Pera's novel featuring Nabokov's Lolita (*Diario di Lo/Lo's Diary* 1995) experienced a difficult road to publication in translation in the U.S. because of the objections of Nabokov heir (and copyright beneficiary), Dmitri Nabokov. Pera responded to the infringement suit by claiming that the character of Lolita had become part of contemporary society's cultural consciousness, a claim that pertains perhaps more to series characters than to Lolita. Ms. Pera's troubles did not end with the resolution of the copyright infringement case. Reviewers, who in many respects function as the guardians of the sanctity of original works of art and literature, generally accused her of vandalism. Few people, however, would accuse creators of new adventures for Nick Carter of vandalism, of violating the integrity of the original. J. K. Rowling, the author of the immensely popular Harry Potter series of novels, responded to an interviewer's query regarding rumors that two of the series's central characters would die in the seventh and last installment, by saying that, although she was not motivated by the same considerations in bumping off her characters, she understood "the mentality of an author who thinks, 'Well, I'm going to kill them off because that means there can be no non–author-written sequels'" (McGrath 12).[18] Killing off a series character does not always represent the end, since he can always be resurrected, as Sherlock Holmes was, eight years after Sir Arthur Conan Doyle had finished him off at the Reichenbach Falls, or an earlier or different period of his life can be explored, as in the life of Young Sherlock Holmes. What Rowling refers to, perhaps, is not the attempt by others than herself to continue telling Harry Potter tales (given the popularity of the character, this is going to happen regardless of her efforts), but to the unofficial creations of fans, which rarely enter the market. As long as the creators of unofficial works receive no financial compensation from their versions, they can basically continue to produce and distribute them with impunity. It is to be noted, however, that even fans police each other, expecting all who interact with a series to adhere to the traits of its characters and the narrative constraints of its formula.[19]

For critics, writers who write for series films, whether or not they are the original authors, generally forfeit claims to originality precisely because they write for a pre-existing format, for pre-developed characters, and, by association, within a formulaic genre. Indeed, Hagedorn and Oltean see series and seriality as establishing a relationship, not between author and audience, but for Oltean, between medium and audience/reader (if a series dies, "[i]t is a series that dies, not the series as paradigm"), and for Hagedorn, between media industries and audience/reader (Hagedorn 5, Oltean 13–14). This non–author-centered relationship presents "series and seriality as a condition of media culture," as formats suited to and exploited specifically by media industries "in order to cultivate a dependable audience of consumers" (Hagedorn 5). Hagedorn's argument offers the image of a passive public groomed to consume a product by a predatorily capitalistic industry (12). Oltean contends that "serial narratives reflect the structure of our world" (27). His position differs from that of Hagedorn in that he sees in the recourse to the form, not the exploitation of a passive consumer (this is not the focus of his essay), but an attempt to "seduce it [the audience] as a co-author of the whole" (27, 11). However limited in scope, the audience is engaged in the basic "creating and recreating [of] fictional worlds" (Oltean 12). On a very basic level, the audience does the work of actualizing the series mode by filling in the gaps that have been furnished by viewings of prior (or, out of sequence, as often is the case in serials) episodes, as well as the intervals between films, or in a first-time viewing, in actualizing the generic conventions. On a more complex level, the need that producers/creators have for the audience's work of "recreating" limits the amount of freedom that authors have in imposing their own vision on the spectator: the prior knowledge that the audience brings to bear on subsequent entries in a series constrains the producers/creators as well to respect and not deviate from the logic of the series's world as well as that of its generic conventions. It is to the advantage of both to adhere to the narrative cohesiveness of the series's world since neither the producer/creator/capitalist nor the spectator/recreator/consumer of a popular series wants the series to end.

Because patrons of a particular series are usually repeat viewers (repeating a viewing of the same film or viewing a new entry within a series, and therefore familiar with the conventions of that series), once the conventions of the series have been established, viewers' interest shifts from a focus on the unfolding of the narrative and its resolution to a focus on the characters' idiosyncrasies, on relations between characters, and on non-essential details (all the little winks and nods directed at the audience by a series's creators) that bind all entries in a series. To disparagingly dismiss series films based on their repetitive narratives is to misunderstand how they function: the narrative is just a vehicle for other activities whose fundamental quality is difference. On a very basic level, in the Torchy Blane series, viewers await the moment when Sergeant Gahagan will ask Lieutenant McBride if he can put on all the sirens in the police car, or for when he improvises a poem; in the Dr. Kildare series we await an event that will require ambulance driver Hayman and his trusty wrench to persuade someone not initially inclined to cooperate with Kildare; one looks forward to the kind of situation that will provoke one of Dr. Gillespie's outbursts; in the Charlie Chan films, the viewer anticipates one of Chan's humorously pithy sayings; in the James Bond films, fans anticipate the comic quip that always follows Bond's dispatching of a villain, or a new gadget and its eventual implementation. The moment must not, however, duplicate another moment from a different story. On a deeper level, audiences look forward to those moments in which Torchy Blane mutters disparaging, irreverent comments to her fiancé or other authority figures, comments that the viewer has clearly understood, comments that, when she is asked to repeat them, are displaced onto similar sounding words. This is not passive consumption, but play, on the part of the audience member who anticipates such recurring (yet contextually different) moments. And this is not assembly-line production, but play, on the part of writers, directors, and the rest of a series's creative team, not only with the conventions of the series and its genres, but with the codes of common cultural experience (series often parody other series, but especially works enjoying a certain cultural cachet).[20] The generic narrative resolution with its reinstatement of law and order at the episode's end, that same law and order that are said to provide the audience with vicarious and temporary deviation from social norms, and that are said to be that which attracts popular audiences, becomes only a structural vehicle that masks an array of disorderly, unpoliced activities. The sites of disorder are precisely those that are "open to any possible 'aberrant' decoding," that are open to any interpretation, counter-interpretation, or use because these texts have no intention of leaving a trail leading back to an author (Eco 8). The author is multiple — producer, writer, director, and spectator — and has no intention of being located.

Conclusion — Neverending Stories

Unlike serials, which postpone the narrative resolution (but not indefinitely) that will signify its technical end, the film series rarely ends in either a theoretical or a real sense. James Bond never retires (because he never gets old); Indiana Jones may have yet another adventure; Ripley may not have successfully destroyed the alien monster's offspring; Nancy Drew will never grow up. Actors may die prematurely, like Warner Oland and Sidney Toler, Charlie Chans number one and two respectively, and the series may never recover from that loss (as it was able to do the first time with the death of Chan number one); actors associated with a particular role may become too old to play their signature role (Kwan Tak-hing as the legendary Huang Feihong); novelists like Leslie Charteris may refuse to allow a studio to produce further entries in a series (the Saint series died, only to be replaced by a carbon copy series, the Falcon). Other factors may seemingly put the future of a series in the balance: Glenda Farrell decided not to continue as Torchy Blane; Timothy Dalton only agreed to portray James Bond for a few films (he was replaced by Pierce Brosnan in six films, who himself has been very successfully replaced more recently by the blond Bond, Daniel Craig); MGM decided not to renew Ann Sothern's contract, and so Maisie disappeared; a studio may kill a series due to sagging receipts. Oltean's remark that a series may die, but not the series paradigm, was in error. Series never really die: they merely go in (and sometimes are brought out of) a state of suspension.

Notes

1. In only one film is McBride the source for the deferment: *The Adventurous Blonde* (Frank McDonald, 1937).
2. "A garden, and a fence, and the patter of little typewriters" (*The Adventurous Blonde*).
3. The precise generic affiliation of the Torchy Blane series, as with a good number of series, is difficult to pin down. Depending on which source one consults, the series is described as generically mixed, drawing upon a combination of the mystery, crime, drama, or comedy genres.
4. Unless otherwise indicated, all translations from the French are mine.
5. See Richard Abel's "The Thrills of *Grande Peur*: Crime Series and Serials in the Belle Epoque" *The Velvet Light Trap* 37 (1996): 3–9.
6. One finds irony in the idea that the exportation of "finer" works is somehow less imperialistic. What "fine" art loses in apparent commercialization as it travels across borders, it gains in its mission of civilizing.
7. Eco's use of the words "text" and "reader" connotes any continuous discourse (including film, radio broadcasts, comic books, etc.) and any person receiving the communication of that discourse, respectively.
8. Devotees of particular film series (as well as those of novel, radio, comic book series, etc.) have demonstrated that the contrary is true. True fans revisit series material on a regular basis, but not in the same way as the reader for "open" texts seeking a text's transcendent qualities. Fans engage in active play with series, one component of which is the ability to reproduce lengthy dialogues and provide details, often seemingly insignificant, on

demand. The truths that fans find do not ultimately go beyond the text, but rather are anchored wholly in the commonplace world of that text.

9. Esslin dates the first recorded instances of serial form (although his discussion and title specifically references series, not serials) as far back as antiquity: "The *Iliad* and the *Odyssey* are distillations of hundreds and thousands of crude episodes that were not worth preserving. And there are whole centuries of such popular products which have not survived at all, because they brought forth nothing worthy of survival" (195).

10. Hagedorn uses the term "serial" to refer to a continuing narrative cut into episodes, serials with cliffhangers (the "serial proper"), and independent episodes with recurring characters (the "series proper") (8).

11. The first *feuilleton-roman* was actually Alexandre Dumas's *La Comtesse de Salisbury*, which was serialized in *La Presse* from July 15 to September 11 of 1836. Balzac's novel appeared from October 23 to November 30.

12. The *roman-feuilleton* can refer to both serial and series literature. Today the term "paralittérature" is used to refer to, among other things, this lower form of literature that doesn't aim toward the recognition of its literary value.

13. There are roughly twenty-seven extant stories in the *Roman de Renart*.

14. The *commedia* was well established in Italy by the end of the sixteenth century, and soon spread in popularity across Europe.

15. Two more Saint films were made.

16. This was the first film adaptation of the novel, making Edward Dmytryk's *Murder My Sweet* (1944) a remake. This film also references its filiation to the earlier Saint series by appropriating its title: *The Saint Takes Over* (Jack Hively, 1940). George Sanders's brother, Tom Conway, took over the role of the Falcon until the end of the RKO series, once he tired of the series. There were three final entries produced by Film Classics and starring John Calvert.

17. See Gary Westfahl, "Where No Market Has Gone Before: 'The Science-Fiction Industry' and the *Star Trek* Industry," *Extrapolation: A Journal of Science Fiction and Fantasy* 37.4 (Winter 1966): 291–301.

18. Rowling, herself, was the target of many attacks by critics in the early stages of the Harry Potter series's popularity, many of which cast doubt on her authorship, first, by claiming that she plagiarized other, presumably better, children's literature authors, and by extension, by defining the lead character as a generic type to be found in any number of children's novels.

19. For a discussion of fan culture, see Henry Jenkins' *Textual Poachers: Television Fans and Participatory Culture* (New York: Routledge, 1992).

20. For example, the Scary Movie series does not only send up horror flicks. The first two entries (2000, 2001) did, indeed, spoof horror movies like the Scream series, but the 2003 and 2006 installments have branched out of the horror genre (and expanded the audience to include those may not go to horror films) to include lampoons of action/adventure/science fiction films (the last one parodied primarily Steven Spielberg's *War of the Worlds* [2005]).

Works Cited

Balio, Tino, ed. *Grand Design: Hollywood as a Modern Business Enterprise, 1930–1939.* Berkeley: University of California Press, 1993. Vol. 5 of *History of the American Cinema.* 10 vols. 1994–2006.
Banville, Théodore de. *Mes Souvenirs.* Paris: Charpentier, 1882.

Bordwell, David. *Planet Hong Kong: Popular Cinema and the Art of Entertainment.* Cambridge, MA: Harvard University Press, 2000.
Eco, Umberto. *The Role of the Reader: Explorations in the Semiotics of Texts.* Bloomington: Indiana University Press, 1979.
Esslin, Martin. "The Television Series as Folk Epic." *Superculture: American Popular Culture and Europe.* Ed. C.W.E Bigsby. Bowling Green: Bowling Green University Popular Press, 1975. 190–198.
Fiske, John. *Understanding Popular Culture.* Boston: Unwin Hyman, 1989.
Fournel, Victor. *Les Rues du vieux Paris: galerie populaire et pittoresque.* Paris: Firmin-Didot, 1879.
Hagedorn, Roger. "Technology and Economic Exploitation: The Serial as a Form of Narrative Presentation." *Wide Angle: A Film Quarterly of Theory, Criticism, and Practice* 10.4 (1988): 4–12.
Krymko-Bleton, Irène. "Du 'Déjà-lu': la répétition au service du principe de plaisir." *Etudes littéraires* 30.1 (Fall 1997): 37–44.
Malkmus, Lizbeth, and Roy Armes. *Arab and African Film Making.* London: Zed, 1991.
McGrath, Charles. "And They All Died Happily Ever After." *New York Times* 2 July 2006, sec. 4:12
Oltean, Tudor. "Series and Seriality in Media Culture." *European Journal of Communication* 8.1 (1993): 5–31.
Pitts, Michael R. *Famous Movie Detectives.* Metuchen, N.J.: Scarecrow, 1979.
Priestman, Martin. "Sherlock's Children: the Birth of the Series." *The Art of Detective Fiction.* Ed. Warren Chernaik and Robert Vilain. New York: St. Martin's, 2000: 50–59.

EARLY CINEMA

2

The Intertextuality of Early Cinema: A Prologue to Fantômas, *Film and Novel*

TOM GUNNING

Before Adaptation

I would claim that there was no such thing as film adaptation of literary works during the first decade of the cinema's existence. Cinema emerged at the end of the nineteenth century within a welter of popular entertainments recently transformed by new technologies of mechanical reproduction into a complex environment of mass entertainment. In spite of the best efforts of film historians to identify the personnel behind the first films issued by the Lumière and Edison companies (and a flood of individual film companies around the world), these films were issued as unauthored works, in most countries barely protected by copyright. For the most part, films in the 1890s functioned as the software used by exhibition companies (such as the Lumière Company and the American [or British] Biograph Company) to demonstrate the hardware of their projecting machines. The first film audiences crowded into exhibition halls and vaudeville theaters to see the Biograph, the Vitascope, or the Cinématographe, rather than a particular film, let alone the work of a specific filmmaker. This was an era of technical marvels and mechanical novelties, rather than of individual authors or texts.

Yet far from being a primitive form of folk art, this modern form of entertainment issued primarily from highly capitalized and sophisticated

---

First published as "A Tale of Two Prologues: Actors and Roles, Detectives and Disguises in *Fantômas*, Film and Novel," by Tom Gunning from *The Velvet Light Trap* 37, pp. 30–36. Copyright © 1996 by the University of Texas Press. All rights reserved.

corporations, who utilized cutting-edge technology and were well aware of the business practices of high capitalism. During cinema's first decade, while films were hardly regarded as individualized works of art, their production companies aggressively sought to guarantee their profit-making potential and employed legal means to protect their right to their exclusive exploitation. Conceiving of films as commodities rather than authored works, early film companies utilized trademarks (included in film intertitles and sometimes actually placed within sets themselves) and company brand names to legally claim ownership, rather than employing discourses of authorship or claims of intellectual property. The copyright law in the United States, for instance, did not recognize films as examples of dramatic or narrative work. Before the law was amended in 1912 to include motion pictures, films were copyrighted as photographs, and it was their exact visual appearance that was granted legal protection.[1] It is nearly impossible to "adapt" a photograph.

Thus when the Edison Company was sued by the American Mutoscope and Biograph Company in 1904 for having produced a film entitled *How a French Nobleman Found a Wife through the New York Herald Personal Columns*, which re-staged shot by shot their successful film comedy *Personal*, the court found that no copyright was violated, since the Edison film, while containing the same plot, characters, and action, did not actually reproduce the photography of the earlier Biograph film.[2] It was not until 1909, when a lawsuit brought against the Kalem Company for their 1907 film version of *Ben Hur* was finally decided, that a United States court recognized the possibility of copyright violation by a film version of a copyrighted narrative work in another medium.[3] This date corresponds with the period in which the film industry worldwide underwent an enormous economic reorganization (typified by the Motion Picture Patents Company in the USA and by the Congress [sic] de Paris and formation of the Congrès International des Editeurs du Film in Europe), bringing economic organization and predictability to the film market.[4]

It was also at about this time that film production companies recognized the fictional narrative as the major genre of film and storytelling and as the stylistic dominant guiding how they were made. The nickelodeon revolution had begun a very few years earlier in the United States, as thousands of film theaters opened nationwide charging a cheap admission price and attracting a mass audience. This transformation in film exhibition paralleled a marked rise in the popularity of story films over the actualities, magical trick films, and brief gags that had dominated film programs during cinema's first decade.[5] With the appearance of new character-driven stories, filmmakers began to employ styles of editing, staging, and acting, as well as intertitles, that made the stories and their characters easier to follow and emotionally involving even to unsophisticated audiences. Thus a cinema of narrative integration arose in which the idea of adaptation from literary sources became a possibility.[6]

My claim that there was no literary adaptation in cinema before roughly 1907 does not mean that there were no films based on famous novels or plays before that date. On the contrary, scores of films took their action or characters from such classic or popular works as *Ten Nights in a Bar Room, Faust, Uncle Tom's Cabin, Hamlet, Robinson Crusoe,* or *Rip Van Winkle*. However, calling these early films "adaptations" only confuses things and threatens to superimpose later categories onto an early practice with a different cultural background and intention. Rather than attempting to realize a literary work in the new medium of film, these early films *make reference* to famous works, often relying on what Charles Musser calls "audience foreknowledge."[7] Thus a film version of *Ten Nights in a Bar-Room* might only include five famous, but rather brief, moments from the well-known temperance drama, each a separate film (*Death of Little Mary, Vision of Mary, The Fatal Blow, Murder of Willie,* and *Death of Slade,* all copyrighted by the American Mutoscope and Biograph Company in 1903 and none lasting more than a minute). A film might be made of only the duel scene from *Macbeth*[8] or a series of scenes from *Rip Van Winkle*.[9] This "peak moment" approach, excerpting a famous action from already well-known works, paralleled similar treatments of well-known material in vaudeville programs (which might present a famous speech, song, or action-packed moment from a famous play, usually performed by the actor who made it famous), or even the illustration of famous gestures or *tableaux* from plays in journal illustrations and popular prints. We might call this strongly intertextual practice, which has little interest in the integrity of the text, a cinema of reference rather than adaptation, the goal being to recall a famous work or even a specific performance, rather than give a treatment of its narrative or dramatic content.

Even the longer films that seem at least to summarize (usually in a ten-minute version) the whole action of a work (such as Edison's film of *Uncle Tom's Cabin* from 1903 or Méliès's 1904 *Faust and Marguerite*) would be best approached as traditional adaptations. Instead of a relation to a single ur-text, such films relate to a process and history of absorption and reference in which the original novel or verse drama can only be glimpsed (sometimes much transformed) through a variety of appropriations, including stage melodramas or operas and a variety of other popular forms (parodies, popular songs, visual illustrations, and prints). Porter's *Uncle Tom's Cabin* or Méliès's various Faust films work less as adaptations than as palimpsests of references caught within an echo chamber of popular memory.[10]

Further, one should not focus exclusively on the relation of early film to literature, as the lens of adaptation would encourage us to do. Early films find inspiration and material in diverse sources: vaudeville acts, dance crazes, political cartoons, comic strips, musical revues, popular songs, famous paintings, commercial advertisements, catch phrases, minstrel shows, verbal jokes, and clown gags. Such a range of sources affirms not only the place of early film within an unstable environment of popular commercial entertainments, but also the process of multiple reflection and reverberation, creative appropriation, self-conscious parody, and unconscious theft that dominated this world, blurring distinctions between individual works in favor of a promiscuous intermingling. Thus a Biograph film, *Foxy Grandpa and Polly in a Little Hilarity* (1902), not only refers to a popular comic strip of the era (about which the Biograph Company made a series of films besides this one), but also to a musical review based on the comic strip (whose star, Joseph Hart, appears in the film) and to a popular dance (the "little hilarity") which he performs in the film. To trace an early film back to a single source would not only be difficult, but also efface the actual context of free borrowing across and within media which characterizes early film production and much early popular commercial entertainment.

But with the transformations (which Yuri Tsivian, tracing a similar change in Russian cinema of the time, calls a "reception shift") that occurred around 1909, the meaning of adaptation changed (23–24). Literary rights were recognized legally in the USA, and, internationally, the prestige of an adaptation for a burgeoning industry desirous of middle-class acceptance became obvious. The French *Films d'art* premiering in 1908 produced both original works and filmic adaptations of classics, proclaiming that cinema was a new art form (whose artistry was based not so much on its originality as on its pedigree, with the new company employing actors and authors well known from the theater).[11] During 1909 nearly every film company around the world was influenced by the *Films d'art* innovations and produced what William Uricchio and Roberta Pearson have called "quality films" whose mark of distinction came from the cultural capital of either portraying events of history or mounting adaptations from literature.

However, these same film companies (especially in the USA) generally recognized the need to retain a large, popular, working-class audience, even as they pursued their middle-class aspirations, playing to the masses while attracting the classes, to paraphrase early film entrepreneurs. Thus, adaptations began not only of classic or culturally recognized works, but also of the popular literature with which cinema had much in common. Somewhat redefining the promiscuous intertextuality of the previous era, popular film genres emerged — Westerns, melodramas, and detective films — whose repetitive formulas reference a domain of shared plots, character types, and situations that exceed the boundaries of one-to-one adaptation from a single text. But the prestige of certain works of popular fiction, along with the tightening of legal protection against unacknowledged adaptation, led to film versions of, for instance, the Sherlock Holmes stories of Arthur Conan Doyle (often filtered through the various stage adaptations of Holmes) and of the work I will focus on in this chapter, the serial novel *Fantômas* by Marcel Allain and Pierre Souvestre.[12] Here the one-to-one comparison of the literary text to its filmic adaptation shows both the elements that film genres were absorbing from popular literature and also the difference in narration that film, as a visual form, seemed to offer filmmakers such as Louis Feuillade in 1913.

Spreading Terror: Popular Crime Fiction and Cinematic Narrative

"Fantômas."
"What did you say?"
"I said 'Fantômas.'"
"And what does that mean?"
"Nothing.... Everything."
"But what is it?"
"Nobody ... and yet, yes, it is somebody."
"And what does the somebody do?"
"Spreads terror" [Allain and Souvestre 11].

With this unattributed dialogue, Marcel Allain and Pierre Souvestre began the first chapter of the first volume of their narrative of the exploits of Fantômas, a narrative which would extend to thirty-two volumes. As the source of such a Niagara of literary production, it is worth lingering over. In fact, the authors withhold the identity of the speakers in this dialogue for two pages, delaying their appearance through an accumulation of Balzac-like details of setting and character description. Through this separation from its enunciating characters, the opening dialogue seems suspended above the narrative, functioning almost like an epigraph, a prologue, or the argument for the piece.

And this is undoubtedly the intention. The stylistic device accomplishes, with great economy and elegance, a number of narrative tasks. By avoiding immediate identification of the speakers, it announces formally, through a sort of mini-enigma, its allegiance to the genre of mystery stories, tales of suspense. Further, the lack of attribution of the words spoken raises in narrative form the very issue discussed in the conversation, the tremulous nature of identity and names — the phantom-like obscurity of the figure Fantômas, who appears in much of the novel as little more than a name. The terror that name produces derives to a large degree from the mystery that surrounds its uncertain identity so well described by this opening dialogue: nobody, yet somebody, nothing and everything.

The initial speaker is eventually identified as President Bonnet, a retired magistrate (and fairly minor character in the tale). He soon extends his opening enigmatic remarks with a further description of this mysterious figure:

> It is impossible to say exactly what or to know precisely who Fantômas is. He often assumes the form and personality of some particular and even well-known individual; sometimes he assumes the form of two human beings at the same time.... That he is a living person is certain and cannot be denied, yet he is impossible to catch or identify. He is nowhere and everywhere at once [14].

But the exact identity of Bonnet's interlocutor in the opening dialogue is never firmly established. It could be any one of the guests whom the president regales with his description of the mysterious criminal at the dinner party given by the Marquise de Langrune that evening. This lack of a specifically named addressee seems designed to encourage the reader to insert him or herself in this unknown questioner's position. Like the interrogator, he or she knows nothing yet of Fantômas, is curious to know more, and is eager to formulate the enigmas which express this curiosity and which will fuel the act of reading and decoding that the mystery genre demands.

However, among the assembled audience of guests for Bonnet's invocation of the name of Fantômas, a young man named Charles Rambert expresses the greatest interest, paralleling the ardent questioner of the opening dialogue. Charles displays a curiosity so intense that Bonnet finds it excessive and even distasteful. "I fail to understand your attitude, young man," he says reproachfully. "You appear to by hypnotized, fascinated" (19). And, indeed, that night, trying to sleep at the Marquise's chateau, Rambert seems to be haunted, not simply by the name Fantômas, but by a protean series of images it summons up:

> In his imagination Charles saw all sorts of sinister and dramatic scenes, crimes and murders. Hugely interested, intensely curious, craving for knowledge, he generally was given to concocting plots and trying to unravel mysteries. If for an instant he dozed off, the image of Fantômas took shape in his mind, but never twice the same way. Sometimes he saw a colossal figure with bestial face and muscular shoulders; sometimes a wan, thin creature, with strange and piercing eyes; sometimes a vague form, a phantom–Fantômas [21].

Rambert, in fact, awakes in the morning to find his hostess, the Marquise, dead. Wakening into a nightmare, as the latest victim of Fantômas's histrionic machinations, he becomes the key suspect in her murder. As if immersed in the hallucination brought on by his fascination with Bonnet's invocation, he loses his own sense of identity, becoming an accused murderer, forced for a time to hide disguised as a chambermaid, while a drowned body without a recognizable face is identified as his own. Eventually taken under the protection of Detective Juve, his new mentor fashions for him a new identity a and a new name. He asks Juve to make it "something arresting — like Fantômas" and takes on the name Jerome Fandor, the investigative journalist sidekick of Detective Juve in many of the succeeding volumes (210). However, this rescue through the agency of Fantômas's detective nemesis only underscores Charles's brush with oblivion, a fitting punishment perhaps for his over-susceptibility to Fantômas's fascination.

If the reader seems at first to be identified with this too-impressionable victim of Fantômas's spell, readers familiar with the genre soon recognize their preferred surrogate in Detective Juve, who sees through appearances in order to sketch with clarity the shadowy figure of the master criminal. The opening of the novel, therefore, first proposes a dangerous way to receive its tale of villainy: Charles's dream-like submission to its thrill of evil; then the proper alternative: Juve's both rational and intuitive scrutiny and detection. Following genre tradition, it is Juve who at the climactic trial of Fantômas (under his alias of Gurn) will provide the interpretation which converts the events of the mystery *syuzhet* into a solution *fabula*, the position of final knowledge which the reader shares with satisfaction.[13]

To note that *Fantômas* makes use of shifting identities simply fixes its place in the already established genre of detective adventures in which both criminals and detectives ply their trades through a mastery of disguise. But the particular care with which Allain and Souvestre keep the actual identity of Fantômas intangible beneath his various avatars produces an elaborate and somewhat unique game for mystery readers, focused less on the traditional mystery riddle of naming the culprit than on recognizing the already named villain beneath a succession of aliases: Etienne Rambert, Gurn, Professor Swelding, plus a variety of unnamed walk-on (or rather run-through) parts. Throughout the first two volumes at least, Fantômas remains a truly ambiguous figure, little more than a name whose presence is suspected behind his actions. The novels present a series of crimes and a cast of characters, and only gradually is the figure of Fantômas revealed beneath his disguises. As Juve laments to another police officer in the second volume in the series, *Juve versus Fantômas*:

> "We see the puppets moving — Loupart, Chaleck, Josephine, others maybe — but we don't see the strings."
> "Perhaps the strings that move them are none other than — Fantômas," ventured Michel" [106].

This conversation provides the structure of the first eight novels.[14]

Through a restrictive narration, which is designedly uncommunicative, readers are kept in the dark about the true nature of characters. In *Juve versus Fantômas*, for instance, Chaleck and Loupart turn out to be the same character, and both of them are revealed to be disguises assumed by Fantômas. However, they are presented on the *syuzhet* level as if they are separate characters, and their identity with Fantômas is only revealed toward the very end of the tale. Allain and Souvestre supply in the first installment of *Fantômas* a wonderful image for this now-you-see-it-now-you-don't figure (which appears in the first of the Feuillade film series as well): the initially blank calling card he leaves with Princess Danidoff after stealing her jewels and cash which after a time slowly displays the legend "Fan-to-mas."

In adapting Allain and Souvestre's novels to the screen, Louis Feuillade skillfully streamlined a plot designed for extended reading in a serial publication into a series of fast-paced, semi-independent, multi-reel films. As Jacques Champreux points out, Feuillade cannily eliminated the complex plot elements dependent on interlocking railway timetables (a frequent device in turn-of-the-century detective novels) (256). Even more crucial to the simplifying of the narrative line, he also cut the complicated plot of Charles Rambert and his supposed father, picking up the character already transformed into the journalist Fandor. But perhaps most fundamentally, Feuillade transformed the narrative role of the reader/viewer by immediately imaging Fantômas beneath (and alongside) his disguises.

He does this by opening both of the first two installments of Gaumont's Fantômas series, *Fantômas* and *Juve contre Fantômas*, with prologues which play a complementary role to the opening dialogue of the series of novels. Like the opening dialogue, these sequences deal with events and characters within the fictional world yet stand outside them. They also rehearse for the audience, before narrative events get under way, the films' themes of identity and illusion and formally indicate the reader's relation to these mysterious transformations. In the films these sequences act as peritexts on the threshold of the diegesis.[15] They function more as title sequences than as part of the unfolding narrative. Each of these opening sequences introduces the actor René Navarre as Fantômas and presents Fantômas in the disguises he uses in the film. In *Fantômas* these are Dr. Chaleck, an unnamed hotel porter, and Gurn, and in *Juve contre Fantômas* these are the apache Loupart, Chaleck, and the hooded and robed "man in black."[16] In the second film, a similar sequence is also devoted to Bréon, the actor who portrays Juve, who is shown in several of the disguises he employs in his pursuit of Fantômas.

What are we to make of this essential change in narrative address between film and novel? I believe that, like all significant textual nodes, it reflects the intersection of several concerns. First, the most frequent narrative approach in early feature films is one that rarely withholds knowledge from its audience. Although enigmas occur in early feature films, they tend to result from questions about the proairetic events (in other words, questions about how things are going to turn out) rather than from withholding knowledge from the audience, particularly "back stories" of events shown on the screen.

This narrative strategy undoubtedly has several motivations. A linear story line is easier to follow in a medium whose use of flashbacks in this period remains primarily limited to brief inserts of character (or viewer) memory. Apparently, early filmmakers had doubts about the ability of audiences to follow a nonchronological exposition of earlier events via an extended flashback (which could actually reconfigure the meaning of events already shown) and therefore limited the play in early films between *fabula* and *syuzhet* on which mystery narratives often depend. The narration of early features tends to be extremely communicative. Therefore, films adapted in the 1910s from literary sources often unscrambled the events of the *syuzhet* and presented them in a chronologically linear fashion. For instance, the 1919 adaptation that Léonce Perret (Feuillade's former colleague at Gaumont) made in the United States of Wilkie Collins's *The Woman in White*, entitled *The Twin Pawns*, begins with the separation of identical twins, which forms one of the final climactic revelations of the novel. Likewise, Vitagraph's *A Tale of Two Cities* begins with the romance which causes the imprisonment of Dr. Manette, an enigma the novel reveals only gradually.

Further, as Richard Abel reveals in his treatment of the French crime film in his work *The Ciné Goes to Town*, crime films were subject during this period to special scrutiny by censors and government officials. It is possible that Feuillade's opening could reassure censors by providing viewers with a more secure orientation toward this rather anarchistic drama than its literary source provided.[17] One might return to the novel's original dialogue on Fantômas. The lack of a secure identity for this master criminal sparks Charles's fascination and brings on the disturbing hallucination/nightmare of Fantômas's protean power. A film with a similarly disorienting narrative address might threaten to turn viewers into victims of fascination (if they were not undone by narrative confusion). Instead, Feuillade immediately places them into a secure and knowing reading position, like that of Detective Juve, who sees the figure behind the disguises and is able to see through Fantômas's powerful visual illusions.

The legal apparatus of the Third Republic showed great concern to maintain stable identity, particularly of malefactors. The Bertillon method of identification through carefully cross-indexed photography and anthropometry was aimed primarily at establishing scientifically certain identification of those arrested in spite of attempts at disguise or false names. Such clear identification would allow law enforcement officials to isolate recidivists, the repeat offenders who so obsessed the criminologists of a society terrified of "degenerate" criminal types.[18] Fantômas plays on these fears with delight and thumbs his variety of nose types at any attempt to fix identity and culpability. However, the opening sequence of the Gaumont film reveals what the criminal conceals, and creates for the film viewer a reassuring sense of the underlying unity of Fantômas's character, whose equivocal nature in the original novels provides many of their narrative enigmas. Important as this play with the social regulation of the identity of social deviants is in explaining the structure of *Fantômas*, this film sequence appears overdetermined. As a prologue it strikes viewers familiar with the devices of early feature films less as a unique opening than as a variation on a form of prologue quite frequent in this period in both American and French films: the introductory sequence that presents both actors and their roles. The sequences in the first two Fantômas films not only reveal Fantômas beneath his disguises; they also introduce the actor Navarre alongside his fictional roles. Indeed, one could argue that the identity the prologue reveals as underlying the various roles embodied by these disguises is less that of the character Fantômas than that of the actor Navarre who plays all these roles, including Fantômas.

These actor-centered introductory film sequences seem to appear first in France and to serve several functions. Most obviously, they mark a change in modes of production and reception, moving from the previous anonymity of players to a new emphasis on the presence of actors, often stars previously known from theatrical careers, in films. Following the logic of the *Films d'art*, these prologues announce the importance of the actor and bring to films the imprimatur and cultural capital of theater, while they instruct audiences that they should receive the film partly as a performance in which the actor's skill is appreciated beneath the role.[19] In the Fantômas films, this relatively new protocol of film viewing as actor watching becomes doubled (or tripled) as one admires not only the actor's but also the character's skill at role-playing. If film viewers (at least in France) had already learned to recognize performers, a film like *Fantômas* redoubled these pleasures by cueing them to recognize actors like Navarre or Bréon in a variety of roles and also to note the power of make-up and costuming, elements of showmanship fully recognized in theater.

After the initial introduction of the concept of the actor (that is, a person recognizable from several roles, not simply a performer) to cinema around 1908–09, a number of techniques in early feature films from around 1912–14 seem to renew this novelty of actor recognition through a series of baroque variations. Actors play multiple roles or even appear as twin characters through devices of re-photography in a number of highly publicized early features. The multiple disguises of Fantômas and Juve can be seen as one of the ways in which early feature films drew audience attention to the still relatively recent phenomenon of the film actor separate from (or underlying) specific roles.

Yet, at the same time, the position of Navarre in these prologues remains somewhat paradoxical. The opening shot of the actor without disguising make-up asserts his stable identity as a performer. But the succession of disguises seems to progressively obscure his identity as much as it affirms his skill as an actor and his ability to merge with his role. This sense of vanishing identity is clearest in the prologue of *Juve contre Fantômas* as we move from the undisguised, hairless face of Navarre to the hirsute disguises of Loupart and Chaleck. It then reaches its climax (marked by a change in lighting and possibly tinting) with his apotheosis as the "man in black" when he pulls the hood over his face and becomes concealed from the viewer. This figure, masked and hooded with all individual features concealed, stands in the film series as the ultimate image of Fantômas, even more than the domino-masked titan looming over Paris that Gaumont adapted from the cover of the first Fantômas volume for the film poster.

We find in these film prologues, then, two identities being formulated for audiences to follow. On the one hand, they inscribe the figure of Navarre the actor, who might be remembered from a number of previous performances at Gaumont (and who could be followed in a number of non–Fantômas roles to come). On the other hand, they also fix the image of Fantômas, criminal genius and master of disguise, who can also be followed in a series of films. If the identification of actors as figures existing beneath their roles is a general strategy of the French film industry of this period, the creation of a consistent character, tied to (but not restricted to) a performer, was also essential to achieving the equally important marketing strategy of the film "series."[20] The series appears in its most obvious form in the comic films produced in the 1910s by French studios. Gontran, Onésime, Rigadin, Bébé, Rosalie, and others all name characters in series of films whose titles invariably included their character names.

The early French detective film genre also used recurring characters to define series. Several studios had recurring detective heroes (occasionally based on a literary prototype) with a string of separate film adventures: Eclair's Nick Carter, Pathé's Nick Winter, Eclipse's Nat Pinkerton. This genre dealt in a more complex way with the nature of a recurring character than the comedies were able (or needed) to. Most of the detective characters employed disguises which endowed their recurring characters with a range of appearances. The fairly simple approach to recurring characters in the comedies, the immediately recognizable physique and physiognomy of rotund Rosalie, goofy Rigadin, or dapper Max which quickly established audience familiarity and expectations, was given a baroque variation in the detective genre as audiences recognized an established figure often hidden beneath a deceptive appearance.

Further, the dangers endemic in the detective genre made the detective's continued appearance from film to film the result of a nearly preternatural invulnerability, rather than the irrepressible suite of reappearance of the comedians. The dramatic overcoming of death by detectives or criminals provided a way of intensely dramatizing the continuation of the series. Recall that both the last lines of *Juve contre Fantômas* and the final title of Feuillade's film version (which comes after Fantômas triggers the dynamite explosion of Lady Beltham's villa with Juve and Fandor within) equivocally close their narratives with the words: "But were Juve and Fandor among the dead?"

Thus, Eclipse's publicity announced in December 1911, after a series of Nat Pinkerton adventures: "No. He is not dead. The famous detective, the police agent so loved by the public continues the series of his exploits in *Nat Pinkerton l'emmuré*."[21] Eclair also announced a new film in its Nick Carter series with a full-page advertisement containing a dramatic black-bordered announcement stating simply: "Nick Carter is not dead."[22] Similarly, when Eclair began its publicity for its second Zigomar film, it immediately addressed the fact that in its first feature Zigomar had seemed to perish in the explosion of his subterranean criminal lair. The first advertisement hinting at the second Zigomar film addressed this question to its readers: "Who, then, has claimed that Zigomar was dead — under the smoking rubble of his mysterious hideout — after the explosion of the crypt? A slight noise."[23]

We recognize here a familiar narrative device of both the adventure film serial and the character-based thriller series: the redefinition of narrative closure in which what seemed in one film a definitive demise becomes redefined in a sequel as somehow less than fatal. In this structure, character recognition and popularity overrule credibility and discrete narrative form. The heroes of these crime film series display not only an ability to appear in various roles and guises, but also a near immortality based less on verisimilitude than on popularity and profitability. The mysterious identity and powers of these characters could be used to motivate their continued appearance in a succession of films even when their mortality appeared to have been tested to the limits. But the longevity of such characters, especially of the master criminals such as Zigomar or Fantômas, was partly naturalized by the very malleability of their ambiguous identity. They could *play* dead because they were so good at disappearing under assumed identities. They could be resurrected because their power of disappearance entailed a complementary ability to materialize unexpectedly.

If Feuillade avoided the incommunicative narrative structure that defined the ambiguous nature of Fantômas's character in Allain and Souvestres's novels, he nonetheless found in the figure of the "man in black" (Fantômas in his tight-fitting leotard and *cagoule*) a visual correlative to an anxiety-causing effacement of individuality. While the visual appearance of this figure undoubtedly has many antecedents, at least one of these would seem to be the dark-robed and hooded figures of the theater of illusions that allowed the magical manipulation of props in the "black box" magic practiced by Méliès and others. With the proper lighting, these dark-shrouded figures remained invisible to the audience against the black backgrounds of the stage sets, thus creating magical illusions of levitation and disappearance.[24] This ancestry is particularly clear in Eclair's predecessor to Fantômas, Zigomar, whose robed henchmen use their dark habits to literally disappear into the darkness of the unlit backgrounds of their hideouts. What in the magic film functioned as a technical device intended to remain invisible to the viewer, in the crime thriller became a dramatized process as these dark-robed figures merge into darkness to become invisible or emerge from the shrouded background like terrifying apparitions. Once again the genre discovers a visual means to play with identity and presence.[25]

The terror inspired by Fantômas and Zigomar resides not only in the ability they share to become a range of other characters but in their apparent power of disappearing entirely, leaving only their name, like Fantômas's mysterious calling card. In fact, the literary source for Zigomar, Sazie's *feuilleton* in *Le Matin*, was launched by a publicity campaign which plastered posters inscribed with the mysterious and vaguely distressing name of the anti-hero in nearly every public place without further explanation. Like the opening dialogue of *Fantômas*, the lack of attribution or context for the name inscribed the enigmatic structure essential to the mystery genre in the very form of its publicity.

Eclair's first publicity for its film of *Zigomar* continued this announcement of a name rather than a character, showing against a black background a contorted face shouting, "Zigomar."[26] The name of Allain and Souvestre's Fantômas was conceived to have a similarly anxiety-causing effect on both characters and readers, as skeptical police agents speculate that Fantômas is nothing but a legal fiction, as phantasmatic as his name.

Other than for publicity purposes, a name without a body remained a literary conception of dubious value to a filmmaker in the early 1910s. But the creation of a character whose face, identity, and even name remained malleable and uncertain provided devices of mystery which could have a direct visual impact. The fascination that the crime films of the period showed with nameless and often faceless characters certainly reflects not only the inherent mystery convention of uncertain identities but also a cinematic play with establishing and complicating the viewer's ability to recognize consistent characters and actors. This is evident in the recurring icon in the genre of the masked figure with a mysterious name (see, for instance, Eclair's advertisement for *Tom Butler*[27] or Lux's advertisement for "*X le mystérieux*"[28]). However, Feuillade (and Jasset in *Zigomar*) achieved something with more visual power than the domino masks that disguise these figures: an image of an actor whom we see transform himself into a variety of identities and ultimately efface himself into darkness through his dark *cagoule*.

It is certainly true that the viewer of the Fantômas series possesses, via the prologues to these films, knowledge of the identity underlying Fantômas's disguises, a knowledge denied the mystery reader. However, we might also point out that the visual power of these shifting identities, and especially of the "man in black" (so much more important in the film than in the novels), possesses an unsettling impact which the security of narrative knowledge may not entirely outweigh. The approach of the mystery film genre in the early 1910s seems to rely more on the power of visual transformations than on the unraveling of carefully crafted enigmas. It remains a genre based on visual effects and attractions rather than intricately crafted plotting. The visual effect of such scenes may have been such that film viewers felt more like Charles Rambert, subjected to his nightmare hallucination of shifting images, rather than sharing the sangfroid and perspicacity of Inspector Juve. How many of us, even today, can imagine the nightmares provoked in a darkened theater by the triumphant gesture of the "man in black" at the explosion which ends *Juve contre Fantômas*?

The first volume of *Fantômas* climaxes with the guillotining of the criminal under his alias Gurn. However, the deceptive nature of this public demonstration of justice is subverted by one of Fantômas's most devious ruses. The scandalous nature of Gurn's crimes and trial has prompted Valgrand, a Parisian actor, to star in a theatrical recreation of the criminal's career employing a detailed make-up patterned on the actual criminal. Valgrand is manipulated by Fantômas when Lady Beltham convinces him to meet her in his make-up near the prison for a romantic tryst. The vain and somewhat perverse actor remains unsuspicious, seeing this arrangement as "a positive refinement in erotic delight. See? The lady and I — the double of Gurn — and right opposite, the real Gurn in his cell" (299).

Like Charles Rambert in the opening, only more seriously, Valgrand pays for his fascination with devious role-playing. He is drugged and, with the aid of a corrupt prison guard, replaces the real Gurn in his cell. Despite his protests ("I am not Gurn ... I am Valgrand the actor. Everybody in the world knows me"), it is Valgrand who loses his head on the scaffold (308). On examining his remains, Juve alone discovers the greasepaint that reveals Fantômas's final disappearing act. Feuillade uses this climax as well but substitutes a milder ending as Valgrand is saved at the last moment. However, seemingly inspired by Valgrand's perverse scenography of the tryst in the novel, Feuillade adds an original element: Fantômas and Lady Beltham watching the execution from a nearby window, their spectatorial position underscoring the theatrical nature of the scene. While both endings complicate the theme of the genre's identity through play-acting, Feuillade's film gains an additional complication, in spite of its seemingly more conventional moral ending. This film, which begins with a nondiegetic prologue demonstrating the actor's skill in assuming identities, ends with a fictional sequence demonstrating the danger of playing roles too well, while also visualizing the perverse pleasures of spectatorship. Again, while the film version may possess a more reassuring narrative, the cinematic context complicates and plays with the new regimes of film viewing and actor recognition, arousing anxieties from other sources.

Conclusion: Adaptation, Identity, and Genre

The Fantômas series, like many other features, serials, and films in series released in the era of cinema's increased narrativization, acted out a drama of mysterious disguises and multiple identities. The prologue to the Fantômas films, like many similar prologues displaying actors and roles that open films from this period, seemed designed to assist viewers to recognize the actors beneath the roles. As such, these prologues stimulated the newly appearing star system in which recognizable actors became a major attraction to audiences. But the *Fantômas* prologue reveals, not only René Navarre, but also the mysterious Fantômas, the phantom-like presence that underlies all the disguises, in some ways like an actor underlying roles. But, as we have seen, with a master of disguises, this relation becomes more complex and fraught with peril. It might not always be so easy to divide actor from role, and one might not be sure whether there was something tangible left over once the disguises were torn away.

In a curious way this paradox of actor/role and disguise/identity parallels the act of transformation that literature was about to undergo at the hands of cinema. On the one hand, in search of middle-class respectability and cultural capital, the cinema worked its newly founded publicity machines to stress that works of classical literature were now being offered in cinema versions. Thus, individual film adaptations (and cinema in general) gained status through relation to a higher art form. In fact, filmmakers responded to more complex narrative material with developments in film language in order to express subjectivity of characters and the temporal re-organizations of literary plot. But, like issues of disguise raised by the detectives and mysterious super-criminals brought from the dime novels to the cinema, issues of adaptation might confound issues of identity rather than resolve them. Was a successful adaptation one in which, as in one understanding of the actor's responsibility to role, faithfulness to an original model was paramount? Or, as the film of mystery hinted, was such faithful imitation only a sign of clever deception, and the truly cinematic adaptation in fact a film in which the original source material has been wholly absorbed by the new medium, so that no original identity could be said to persist? Generations of argument about the relation of identity and adaptation, faithfulness and invention and the interrelation of media appear here.

It is perhaps important, however, to recall that cinema's borrowing from pulp literature provided it with some of its most powerful visual metaphors and filmic practices. Visualizing the detective or mystery story opened up for cinema a tradition of narrative so attuned to the visual devices of the medium — and often so distant from the emphasis on character psychology of the realist novel — as to seem to be inherently cinematic rather than "literary." But it all depends on what literature one refers to. In adapting the devices of the mystery story, the cinema created a genre rather than, primarily, a reference to singular pre-existing literary works. Thus, the single identity of a source dissolves into a series of devices, plot templates, character types, and dramatic situations. Instead of the body of a singular canonical work, the cinema appropriated parts and elements from many works, much like the scene in *Fantômas contre Juve* in which Dr. Chaleck escapes from the police who have grabbed him, leaving them astonished, holding only an evening coat and a pair of artificial arms.

Notes

1. The copyrighting process which resulted in the Library of Congress Paper Print Collection is discussed in detail in Patrick Loughney, "A Descriptive Analysis of the Library of Congress Paper Print Collection and Related Copyright Materials," unpublished dissertation, George Washington University, 1988.

2. André Gaudreault, "The Infringement of Copyright Laws and its Effects," in *Early Film: Space—Frame—Narrative*, Thomas Elsaesser and Adam Barker, eds., (London: British Film Institute, 1990) 114–22, covers this and other early copyright suits in early cinema. He places the emphasis somewhat differently from the way I do. The lawsuit over *Personal* is also discussed in Charles Musser, *Before the Nickelodeon: Edwin S. Porter and the Edison Manufacturing Company* (Berkeley: University of California Press, 1991) 280–82. As Musser notes, there was another solution, which the Biograph Company followed after this lawsuit, which was to copyright the scenario for the film as a dramatic work as well as the film roll itself. However, this was a separate and — importantly — a *written* document, filed with the copyright office (281).

3. See the decision in this case by K. S. Hover reprinted in *Nickelodeon* (September 1909), 81–82.

4. On the Motion Picture Patents Company, see Robert Jack Anderson, "The Motion Picture Patents Company," unpublished PhD dissertation, University of Wisconsin, Madison, 1983. On the CIDEF, see Georges Sadoul, *Les Pionniers du cinéma (de Méliès à Pathé), 1897–1909*, vol. 2 of *Histoire générale du cinéma* (Paris: Denoël, 1948) 483–96.

5. On the rise of the story film, see Charles Musser, *The Emergence of Cinema*, vol. 1 of *The History of American Cinema* (New York: Scribners, 1990). Musser dates this slightly earlier than I do, but does not include in his conception of the story film the importance of character-driven action. With this in mind I stick with the later date of 1906–1907.

6. I discuss the change from an earlier cinema based in attraction to one founded on narrative integration in my *D. W. Griffith and the Origins of American Narrative Film* (Urbana: University of Illinois Press, 1991).

7. Charles Musser, "The Nickelodeon Era Begins: Establishing the Framework for Hollywood's Mode of Representation," in Elsaesser and Barker 256–73.

8. *The Duel Scene from Macbeth*, American Mutoscope and Biograph Company, copyrighted 1905.

9. In 1896 the American Mutoscope and Biograph Company filmed the famous aging actor Joseph Jefferson in his signature role as Rip Van Winkle. Again, a series of peak moments were shot: *Rip Meeting the Dwarf, Rip and the Dwarf, Rip Leaving Sleepy Hollow, Rip Passing over the Hill, Rip's Toast, Rip's Toast to Hudson and Crew, Rip's Twenty Years' Sleep*, and *Awakening of Rip*.

10. On *Uncle Tom's Cabin* particularly, see the discussion of dramatic sources by Janet Staiger in *Interpreting Films: Studies in the Historical Reception of American Cinema* (Princeton, NJ: Princeton University Press, 1992) 105–19.

11. On the *Films d'art* as a company and as a movement, see Sadoul 497–512.

12. For background on *Fantômas* as a literary source, see Robin Waltz, "Serial Killings, *Fantômas*, Feuillade and the Mass-culture Genealogy of Surrealism," *The Velvet Light Trap* 37 (1996) 51–57.

13. My point in using these terms from Russian Formalism is that as *syuzhet*, that is, the mystery story as actually written, the mystery genre needs the re-reading of events by the detective to provide the actual story (*fabula*), with the elements previously withheld now filled in by the detective's interpretation. The most thorough discussion of these terms in relation to the mystery narrative in film is given in David Bordwell, *Narration in the Fiction Film* (Madison: University of Wisconsin Press, 1985), esp. 64–65.

14. Robin Walz's chapter on *Fantômas*, "The Lament of *Fantômas*: The Popular Novel as Modern Mythology," in his "Imaginary Paris: Surrealism and Popular Culture in Early Twentieth-Century France," diss. University of California at Davis, 1994, 80–137, provides an excellent overview of the series of novels as a whole. In his section "Modern Masks" (106–112), he details the complex exchanges of identity which pervade the whole series, with at points even Juve being taken for Fantômas or masquerading as Fantômas. I thank Professor Walz for sharing this chapter with me.

15. The term *peritext* comes from Gérard Genette, who uses it to refer to aspects of a work which are on the threshold of a text, such as the title, preface, and so on. See Genette, *Seuils* (Paris: Editions du Seuil, 1987).

16. [Editor's note: *apache* was the term used to describe hooligans and criminals of the Paris region from roughly 1900 to 1920.]

17. Richard Abel, *The Ciné Goes to Town: French Cinema 1896–1914* (Berkeley, CA: University of California Press, 1994) 364, makes the point that in 1912 the coincidence between actual anarchist violence (for example, the *Bande à Bonnot*) and films supposedly celebrating criminal heroes led to the banning of a number of crime films. This may have caused Gaumont to be cautious in their adaptation of *Fantômas*. Champreux indicates that the Fantômas films did encounter bans in some areas of France (262).

18. For a thorough discussion of Bertillon and the use of photography to establish identity in France, see Christian Phéline, "L'Image accusatrice," *Cahiers de la photographie* 17 (1985) 1–169. For a discussion of French concerns about degeneration and recividism, see Robert A. Nye, *Crime, Madness and Politics in Modern France: The Medical Concept of National Decline* (Princeton, NJ: Princeton University Press, 1984).

19. My thoughts on these prologue sequences have been influenced by a very fruitful exchange with Livio Belloï of the University of Liège who is undertaking a study of such sequences. I have found our correspondence invaluable and thank him for sharing his insights with me.

20. Abel discusses both the comic series and the detective and crime series and their role in the French film industry in *The Ciné Goes to Town*.

21. Eclipse advertisement in *Ciné-Journal* 19 December, 1911: n.p.

22. Eclair advertisement in *Ciné-Journal* 25 November, 1911: n.p.

23. Eclair advertisement in *Ciné-Journal* 29 July, 1911: n.p.

24. Méliès describes one instance of his use of such shrouded manipulators of props in his description of his illusion "Les Phénomènes du spiritisme" performed at the Théâtre Robert Houdin, reprinted in Pierre Jenn, *Georges Méliès cinéaste* (Paris: Albatros, 1984) 165.

25. I have discussed the use of devices from the magic theater in Zigomar in my article "Attractions, Detection, Disguise: Zigomar, Jasset, and the History of Film Genres," *Griffithiana* (May 1993) 111–36.

26. Eclair advertisement, *Ciné-Journal* 25 March, 1911: n.p.

27. Eclair advertisement in *Ciné-Journal* 27 April, 1912: n.p.

28. Lux advertisement in *Ciné-Journal* 11 May, 1912: n.p.

Works Cited

Allain, Marcel, and Pierre Souvestre. *Fantômas*. New York: William Morrow and Co., 1986.

———. *The Silent Executioner* (translation of *Juves contre Fantômas*). New York: William Morrow, 1987.

Champreux, Jacques. "L'Année du 'maître de l'effroi.'" *L'Année 1913 en France*. Ed. Thierry Lefèbvre and Laurent Mannoni. Special issue of *1895*. 1993: 244–263.

Elsaesser, Thomas, and Adam Barker, eds. *Early Film: Space—Frame—Narrative*. London: British Film Institute, 1990.

Sadoul, Georges. *Les Pionniers du cinéma*. Paris: Denoël, 1948. Vol. 2 of *Histoire générale du cinéma*.

Tsivian, Yuri. *Early Cinema in Russia and Its Cultural Reception*. London: Routlege, 1994.

Uricchio, William, and Roberta E. Pearson. *Reframing Culture: The Case of the Vitagraph Quality Films*. Princeton, NJ: Princeton University Press, 1993.

CLASSIC HOLLYWOOD CINEMA

3

Tarzan in Novel and Film
MICHAEL HARNEY

Tarzan movies are ultimately based on the literary personage first appearing in a story by Edgar Rice Burroughs in the October 1912 issue of *The All Story* magazine (Zeuschner 184). Since then Tarzan has figured in more than forty films. Only a few of these — including the earliest filmed version, with Elmo Lincoln, and the recent Disney animated version — have been based on any of the Burroughs novels. The work most frequently adapted is *Tarzan of the Apes* (1914), the first of the series. The film adaptations depart considerably in narrative structure and characterization from the original novel.

Understanding the place of Tarzan movies in cinematic history and popular culture implies several investigative emphases. One involves the ways in which the movie Tarzan diverges from or agrees with Burroughs's novelistic depiction. Another outlines the various transformations of the character in the movies themselves. Yet another demonstrates how the trademarked Tarzan varies from medium to medium within the entertainment industry and its affiliated markets. To one degree or another, all these problems are interrelated. This essay focuses on the first two, with occasional reference to the third.

The early novels of Burroughs were published during what might be called the extended Edwardian era, a time that witnessed pivotal geopolitical events and cultural developments: the Spanish American, Boer, and Russo-Japanese Wars; the Chinese, Mexican, and Russian Revolutions; the birth and early development of the automobile and of aviation; the escalation of such interrelated trends as state-centralization, propagandistic media, and the growth of industrial complexes; the consolidation of methodologies, such as assembly-line production, mass marketing, and statistical demography.

The Tarzan novels, along with those of several other popular series authored by Burroughs, continued to be published and reprinted throughout the years in which Tarzan movies were one of Hollywood's most successful cinematic franchises. Tarzan became an icon of American popular culture, and a notable commodity in the emerging entertainment-industrial complex and its commercial affiliates. Since Burroughs registered "Tarzan" as a trademark in 1913, the character, as Walt Morton observes, has been licensed not only into narrative and entertainment media (comic books, cartoons, movie serials, board and video games, etc.), but into many commercial products as well: candy, trading cards, bubble gum, toys, bathing suits, wrist watches, etc. (Morton 106). Each rendition of the "trans-media Tarzan" resembles the Tarzan of the novels to a greater or lesser degree according to the "specific devices" required by a given medium or technological platform (Morton 107).

An outright superhero, the Tarzan of the novels is more "comic-book-ish" than his facsimile of the movies. In more or less exaggerated form, this is the dominant image of Tarzan in the multi-media domain. By contrast, the movies, for several decades, and intermittently in recent years, have tended to represent a somewhat more naturalistic and understated (i.e., more conventionally literary) concept of the character. This aspect is confirmed by a survey of the first half-century of Tarzan movies. Derral Cheatwood presents a typology of Tarzan films made between 1918 and 1970. The first group he discerns, the MGM series with Johnny Weissmuller, includes six films made between 1932 and 1942. Another group comprises films from the 1930s that sought to compete with the MGM series. Among these were films made by Sol Lesser between 1933 and 1938. Like MGM's Tarzan series, Lesser's films starred Olympic athletes (Buster Crabbe, like Weissmuller, a champion Olympic swimmer; Glenn Morris, an Olympic hurdler). Films produced in the 1930s by Edgar Rice Burroughs himself constitute yet another set of films competing with the MGM productions. These also starred an Olympic athlete, Herman Brix, a shot putter who, later in his career, under the name Bruce Bennett, appeared in such films as *Mildred Pierce* and *The Treasure of the Sierra Madre* (Fury 142). Other distinct groups are Tarzan films produced by Lesser between 1943 and 1958, and by Sy Weintraub between 1959 and 1968. Several films—such as the very first Tarzan movie, starring Elmo Lincoln, and a number of films made since the last of the Weintraub series—are productions whose only shared factor is Burroughs's trademark protagonist (Cheatwood 129).

While he cogently demonstrates the thematic continuities, shared cast, and production staff that define the sets of films in his schema, Cheatwood perhaps underestimates the significance of the films made between 1953 and 1959. The films in question (*Tarzan's Hidden Jungle* [Harold D. Schuster, 1955], *Tarzan and the Lost Safari* [H. Bruce Humberstone, 1957], *Tarzan's*

Fight for Life [H. Bruce Humberstone, 1958], *Tarzan and the Trappers* [Charles F. Haas and Sandy Howard, 1958], *Tarzan's Greatest Adventure* [John Guillermin, 1959]), for one thing, all star a new Tarzan, Gordon Scott. Scott was among the first bodybuilders, along with Steve Reeves of the Hercules films, to play a superhero. The films — all but the last produced by Sol Lesser — are significant because they re-imagine Tarzan in terms much more compatible with Burroughs's original vision of a superman in mind as well as body. The disavowal of the Weissmuller "me–Tarzan" legacy, already undertaken in Lesser's Lex Barker films, embraces a hero who is articulate, eloquent, and erudite, as well as muscular and athletic. In aligning themselves with Burroughs's original concept, the makers of the Gordon Scott films adhere to the renewed superheroic tradition of the late-twentieth and early-twenty-first centuries.

Tarzan could be regarded as the archetypal superhero of modern popular culture. A loner who does not work well with others, Tarzan typically defies villainous gangs of poachers, spies, and slave traders. Although he occasionally makes friends, or has associates and allies, Tarzan is a solitary champion who never has what could be called a sidekick. Preternaturally strong, agile, swift, tireless, and alert, the Tarzan of the books is superhumanly stealthy, capable of moving about unseen, whether swinging through the upper terraces of the forest or prowling under the very noses of unsuspecting enemies. A typical interlude shows him infiltrating a German camp, listening undetected at the backs of tents, then following and silently attacking his quarry: "the man beast sprang upon the back of his prey and bore it to the ground for steel fingers closed simultaneously upon the soldier's throat, effectually stifling any outcry" (*Tarzan the Untamed* 23). Very numerous scenes in the films depict this characteristic predatory invisibility.

Weissmuller's famously monosyllabic, agrammatical rendition highlights the most significant difference between the Tarzan of the novels and the MGM Tarzan — arguably the most culturally influential cinematic interpretation. The novels' Tarzan is as preternaturally intelligent, multilingual, and cultured as he is impossibly brave, strong, and agile. By contrast, the MGM movies, and other, similarly understated or de-mythologized versions (e.g., *Greystoke: The Legend of Tarzan, Lord of the Apes* [Hugh Hudson, 1984], and, to a certain degree, the recent Disney reincarnation [Chris Buck and Kevin Lima, 1999]) reject the mentally superior Tarzan, positing instead the somewhat less fabulous scenario of a mysterious wild man, presumably raised in the jungle in isolation from his own kind, who only learns to mimic human speech when he meets Jane. Disendowed of the original character's cerebral prowess, the stereotypically influential MGM exemplar only retains the strength, speed, agility, and sensory acuity of Burroughs's hero. However, since the time of Weissmuller's last Tarzan movie, in the late forties, the character has occasionally been reassigned some of the superhuman characteristics of the original Burroughs concept. The effort of some later Tarzan movies to re-imagine the hero according to the original, novelistic conception — yielding, for instance, the laconic but sophisticated and articulate Tarzan portrayed by Lex Barker and Gordon Scott — is best understood as a rejoinder to the dumbed-down interpretation embraced by the Weissmuller films, and as a rapprochement with Burroughs's superhuman conception.

Other Burroughs characters — John Carter of the Mars series; Carson Napier of the Venus series; David Innes of the Pellucidar novels — contributed to the modern superhero's profile, establishing, along with Tarzan, the basic motifs and narrative formulae that mark a thematic range for subsequent variations. As Everett Bleiler points out, the standard Burroughs hero is, like Tarzan, an exile, a solitary underdog who shows dauntless virility as he "triumphs over a hostile environment" (Bleiler 63). Tarzan, however, is a "unique superman" in that he "reconciles" elitism and democracy, renouncing both his class and his species. As Bleiler points out, Burroughs's jingoism nonetheless insures that Tarzan's enemies — Russians, Germans, Arabs, anarchists, etc. — are usually from the index of least-favored types in the current Anglo-American geopolitical and cultural hit list (Bleiler 64). Whether in the interplanetary reaches of space opera, or in Tarzan's vaguely situated African wilderness, Burroughs's narrative universe is dominated by unfettered jingoism and macho derring-do. His Martian and Venusian novels perfected that peculiar blend of the primitive and the super-advanced — an "erratic, structured decadence" linking swords and ray guns — that has come to be identified with science-fiction fantasy and romance (Bleiler 64). Combining elements of medieval chivalric romance and speculative science fiction, Burroughs's earlier adventure fantasies are the origin of the Star Wars universe, by way of the Flash Gordon and Buck Rogers serials of the thirties. Along with amusement parks, video games, and other escapist entertainments, such modern-day analogs of late-medieval and early-modern chivalric narratives function, like their predecessors of earlier phases in the evolution of modern popular entertainment, as a kind of utopia. The latter mode, for Louis Marin's model, is "the imaginary correlation between individuals and their real conditions of existence." An "ideological locale," a "category of ideological discourse," it facilitates the establishment of a "a theatrical setting" where mythic ideology ("a narrative structurally formulating the solution to fundamental social contradictions") is validated (297).

Using the example of musicals, Richard Dyer explicates the escapism and wish-fulfillment purveyed by mainstream commercial entertainment in terms of images of "abundance, energy, intensity, transparency and community" that compensate for the perceived "specific inadequacies" of quotidian existence (19–20). Entertainment is performance for profit, "before a generalized audience" for the specific purpose of providing the utopic pleasure of escape (19). While allowing that capital and labor dispute control of this product, Dyer regards professional entertainment as, in the aggregate, the "dominant agency" determining what entertainment is. The utopic content of entertainment utopia, expressed in the "feelings it embodies," is conveyed, in musicals, by "non-representational signs" (e.g., color, texture, melody, movement, camework, etc). But these signs, like the representational signs in literally utopic works, is iconic. Escape is enabled through "non-representational icons" (20).

The chivalric utopia of the medieval and early-modern romances, and of Victorian and Edwardian times, encloses not one central locale, such as Amadís's marvelous Firm Isle, or H. Rider Haggard's African realms, or Tarzan's jungle estate. Rather, it is a notional topography, staked out by the hero's exertions and the justice of his cause. The romance's mythogenetic playground grants a reprieve from real-world concerns and contradictions, nurturing the momentary illusion of an ideological resolution, on various levels, of the contradictions inherent in the real-world status quo—a stratified reality whose upper echelons entice readers while excluding them—exonerated by the fantasy (M. Harney, "Economy" 383–87).

D.W. Griffith's *Birth of a Nation* could be regarded as the cinematic expression of the themes prefigured in chivalric romances and their more recent imitators. The notions of chivalrous guardianship and heroic resistance to invasion animate *Birth of a Nation*, released in 1914, the year the first Tarzan novel was published. The cause to which good men devote themselves, for both Burroughs and Griffith, is the safeguarding of protected categories—damsels in distress, widows, orphans, favored social or ethnic groups. The modern romance's revived chivalry, with its selective altruism, was fated to exert authority in the fabrication of nationalist ideologies in all countries involved in the two World Wars and their subsequent localized reiterations. Amy Kaplan demonstrates, for example, America's historical tendency to employ a mythologized "narrative of liberation" in order to legitimate "the exercise of imperial power" (92). Paraphrasing late-medieval chivalric protectionism, this liberationist narrative is the frequent pretext of American intervention and hegemonic interference, and the ideological justification of America's military-industrial complex. Kaplan shows how late–nineteenth-century historical romances, set in the middle ages or the ancient world, provided exotic settings for manly adventures, including a rescuing of distressed damsels that served as the core metaphor of allegedly salvific ideologies (93–94).

Such service-based ideologies, including the medieval estates schema, early-modern chivalry, and late–Victorian gallantry, legitimate elite prerogatives while vindicating the greater social order. C. Wright Mills succinctly characterizes the tendency of elites "to define themselves as inherently worthy of what they possess," and to regard "their possessions and their privileges as natural extensions of their own elite selves." Notions of the elite "as composed of men and women having a finer moral character" inspires an "ideology of the elite as a privileged ruling stratum ... whether the ideology is elite-made or made up for it by others" (14).

Birth of a Nation expresses this mentality, channeled through the spirit of chivalric romance. The great early exemplar of the latter genre, *Amadís of Gaul*, was the first fictional best seller of the international publishing trade. Providing the prototype for the sixteenth-century romances which knew such extraordinary success throughout Europe (Whinnom 193; Sieber 204–209; M. Harney, *Kinship* 249–53), *Amadís* found an eager audience in Elizabethan England, inspired an elite of cognoscenti in the eighteenth century, and was translated by Robert Southey in the early nineteenth (John J. O'Connor 131–33; L. Harney 4–5).

While his stylistic and thematic debt to ancient authors, including Homer and Virgil, is undeniable (see Holtsmark, *Edgar* 3; *Tarzan* 55–57), Burroughs's verified education and reading preferences suggest at least the indirect influence of medieval and early-modern romance authors. The romance lineage can be traced from *Amadís*, through Sir Walter Scott (known to be attentively consulted by Burroughs; see Galloway 100–104) and numerous congeners in the Romantic and Victorian eras (including Haggard and Rudyard Kipling), down to Burroughs in the early twentieth century (Nesteby 484–86). Meanwhile, as Steve Neale points out, filmmakers, especially producers of the many types of adventure film, have always adapted, imitated, or incorporated elements from the medieval romances (Sobchak qtd. in Neale 55).

Hence the similarity of story-telling style and chivalric themes in the Mars novels of the Chicagoan Burroughs and the cinematic romance of the Virginian Griffith. Burroughs's John Carter, savior of the good Martians from the depredations of the Black Pirates of Barsoom, is a Virginian and one-time officer in the Confederate army. He is, in effect, a knight-errant of the Martian sea bottoms and highlands. The Klansmen of Griffith's most famous film are knights crusading in white sheets instead of armor, defending Southern womanhood and gentility against similarly savage hordes. Woodrow Wilson, another Virginian, famously described *Birth of a Nation* as "history written with lightening" (qtd. in O'Connor and Jackson xix). Replacing "history" with "romance," we may see in the pastorally imagined Ante-Bellum South — so fancifully glorified in *Gone with the Wind* (Victor Fleming, 1939), so sympathetically depicted in films from Griffith down to and after Clint Eastwood's *The Outlaw Josey Wales* (1976) — the image of an organic society futilely but splendidly defended, brutally defeated and invaded by opportunistic hordes overthrowing a way of life that is doomed as if by a fatality. The neo–Victorian chivalries and pastoral visions of our own time (as in "the few good men" of Marine Corps recruiting ads) shed light on the ur–Victorianisms of a century ago. Images of the invading horde of devilish minions, enacting the inscrutably predatory agendas of invading masterminds, are reincarnated by the invading orcs and trolls of Tolkien; by the imperial storm troopers of the Star Wars films; by the endless parade of villains whose depredations provoke and justify the exploits of superheroes like Superman, Batman, and Spiderman; by the demon hordes of television's *Buffy the Vampire Slayer*.

The Tarzan of the novels, channeling earlier literary heroes, including the late-medieval knight-errant, is the paradigm and direct precursor of modern superheroes. Folkloric orphaned saviors (e.g. Oedipus, Theseus, Jason, Moses), or founder-heroes (e.g. the epic Cid, Robin Hood, the folkloric Jesse James) are defined by the singular deeds they perform and the specific communities they serve. Their unique, salvific scenario is the essence of their myth (M. Harney, "Movilidad" 68–72). The traditional mythic hero's story, observes Umberto Eco, "has taken place and can no longer be denied." The pop-cultural hero exemplified by Superman, by contrast, is "typical" rather than mythical, undergoing adventures that "proliferate as much as possible *ad infinitum*" (332). Superheroic cycles, whether played out in multiple issues of comics, in numerous episodes of television shows or movie serials, or in several films in a series, continually re-enact the salvific premise. Superheroes have a caseload rather than a single mission. Thus the repeated melodrama of deliverance, the inexhaustible supply of oppressed victims: widows, orphans, damsels in distress, hostages, oppressed natives, lost explorers. The episodic renewal is exemplified (and parodied) in Buffy the Vampire Slayer's epitaph, engraved on her tombstone in the concluding episode of the series's fifth season, after she has given her life to avert (yet another) apocalypse: "she saved the world — a lot" ("Chosen"). Naturally, Buffy is resurrected at the beginning of the following season, exemplifying what Eco calls the "device of iteration," that deploys familiar characters, formulaic episodes, and stereotypic escapades, reversing "the development of events," and focusing on an "*instant*, which is loved because it is recurrent." The superhero's synthetic mythology, sustained by this "narrative of redundance," gratifies the popular craving for formulaic reiteration, insuring the superhero's intimate association with mass production and the capitalized entertainment industry. The initiator of a numerous progeny of sequels and imitators, the first Amadís romance sets a precedent, in the early days of the printing industry, for narrative tinkering that yields a harvest of superheroic sequels, spinoffs, episodic proliferations. The pattern intensifies in the modern entertainment industry's expanded distribution networks and diversely interconnected media, including pulp magazines, radio, film, television, comic books, graphic novels, video cassettes, DVD's, video games, and various emerging web-based platforms.

Tarzan, the modernized avatar of the knight errant, is a made-to-order performer in the superheroic marketplace. In many ways epitomizing the late–Victorian chivalric gentleman profiled by Mark Girouard, the Ape Man is a protector of women, of the innocent, and of the helpless. Like the stereotype described by Girouard, Tarzan is fearless in war and in the hunt; athletic to a preternatural degree; "tough with the tough," but gentle with the weak; naturally "tender, respectful and courteous to women." Modest, altruistic, and benignly paternalistic to his dependants, he is also, apparently, an "ardent and faithful lover." Above the dirty business of politics and partisan strife, he prefers the countryside and the wilderness to the town (Girouard 260).

However, there is more to Tarzan, in both film and novel, than Victorian neo-chivalry. In his constant differentiation of savagery and civilization, Tarzan, argues Eric Cheyfitz, invokes not the Anglo-Saxon heritage, but its distilled quintessence, "the frontier individualism of Natty Bumppo" (4). Tarzan's intellectual and moral superiority is inherent; black Africans are frequently classed as "debased," "mongrels," "depraved," etc. It is Tarzan who recovers the truly primitive, and thus the truly pure. Even the Waziri of the novels, relatively unspoiled by the corruptions that degrade their fellow Africans, are diminished by their very acculturation within human society. Only Tarzan is possessed of sovereign, untainted primitivism. In this he is similar to mythologized historical personages like Davy Crockett, Daniel Boone, Kit Carson, and Fenimore Cooper's fictional pathfinder. Such folk heroes act as mediators between civilization's complexity and nature's simplicity. Tarzan, argues Gary L. Harmon, "outdoes them all," owing to the genetic superiority of his upper-class British lineage (122). Embodying a "harmonic coupling" between nature and culture, Tarzan represents "a compressed archetypal history of human evolution," and a viable balance between chaos and order, progress and degeneracy (123–24).

Ruth Mayer characterizes cultural encounters in Kipling and Rider Haggard, Burroughs's influential predecessors, in terms of lopsided "negotiation and communication" between hegemonic colonizers and subaltern natives (247). Burroughs, she argues, narrates from a perspective of misanthropic detachment. Assuming the futility of Western civilization's "refinements," he highlights such elements as the pathetic ineptitude of Lady Greystoke and Jane with firearms; the ludicrous ineffectuality of "impractical theorists" like Jane's father, Professor Porter; the impotence and irresolution of Clayton, Tarzan's cousin and rival for Jane's hand (*Tarzan of the Apes*, ch. 4 and ch. 13).

Tarzan's power, in both novel and film, derives from his primitivism. Chapter 13 of *Tarzan of the Apes*, prefiguring the movies' adoring photography of the male form, describes him as "Strange and war-like" in appearance. Possessed of a "straight and perfect figure," he is "muscled as the best of the ancient Roman gladiators ... yet with the soft and sinuous curves of a Greek god." His "wondrous combination of enormous strength with suppleness and speed" makes him the "personification ... of the primitive man, the hunter, the warrior," while the "noble poise of his handsome head," the "fire of life and intelligence in those fine, clear eyes," make him the "demigod of a wild and warlike bygone people of his ancient forest." This physical superiority, argues Mayer, does not derive from "archaic masculinity." Unlike the "white warrior," a stock figure of nineteenth-century adventure fiction (cf. Sir Henry Curtis in *King Solomon's Mines*), who benefits from a mystically recovered primitivism that radiates from the wilds, Tarzan possesses a marvelous physique due to the training afforded by his forest upbringing: his is a "built body" (Mayer 249). In this visual aspect, already expressed in the novels, Tarzan is made to order for the movies, whose tradition of enhanced bodily displays goes back to the earliest years of the medium (see Neale 56–57).

The "epitome of the Anglo-Saxon race," the Tarzan of the novels operates in "an American wilderness displaced to a fantasized European colonial Africa" (Cheyfitz 4). Biological determinism, bolstered at first by social Darwinism, then, around the turn of the twentieth century, by the new science of genetics, underwrote Anglo-American racial, political, and cultural hegemony. The White Man's Burden — explicated and justified, for example, by Walter Bagehot (161–62) — remains an important motif for Haggard and Kipling, the Victorian novelists who most influence Burroughs. In its didactic and Westernizing manifestation, this earlier colonialism is officially chivalric (despite a readily demonstrable materialist and hegemonic subtext). It wants to save the native from himself. The Edwardian restatement of the mission recuperates selected, salvageable natives for the white man's use. The projected modernization (i.e., Europeanization) of the non–European world is replaced by an axiomatic "biologization of race," a "petrification of racial hierarchy," and the assumed insusceptibility of racial types "to assimilation or homogenization" (Cheyfitz 5). Jules Zanger expresses it very succinctly: Tarzan "carries no torch of commercial civilization or Christianity to the savages" (84).

The novelistic Tarzan is Edwardian. Enemies are exterminated; Africans are generally either barely tolerated neighbors or worthy vassals. Thus, the black who kills Tarzan's simian foster mother belongs to a typically debased tribe, while the ape man's beloved Waziri are a race of noble warriors whose regularity of features is invidiously contrasted with "the flat noses and thick lips of the typical West Coast savage." Waziri faces, the narrator tells us, are "intelligent and dignified, those of the women ofttimes prepossessing" (*Return of Tarzan* 126).

In addition to the typology that distinguishes honorable from depraved natives, other racial differentiations define Western Europeans, especially the English, the (white) American, and the French, as of the in-group, while Slavs, Italians, and Turks are suspect outsiders. Whether in Africa, on Mars, or at the Earth's core, bad races are to be controlled, good races to be favored. This division is foreshadowed in *King Solomon's Mines*, published thirty years before the first Tarzan story. The Haggard novel distinguishes between good and bad Africans (e.g., the malevolent old witchdoctor, the noble prince Umbopa), and factions which the European interlopers support or oppose (e.g., the royalists and anti-royalists among the Kukuanas visited by Alan Quatermain and his comrades).

The good-native/bad-native dichotomy is more precisely expressed in Arthur Conan Doyle's *The Lost World*. The "good" natives are "small men, wiry, active, and well-built," of an evolutionary and cultural level "considerably higher ... than many South American tribes" (163, 164). This praiseworthy race of "little red warriors," grateful for the explorers' intervention in the war with the bestial ape-men, shows a proper deference: "the whole tribe lay down upon the ground ... in homage" (169). The war between the good natives and their evil, simian-like enemies is justified in Darwinian terms. Its resolution of "the feuds of countless generations" insures that man will reign supreme, while the "man-beast" is ever after assigned "his allotted place" (174).

Arab and Turk, in the T. E. Lawrence legend, exemplify this good-native/bad-native scenario. Lawrence, as Lowell Thomas imagined him, is the gallant deliverer, admired by native crowds, "as blond as a Scandinavian, in whose veins flow Viking blood." He could be, Thomas effuses, "one of the younger apostles returned to life." His expression is "almost saintly, in its selflessness and repose" (4–5). Later, Lawrence is compared to King Arthur and Richard the Lion-Hearted, while Allenby, Lawrence's commander, is celebrated as a leader of "twentieth-century crusaders" (6). Organizing the nomadic tribes of Arabia "into a unified campaign against their Turkish oppressors," Lawrence is the virtual ruler of the liberated territories, including the Holy Land (8). The defeat of the Turkish empire, conceived and carried out by Lawrence and Allenby, is "the most brilliant and spectacular military operation in the world's history" (272).

Similarly, a crusading John Carter, with the aid of native confederates, converts the ancient civilization of an entire planet to a semblance of North American secular capitalism, uniting nomadic tribes, overthrowing a corrupt priesthood, and afterwards allowing a secularized vestige of the old caste society to live on. While recognizing the suffering caused by the abolition of an ancient religion as "a tissue of falsehoods," John Carter, the first-person narrator of *The Gods of Mars*, proposes nothing viable or specific to replace the old ways (142–43).

Not that the real Lawrence imitated Burroughs's fictional John Carter, but that Thomas, in exalting his media superstar, employed a mythographic style similar to that of Burroughs. Thomas's sensationalist scenario yields a never-never land of Bedouin exploits led by the gone-native Englishman in resistance to the evil Turk. The image persists in Robert Bolt's screenplay for the 1962 David Lean film, in which the marginalized English hero out-natives the natives. An example is the scene in which Lawrence, the bandit chieftain and redistributor of loot, struts and dances on the captured train before his chanting Bedouin followers. Similarly, in *Tarzan of the Apes* the hero, among the Great Apes, takes orgiastic part in "the mad whirl of the Death Dance;" he is "one of the wild, leaping horde" (54). In *The Return of Tarzan*, the hero strides among his Waziri vassals "lithe and active as a young forest god." "One of them" except for the color of his skin, he sports ornaments and weapons identical to theirs, speaks their language, laughs and jokes with them, leaping and shouting in the "wild dance." He is "a savage among savages" (130).

Marianna Torgovnick characterizes Burroughs's conception of the primitive as a pretended revelation of the natural state of man. In this she suggests that Burroughs follows the ethnographers of the late-nineteenth and early-twentieth centuries, for whom so-called primitive societies disclose human origins and the outlines of a natural social evolution. This notion, she argues, stems from an ethocentric assumption that primitive peoples "exist in an eternal present which mirrors the past of Western civilization." This makes for a "temporal illusion" persisting in both high and popular culture (46). This illusion notwithstanding, she implies, the Tarzan of the novels embodies not a consistent racism or eurocentrism, but rather a mercurial ambivalence concerning race and culture. Tarzan's virtue emanates from an acultural, ahistorical primitivism which places him above both native and European.

Burroughs sometimes depicts Europeans in harsher terms than those he reserves for natives. For example, the tribe of Kulonga, the cruel slayer of Tarzan's simian foster mother, has fled the Congo Free State owing to the "still crueler barbarities" of that colony's Belgian rulers (Torgovknick 50). Burroughs's ambivalence with regard to the primitive — an ambivalence presumably shared by many of his readers — can be examined in the light of Chris Bongie's dichotomy of imperialist and exotic exoticisms. The former "affirms the hegemony of modern civilization over less developed, savage territories." The latter "privileges those very territories and their peoples, figuring them as a possible refuge from an overbearing modernity" (17). As we will see, the escapism of the Tarzan films somewhat favors the second of these two exotic modes, while occasionally indulging in colonialist nostalgia or neo-colonialist fervor.

Amadís's kingdom of Insula Firme ("Firm Isle") is similar in its idealized hierarchies, social structure, and geographical isolation to Tarzan's African estate and de facto empire. The remote realm of the Spanish hero is a "a most delightful country, abounding in all things" (II: 552). Amadís's great castle ("strongly built, and the only entrance point") along with the island domain it dominates, constitutes a manorial realm very similar to Tarzan's estate and the vast hinterland it governs. Amadís's fiefdom is a "vast and ... well-stocked country ... peopled with inhabitants many and good" (II: 563). The predatory and militarist themes so essential to the manorial fantasy are also expressed: "it was well enough supplied to wage war, using it as a base, against the whole world" (II: 563). Like Tarzan, Amadís comes and goes as he pleases, while the kingdom runs itself. His adoring subjects chant like children long separated from their father whenever the hero returns from his adventures: "Hail to our lord, who so long has been away from us" (III: 905). Amadís's Firm Isle, so like an amusement park in its "many entertainments," is designed to provide the leisure that sets privileged nobility apart from other folk, assuring that the inhabitants and their guests can hunt "deer and wild pig and rabbits, and other wild animals" (IV: 1200).

Amadís is not a race-neutral fantasy. Its conquering hero's greatest enemies include non-human "giants," kings of "Araby" and other infidel realms. Written in its present form in the late-fifteenth century, shortly after the Christian conquest of Muslim Granada, the expulsion of Spanish Jews, and the opening-up of the New World, it entertains readers steeped in the rhetoric of conquest, conversion, and exclusion. Glamorizing xenophobic/

xenomanical subjugation and possession of pagan otherness, the plot of *Amadís* supplies, as David Boruchoff remarks, a "normalizing element," an "analogic design" for the Conquistadors's acquisitive program (334, 335). This fetishisized exoticism, "the coin in which wealth was calculated" (Boruchoff 338), is famously encapsulated by Bernal Díaz del Castillo: "From the moment we beheld so many populous cities and towns on the water," he recounts, "and on the main land many more great settlements, and that highway, so straight and level leading into Mexico, we were struck with amazement, and said that it seemed like the enchanted things recounted in the book of Amadís" (Díaz del Castillo 159).

In both novel and film, Tarzan incarnates the spirit of the post-medieval adventure story of which *Amadís* is the most famous and influential example. As Daniel Iwerks observes, adventure stories such as those of Burroughs are saturated with "the rhetoric of Eurocentric colonialism" with what Martin Green characterizes as "the energizing myth of empire" (Green qtd. in Iwerks 69). Eurocentrism is experienced by its proponents and practitioners as a faith, recognizable "as best by every right-thinking tribesman" (Orth qtd. in Iwerks 70). Tarzan in the novels is a "forest god," dominating and intimidating native populations, imposing on his empire such "Westernisms" as monetary accumulation and the ideology of private property. His world, argues Iwerks, is "a piece of the jungle Westernized," and he himself "a jungle-fied chivalric knight" who personifies delusional Eurocentrism (72, 73).

The Tarzan of both novel and film, a superior warrior who can only be overcome by treachery or sheer numbers, incarnates the first of Neale's two types of adventure protagonist: the loner (swashbuckler, explorer, great white hunter, lord of the jungle), and the heroic leader of "a microcosmic group" (a lost platoon, hostages, an expedition, a group of castaways) (Neale 56). The Ape Man of the novels is mentally as well as physically superior; he is a loner elevated to the rank of superhero. His superiority is enhanced by, rather than derived from, acquired erudition. The autodidactic polymathy of the superhero is prefigured, as in many other features, by Amadís, as in the scene in which the hero addresses the lady Grasinda: "although the damsel's language was German, he understood her quite well, for he always sought to learn the languages of the lands through which he travelled" (III, 783. 89–94). Similarly multilingual, Tarzan first acquires English as a second language, reading primers he finds in the cabin of his deceased human parents. Isolated from his own kind, and lacking any sort of tutor, he reasons out the significance of the alphabet by correlating pictures with letters and accompanying text. Later in the first novel, Tarzan acquires his first spoken human tongue from his first human friend, the French naval officer Paul D'Arnot. In subsequent novels, the ape man becomes "a phenomenal linguist," learning, in addition to French, English, and many African languages, German and Arabic as well (Holtsmark, *Edgar* 33). Typical scenes from Tarzan's polyglot career portray his unfailing tendency to try out numerous languages on strangers: "she could not understand him, though he tried French, English, Arab, Waziri, and, as a last resort, the mongrel tongue of the West Coast" (*The Return of Tarzan* 168–69). Rarely at a linguistic loss when dealing with any natives, anywhere ("'Make no sound,' he cautioned in the man's own tribal dialect"), Tarzan deals no less masterfully with Europeans: "the apeman called back to the girl in perfect German" (*Tarzan the Untamed* 30, 93).

Burroughs, as Jeff Berglund observes, "arms" his character with literacy, exposing him, in effect, to the Western canon in his dead father's cabin, "the house of literature," which conveys not only a body of knowledge but such values as "white masculinity" and European civilization (54). Tarzan's "inherent intellectual superiority," argues Berglund, can be understood in terms of Homi K. Bhaba's appraisal of Western colonialism's ingenuous credence in the empirical reality of racial and sexual stereotypes, its self-serving double standard of racial differentiation and hierarchic monoculturalism (Bhaba qtd. in Berglund 56). Tarzan's innate gentility, an Americanized expression of English cultural authority, is confirmed by his instinctive repudiation of cannibalism, reinforced by the example of the books he has mastered. This "triumph of civil morality," argues Berglund, is pointedly compared by Burroughs to the savagery of the many blacks who readily consume human flesh (57–59). It is not merely Tarzan's innate British and white–European nobility that distinguish him, but his immaculate primitivism as well. He is the ancient Anglo-Saxon warrior reborn to the uninhibited power and autonomy of primeval nature, unfettered by the inhibitions and arbitrary formalities of sterile modernity. Tarzan's avoidance of human flesh does not, therefore, reflect a merely "civil" morality. He adheres not to law codes or rules of etiquette, but to a warrior's code, a heroic protocol.

The first three Tarzan novels, as William Gleason demonstrates, conformed to a "recapitulatory plot" based on Eurocentric, fin-de-siècle notions of developmental psychology and Lamarckian evolution (41–42). The concept privileges those of noble birth, who maximally benefit from "the return to primitive origins" (44). Realizing how this recapitulatory premise might compromise his serial narrative — Tarzan's son, invented in conformity with the original psychological model, upstages the hero himself — Burroughs renounced the concept. Thereafter, Tarzan's superior powers of mind and body confirm "not evolutionary perfection but exterminatory violence" (Gleason 46).

Such departures from the initial Anglo-centric concept manifest in other ways as well. Tarzan in the novels is more practical than the model British chivalric gentleman. Jules Zanger advances the notion that the "Darwinian garden" of Africa as imagined by the American Burroughs, in which survival ultimately depends on the ability to kill, particularly distinguishes the Tarzan novels from British adventure fantasy. American fantasy, exemplified by Burroughs, blends the fantastic and the mundane, while situating the hero's adventures in contemporary settings. In line with this tendency, Tarzan novels and their cinematic counterparts juxtapose the ordinary ingredients of gazetteers and current technology with lost worlds, hidden civilizations, fabulous races, and living fossils. While British fantasy tends to take the form of historical or futuristic romance, American fantasy, including the works of Burroughs, prefers "distantly imagined, exotic lands" situated in "empty places on the map" (Zanger 83–84).

After the first novel, the books settle into a predictably narrow range of themes: lost civilizations, peoples, and tribes; ruthless, corrupt, ethnically dubious interlopers; damsels in distress; and the perpetually invidious contrast of degenerate civilization and unpolluted wilderness. Beginning with the second novel, *The Return of Tarzan* (1914), the most frequent formula is that of a lost civilization or tribe. In *Return*, and in *Tarzan and the Jewels of Opar* (1918), it is a lost city of the vanished Atlantean empire; in *Tarzan the Untamed* (1920), a lost city of lion-worshipping maniacs; in *Tarzan the Terrible* (1921), the primeval land of Pal-ul-don, the abode of dinosaurs and a civilization of primitive hominids; in *Tarzan and the Golden Lion* (1923), Opar and a neighboring land ruled by gorilla-men; in *Tarzan and the Ant Men* (1924), a race of primitives dominated by females, and a rival kingdom of diminutive warriors; in *Tarzan, Lord of the Jungle* (1928), a lost crusader kingdom; in *Tarzan and the Lost Empire* (1929), a lost outpost of Ancient Rome; in *Tarzan at the Earth's Core* (1930), an inner world of cavemen, pirates, and intelligent reptiles. Except for *Tarzan and the Foreign Legion* (1947), one of the last of the series, subsequent Tarzan novels show the same preference for this theme.

Another characteristic theme of the Tarzan novels is the Victorian notion, amplified by Edwardian ideology, of the gender-based division of labor. Chivalry is man's work. A woman's role is either the appreciative acquiescence to valiant deliverance (e.g., Burroughs's Jane Porter), or the haughty, passive acceptance of male devotion (as in the Mars, Pellucidar, and Venus novels of Burroughs). Bleiler characterizes the trademark gauche masculinity of the Burroughs protagonist in terms of a succession of thwarted abductions, "by lecherous brutes," of "proud and haughty beauties who must be approached with Edwardian circumspection," of "Gibson-girl conventions transplanted to the jungle or the deserts of Mars" (62).

Noting Burroughs's characterization of Jane in terms of the image of a "Venerated Madonna," Jonna Higgins points out the "chivalrous loyalty" and self-sacrifice expected of a gentleman (25; referring to *Tarzan of the Apes* 180). She argues that Burroughs assigns the medieval roles of knight to the man, of lady to the woman, thus objectifying woman, and making her a pawn in the honorific competition among men (25–26). The Jane of the novels, argues Greg Wahl, is subjugated by this sexual commodification, either in terms of simian competition over females, as when Tarzan defeats Jane's abductor, the savage anthropoid Terkoz, or in the even more sinister terms of capitalist-motivated arranged marriage, as when Jane's father seeks to marry her to his debtor, the suavely cynical Robert Canler (Wahl 35–36).

Chesney Baker, pointing to the aggressive patriarchy of such themes and images, notes their promotion of the typical romance novel's assumption that a woman's supreme fulfillment is in finding the right mate (49, 50). Showing the stereotypical femininity of the romance heroine, Jane is "intelligent but guileless, vulnerable but defiant, and sexually immature but sexually responsive" (Baker 55). The ideal object of Tarzan's salvific vigor, the Jane of the novels personifies the double-bind of the typical romance heroine, who seeks an attractive husband of superior social status, but cannot do so too obviously. This guileless irresolution of the conventional romance heroine ("I do not know my own mind," declares Jane) can be explained as a narrative device permitting the heroine to preserve her innocence (Baker 57–58; *Tarzan of the Apes* 235).

Tarzan movies, distancing themselves somewhat from Burroughs's treatment of gender and race, modify the residential fantasy prefigured by the hermetic, proprietary isolation of Amadís's Firm Isle. The novelistic Tarzan's estate and surrounding territory, well stocked with game and loyally guarded by his stalwart Waziri, are the hero's private domain. But the Tarzan of the novels, like the knights-errant of the romances, roams incessantly; we seldom see him at home. He is an absentee landlord. The movie Tarzan, by contrast, is comfortably domestic, living happily at home with his wife and son. Their tree house and its sylvan surroundings are a *locus amoenus* affording amniotic shelter from the wickedness and snares of civilization.

Rebutting the perception of Tarzan as a "a conventional exemplar of white imperial domination," Catherine Jurca argues that Burroughs's hero enacts, instead, a "myth of settlement" and "reverse colonization" (20). The natives Tarzan fights are "unruly newcomers" from the interior whom Tarzan does not want to conquer, but rather to "keep ... at bay." *Tarzan of the Apes*, then, is a segregationist utopia, "a novel of white flight" rather than of white rule. It expresses "the emerging exclusionary logic of the twentieth-century American suburb" (21).

The movie portrayal of the Tarzan/Jane marriage and household embraces a modified version of this suburban scenario. Africans, whether hostile or friendly, live in their own neighborhoods, somewhere off-camera. The focus is on the edenic setting of the couple's world; the architectural ingenuity of the tree house's utilitarian architecture (as in *Tarzan and His Mate* [Cedric Gibbons, 1934], and subsequent MGM films); the organic cleanliness of the forest setting; the blameless harmony of the couple's relationship (and, eventually, that of their nuclear family, following the adoption of Boy in *Tarzan Finds a Son* [Richard Thorpe, 1939]) with their environment (Orth 225–30). Although the theme of defending the estate would seem to allegorize the patriarchal notion of "a man's home is his castle," the films reject the Edwardian model, showing a Jane who, while somewhat deferential, far more actively collaborates with her mate. In most of the novels, Jane is either absent as a character, or off-stage for much of the story. Feistier, less vulnerable, than her literary counterpart, the Jane of the movies is her mate's constant partner. She learns rugged self-reliance from him, as he acquires gentle civility from her (as in *Tarzan and His Mate* and *Tarzan's New York Adventure* [Richard Thorpe, 1942]).

The frequent fairy tale and romance themes of hypergamy and hypogamy — i.e., the woman's marrying up (e.g., Cinderella, Beauty and the Beast) or down (e.g., the Disney *Aladdin, Titanic*) — are minimalized by the Tarzan films, which depict gender in egalitarian terms. In the books, the Ape Man is the scion and heir of an English lord. In becoming his wife, Jane acquires the ideal spouse, as impossibly handsome, strong, virile, and brave as he is incredibly wealthy and aristocratic. The Tarzan of the novels is the "strong but tender romantic hero," who appeals to female readers' fantasies of "fulfillment in marriage with a husband who will finally nurture them" (Baker 64). The paradox of Tarzan's nobility in the novels is that superior status compels him to eschew the luxury and depravity of civilization. The Tarzan of the movies faces no such ethical dilemma. He is, as we have seen, a true wild man, at home in nature. For him and his wife, it is the pastoral setting that matters most, not the hero's origins. The amorous fantasy of the films focuses not on social status or benign sexual domination but rather on adventurous equality. Jane is not only an active partner in the adventure — she sometimes even rescues her endangered husband (as in *Tarzan Escapes* [Richard Thorpe, 1936]).

Tarzan in the novels, unlike the neo-chivalric British gentleman, is not indifferent to money. This is seen in his sensible plundering of the Oparian treasure vaults, with their countless gold ingots, representing a "fabulous wealth" contained in "thousands of pounds of metal" (*The Return of Tarzan* 187). The movie Tarzan, by contrast, is above and outside the system of money and markets. As in the novels, Africa in the Tarzan movies is a vast game preserve, of which he is the warden. More frequently than in the novels, however, villains personify capitalist exploitation. The favorite plot is that of greedy white men intruding on the Ape Man's pre-capitalist wilderness. Ivory poachers, wild game hunters, gold seekers, mining surveyors, German spies, slave traders, con men, and plunderers of native artifacts are typical trespassers. In the first two Weissmuller films (*Tarzan, the Ape Man* [W. S. Van Dyke, 1932], *Tarzan and His Mate*), the intruders seek the fabled elephants' graveyard. In *Tarzan Escapes*, a ruthless big game hunter attempts to capture Tarzan in order to exhibit him as a caged public attraction; in *Tarzan Finds a Son*, underhanded schemers connive to gain control of Boy's inheritance; in *Tarzan's Secret Treasure* (Richard Thorpe, 1941), rapacious scoundrels kidnap Jane and Boy and blackmail Tarzan into revealing hidden gold fields; in *Tarzan's New York Adventure* (Richard Thorpe, 1942), a ruthless trapper abducts Boy, taking him back to New York to perform in the circus; in *Tarzan's Desert Mystery* (Wilhelm Thiele, 1943), an opportunistic crook seeks to seize control of a sheikdom; in *Tarzan and the Amazons* (Kurt Neumann, 1945), an underhanded fortune hunter seeks to loot the treasure of a hidden city (a storyline reminiscent of several of the novels); in *Tarzan and the Huntress* (Kurt Neumann, 1947), hunters attempt to capture animals for sale to zoos.

Tarzan in the novels makes war in unsportsmanlike fashion. All enemies are fair game. In the propagandistic *Tarzan the Untamed* (1920), for example, he carries on a one-man guerrilla war against the Huns who have supposedly murdered his wife, slaughtering German soldiers and their native auxiliaries wherever possible (see ch. 2 and ch. 3, in which he strangles a sniper, mows down hundreds with a machine gun, and unleashes a ravenous lion on helplessly cornered troops). It is as if Burroughs celebrated the "death of chivalry" described by Girouard, where the brutal reality of trench warfare quashed all notions of the viability of heroic cavalry charges, the naive fiction of the band of brothers valorously putting the bully in his place (289–90).

Generally a better sport than his novelistic counterpart, the movie Tarzan chiefly campaigns against thugs of one kind or another; even Nazis, as in *Tarzan's Secret Treasure*, are depicted as individual bullies rather than ideological operatives. Significantly, the movie Tarzan is capable of showing mercy even to a sworn enemy (as in the climax of *Tarzan and the Lost Safari* [H.

Bruce Humberstone, 1957], when the hero tries, unsuccessfully, to save the ruthless, greedy, and treacherous Tusker Hawkins). In addition, the villains in Tarzan movies — unlike those in the novels, who generally come from a current ethnic or ideological hit list — are generally white. Africans, although often hostile, even murderously antagonistic, are generally shown to be protecting their country against acquisitive intruders (as in *Tarzan and His Mate, Tarzan Escapes*, and many others). In this aspect, the Tarzan films show a different racial sensibility from most Westerns of the 1930s, 1940s, and 1950s, which portray Indians as dangerously barbaric "hostiles." In Tarzan movies, when a native African collaborates with villains, he is more often than not an innocent stooge (in pointed contrast to the novelistic Tarzan's multi-racial misanthropy). This tendency is typified by a climactic sequence in *Tarzan Escapes*, in which the Ape Man leads Jane and others, including the murderous Captain Fry, through a deadly swamp. As the party reaches safety, Fry's native henchman, Bomba, throws himself at Tarzan's feet, begging for mercy. Tossing his head with kingly impatience, Tarzan, in a Solomonic gesture, orders the African to take his place with the others. The scheming Fry, however, is held accountable, and sternly commanded back into the lethal morass.

The producers and screenwriters of Tarzan movies presumably accommodate gender and race issues in order to avoid offending — or to alienate less intensely — important segments of the viewing public. The adjustments in question do not, of course, reflect a consensus on relevant issues among affected categories or communities, much less a nuanced conception of feminist or African-American spectatorship (as defined, for example, by Mayne 144–45, 154). The Tarzan filmmakers' scruples regarding race and gender are obliquely homologous to their protagonist's tutelary agenda, which is defined by the protected categories that justify it. The Ape Man's physical prowess, his innate ethical and racial superiority (the latter factor overtly expressed in the novels, only implicitly in the movies), support police functions that do not require the consent of served and protected categories. The prototypical modern superhero, Tarzan unilaterally arbitrates, on a case-by-case basis, within his extrajudicial jurisdiction. Heedless of due process, he discloses a moral instinct as infallible as it is self-righteous. Tarzan, whether in movies or novels, intervenes selectively, as when, in *Tarzan and the City of Gold*, having rescued a stranger, he notes the man's "intangible aura," and assumes that "loyalty and dependability [are] innate characteristics" (23). In the movies, this aspect of the character is illustrated by scenes such as the one in *Tarzan's New York Adventure*, in which the Ape Man and the intruding expedition's pilot instantly hit it off. He and the pilot, Tarzan tells Jane, understand each other.

This is another superheroic attribute that may be traced to the first specimen of the species. In one among a very large number of similar incidents, Amadís defends a woman's cause in judicial combat "for the sake of mercy and of upholding justice" (I: 116). The hero prevails "by right and by arms" (II: 567). Exercising unerring judgment, for his people-reading skills are as impressive as his linguistic acumen, Amadís, like his superheroic descendants, usually takes the plaintiff's word at face value. Amadís declares, "I take no vengeance save from those who seek to sustain their misdeeds by force of arms" (IV: 1269).

The foregoing discussion has aimed at characterizing and contrasting the Ape Man in book and film, while attempting some explanation of this protean character's enduring popularity. The iconic appeal of the novels, for Morton, is in their melodramatic empowerment of the orphaned English aristocrat, their exaltation of Tarzan as a master of his fate and transformer and improver of his world (118). The movies' escapist charm, by contrast, derives from their combination of Rousseauvian primitivism, classless American individualism, the visual glorification of "male physicality," the simulation of an "idyllic return to nature" (Morton 118, 121).

Tarzan books and movies represent different aspects of superheroic escapism. The latter may be seen as yet another confection of an entertainment industry widely viewed as trafficking in — as Paul Coates phrases it — "antiart" intended to divert "those ... rendered incapable ... of the aspiration to art." Defined as a therapeutically intermittent recess "incorporated into regimes of exploitation," industrialized entertainment takes no account of "social and psychological depth," thus implicitly defining extremes of " the sub- and the superhuman." As entertainment product, superheroic narratives embody "dreams of redemption [that are] cynically aware of their own unreality" (Coates 3).

The producers and screenwriters who adapt Burroughs's trademarked property carefully temper superheroic hyperbole with naturalistic restraint. They re-process the *outré* Edwardianism, histrionic sexism, and mean-spirited racism of the Burroughs novels in apparent conformity to an aesthetic calculus imposed by censors, ratings systems, audience demographics, and studio oversight. Hence the somewhat restrained (i.e., "family-oriented") depiction of violence in Tarzan movies, their euphemistic depiction of sexuality, and their sensitivity, however crudely expressed, regarding race and gender issues. These exterior factors are abetted, perhaps, by the practitioners' own expedient differentiation of art and entertainment. The conjectured expectations of what Christine Gledhill calls "sociohistorically constituted audiences," of which the screenwriter is also an actual or virtual member, might encourage the marketing of dreams of redemption in terms consonant with such expectations (241). Spectatorship, for Gledhill, is verified by conditions of consumption, while meaning is produced through an exchange effected between "processes of production and reception." Meaning is not "imposed" or "passively imbibed," but rather elaborated through a negotiated collaboration of "frames of reference" (244). Summarizing the work of Gledhill and other analysts of spectatorship, John Storey points to cultural and institutional forces supporting both production and reception, and to the need to go beyond determinist assumptions regarding consumer passivity, and concepts of spectatorship as merely a secondary product of filmic production (68–69).

Such interactive and negotiatory models of spectatorship help explain why Tarzan movies tend to conform, to some degree, with canons of literary taste. Richard Utz compares a passage from chapter I of *Heart of Darkness* with one from chapter 22 of *Tarzan of the Apes*. Both describe French imperialist military actions. The passage from Conrad involves the shelling of a stretch of African coast by a French naval vessel. "In the empty immensity of earth, sky, and water," narrates Conrad's Marlow, "there she was, incomprehensible, firing into a continent" (17). Violent details are muted by distance: the "pop" of the six-inch guns, a "small flame," a "little white smoke," a "tiny projectile," a "feeble screech." The scene from the Tarzan novel, by contrast, portrays the massacre of a native village by French troops in graphic close-up. Burroughs's omniscient narrator shows the French in hand-to-hand combat with the natives, mowing down their victims with "revolvers, rifles and cutlasses." In the end, they survey their handiwork, "panting, blood covered and sweating" (184). A comparison of the two passages, argues Utz, suggests an implicit "binarity of categories" in which certain attributes of Conrad's narrative, juxtaposed with corresponding traits in Burroughs's work (abstract/concrete, complex/simple, connotation/denotation, figurative/literal, etc.) embody cultural values pointing to additional invidious dichotomies. The latter include such contrasts as enlightened/racist, unique/repetitive, original/formulaic, etc., that underwrite notions of "literariness," readability, and aesthetic correctness. An aesthetic canon that hovers over even commercial filmmaking (and that superintends, for example, award nominations) will favor the "modernist textuality" of Conrad over the "visual/iconic" characteristics of Burroughs ("Introduction" 5–6; see also Carey-Webb 124–30).

Despite the many differences between the Tarzan of the novels and of the movies, the two media share the same broad visual/iconic agenda. The movies, while exercising cinematic understatement perhaps prompted by issues of cultural preference or imposed by self-censorship, nonetheless present essentially the same Tarzan originally visualized by Burroughs: a gloriously physical action protagonist who, whether in the imperialist/sexist mode of the novels, or the egalitarian/pastoral mode of the films, remains the superhero who valiantly defends the utopic universe that defines him.

Works Cited

Amadís de Gaula. Ed. Edward B. Place. 4 vol. Madrid: Consejo Superior de Investigaciones Científicas/Instituto Miguel de Cervantes, 1959–65.

Bagehot, Walter. *Physics and Politics, or, Thoughts on the Application of the Principles of "Natural Selection" and "Inheritance" to Political Society*. New York: A.A. Knopf, 1948 [1871].

Baker, Chesney. "And She Liked It: The Romance of Reading Tarzan of the Apes." Utz, *Investigating* 49–68.

Berglund, Jeff. "Write, Right, White, Rite: Literacy, Imperialism, Race, and Cannibalism in Edgar Rice Burroughs' *Tarzan of the Apes*." *Studies in American Fiction* 27 (1999). 53–76.

Bhaba, Homi K. *The Location of Culture*. New York: Routledge, 1994.

Bleiler, Everett Franklin. "Edgar Rice Burroughs, 1875–1950." *Science Fiction Writers: Critical Studies of the Major Authors from the Early Nineteenth Century to the Present Day*. Ed. Everett Franklin Bleiler. New York: Scribner's, 1982. 59–64.

Boichel, Bill. "Batman: Commodity as Myth." *Many Lives of the Batman*. Eds. Roberta E. Pearson and William Uricchio. New York: Routledge, 1989: 4–17.

Bongie, Chris. *Exotic Memories. Literature, Colonialism, and the Fin de Siècle*. Stanford: Stanford University Press, 1991.

Boruchoff, David A. "Beyond Utopia and Paradise: Cortés, Bernal Díaz and the Rhetoric of Consecration." *MLN* 106 (1991): 360–369.

Burroughs, Edgar Rice. *The Gods of Mars*. Chicago: A.C. McClurg, 1918. New York: Ballantine, 1963.

———. *The Return of Tarzan*. Chicago: A.C. McClurg, 1915. New York: Ballantine, 1963.

———. *Tarzan and the City of Gold*. Tarzana (Edgar Rice Burroughs). 1933. New York: Ballantine, 1964.

———. *Tarzan of the Apes*. Chicago: A.C. McClurg, 1914. New York: Ballantine, 1963.

———. *Tarzan the Untamed*. Chicago: A.C. McClurg, 1920. New York: Ballantine, 1963.

Carey-Webb, Allen. "Heart of Darkness, Tarzan, and the 'Third World': Canons and Encounters in World Literature, English 109." *College Literature* 19–20.3–1 (October 1992 October–February 1993): 121–141.

Cheatwood, Derral. "The Tarzan Films: An Analysis of Determinants of Maintenance and Change in Conventions." *Journal of Popular Culture* 16. 2 (1982): 127–142.

Cheyfitz, Eric. *The Poetics of Imperialism: Translation and Colonization from The Tempest to Tarzan*. Expanded ed. Philadelphia: University of Pennsylvania Press, 1997.

"Chosen." *Buffy the Vampire Slayer*. WB Television Network. 20 May 2003.

Coates, Paul. *Film at the Intersection of High and Mass Culture*. Cambridge, England: Cambridge University Press, 1994.

Conan Doyle, Sir Arthur. *The Lost World*. Ed. Philip Gooden. New York and London: Penguin, 2002.

Conrad, Joseph. *Heart of Darkness*. Ed. Robert Kimbrough. 3rd ed. New York: W.W. Norton, 1988.

Díaz del Castillo, Bernal. *Historia verdadera de la conquista de la Nueva España.* 22nd ed. Mexico City: Editorial Porrúa, 2005.
Dooley, Dennis. "The Man of Tomorrow and the Boys of Yesterday." *Superman at Fifty.* Ed. Dooley and Gary Engle. New York: Collier, 1987. 19–34.
Dyer, Richard. "Entertainment and Utopia." *Only Entertainment.* 2nd ed. New York: Routledge: 2002. 19–35.
Eco, Umberto. "The Myth of Superman." *Contemporary Literary Criticism.* Ed. Robert Con Davis. New York and London: Longman, 1986. 330–344.
Fury, David. *Kings of the Jungle. An Illustrated Reference to "Tarzan" on Screen and Television.* Jefferson, NC: McFarland, 1994.
Galloway, Stan. "The Greystoke Connection: Medievalism in Two Edgar Rice Burroughs Novels." *Studies in Medievalism* 6 (1994): 100–108.
Girouard, Mark. *The Return to Camelot: Chivalry and the English Gentleman.* New Haven and London: Yale University Press, 1981.
Gleason, William. "Of Sequels and Sons: Tarzan and the Problem of Paternity." *Journal of American & Comparative Cultures* 23 (2000): 41–51.
Gledhill, Christine. "Pleasurable Negotiations." *Cultural Theory and Popular Culture: A Reader.* Ed. John Storey. 2nd ed. New York: Prentice Hall, 1988. 236–249.
Green, Martin. *Dreams of Adventure, Deeds of Empire.* New York: Basic, 1979.
Harmon, Gary L. "Tarzan and Columbo, Heroic Mediators." *The Hero in Transition.* Ed. Ray B. Browne and W. Marshall Fishwick. Bowling Green, OH: Popular Press, 1983. 115–130.
Harney, Lucy. "*Amadís de Gaula* and Henry Fielding's *Tom Jones.*" *Ojáncano: Revista de Literatura Española* 30 (2006): 3–31.
Harney, Michael. "Movilidad social, bandolerismo y la emergencia del estado en el *Poema de Mio Cid*" ("Social Mobility, Banditry, and the Emergence of the State in the *PMC*"). *Mythopoesis. Literatura, totalidad, ideología.* Ed. Joan Ramon Resina. Barcelona: Anthropos, 1992. 65–101.
_____. "Mythogenesis of the Modern Super Hero." *Modern Myths.* Ed. David G. Bevan. Rodopi Perspectives on Modern Literature 10. Amsterdam: Rodopi, 1993. 189–210.
_____. "Economy and Utopia in Medieval Hispanic Chivalric Romance." *Hispanic Review* 62 (1994): 381–403.
Higgins, Jonna. "*Tarzan of the Apes*: An Ecofeminist Perspective." Utz, *Investigating* 15–29.
Holtsmark, Erling R. *Tarzan and Tradition: Classical Myth in Popular Literature.* Westport, CN: Greenwood, 1981.
_____. *Edgar Rice Burroughs.* Twayne U.S. Authors Series 499. Boston: Twayne, 1986.
Iwerks, Daniel. "Ideology and Eurocentrism in Tarzan of the Apes." Utz, *Investigating* 69–90.
Jurca, Catherine. *White Diaspora: The Suburb and the Twentieth-Century American Novel.* Princeton: Princeton University Press, 2001.
Kaplan, Amy. *The Anarchy of Empire in the Making of U.S. Culture.* Cambridge, MA: Harvard University Press, 2002.
Lupoff, Richard A. *Edgar Rice Burroughs: Master of Adventure.* Rev. ed. New York: Ace, 1968.
_____. *Barsoom: Edgar Rice Burroughs and the Martian Vision.* Baltimore: Mirage, 1976.
Marin, Louis. *Utopiques: Jeux d'espaces.* Paris: Editions de Minuit, 1973.
Mayer, Ruth. "The White Hunter: Edgar Rice Burroughs, Ernest Hemingway, Clint Eastwood, and the Art of Acting Male in Africa." *Subverting Masculinity: Hegemonic and Alternative Versions of Masculinity in Contemporary Culture.* Ed. Russell West and Frank Lay. Amsterdam, Netherlands: Rodopi, 2000. 247–265.
Mayne, Judith. *Cinema and Spectatorship.* London and New York: Routledge, 1993.
Mills, C. Wright. *The Power Elite.* New York: Oxford University Press, 1957.

Morton, Walt. "Tracking the Sign of Tarzan: Trans-Media Representation of a Pop-Culture Icon." *You Tarzan: Masculinity, Movies and Men.* Ed. Pat Kirkham and Janet Thumin. London: Lawrence & Wishart, 1993. 106–25.
Neale, Steve. *Genre and Hollywood.* London and New York: Routledge, 2000.
Nesteby, James Ronald. "The Tenuous Vine of Tarzan of the Apes." *Journal of Popular Culture* 13 (1980): 483–87.
O'Connor, John E., and Martin A. Jackson, ed. *American History/American Film: Interpreting the Hollywood Image.* New York: Continuum, 1988.
O'Connor, John J. *"Amadis of Gaule" and Its Influence on Elizabethan Letters.* New Brunswick, NJ: Rutgers University Press, 1970.
Orth, Michael P. "Utopia in the Pulps: The Apocalyptic Pastoralism of Edgar Rice Burroughs." *Extrapolation* 27 (1986): 221–233.
Sieber, Harry. "The Romance of Chivalry in Spain, from Rodríguez de Montalvo to Cervantes." *Romance: Generic Transformation from Chretien de Troyes to Cervantes.* Ed. Kevin Brownlee and Marina Scordilis Brownlee. Hanover and London: University Press of New England, 1985. 203–219.
Sobchack, Thomas. *An Introduction to Film.* 2nd ed. Boston: Little-Brown, 1987.
Storey, John. *Cultural Studies and the Study of Popular Culture.* Athens: University of Georgia Press, 1996.
Taliaferro, John. *Tarzan Forever: The Life of Edgar Rice Burroughs, Creator of Tarzan.* New York: Scribner, 1999.
Thomas, Lowell. *With Lawrence in Arabia.* New York and London: Century, 1924.
Torgovnick, Marianna. *Gone Primitive. Savage Intellects, Modern Lives.* Chicago: University of Chicago Press, 1990.
Utz, Richard J., ed. *Investigating the Unliterary: Six Readings of Edgar Rice Burroughs' "Tarzan of the Apes."* Regensburg: Ulrich Martzinek, 1995.
_____. "Introduction: Reading/Teaching Against the Grain: Literariness and *Tarzan of the Apes* in the Literary Classroom." Utz, *Investigating* 1–13.
Wahl, Greg. "Me Hero, You Dupe: Gender and the Narrative Division of Labor in Tarzan of the Apes." Utz, *Investigating* 31–48.
Whinnom, Keith. "The Problem of the 'Best-Seller' in Spanish Golden Age Literature." *Bulletin of Hispanic Studies* 67 (1980): 189–98.
Zanger, Jules. "Dorothy and Tarzan: Notes toward a Theory of National Fantasy." *Contours of the Fantastic: Selected Essays from the Eighth International Conference on the Fantastic in the Arts.* Ed. Michele K. Langford. New York: Greenwood, 1994. 81–87.
Zeuschner, Robert B. *Edgar Rice Burroughs. The Exhaustive Scholar's and Collector's Descriptive Bibliography.* Jefferson, NC: McFarland, 1996.

4

Narcissistic Doubling and the Question of Identification in Film Series: The Case of Nancy Drew

CAROLE MARTIN

Preliminaries

Most reader-response critiques would take gender as an essential element in the way readers of texts, in the extended sense of the word, identify what they read and, in part, identify with what they read. In the concluding words of Wendy Doniger's study of duality in mythology, "culture is [but] the shadow of gender" (49). Women readers, especially, have been sensitive to the fact that, despite their gender, they might identify more often with prominent male characters rather than with their lesser female counterparts. Such an identification process would indicate that reading is not a mere ability that one would freely exercise on a vast range of material, but a skill acquired mainly through the deciphering and absorption of works that, through their strategies and assumptions, replicate a patriarchal order. To this significant hampering, if not denial, of *une lecture féminine* ("a female reading"), feminist critics have retorted with the watchword of resistance, the injunction to become a "resisting" rather than an "assenting" reader.

In film theory, if films are assimilated to texts and, likewise, reveal themselves to be highly ideological constructs, a similar interpretation should prevail and warn the female spectator to put on resistance lenses before she becomes absorbed in watching a standard production. However common this stance is among feminist film critics and reviewers indeed, there is an alternative position on which I would like to focus presently. The French film scholar, Raymond Bellour, has articulated it in his groundbreaking collection of essays, *The Analysis of Film*. This position "is founded on the relation of narcissistic doubling between man and woman"—a doubling that "rules the two sexes' relations of desire," as well as their identification processes (12). Represented in the diegetic couple of the textual or filmic narrative, this doubling also produces in the narrative (that sustains the reader/spectator's identification) a "symbolic blockage." Indeed, the narcissistic doubling between man and woman, only partially realized in a couple who remains informed by sexual difference, finds itself displaced onto the structure of the narrative, the formal elements of which compose mirror images of each other. In Bellour's words, "the movement that opens the film is the same that permits it to close, ... and according to an effect of continuous echo, this movement is propagated as much at the level of the global destiny of the narrative, ... as it is at the level of the infinite detail ... this extreme formalization [reflecting] the mirror image of the diegetic couple" (12). If, according to the critic, this structuring determines the configuration of most Western films, especially in classical American cinema, on the one hand, it certainly "naturalizes" female identification to male protagonists who hold a mirror to their feminine counterparts on the screen, while offering it to the women of the audience as well. On the other hand, although sexual difference is now restructured on the basis of the governing representation of a single sex, it does postulate, to a point that we will have to specify, the reverse identification between male spectators and female characters, the "legitimacy" of bisexual fantasy in the quest for the reality of the opposite sex, and the possibility of interpretation across and beyond gender boundaries.

But this configuration should have another range of consequences, as to the structure of classical cinema versus that of B production, especially when it turns to film series. If a classical film is the product of an almost infinite *structure en miroir* ("mirror imaging") that ultimately reflects back to the couple man/wo/man of modern Western culture, a series, in the intentional absence of a positive dénouement that would untie all the corollaries of an original plot, falls into line with another form altogether. Its open-endedness defies the narcissistic doubling model, while its frequent reliance on a single character puts the predominance of the diegetic couple aside. And if it keeps the identificatory couple away from the screen, from the audience, isn't it reasonable to posit that it also transforms the way in which the public "reads" the film and identifies with its protagonists—a process whose gender-based development deserves more attention in this context?

Here are thus four interrelated questions concerning the structure of narration, its type of characters, the identification process and its gender implications, that I would like to investigate in a contrastive approach to film series versus classical cinema. Using Howard Hawks's *The Big Sleep* to illustrate the concept of narcissistic doubling,[1] I will contrast it with the way in which repetitive sequencing and the framing of a single, eponymous character typify serial production, as exemplified by William Clemens's adaptation of the *Nancy Drew Mystery Stories*.[2] Before considering these specific works, however, it is judicious to retrace the formation of our reference concept. Borrowed from psychoanalysis, "narcissistic doubling" finds its source in the Greek myth of Amphitryon, or Alcmena.[3]

The Case of Amphitryon

So, Amphitryon or Alcmena? Whose myth is it indeed? To whom shall we attribute the first role in this story of Jovian seduction? Who is seduced, misled, and deceived here? Alcmena or Amphitryon? The undecided attribution points to the fact that gender representation is of central importance to the myth, even though it has come to convey one and only meaning — "le jeu du double" ("the double's interplay"). It is this apparent paradox that puts the double, as one of the first representations of the other, at the core of the problematics of sexual difference and associates narcissistic doubling not only with the discovery of oneself in one's mirror image but in/as another, the other, man or woman. To examine the corollaries of this configuration in which my double is both same and other, let's now revisit the development of the legend.

The myth's first traces in Hesiod's *Theogony*, in the *Iliad* and the *Odyssey*, all evoke Alcmena, the last of the mortals to be possessed by Zeus and the future mother of Herakles, while barely mentioning the existence of her husband, Amphitryon. The story seems to have focused on the supernatural order, the god's procreation of a son who would become a hero among men. In a later Hesiodic poem, the *Shield of Herakles*, Alcmena, although married to Amphitryon, has denied herself as wife to remain the pure vessel that both the god and his progeny would soon fill.[4] During the same night, first Zeus, then Amphitryon who is just back from war, possess her, and twin sons are subsequently born — Herakles, Zeus's heroic child, and Iphikles, Amphitryon's son. No mention is made of Zeus taking the shape of Amphitryon to seduce his spouse. The motif of the double characterizes only the act, twice consummated, and its results, the twins. Neither Alcmena nor Amphitryon play much of a part as individuals. They facilitate the relationship, literally and figuratively, between one order (that of the gods) and another (our worldly sphere of action).

From this original plot, let's see how the doubling-up mutates to have Zeus assume Amphitryon's appearance in a Late Greek work, *The Library*.[5] Besides lengthening the night of possession — thrice the normal length — the narrative has Amphitryon come back on the subsequent evening to learn from Alcmena that, in fact, he returned the preceding night. With the doubling of the male protagonist, this version moves the focus from the supernatural to the human order, both man and woman being abused here — the former seeing his shape taken over by Zeus, the latter her body. Identity, rather than deed, is now what is at stake. Actually, three levels of identification between the characters are already in place: Zeus/Alcmena, Zeus/Amphitryon, Alcmena/Amphitryon. Whereas the couple appeared to mediate between gods and men in previous accounts, Zeus has become the mediator of their identification to one another. The triangulation necessary to the formation of the couple-in-love is present, with almighty Zeus the figure of Desire. The configuration of narcissistic doubling is displayed, although having oneself act unbeknownst to one's consciousness, picturing one's body inhabited by another, losing one's sense of inner feelings as truthful and integral to oneself, in other words being possessed, is experienced as hubris. The shape-shifting allows the internalization of desire, however estranged it is from the self, so that, from now on, desire assumes its ambiguous nature as both inseparable from the person and yet foreign to her.

Tragedians of the classical era seize on this ambiguity to explore psychological formations. Twenty or so fragments from an *Alkmene* by Euripides subsist, in which Amphitryon is about to burn Alkmene alive as an adulteress when Zeus, as *deus ex machina*, interferes by "storming" the stage to prevent the death of the blameless heroine. Internalized as hubris, the motif of the double turns into a catalyst for the play of adultery and jealousy against virtuousness. Eclipsed by these highly dramatic behaviors, it almost escapes the spectator's grasp, while Zeus's new role, as the *deus ex machina* who prevents a calamitous ending through the exercise of his formidable powers, also detracts from his more discrete demonstration of omnipotence as Amphitryon's double. If it virtually dissolves in the tragic mode, the theme owes its expansion to the opposite genre of comedy, notably to the adaptation of *Amphitruo* that Plautus wrote presumably from Greek originals around 190 B.C. The playwright introduces a significant change: he doubles the Zeus — in Roman translation — Jupiter/Amphitryon pair with a Mercury/Sosia doublet, a multiplication that characterizes the very movement of the play.

As a "translator" of Greek drama, Plautus is interested in re-presentation, unconcerned with either heroic deeds or psychic intricacies. *Amphitruo*'s prologue, given by the messenger-god, Mercury, is a tribute to Representation, its conditions, type, and process. In this context, the double that Mercury first impersonates is also to be understood as a signifier of the re-presenting apparatus; it is a key to the understanding of what exactly is being represented in this myth-become-play. In more than the obvious way — Plautus's work being the first "full" relation of the legend that survives — the reader needs his invention of the Mercury/Sosia double to illuminate the narcissistic doubling of Jupiter/Alcmena/Amphitryon. Let's examine the text closely before we interpret it as an unexpected blueprint, centuries apart again, of yet another form of representation: film, especially in its serialized mode.

In the prologue, Mercury first evokes the basic components necessary to any representation: a "reporter," just like him, who addresses an audience, whose concerns are identical to those of the portrayed, feeling — himself and the mastermind of the plot, Jupiter, included — as afraid of trouble as any of the spectators. Were this initial identification between addressor and addressee lacking, representation would not exist. Mercury goes on with the type of representation that is about to be given: not a "tragedy"—*Amphitruo*'s prototype both in terms of form and content — for, since he is a god, he will turn the play from a tragedy to a comedy without altering a line. Or rather, reading the mind of his skeptical audience, he will settle for a combination, a "tragicomedy." Here as well, re-presentation is understood as a function of sameness, comedy being but a transfer of the prototypical tragedy, "without a single change of lines," while tragicomedy is no more than a blend of the two (Mantinband and Passage 42). How to account in that case for the prefix of "re-presentation"? In the simplest way, by multiplying the motif of the double conveyed by this prefix. Plautus transforms Euripides's play into a farce by having his spokesman, Mercury, take the shape of Sosia, Amphitryon's slave, just as the messenger's father, Jupiter, takes the appearance of Amphitryon, Sosia's master. From this new "spit-and-image," a new "face to face" will also derive, this time between Amphitryon and Sosia — a confrontation to become one of the highlights of the play and a new duplication of the addressor/addressee or performer/beholder connection. In fact, Mercury's prologue continues precisely with a discussion of the relationship between actor and spectator, one that cannot be corrupted by claques awarding uncritical praise and support, or sneaky cliques using subornment and subterfuge, "for Jupiter himself has turned to histrionics" (Mantinband and Passage 43). Although comic, the play's plot is a serious affair, worthy of divine delivery, in that it still accommodates its tragic origin, an uncanny metamorphosis of hubris into fun, but also because this *dédoublement* ("redoubling") changes the status of the work to that of a meta-play.[6]

Notes on Derivative Representation

What I would like to argue at this point is that Plautus's *Amphitruo* can be read as a model (for both creative and analytical purposes) of derivative representation. The way it derives comedy from tragedy in the context of classical theater can be traced in other genres as well, namely the novel, as it appeared in the late 17th century to reach its climax two centuries later, and the heir it found in narrative cinema. This derivation pattern especially applies to the relationship between novel, or film, and their respective serialization. *Amphitruo* makes clear two fundamental points: (1) there is always an element of parody in the derivative that encompasses both the original and its transformations, and in this capacity the offshoot, operating on a meta-level, serves as a "developer" of the prototype; (2) duplication is the developer's favored technique, but duplication with a difference so as to reveal through this difference the original's structure and modify it into a new one. Hence, the doubling of the double motif in *Amphitruo*, a doubling that brings a comic or satirical bend to the derivative. It is an age-old story, but in a new garb — a servant's outfit, jokes Mercury — a downscale version from which the narcissistic element has disappeared, strictly consigned to the mock-up costume, a repeat wherein doubling is formulized, reduced to its purely formal function. Mirror imaging is replaced by mere repetition. Narcissistic doubling, as the core process of both classical novel and film, becomes serials' and series' repetitive sequencing. At the same time, it is this repetitious structure that underlines the original's complexity through its lack. It is thanks to the unisex coupling of Amphitryon and Sosia that we apprehend the stakes of having one sex mirror the other in the legend to configure desire as *désir de l'autre* ("desire of the other").

Now what does this structural transformation entail in terms of the derivative's content? Among other things, how does it affect the gender issue? Again, let's look at *Amphitruo* as the theoretical model whose elements we will be able to map onto our later serial derivatives. When Jupiter takes the shape of Amphitryon to enjoy the love of his wife, to lie "rapturously" in her arms, desire is clearly what is at stake, whereas, if Mercury impersonates Sosia the slave, it is to work as a servant, do chores, and run errands all day like one of the "house-slaves." Labor and class relations are what matters here, the master-slave relationship taking center stage with Sosia's entrance in Act I as the play's first "real" character. The slave's lead role as Amphitryon's messenger, spokesman, interlocutor, and even alter ego, since they will be sharing the same *dédoublement* with Sosia's doubling instrumental in revealing his master's curse, largely displaces Alcmena's traditional part as Zeus/Amphitryon's cohort. Her actual presence on stage dwindles; she is relegated to merely three scenes, two of which are short, three-page long dialogues with Jupiter, while she shares the stage with Sosia for her longer confrontation with her husband (13 pages in my edition). Her tragic posture at the end of Euripides's version is not only modified but altogether eliminated. Alcmena is absent from the play's conclusion, replaced by a maid who announces the birth of the twins. In fact, more than a presence, Alcmena has become the subject of one's discourse, the figure of one's fantasies, the reified object of desire, while desire itself has lost its central position to power relations between master and servant. In this shift from the original focus of the plot to Plautus's *inventio* we see one sex evicting the other, now objectified as an imaginary figure, to take control over representation not through mere domination but via a discrete change of subject matter: from possession (always involving the two parties) to division of labor (a process that separates them). Sosia remarks on the opposition-as-equivalence that allows the substitution — "All's fair in love and domestic service"— before he details his condition's blight (Mantinband and Passage 46):

> It's a hard life being a rich man's slave... Night and day, they never end it; No rest for the weary.... The rich man, not a thing does he do, But whatever he says, that goes for you.... But that rich man — how great his nerve is! Always thinking up extra work, that's their very favorite quirk. Well, grin and bear it, that's the ticket [46].

Transformed into class relations, gender issues as central to individualization subside, and a man's world structured by the fight for power takes the front stage. When Alcmena reappears in the fuller light of Heinrich von Kleist's "romantic" adaptation of *Amphitryon* in 1807, the questioning of her relation to the other sex according to the recurring paradigm of narcissistic doubling is tainted by madness and has to yield to the schema of sexual difference, as reorganized upon the model of the dominant representation of the male sex. Alcmena's absorption in her lover does not bestow a richer, cross-gendered identity on her but generates an inflated portrayal of him.[7]

Now, two centuries later, with gender politics in fashion, feminists still have to confront the same relational mode. Film series exemplify this pattern of domination, as they reshape the narcissistic doubling between man and woman that characterizes classical cinema into a master-slave formula or the deflected form of the good-and-evil struggle.[8] If the latter relationship sheds light on the former configuration, demonstrating that gender interactions are power dealings, it also pushes the gender question aside, simplifying it, neglecting its hubris-like, almost tragic aspect to transpose it into the satirical vocabulary of the strong versus the weak. In that, it reinforces each sex's stereotyping on the tautological model of the rich man getting richer. Easier to apprehend than the original construct of the double as other ("how can a man be a god, a woman a man?" was the question borne by the myth), the derivative formula (following the parody's answer that a man is a man ... more or less) has indeed taken a life of its own and altered, if not obscured altogether, the initial paradigm. Whereas narcissistic doubling could, in theory, integrate the figure of the other and initiate cross-gender identification, the master-slave model upholds sexual difference, even as it offsets gender identity, even when the "master" is a female protagonist.

The Case of Nancy Drew

To come to the case of Nancy Drew, where this model applies to perfection, it is not despite, but because of the fact that the series's heroine is seen as a figure of empowerment that the patriarchal order is reinforced, boosted with the audience's full adhesion — a paradox that ultimately attests to the quixotic, if not conservative, nature of gender politics. The couple that Nancy (played by Bonita Granville) and Ted (Frankie Thomas) make in the series is indeed modeled after the oppressive master-slave relationship, with Ted playing the comic, recalcitrant but always yielding servant to Nancy's every whim and wish. This structure obviously obliterates any trace of sexual innuendo between the two, even if Ted is formally portrayed as Nancy's boyfriend. Supposedly, it makes it safe material for children to enjoy, although the enigma of "sexual difference"— that repressed narcissistic doubling — does materialize as a "corpse in the attic."[9] The original configuration remains in a number of gender transfers. In the first film, *Nancy Drew — Detective* (William Clemens, 1938), to "penetrate" in the mystery house where the victim (an older woman) is being held captive, Ted dresses up as a nurse. After an almost successful "reconquest" is performed, needless to say, by Nancy-the-master-sleuth, it is again Ted's im/potency that is made patent when his "undone" pants drop from under his skirts, an "exhibit" that unfortunately betrays the reconquest and has the two characters arrested by the villains. Over-determined by the master-slave compound, by the opposite traits of mastery and helplessness it associates respectively with Nancy, the girl, and Ted, the boy, in a reversal that can easily be swapped again, this caricature of cross-gender identification is repeated in the second film of the series, *Nancy Drew — Reporter* (William Clemens, 1939), the only one to follow a fully original script.

While ensuring continuity despite a plot unfamiliar to Nancy Drew's readers, the repetition of the travesty set also identifies the major structural device of the series, the ingredients of which are systematically repeated from one scene to the next, and from one episode to the other. The travesty in *Nancy Drew—Reporter* falls onto a male detective, whom the teenagers have persuaded to share in their glorious capture of the criminals they have ensnared in a trap. Again, the dress-up scene is the catalyst for the plot's last turn, which will lead to the story's resolution, a position that points to the significance of cross-gender identification in the elucidation of the enigma of sexual difference — the mystery's "true" object, the series's repressed subtext, the displaced topic of both novel and film. Marie Bonnafé, in her article on Sosie, Oedipe, and Alcmène quoted above, paraphrases Freud:

> The quest for truth has its origin first in this question: What is the reality of the other sex? ... The mother is going to lead there first, and at the end, the little boy "will solve" the oedipal complex by seeing [in] "the little girl a being just like him" at whom he looks and about whom he *realizes* the difference[10] [150].

Indeed the detective, by a condensation process familiar to psychoanalysis, is dressed up as an older woman, the teens' grand/mother whose role it is this time, not to be "conquered" as in the previous episode, but to help in the conquest of the truth. Together with watching the series, we are moving along the Oedipal complex. Yet, just like in *Nancy Drew—Detective*, the transvestite's outfit gets loose, revealing his belittled pants, before the villains tie him up. Condensed in this bondage scene, the master-slave formula once again covers up the cross-gendering before its reversal, the freeing of the "slave-in-drag," determines the mystery's resolution.

In the last episode of the series, *Nancy Drew and the Hidden Staircase* (William Clemens, 1939), we will see Ted himself becoming the older woman (having apparently solved the Oedipal enigma) and being arrested for it as he goes across town in full dress, wearing a Victorian gown as the only garment left to him at the close of a spellbinding night. Interestingly, this passage repeats an incident that marked the first part of the film when Ted, after losing his "belt" in the hands of Nancy, who is engrossed in the middle of her sleuth act, is apprehended for running "naked" by the roadside. This initial impropriety (hinting at the substance of the second transgression) is compounded by the fact that, presently, Ted should have been at work — he delivers huge blocks of ice around town — rather than "working" for Nancy again. The substitutive equivalence between labor and sex comes out clearly: Nancy's enslaved boyfriend is caught in the act of "assisting" her, meanwhile consuming all of his vigor to her benefit and remaining helpless, pants down at the side of the road. The travesty scene will follow the same pattern. By quite a cruel order of the "teenage sleuth," Ted has to "sleep" alone in the basement of another of these big mystery houses where the stories take place, so he can catch unawares the potential visit of a "ghost."[11] Before going to sleep, Ted has undressed at Nancy's initiative and, after her departure, tied a web of string around him so as to awaken him as soon as somebody walks in.[12] He wakes up the next morning with his clothes gone, the ghost having left his trace — a written threat of murder — on his chest instead. The passage articulates what the first one eluded, the act of possession symbolized by the ghost's approach of Ted's body, his shadow covering the teenager lying still on a makeshift bed, while his hand seizes from Ted's a rather virile axe the latter was holding for protection. The connoted homosexuality is both obvious and transformed into a heterosexual relation not only because of the eluded intercourse with Nancy for which it stands, but also because of Ted's feminization throughout the scene.[13] "Afraid," he reluctantly accepted the "job," all the while wishing that it would be "somebody else's." Actually, when we first discover the cot on which Nancy will make his bed, a headless female mannequin, lying where Ted is about to sleep, frightens him.[14] The "ghost" is not merely male here, it is female just as well, and bisexuality — or rather cross-gender identification — is what is at stake. In fact, while being deflected by the comic mode and the master-slave overarching script, this caricatured exploration of desire as anchored in bisexual identification exposes what a serious and straightforward approach would mask. The narcissistic doubling between man and woman is presently achieved through the "mating" of both ghosts, when the specter's hand-become-camera transfixes the smile of Ted-as-mannequin. Beyond difference, one is the image of the other, literally, while the other is to take one's likeness: to Ted's bed is attached Nancy's camera, which, as soon as the ghost crosses over, goes off to capture his image. We will come back below to the meaning of this technological appendage projecting from the protagonist's body.

The next morning, Ted loses his job to this episode of cross-gendering, after an officer has stopped and jailed the "law offender" in full drag. Coming to his rescue, Nancy and her father cannot resist laughing at his attire, while the amused police captain releases the poor "lady-like-sir." Entertained as well by these antics, disengaged by the meta-discourse of the parody, the spectator identifies what they imply, rather than with the implied.[15] Narcissistic doubling is circumscribed to the safe zone of childish entertainment. Nonetheless, the structure is operative and, thus, laden with its antidote. It refocuses the spectator's attention on the male protagonist rather than on the female heroine, in a shift closely related to that of Plautus redirecting the spotlight from Alcmena to Sosia. The comic slave steals the show from the powerful eponymous character, man and/or woman. He steals the show away from desire, reinstates it as labor, which, independently from the heroes' sex, will insure a male-dominated form of representation. Desire, in the slave's vision of the world, can only be venal and, as such, it is aligned with labor indeed.[16]

Technological Substitutes

We see the same dismissal operate in Ted. Always busy with work, he never shows the slightest "desire" to unravel Nancy's mysteries, participating in her interest only insofar as it is relabeled a "job" for which he is compensated. Nancy has a number of gifts — a hat in the second film, a watch in the third (both of which you have to beat or bang for them to perform as expected, just like their future owner) — to entice Ted to join in her escapades and abandon his devising some technological contraption or other. For Ted has this remarkable inquisitiveness as to technology, an interest that, combined with or substituted for Nancy's curiosity, will contribute to solving the mysteries. Symptomatically, *techne* takes over from *eros*. We have already mentioned the photographic appendage that prolonged Ted's body in the "mating" scene and performed what he himself did not, capturing the other, if only on film. Or rather, precisely on film, for this capture of the "truth" thanks to the camera serves to remind the spectator of the filmic apparatus itself. It is thanks to the relationship between film and reality — one "duplicating" the other — that film can "see through" reality, that its mysteries (especially that of desire) can be resolved by the manipulation of film or one of its metonyms. The series's opening installment, *Nancy Drew — Detective*, owes its resolution to the aerial "pictures" taken from a plane in "motion" and developed in Ted's darkroom to reveal the elusive location of the mystery house. Old-style sleuthing with the help of a homing pigeon that leads to the wrong mansion is outperformed by the consummate handling of technological equipment, the profusion of which ultimately represents cinematic means, assets, and resources, at a time when the latter have coalesced into the form of entertainment par excellence. There is no need to insist on the purpose of Nancy's car, cast in one chase after another, from one film to the next, although to possess a car at sixteen in 1938 must have been a rather rare occurrence.[17] As mentioned above, Ted also flies airplanes and operates all sorts of machines starting from his own radio system to an x-ray device that he transforms into a Morse transmitter, to a tape recorder together with its miniature mikes, to a fuse box the wires of which he disconnects to create an illuminated message from a hotel sign. In this peripeteia, the hotel's name suddenly changing to that of Bed Bug Hotel alerts a laughing street crowd to the presence of the imprisoned kid-detectives in the building's electrical room, while the mother-sleuth is in bondage in one of the rooms below.

A "bed bug" it is indeed, for in all these instances the technological device (be it a camera or its stand-in) is used for eavesdropping on the forbidden fruit before it causes the characters to escape and evade the shadows of desire that cross-dressing had exposed. Again bright, spotless technology steals the show away from dark, murky desire, or rather, the yearning for technology that film actualizes so well stands for the other's desire that it strategically veils/unveils. Self-aware, the derivative genre that is the film series uncovers the "truth" of film, its systemic shift of focus from the nucleus of desire to conditions of production. The camera becomes *l'objet du désir* ("the object of desire"). As such, technological appendages are not only the cinematic *dei ex machina*, miraculously resolving the schemes at stake, while literally coming, as symbols of the filmic apparatus, from the machine itself, they also represent *le dieu de la machine* ("the god of the machine"), the "corpse in the attic" whose fascinating limbs the spectator will fetishize for want of a fuller, forbidding encounter with his other.

In Plautus's *Amphitruo* and even more in Molière's enduring adaptation, with its self-conscious emphasis on the circumstances of representation typical of Classicism, the conditions of production already took center stage.[18] In the former, Mercury alludes to the longer than usual night that auspiciously factors in the seduction. In Molière, the prologue has Mercury request a personified Night to "satisfy his [master's] amorous wishes, Stretching a night that's most delicious Into a night that's long indeed [to] allow his fires more time to burn" (10). Night appears as the facilitator of the pleasure-enticing doubling process, as its effect "sends to sleep" consciousness and allays conscience, beguiling humans in its dream world to let desire take over. Indeed, Amphitryon will repeatedly accuse Sosia of being "asleep and dreaming" when his slave first tells him about his double, and Sosia will return the compliment to Alcmena:

> SOSIA: Leave her alone, Amphitryon, till she sleeps it off. Clearly she's having nightmares.
> AMPHITRYON: What do you mean, awake and yet asleep? ...
> SOSIA: She's telling you her dream, to the best of her memory. Listen here, Alcmena, after you woke up you should have sacrificed to Jupiter ... he's the god in charge of dreams [Mantinband and Passage 72–74].

The character's state, "awake and yet asleep," pointedly alludes to that of the spectator, seeing his dream come alive, while Jupiter, the *deus ex machina* who had ordered the night to stay awhile, is designated both as the dream's object and "director-in-charge." As Jupiter is to Alcmena, so is the director to the spectator, the agent of representation mesmerizing the latter's attention. Such shift to the conditions of creation had already been underlined by Plautus's Mercury who called his doubling of Sosia a "costume," assimilating the plot's nucleus, the replication process itself to a production proviso. Now, although "darkness" was more of a psychological condition than a concrete situation, given the fact that Roman theater was always performed in daylight, and that the duplication it made credible was virtual rather than actual, both provisions certainly echo in the realm of cinema duplicating reality in the dark of the projection room. The beholder's interest has effectively deviated from the seduction intrigue to the means of its production, from the Alcmena/Amphitryon/Zeus story to the Jupiter/Amphitryon doublet repeated as Mercury/Sosia.

This shift from the tripartite structure of desire to the structural device of repetition clarifies to a great extent what Raymond Bellour defined as the "symbolic blockage." The critic posited a subject of desire, historically determined "by a series of constraints ... shifted and regulated at once" in fictional production, the purpose of which is to inscribe the yearning couple within a structure:

> I have called this effect "symbolic blockage." By this I mean to suggest, first, that the movement that opens the film is the same that permits it to close, according to a program in which contingency is [a function of] a determinant relation between repetition and its resolution; second, that through a skillfully orchestrated hierarchization and according to an effect of continuous echo, this movement is propagated as much at the level of the global destiny of the narrative, of its massive and manifest design, as it is at the level of the infinite detail of each of its components; and, finally, that this extreme formalization is not content until it almost infinitely ... reflects the mirror image of the diegetic couple devoted to the final reconciliation of desire and the law, or to their impossible conjunction [12–13].

Symbolic blockage, summarized Bellour, regulates desire "according to a properly infinite process of expansion of the same, of repetition subordinated to its resolution." Hence, the allegoric nature of Amphitryon's legend through the development of which the structure of desire has become the desire for structure, or again the "impossible conjunction ... of these two forces conjugated as one" (13). *Amphitryon*'s Jupiter as both the impersonator of passion and the king of gods, who has jurisdiction over supernatural as well as human beings, is the figure that represents this conjunction. The one who "had his fill of love with the lady in there" and the one who "will restore love and peace and harmony" are the same in representation, if not in real life (Mantinband and Passage 61).[19] What reflects "the desire of the Western subject" in making the "impossible" union of law and desire possible is the *deus ex machina* nature of Jupiter, his belonging to the machine, but a machine that can mimic life itself.[20] Rather than with any of its specific characters, the spectator thus identifies with the representational "machine." And if film, to an extent unmatched in the history of representation, fulfills the machine's double bind as worlds apart in terms of its mechanism and life-like in terms of its product — just like Jupiter is both Zeus and Amphitryon — the film spectator's primary identification falls on the filmic apparatus itself. However, along with the "truthful" representation the machine grants us, there is a by-product, outside our direct reach, resulting from its inner works. As Plautus's *deus ex machina* acknowledges, he will even perform the delivery for Alcmena. His attributes of deafening thunder and dazzling light shield the painless birth of two boys, soon to be threatened by a couple of enormous serpents. Before anyone can prevent the danger, the biggest child has jumped right out of his cradle and strangled the crested reptiles, while his father's voice claims that he is Alcmena's secret lover, the infant who killed the snakes his son, and the other Amphitryon's.

Narcissistic Doubling Versus Formulaic Repetition

Now, how to account for this conclusion to the legend? What to do with this birth of both a human child and a godlike offspring with "only one confinement"?[21] And what about the strangled snakes? As usual, Mercury, the Roman Hermes, helps us interpret the condensation at work here. He explains how the *deus ex machina* has "seen to it that only one confinement — a single parturition — will do the job for two. So no one will suspect her of adultery" (Mantinband and Passage 61). It is the logic of desire, a logic that makes one of two (or vice versa) and two of three (or vice versa), which is the by-product of the machine of representation. Alcmena's object is either single (Amphitryon) or dual (Amphitryon and Jupiter, as both the same and other) in an undistinguishable configuration, while the Alcmena/Amphitryon couple mirrors itself in an endless combination where Alcmena's partner can be Amphitryon as Jupiter,[22] or Jupiter as Amphitryon,[23] where Amphitryon can identify with Jupiter (hence his jealousy) or Alcmena (hence his folly), and where Jupiter identifies with one for the sake of identifying with the other, man or woman. The machine's by-product is the narcissistic double as structure of desire that we see reconfigured in the twins-who-are-not-twins but who are able to come to grips with the archetypical snake. The union between "desire for structure" and the "structure of desire," if rather monstrously, has been fruitful. In associating with Jupiter, the amalgamation engine, the god of metamorphosis, the spectator's identification works three ways: (1) with the machine, (2) with both of the couple's characters, Jupiter uniting with Amphitryon to take his shape as well as with Alcmena to take her love, and (3) with the split, the hubris inhabiting the characters as they see each other mirrored in a third party. Sosia, the initial witness of Jupiter-doubled-as-Mercury's "superspectacle of fooling," describes the uncanny feeling quite plainly (Mantinband and Passage 86):

> I *am* right here, and I *am* at home ... I didn't really believe that it was my own self there, not until the other me, that other Sosia convinced me.... There I was at the house before I even arrived.... That's the long and short of it — I've become a set of twins [Mantinband and Passage 66–67].

Again Sosia's "set of twins" exposes in its comic ways Jupiter's delivery of the false twins to which desire gave birth: when desiring, I (Jupiter) am both "my own self" and "the other me" (Amphitryon), the one who has access to you (Alcmena), who is reflecting you and, as such, is able to convince you to reciprocate, to come to coincide with me so I can be one again. When watching any one of the numberless renditions of this narrative, likewise, I identify with Jupiter, now *dieu-machine* ("god-machine") as well as desiring subject, and through him with the characters he produces to impersonate the script. This elucidates the cross-gendered identification typical of spectatorship (or readership as we noted in our preliminary remarks), whilst it is absent from customary interactions between men and women. But is this identification, which is elicited by the tripartite structure of desire, and which is the narcissistic doubling between man and woman that we find epitomized in classical cinema, operative when desire, if still latent, is largely cancelled out, as is the case in film series? Molière, by giving Sosia a wife and apparently redoubling the Amphitryon/Alcmena couple, in fact points out, via the wives' opposite treatment, the radical negation of desire conveyed by the slave.[24] His mirroring in Mercury is not a reflection through which he can harmonize with her. In his likeness, she finds a stranger "chilly and severe, As if I were not anyone you knew.... I expressed to you a tender, wifely love, but to all I said, you were as cold as stone; And you never spoke one syllable of Affection, in answer to my own.... And so extreme was that cold mood of yours, That you wouldn't even join me in our bed." There goes her long series of complaints to which Sosia replies "Well done, Sosia! ... I feel profound self-satisfaction" (Molière 77–79). He will confirm a third time his lack of interest when he declines to make amends ("it's my turn now to let my temper flare") and exits the stage alone (97). No, the mirroring effect is all about the reinforcement of his very own traits:

> I saw that he was I, and no mistake; From head to foot he's like me — handsome, clever, Well-made, ... In short, two drops of milk were never So much alike as we are, [but] The me whom I have met of late Excels the me you see, in one respect; His arm is strong, his courage great; ... That me whose rage could terrify My craven self, and make me flee[25] [Molière 54–57].

From the description of "identical twins," the passage has moved to the depiction of an aggrandized original — here, the other is not other but the same, only better. It is the ideal self. Indeed, in Sosia and Mercury, one sees a tit for tat matching pair. Mercury is the messenger-god, just like Sosia is Amphitryon's messenger; Mercury is the god of poetic *inventio*, just like Sosia shall present to Alcmena his own reconstitution of a battle in which he did not participate; Mercury becomes an actor in his father's footsteps, just like Sosia plans to perform for his master's wife. Mercury, in taking Sosia's appearance and behavior, borrows his devious character as well, just like Sosia-become-actor takes on Mercury's sharp-witted attitude. The mirror image is so perfect that they can only fight for this one and unique identity. Says Mercury: "You'll never get away with pretending I'm anyone but Sosia." To which Sosia replies, echoing his image: "And *you* will never get away with making me out to be someone else." (Mantinband and Passage 57). Repetition is aligned with authenticity: re-presentation (although deceptive in itself) serves as the catalyst for truth. Sosia's description of Amphitryon's victory, which he pretends to have watched, when actually construing a way to spin it, is "every bit" true, attests Mercury, eyewitness to the fight, in a straightforward (or is it disingenuous?) manner. In fact, it does not even matter.

What does matter is that the repetitive structure strengthens the notion of identity on the model of the ideal self, underlining the genuineness and legitimacy of that notion, despite the very fact that it is based in deception.[26] In that, the film series's foremost structural device plays a major part in anchoring the ideological value of identity and authenticity in the face of difference and untruth, even though the former might themselves result from make-believe, leaving "difference" as the series's foe, the very difference that is the object of narcissistic doubling. Instead of gender cross-identification, parodied in travesty scenes to the point of eschewing the beholder's empathizing, the spectator will see gender reification take place on a wholly didactic level and underpin not only each sex's set of stereotypes but also promote them to an ideal configuration, whose redundant traits warrant inner veracity. Thus, "*Nancy Drew*, WASP Super Girl of the 1930s" becomes the truth of any woman-to-be and takes on a progressive fight, despite her conservative gear.[27] While cross-identification in classical film narrative will have to be compensated by a strong differentiation molded on the dominant representation of the male sex, no such danger exists in film series, leaving room for experimentation with gender roles. Nancy rights the wrong not only by fighting crime but also in bettering her sex. It's all about "taking the law into our hands," including that which rules gender attributes, even though gender is no longer assessed through the idea of difference but that of identity, as if deactivation of desire had disentangled it from sexual difference (Jones 710).[28]

James Jones points out the relentless defacement of people apprehended as "different" in the book series. "Racial and national stereotypes abounded," including those denigrating black "menial" characters, Italian and Asian criminals, Jewish and Irish protagonists. Not only did "the treatment of national groups read like a quota chart of the 1920s immigration law," but there was also much "class snobbery," anchored in the master-slave relationship previously discussed (Jones 710–12). In short, shifted onto maligned ethnic peculiarities (the Polish woman's brawny arms fresh "with washtub's suds") and class aberrations (the defamed nouveau riche who cast doubt on the social status quo), sexual difference has been ousted from the characterization of the series's eponym. Nancy is a superwoman to the extent that she is utterly desexualized, totally indifferent. In the seventh novel, *The Clue in the Diary*, she meets her boyfriend, Ned, who just like Ted, his film homologue, will never be allowed to romance his non-other, the only relation that exists between him and Nancy being one of identity with a twist — the twist the master-slave bond gives to matching-but-not-mating partners.

The Big Sleep

It is easy to oppose the Nancy/Ted detective couple to its contemporary Lauren Bacall/Humphrey Bogart mystery duo. If one is a product of the structure of duplication typical of derivative formula fiction, the other must be the epitome of narcissistic doubling as exemplified in classical Western cinema. The latter demonstrates to the outmost the very paradox of this structure, in which one recognizes oneself in an other whose nature is thoroughly alien to one's own, an identification with which the spectator will intimately associate in the dark of the theater. I always wondered about the film's title; it seems to collect meaning from Jupiter's long night, from "blond Phoebus drowsing over-long in dreams" (Mantinband and Passage 141). Similarly, I often pondered about the plot, "so convoluted even Chandler didn't know who committed one murder, but so incredibly entertaining that no one has ever cared" (Maltin 121). Obviously, the movie's power (like the fascination for the myth) did not lie in the story line, as Leonard Maltin confirms when he notes that the pre-release version "has less of Bogie and Bacall and a more linear plot, but is somehow less exotic and interesting" (121). As the myriad of adaptations shows the lure vested in the Greek triad, the attraction rests here with the characters' intimate though adversarial, "exotic" relationship. Desire indeed is what is at stake in *The Big Sleep*, not concordance. The 18 minutes of scenes re-shot or unused in the official release left undermined the "integrity" of the story to the sole benefit of the characters' sexualization.

Reminiscent of *Amphitryon*, there is a startling line uttered by the murder suspect, the casino owner, to Marlowe/Bogart, the detective, that summarizes in a perfect condensation the narcissistic doubling characteristic of the male/female relationship in the film. Just as Philip Marlowe is leaving Eddy Mars's office after a sterile conversation, he finally asks the question that will determine the end of his investigation. Speculating on the whereabouts of Mars's wife, he gets a rather defensive response — "What is between me and my wife is between us." Let's undo the various meanings encoded in this brief, ambiguous though final, statement. It can mean that, indeed, the couple's relation is privy to them, with Marlowe having no right to interfere in between. In other words, Amphitryon is facing Alcmena, and that's that. However, it can also signify the opposite: what exists between my wife and me also exists between us, Marlowe and Mars. From a heterosexual rapport (me/my wife), we have switched to a *relation homosexuée* ("homosocial relation") involving Philip and Eddy, analog to that of Jupiter and Amphitryon, the homosocial bond exactly mirroring the heterosexual one and already inferring cross-gender identification. Finally, to complete the structure, we can understand the reply as holding yet another meaning: what is standing between me and my wife is standing between us two as well, and this time it is Vivian/Bacall. Singing in the room adjacent to the office, her presence at the casino is evidently what has motivated Marlowe's visit to Mars. From the homosexual transfer, we return to a man/wo/man relation, although now it is tripartite, shaped on the Jupiter/Amphitryon/Alcmena paradigm. The twofold identification process, to both man and woman, that desire implies (Jupiter becoming Amphitryon to possess Alcmena), as unfolded above, clearly exemplifies the narcissistic doubling the film illustrates so well.

Now, if this is so, if cross-gender identification is at the core of the mystery, for characters and spectators alike, why is it that Vivian comes out poles apart from the self-possessed Philip? How paradoxical it is that the two major scenes shot for the 1946 release were redone expressly to remove any resemblance between the novel's heroes and accentuate Vivian's take on femininity! The first scene moves the stage from Marlowe's rather dreary office — not a setting for the radiant figure Vivian is to become — to an evening bar full of potential admirers. Likewise, her dark business suit in the original version, an outfit that merged into the décor just as well as Marlowe's own attire, is replaced by a shimmering, long and glitzy gown that displays Vivian's glamorous stature as she enters from the far end of the bar to come to the foreground and sit next to Marlowe — a gleaming, oblong, mesmerizing profile. With Bacall's deep voice and emancipated speech encased in this ultra-feminine garment, the actress embodies on the one hand the ideal woman of your dreams, on the other a flamboyant, androgynous blend in which figure and behavior seem at odds with each other, unless it is precisely the Androgyne in her that makes her ideal — a phallic woman.

Such transformation of the female protagonist according to the dominant representation of the male sex is confirmed by the second significant passage to be altered for the official release. In this scene, Marlowe has been taken prisoner to the quarters of Eddy Mars's accomplice. Waking up after having been knocked out and finding himself between two women, Mars's wife and Vivian, he is now the one "standing" between them. In the first version, Mrs. Mars is a petite, curly-haired actress with a high-pitched voice, who neither looks nor sounds anything like Bacall. In the 2nd version, a performer who bears a singular resemblance to the star — same stature, same hairdo and same voice — will replace the miscast one. Even their shared bony facial features make them look twin-like. As this new double shows, the woman is transformed into an object of desire inasmuch as she is phallicized, modeled as an all-powerful yet familiar, unattainable yet available figure, half-mirroring, half-distancing her partner, both same and other in a flickering alternation that the cinematic apparatus perfectly conveys in its *film noir* manifestations. Following a parallel if reverse move, Vivian and Marlowe's common goal ("I want to find out what you want to find out"), positioning the two characters as doubles of one another, becomes the object of his investigation while taking on a fresh turn — "what is to be found out I, Marlowe, want to find out from you, from what you, Vivian, want." The purpose of the quest has shifted from the "what" question to the "you" riddle, leaving the mystery's solution an issue second to the inquiry into female inscrutability on the part of a seer whose job it is now to identify her, to identify with her, and identify (with) the people — father, sister, racketeer — she associates with. Infallibly, we come to perceive the thriller's plot as invaded by the structure of desire that narcissistic doubling has ignited.

Conclusion

Going back to the legend of Alcmena, which at first did not mention Zeus/Amphitryon's doubling and afterwards still characterized it as a function of desire, we have seen the myth evolve so that the characters' duplication (starting with Plautus) has taken precedence over the god's "uncivil/ uncivilized" possession of Amphitryon's young wife. In other words, desire has submitted to empathy, to one recognizing rather than enforcing his own drive in another being—a reversal that offers us an index of "civilization's" progress.[29] This primary shift is supplemented by a second form of "repression," also found already present in Plautus: recognizing oneself in an other does not necessarily mean "falling in love" if desire is short-circuited by labor, if it is re-channeled as the "labor of love" both one and the other share in.

Nancy and Ted do well in this regard, their "workaholism" being exemplified at its best when pitted against the parodied romance for which Nancy's father falls in the series's third film, *Nancy Drew—Troubleshooter* (William Clemens, 1939). As the title indicates, Nancy has become the indispensable problem-solver whose dedication to the job makes for her father giving way to fancy. Together with Ted she solves the mystery behind the imprisonment of Mr. Drew's old friend, while her dreamy father, although the one called for help, remains desperately idle, smitten that he is by his female lodger. The parody of narcissistic doubling that Plautus initiated through the creation of his Mercurial mock-up pair is here "redoubled" by the fact the romance itself is but a caricature, bringing puzzlement and disgust to the youngsters' couple who cannot associate with so distortedly romantic an image. In the scene where Nancy attempts to break that bad mirror, by emulating and supplanting the female "role-model" her would-be stepmother incarnates, she eminently fails. She ruins all the courses of the meal she intended for a father whom she can replace at work but not gratify at home. Obviously (incest being far worse than teenage sex), she is no substitute for the charming lodger, and her place is not in the kitchen, but in the field where she finds the clue to the crime—the exotic flower, which she definitely is not. "The 'true daughter of the middle west' [who] symbolize[s] the verities of middle America," "the little girl [who] has to keep out,"[30] is both much too "near and dear" and much too busy to become *l'objet du désir* (Jones 715–16). Meanwhile, she reflects a safe model of identity for teenagers, an example of the working girl, who "made a daring stride into adulthood" and "trespasse[d] into male territory" but only in terms of labor, that secondary outlet which leaves the structure of desire untouched (Mason 53).[31] An index of productivity, her instrumental roadster adequately materializes her newfound independence and autonomy. As Carolyn Heilbrun argues against Bobbie Ann Mason, what "the mystery Nancy Drew is really about [is not] the mystery of sex," rather that "of overcoming gender expectations and *doing* something in the world ... I think," continues the feminist critic, "she comes out pretty well. She has a gun, but she doesn't shoot it, she risks danger, she survives without falling into any man's arms ... and she avoids romance" (18–20). But there, I would argue, is also her Achilles's tendon, the shortfall of her gender reassessment. Work, although it is no longer restricted to the kitchen, has never "freed" anyone, and certainly not the women enlisted in the 20th century workforce.

So, we are left in a double bind. Either women face the disintegration of the structure of desire, as sexual difference is outdone by gender roles' redefinition according to the paradigm of identity, or cross-gender identification, which results from the narcissistic doubling integral to desire, does occur but concurrently gives rise to a remodeling of the female subject onto the phallus, as the male's object of desire. Whichever scenario comes about in our lives, we linger short of a third way to divest gender politics from ineptitude or perversity.

Notes

1. Filmed during the war, *The Big Sleep* was pre-released in 1945, before a number of scenes involving its main actress, Lauren Bacall, were re-shot for the official release in 1946. The film is an adaptation of Raymond Chandler's first novel, with Humphrey Bogart as detective Philip Marlowe.

2. Produced in 1938–39, after Warner Bros. purchased the screen rights in 1938, the four films of the series "are very much of a piece, and hew to a Hollywood formula" (Maltin 967). Only the first, *Nancy Drew — Detective* (1938) from *The Password to Larkspur Lane*, and the last, *Nancy Drew and the Hidden Staircase* (1939), are adapted from actual novels, whereas the other two, *Nancy Drew — Reporter* and *Nancy Drew — Troubleshooter*, filmed in 1939, are combined from incidents found in various titles of the book series.

3. Here as elsewhere, Freud has used mythology and its literary derivatives to develop his conceptual apparatus. See Marie Bonnafé, "Entre Sosie et Oedipe, Alcmène: jeu du double, fantasme bisexuel et réalité psychique."

4. Appended to the *Theogony*, as it has been transmitted, are two poems by later writers, *The Catalogue of Women* and *The Shield of Herakles*, which provide the legend with more details.

5. Based on a 5th century B.C. fragmentary handbook of mythology composed by Pherecydes of Leros, a contemporary of Aeschylus and Sophocles (whose tragic adaptations of the myth are lost), it is likely to have presented the tale still untouched by the dramatic poets.

6. See Amphitryon's bewilderment and Sosia's deflation of his dismay: "I don't even know who I am any more!— You're Amphitryon. Just watch out that somebody doesn't jump your claim" (Mantinband and Passage 80).

7. See Alcmena's anxious probe into the depths of her psyche and following glorification of her lover/husband: "I'd sooner be mistaken in myself! I'd sooner take this feeling deep inside me, this feeling I drank at my mother's breast, that tells me I'm Alkmena, and

deny it.... Is this my hand? Is this my breast? This mirror image — is it mine? He'd have had to be stranger to me than myself! Take my eyes, I'd hear him; my ears, I'd feel him; my touch, I'd still breathe him; take eyes and ears and touch and smell — take all my senses, but leave me my heart: and with that I'll have the bell I need to find him anywhere in the wide world. [I found] him more beautiful last night than ever before. I could as easily have taken him for his portrait, for a painting by a master's hand, as true as life itself, and yet as if in the figure of a god! He stood before me as if... in a dream.... I would have asked him if he had descended from the stars, except that to me he already seemed glorified" (Kleist 126–27).

    8. Interestingly, the villains in the *Nancy Drew Mystery Stories* are most often disenfranchised laborers, "undeserving, nouveau riches with no class. They were mean and sly, inevitably wore loud clothes, had bad manners, and used bad grammar" (Jones 709).

    9. See Michael Bronski's epitaph for Mildred Wirt Benson, the author of 23 of the first 30 Nancy Drew novels: "The dirty secret of Nancy Drew ... is that it's all about sex. Sure, it's often sublimated sex aimed at an audience between the ages of nine and fifteen — but it is in fact smoldering with unmistakable eroticism.... The idea that these series contain a simmering sexuality was not lost on people at the time. Indeed, most public and school libraries would not even carry them until after World War II because they were seen as junk writing, or worse, dangerous to children's imagination" (31).

    10. "La quête de la vérité a d'abord son origine dans cette question: Quelle est la réalité de l'autre sexe? ... C'est la mère qui va d'abord y conduire, et à la fin, le petit garçon 'résoudra' la problématique oedipienne en voyant [dans] 'la petite fille un être tel que lui' qu'il regarde et dont il *réalise* la différence." Marie Bonnafé quotes from Freud's 1917 text on "La disparition — ou résolution — du complexe d'Oedipe." [Editor's translation].

    11. Here is the command: "I only have one little job for you, then you're all through, states Nancy. — You're sure it's just one? replies Ted [afraid of the dark, just like Sosia when his master ordered him to leave by night and announce to Alcmena his imminent arrival at dawn]. — Certainly. — Well, let's get it over with" (*Nancy Drew and the Hidden Staircase*). None of these incidents is found in the corresponding novel, in which Nancy's helper is not her boyfriend but a girlfriend about to be married. Of the several "midnight watches" they carry out to catch "an elusive ghost," not one is set up this way.

    12. As we shall see below, his body is "prolonged" by a camera whose lens is fastened to the string.

    13. Let's note that in the first film, while Ted plays the nurse in disguise, Nancy takes the part of the older woman to be "reconquered" from the villains. The same pattern obviously defines the travesty sequences from one episode to another.

    14. "Oh, for goodness's sake, only a dress dummy!" teases Nancy, while taking it off the bed. However, it is precisely Ted's function when, in the morning, he has to put on the Victorian gown. See *Nancy Drew and the Hidden Staircase*, the film.

    15. As they leave the station, Nancy, grasping Ted by the skirt, calls him "Sir," when he suddenly stumbles and falls in the arms of an officer who exclaims: "Watch your step, Lady! — Lady [yourself]" replies a dismissive Ted, in a wink at the policeman's cross-dressing of the previous episode. See *Nancy Drew and the Hidden Staircase*, the film.

    16. In Sosia and Mercury's opening dialogue, the former alludes to the fact that the idling night would be just the right time to spend with a "call girl."

    17. In *The Hidden Staircase*, the series's second book, Nancy establishes how experienced a driver she is as she "flashes into the garage with a skill born of long practice" (Jones 708).

    18. First performed in 1668 in Paris, with Molière himself playing Sosia, the comedy is an instantaneous and lasting success. Three hundred sixty-three presentations to both city and court are recorded down to 1715 and, in 1772, the aging Voltaire still recalls reading the text as a boy and "almost falling over backwards" from uncontrollable laughter (Mantinband and Passage 125).

19. Says Jupiter: "The reason I'm here today is on account of you, so as not to leave this comedy unfinished. Also to help Alcmena in her innocence — she's been accused by her husband of adultery. It really wouldn't be right if I got her into trouble all because of something I alone had done" (Mantinband and Passage 82).

20. His machine-like quality has become manifest ever since complex stage machines have been in use. Replicated in some sixty versions or so, in the form of opera, ballet, vaudeville, or drama, *Amphitryon* with its flying gods descending on earth has proven a popular script for the display of theatrical special effects.

21. Mercury even tells us that Amphitryon's son is a ten-month baby, Jupiter's a premature infant of seven months.

22. See Kleist's interpretation above.

23. See Jean Giraudoux's *Amphitryon 38*. First performed in Paris in 1929, the comedy "humanizes" Jupiter and has Alcmena confound the god, rather than feel mystified by the soulful deity.

24. Indeed Mercury perceives Sosia as a threat to Jupiter's pleasures: "that damned babbler there, I'll drive him off ere he ... mars the joys Now savored by our loving pair" (Molière 19).

25. Mercury is Sosia as superhero. When the latter first encounters his double, he marvels at his size, voicing a sense of awe that Mercury fosters at once — "Let's go now, Fists! It's a long, long time since you've had a good square meal. When was it, yesterday? when you laid out and stripped *four* big strong men" (Mantinband and Passage 51). I will not discuss here the function of faked violence in farce and its exploitation in film series, but the pretend-fights of the comic stage, the masks of Roman comedy forbidding real fighting, have certainly found their contemporary analogs in action movies — a genre we often see represented in series.

26. Such is the superhero's dilemma of so many a series, as exposed in *The Incredibles* spoof. In this 2004 animation milestone, written and directed by Brad Bird, a family of undercover superheroes hopelessly tries to emulate suburban life before resuming their station and saving the world from a superhero mock-up turned evil.

27. I borrow the title of James Jones's article on Nancy Drew, the "'clever, capable, popular, athletic, unusually pretty, friendly, attractive, skillful, kind, modest, good, brave, poised, keen-minded, plucky, self-reliant, unforgettable, distinctive, forceful, wise, splendid, observant, healthy, responsible, remarkable,' and amazingly, 'normal'" heroine (Jones 707).

28. Jones quotes from *The Message in the Hollow Oak*.

29. In their comparative account of the legend, James Mantinband and Charles Passage have also suggested that Zeus's metamorphosis, aimed at easing Alcmena's possession, civilizes the brutal, older version of the story.

30. As threatens one of the film's villains, who restates a recurring complaint about the character's nosiness.

31. See also Mason's "*Nancy Drew*: The Once and Future Prom Queen," *Feminism in Women's Detective Fiction*, ed. Glenwood Irons (Toronto: University of Toronto Press, 1995) 74–93.

Works Cited

Bellour, Raymond. *The Analysis of Film.* Ed. Constance Penley. Bloomington: Indiana University Press, 2000.

Bonnafé, Marie. "Entre Sosie et Oedipe, Alcmène: jeu du double, fantasme bisexuel et réalité psychique." *Revue Française de Psychanalyse* 59.1 (January–March 1995): 149–62.

Bronski, Michael. "Sex and the Teenage Sleuth." *Gay and Lesbian Review Worldwide* 9.5 (September 2002): 31–32.
Doniger, Wendy. "Sita and Helen, Ahalya and Alcmena: A Comparative Study." *History of Religions* 37.1 (August 1997): 21–49.
Heilbrun, Carolyn G. "Nancy Drew: A Moment in Feminist History." *Rediscovering Nancy Drew*. Ed. Carolyn S. Dyer and Nancy T. Romalov. Iowa City: University of Iowa Press, 1995. 11–21.
Jones, James P. "*Nancy Drew*, WASP Super Girl of the 1930's." *Journal of Popular Culture* 6 (1973): 707–17.
Kleist, Heinrich von. *Three Major Plays*. Trans. Carl R. Mueller. Hanover: Smith and Kraus, 2000.
Maltin, Leonard. *Leonard Maltin's Movie and Video Guide*. New York: Signet, 2000.
Mantinband, James H., and Charles E. Passage, trans. *Amphitryon: Three Plays in New Verse Translations. Plautus: "Amphitruo," translated by James H. Mantinband. Molière: "Amphitryon," translated by Charles E. Passage. Kleist: "Amphitryon," translated by Charles E. Passage. Together with a Comprehensive Account of the Evolution of the Legend and Its Subsequent History on the Stage*. Chapel Hill: University of North Carolina Press, 1974.
Mason, Bobbie Ann. *The Girl Sleuth: A Feminist Guide*. New York: Feminist, 1975.
Molière, Jean Baptiste Poquelin de. *Amphitryon*. Trans. Richard Wilbur. New York: Harcourt Brace, 1995.

5

The Trouble with Maisie: Insubordination and the Empowered Woman Series

JENNIFER FORREST

The standard assessment of Classic Hollywood films in general, and its genre films in particular, is that they reflect and promote the prevailing ideology of American culture, which is in turn associated with the ideology of the prevailing class in American culture. That movies do reflect this relationship, Robert B. Ray contends, springs both from the nature of Hollywood movies as a big business that tries to reach the greatest audience possible, and from the studios' "financial servitude to the politically powerful eastern banks" that are traditionally conservative (13). Add to this mixture the way in which the studios established the aesthetic conventions of a "seamless" film narrative, and you have a powerful medium that creates the illusion of the naturalness of its worldview. In this light, Ray wonders, "Have dissident variations (thematic or stylistic) *any* chance of disrupting or subverting a movie's intended ideological effect?" (18). If the spectator is jarred out of complacency by an odd camera angle that isn't readily recognized as motivated by the elements leading up to it, we can say that that is an instance of stylistic dissidence. Similarly, thematic dissidence emerges when there is, for example, an emotion or reaction that seems unmotivated in the context established by the film (Ray 18). "For the most part, however," Ray concedes, "those dissident elements have been contained." He wonders, however, "If they had not been, would the movies in which they appeared have been popular?—a devilish question since it points to the great uncharted area of film criticism, the audience" (19–20).

Before addressing Ray's question, it is important to identify the context in which it is posed. Ray refers specifically in his book to A-class productions from *Casablanca* (Michael Curtiz, 1942) to *The Godfather* (Francis Ford Coppola, 1972), and assesses the dissident features they manifest according to high art criteria. B-class series films from the Classic Hollywood period, which are by nature thematically and stylistically conservative because of the conditions of their production (low-budget, low production values, heavily formula-laden, etc.), are not generally perceived as offering instances of dissidence, aesthetic or otherwise.[1] B series and genre films were commercially popular — audiences liked the characters or character types so much that they wanted to see them perform in their own peculiar way the same actions again and again in new adventures — and they were characteristically conservative in their resolution of the narrative's conflict in the ending's reestablishment of a community in which law and order reign. In addition, B-class film series were produced on low budgets and generally each film in the series lasted 60 to 70 minutes. In order to communicate a maximum amount of information in a minimum amount of time, film series relied heavily on a variety of factors: the persona of its characters and/or its (usually) character actors[2]; audience familiarity with the conventions of the genre and of the series; references within the film to other films (e.g., dialogue, set decor, story), to other films in the series, etc. So, given the context of Ray's question about whether a film whose dissidence is uncontained can ever be popular with mainstream audiences, the answer would probably be no: if the amount of dissident material exceeds that of familiar narrative devices, the film would be illegible to the majority of spectators.[3] Any film in which such unrestrained dissidence manifested itself would cease to be commercial. Therefore, it follows that the prevailing social class, whose economic ideology happens to be capitalist, will regulate as much as possible any deviations from filmic and cultural norms in popular films.

While they are defined by an economy of repetition, however, B series films, hardly merit summary dismissal as a medium wholly unsuited for the expression of unresolved dissidence. Dissidence of the order to which Ray refers, however, will rarely be a part of that equation. Surprisingly film series, which during the Classic Hollywood period were generally B-genre movies, and which perhaps by their very repetition, not only of generic formula but of the series formula as well, were the most conservative of all, created a space conducive to expressions of cultural dissidence in ways unavailable to A productions. While the hyper-formulaic structure of any *one* given film in a series seemingly defuses and contains potentially disruptive elements, it is this very same formula that is ill-equipped to defuse and contain disruptions when it is a question of examining together *all* the films constituting a particular film series. Dissidence does emerge in a surprising number of B series films, and recognition of it necessitates a solid familiarity with the conventions of both the genre and the film series in which it appears. Its very repetition puts into question the cinematic and cultural codes within and outside of which it simultaneously finds itself, thereby stripping the "seamless" narrative of its apparent naturalness. This is an action that an individual instance of a film, by virtue of its very individuality, A- or B-class, can never accomplish.

An example of this practice is found in a series from 1930s–1940s empowered woman series: Maisie.[4] The standard feminist stance regarding Classic Hollywood cinema is that its privileging of patriarchy deprives women both as characters and as spectators of agency. According to this logic, B woman's film series, even other empowered woman series, should exhibit a textbook subordination and reintegration of the heroine (who has been seeking individuation throughout the film) back into the community and into her second-class social role within that community. But, while each individual film within the series most often does just that, it is in reviewing either a few installments in the series or the series as a whole that it becomes clear that the final scenes' subordination of the heroine is, in the overall context of the series, indicative of her insubordination. While series films like sequels, are "forms that seem to deny [narrative] closure" precisely because one film in a series "always posit[s] another film in the series," the primary generic format for the Maisie movies is that of the romance, which, unlike the detective, western, or domestic drama series, normally demands closure in the union of the hero and heroine in marriage or its equivalent at film's end (Russell 129–30). But, whereas each Maisie movie ends in anticipated marriage (the desired outcome of the romance genre), each subsequent installment opens with a very unwedded Maisie. If each film in a series "always posit[s] another film in the series," then each Maisie movie not only promises a new adventure, but more problematically a new amorous adventure for its heroine as well, an idea unheard of in Classic Hollywood film history.

Maisie and the Empowered Woman Series

It has been said that *Maisie* (Edwin L. Marin, 1939) was conceived initially as a vehicle for Jean Harlow, but that the project was shelved after Harlow's death in 1937 (Schultz 6). If so, that would mean that the film was not conceptualized in its early stages in terms of a B film, much less a B series (Harlow was an A-class actress). What is certain is that Jean Harlow's death left a casting gap in "tough-girl-with-a-heart-of-gold" scenarios, and MGM tried out its new contract hire in a Harlow role.[5] Although Ann Sothern had played sophisticates just as often as brassy dames, Margie Schultz contends that it was Sothern's interpretation of tough and sassy broads like Mimi in Roy Del Ruth's *Folies Bergere* (1935) and Jean Livingston in Tay Garnett's *Trade Winds* (1938) that caught the attention of producer J. Walter Ruben and destined her to being cast in the role of Maisie (Schultz 6).[6] While the persona Sothern established through these roles was certainly a factor in the matching of actress with role, the reality is perhaps a little more complex given that MGM threw several series Sothern's way in the early stages of her contract, yet another indication that upper management increasingly perceived her as primarily B talent.[7] Sothern starred with Franchot Tone in *Fast and Furious* (Busby Berkeley, 1939), the third and last installment of the Joel and Garda Sloane mystery series, whose initial feature starred Melvyn Douglas and Florence Rice (*Fast Company* [Edward Buzzell, 1938]). She starred with William Gargan in *Joe and Ethel Turp Call on the President* (Robert B. Sinclair, 1939), which "was proposed as another possible series" while MGM "await[ed] the returns on *Maisie*" (Miller 192).[8] Like Maisie Ravier, Ethel Turp was pure Brooklyn. *Time* magazine's reviewer described Sothern's interpretation of Ethel as in the "Joan Blondell style" (qtd. in Schultz 65).[9] The reference to Joan Blondell was perhaps equally as pertinent as the ones to Jean Harlow, since the former played primarily no-nonsense-blonde roles, and had starred with Melvyn Douglas in the first entry of the Bill and Sally Reardon sleuth series, *There's Always a Woman* (Alexander Hall, 1938).[10] Both the Joel and Garda Sloane and the Bill and Sally Reardon series were attempts, by MGM for the former, and by Columbia for the latter, to come up with a Nick and Nora Charles sleuthing pair (the very successful A-class MGM Thin Man series). Like the other studios, MGM relied just as heavily on actors' personas as on tried and true genres to launch series to feed the "maw of exhibition." The logic that dictated that not just any actor could play the lead in an A production pertained equally to B series productions.

Leonard Maltin describes the Maisie series (1939–1947) as a "middling series" featuring a "progression of topical if trivial situations encompassing the changing role of American women during WW2 America" (858). Film series rarely get rave reviews, and the Maisie series was no exception. This is partially because film series of the Classic Hollywood period primarily fall into the B and below category, an indication that little creative and financial energy went into production. Indeed, Maltin faults the Maisie series for its low production values, which "were too often static, utilizing rear projection and indoor sets to establish the varied locales of the episodes."[11] In addition, film series, Classic Hollywood or otherwise, always develop within the conventions of film formulas (western, detective, horror, adventure, science fiction, etc.), which generally rate among critics as nothing more than good entertainment, but rarely rise to the level of art. And accordingly, while including the Maisie series within the group of "Great Movie Series," James Robert Parish called it a "forgettable but entertaining product" (243). While denigrated for their lack of A-class production values, originality, and psychological depth, successful film series usually stand out for the stars or character actors that are perceived as carrying the all too familiar narratives by their charisma alone. For Maltin, as for many of Maisie's critics, the quality of the films' stories varied too much from film to film, forcing them to "rel[y] almost exclusively on Miss Sothern's vivacious personality to carry the slight tales of the conventional tough-girl-with-a-heart-of-gold" (858). And as for her abundance of talent, said the critics, Ann Sothern's was wasted on this "formula-laden" series (Parish 243).

Women have been the central characters of series such as Torchy Blane, Hildegarde Withers, Miss Jane Marple, and Nancy Drew for the detective film, and Blondie Dagwood for the domestic comedy, to name a few, and while drawing from other genres, are identified as woman's films. Thomas Schatz defines the Classic Hollywood woman's film: "Focused on female protagonists and targeted primarily at female audiences, these films traced the seemingly inevitable loss or self-sacrifice that was woman's fate in a man's world — thus the term 'weepies' to describe not only the films but the viewer's presumed emotional response to the heroine's plight." He divides the woman's film into three categories: "ill-fated love stories," "sagas of marital or maternal sacrifice," and "lighter working-girl romantic dramas" (109–11).[12] Schatz's classification of the woman's picture is problematic in that these series also replicate male-oriented formulas. As Jeanine Basinger notes, movies centered on a female lead can be found in a wide range of genres, from detective films, comedies, musicals, war movies, bio-pics, to westerns (7). And although it is assumed that the woman's film is "designed to appeal mostly to a female audience," the empowered woman series had ingredients that appealed equally to male audiences. The first Hildegarde Withers entry (*The Penguin Pool Murder* [George Archainbaud, 1932]) made explicit the playful confrontation of both male- and female-oriented formulas (detective fiction *and* romance) within the series itself in the discussion between schoolteacher Withers/Edna May Oliver and Inspector Oscar Piper/James Gleason about the innocence/guilt of the young ex-lovers Gwen Parker and Philip Seymour[13]:

> WITHERS: And you're willing to send them to the chair on the evidence you have?
> PIPER: Loving couples are not always reunited in the last chapter, Miss Withers. You've taught too much Walter Scott.

WITHERS: Well, if I've taught too much Walter Scott, you've read too many detective stories. All you're after is a conviction, anybody's conviction. I never saw such a man.
PIPER: How many men have you seen?
WITHERS: Plenty of them, that is ... I...
PIPER: Well, maybe if you'd seen more men, Hildegarde Withers...
WITHERS: I've seen enough men today, Oscar Piper, to know that if this murder is to be solved, a woman's got to do it. (*She exits Piper's office.*)
PIPER: (*With noticeable admiration*) Boy, and she can cook, too![14]

Rather than work towards steering Miss Withers away from amateur sleuthing and reintegrating her back into conventional female space (the schoolroom) as the initial exchange promises, Piper's final appraisal of Miss Withers redefines her "womanly" abilities (cooking, housekeeping, sewing, etc.) as nonessential, but not unwelcome, in an appraisal of her attraction for him. The Hildegarde Withers series interests both male and female audiences precisely because it combines two narrative perspectives: the woman's film (woman as center of the film's action) and the detective story (male-oriented action genre). The second entry in the series even brings the male formula into a female space when a murder is committed in the very school where Hildegarde Withers works (*Murder on the Blackboard* [George Archainbaud, 1934]).[15] To define these female-lead series solely in terms of the woman's film is further complicated by exceptions like Torchy Blane, a series "based on *Black Mask* stories written in the 1920s and 1930s by Frederick Nebel" which involved a gender transposition of the stories' male reporter, thereby clearly marking the space occupied by Torchy Blane as male (Pitts, *Detectives* 274).[16]

While technically woman's films in that Maisie is the central focus of the narratives, and while the films privilege the romantic comedy formula (there is usually a male love interest and the promise of marriage at film's end), at the same time, like the Nancy Drew, Torchy Blane, and Hildegarde Withers movies, they sample bits and pieces from a variety of genres and refer to other popular A and B films (in the interest of parody and narrative economy), making it difficult to pin the series down to one formula. A brief overview of the Maisie films highlights the nature of their intertextuality. To Don Miller, *Maisie* (Edwin L. Marin, 1939) was a B remake of the A film *Red Dust* (Victor Fleming, 1932), as was *Congo Maisie* (H.C. Potter, 1940).[17] This latter film in particular recalled all the "hot-love-in-the-isolated-tropics" plots in the *Red Dust* mold: *China Seas* (Tay Garnett, 1935), *Trade Winds*, and even *Torrid Zone* (William Keighley, 1940), the latter of which is said to be a variation on *The Front Page* (Lewis Milestone, 1931), but which replicates remarkably *Red Dust*'s narrative structure (Balio 242). In addition, the first Maisie film borrowed from the western for its overall flavor, and from the sleuth film for its format, the second from the adventure film. *Gold Rush Maisie* (Edwin L. Marin, 1940) was a Depression era/dust bowl movie in the pattern of *The Grapes of Wrath* (John Ford, 1940) and *Three Faces West* (Bernard Vorhaus, 1940). Although a thematically darker movie than its predecessors, *Gold Rush Maisie* counters this darkness by recalling in its title Charlie Chaplin's *The Gold Rush* (1925) so as to inform viewers not familiar with Maisie movies that the mode is comic, not dramatic. *Maisie Was a Lady* (Edwin L. Marin, 1941) parodied those movies featuring the travails and foibles of a society family (e.g., *My Man Godfrey* [Gregory La Cava, 1936], *Holiday* [George Cukor, 1938], *Merrily We Live* [Norman Z. McLeod, 1938], and *The Philadelphia Story* [George Cukor, 1940]). Indeed, the film's set included the very recognizable pool from *The Philadelphia Story*.[18] *Ringside Maisie* (Edwin L. Marin, 1941) drew from the boxing movie for its setting (*Golden Boy* [Rouben Mamoulian, 1939], and *Mr. Moto's Gamble* [James Tinling, 1938]).[19] The *New York Times* described the structure of *Maisie Gets Her Man* (Roy Del Ruth, 1942) as taking off on "A. J. Liebling's Jollity Building series in the New Yorker" (T. S.), while Variety saw it as drawing on the "Broadway theatrical hangout" formula, from the Gold Diggers movies of the 1930s, as well as the A-class *Stage Door* (Gregory La Cava, 1937).[20] The teaming of Sothern and Red Skelton (and Rags Ragland) anticipated, and gave advance publicity to, the soon to be released *Panama Hattie* (Norman Z. McLeod, 1942), even using the song "Cookin' with Gas" that was cut from the latter film.[21] *Undercover Maisie* (Harry Beaumont, 1947) jumped on the bandwagon of the popular B undercover cop movies of the 1940s.

There were three other Maisie movies sandwiched in between the others: *Swing Shift Maisie* (Norman Z. McLeod, 1943), *Maisie Goes to Reno* (Harry Beaumont, 1944), and *Up Goes Maisie* (Harry Beaumont, 1946). While "doing it for defense" by promoting the work of women airplane assemblers, *Swing Shift Maisie* also draws loosely on the saboteur movies of the early 1940s, with Maisie accused of being a Nazi sympathizer. *Maisie Goes to Reno*, while addressing the high rate of divorce in America, was essentially a screwball prevention-of-a-crime (and a divorce) movie. Divorce capital Reno was the locale for many a film during the thirties and forties, from A pictures like George Cukor's *The Women* (1939) to B films like *Charlie Chan in Reno* (Norman Foster, 1939) and John Farrow's *Reno* (1939). And *Up Goes Maisie* turned to industrial theft and the screwball comedy for its narrative. While *Undercover Maisie*'s embezzlers were bilking soldiers and their families out of their savings, it did not possess the other three films' solid backdrop of World War II. *Swing Shift Maisie*, *Maisie Goes to Reno*, and *Up Goes Maisie* (and to a lesser extent, *Maisie Gets Her Man*) were converted to the war effort and later to postwar demobilization.[22] Given the cooperation of the film industry with the war office, and the aggressive recruiting of women into the work force, it is understandable that a popular female series character like Maisie would have been enlisted in the war's defense campaign.

From Maltin's and Parish's comments on the legacy of the Maisie movies, it is evident that the three wartime conversion films are responsible for the association of the entire series, and female empowerment particularly, with the "changing role of American women during WW2 America" (six Maisie films, however, precede the conversion films). The wartime conversion of Hollywood film narratives led to the depiction of a dramatic change in lifestyle offering their cinematic heroines as role models for real women: temporary suspension of plans for marriage and family until after the war, an acceptance of rationing and of the deprivations required by a country at war against Nazi evil, a willingness to work for war defense and to relocate for one's job, etc. In 1946, Margaret Mead noted that "moving about" was a new and important experience for women: "Girls who would have lived and died in the same town, knowing the same people, and thinking they were eternally disgraced if the cake fell, the custard broke, or the curtains weren't laundered every six weeks, have seen how many different ways life can be lived—when necessary" (284–85). Mead also pointed out how notions regarding the sexual division of labor were challenged because "women have done jobs which no one thought they could do, become welders and machine setters, railroad conductors, taxi starters and taxi drivers" (281). Regarding the remarkable but temporary strides made by women in such a short period of time, Michael Renov notes, "It is a distressing revelation that in terms of stature of job classification and equity of pay scales, the contemporary working woman has yet to equal the achievements of her wartime predecessor" (47). Ironically, while Maisie seeks a job in the postwar period as a more stably employed pink collar worker in *Up Goes Maisie*, giving up her aircraft factory job to a returning soldier, her skills as an assembly worker on bombers and not her secretarial skills land her a job with Joe Morton/George Murphy.

Maltin and Parish are, therefore, partially correct in identifying a relation between Maisie and World War II women. Ann Sothern, primarily because of her popular portrayal of Maisie, did become a poster woman for the feminine component of the war effort.[23] In many wartime articles, Sothern (who the editors identified as Maisie) offered advice to the women who wrote her (or, more specifically, Maisie) letters. Most important perhaps, wartime Maisie did her bit for defense as well, particularly in the toning down of her signature style of dressing: she exchanged her lacy dresses, impossible hats, and gaudy jewelry for factory overalls, braids, and an unflattering kerchief in order to work in an airplane plant; she volunteered in the children's nurseries (however little they were actually used by real working women during the war) helping out working mothers during the hours when she should have been getting some much needed sleep; she respected blackout rules, and so on. And at war's end, the "reconverted" Maisie gave up her factory job to a returning soldier.

The War Department and its various commissions worked hard to disseminate propaganda for getting women into the war effort, trying to make directives seem natural so that they didn't ruffle too much the traditional values of women as housewives and mothers (Renov 85). But if it is true that Maisie as role model for American women collaborated with such propaganda and was "doing it for defense" during the war, her character as she was developed in the series wasn't one of the "six million new female recruits joining the labor force by 1944" (Walsh 1). On the contrary, she was one of those women who had worked before Pearl Harbor and had every intention of working afterwards: she wasn't doing anything radically different than what she and most working class women had done before.[24]

While the world created by formulaic films is generally fantastic in nature (they offer simple worlds where problems are easily solved), and while the general structure of any given genre repeats that of universal archetypes (a hero vs. a villain, etc.), series films are just as importantly the products of a particular culture at a particular time. Accordingly, the empowered woman series did not continue past the postwar period. As regards the Maisie movies in particular, the series's ten-year run ended because MGM did not renew Sothern's contract.[25] Other important factors were the anti-trust suit against studios and their theater holdings (no more blockbooking) and the transposition of the series unit and format to television (most Classic Hollywood series did not last beyond 1955). In addition, the Maisie series's demise coincided with the end of the empowered woman series in general: Maisie reflected the spirit of equality among the sexes inherited from the flapper era — she could certainly hold her own with any man — and while the war prolonged her screen life temporarily by capitalizing on her influence on women, the increasing conservatism in the division of labor between the sexes in postwar reconversion reduced the cinematic empowered woman to an anachronism.[26] While not enjoying quite the type of freedom of the better heeled and better educated characters played by actresses like Kay Francis in the 1930s, Maisie's ambulatory existence endowed her with as great mobility, determined by her principle profession (chorine) and the extreme precariousness of a career in show business — she often has only two dimes on her at the beginning of each film (unlike the Kay Francis roles who often possess an unlimited bank account) — and by the need to find a job, any job, quickly. Apart from working as occasional lead chorus girl in reviews like Frawley's Frolics, she was a lady's companion and cook, a gold prospector, a taxi dancer, a maid, a headless woman in a sideshow, a barker at a rifle gallery, during the war a welder/riveter in an airplane plant, and, after the war, a secretary-helicopter assembler, and an undercover cop. As regards these last two jobs, as the empowered woman films became increasingly endangered, Maisie's employment options moved increasingly towards those representative of the more socially conventional.

In terms of self-presentation, Maisie was decidedly unconventional. For most of the series, she countered her own brand of femininity to the accepted norms of woman. She had curly blond hair that she constantly had to defend as her natural color, while the deceitfully "decent" women in the Maisie movies usually had fashionably darker hair.[27] Of short stature, Maisie also possessed a sensuous and curvy figure that stood out against the tall, rather asexual physiques of the standard Hollywood goddess. She wore an extremely low neckline that revealed a very ample bosom, the object of many a male character's gaze. Maisie was also much plumper than the average starlet, a fact even cruelly commented upon in the *Variety* review of *Maisie Gets Her Man*: "she appears a little more plumpish than usual" (Naka).[28] She had a bouncy way of walking that emphasized the swing of her hips. In short, Maisie was hardly the product of Swiss finishing schools.[29]

For the middle-class spectator of the Maisie movies, every aspect of Maisie advertised her as a low, ridiculous other, and overdetermined all the negative markers of her class. In addition to her working-class background, her chorus-girl career pegged her, if not as a prostitute, than as a gold-digger, accusations that she is quick to refute.[30] Slim Martin/Robert Young (*Maisie*), Dr. Michael Shane/John Carroll (*Congo Maisie*), Bill Anders/Lee Bowman (*Gold Rush Maisie*), Skeets Maguire/George Murphy (*Ringside Maisie*), and Flip Hennahan/John Hodiak (*Maisie Goes to Reno*) at first perceive in Maisie all the telltale traits of the gold-digger, but by film's end she has proved her mettle.

Or has she? A lower-class woman's existence is precarious: women, Maisie acknowledges in *Gold Rush Maisie*, often don't earn enough to be entirely self-sufficient. She advises the young okie, Jubie Davis, who idolizes her, that while she may have to accept things from men when she grows up, she should never settle for second rate:

> MAISIE: Well, anyway, if you work for what you get, it can be anything and you don't have to apologize for it. But if you ever take anything from anybody, be sure it's the best.

JUBIE: You mean, if someone was to give me a dress, it would have to be a real nice dress?
MAISIE: You bet. Listen, as soon as you take something from somebody, you've lost part of your right to tell them to go jump in the lake, and that's awful important for a girl on her own. So you gotta be sure what they're offering is tops. If it's a fur coat, it's gotta be the genuine article, one that's by an ermine, not by a white cat. And if it's love, well, if he gives you his whole heart, grab it quickly. There's nothing better than that. But don't ever go shares.... You don't know what I'm talking about, honey.
JUBIE: Well, it does sound a little bit mixed up. But all I know is when I grow up, I'm wanna be just like you.

The entire conversation visually constructs Maisie as a comic low other that couldn't distinguish the "genuine article" from its cheaper version. For middle-class audiences, Jubie's desire to be like Maisie offers Maisie not as the model of the emancipated woman, but as a working-class woman with singular bad taste, and therefore as a ridiculously (but not dangerously) unsuitable model to emulate. Jubie says to Maisie, "And when I'm grown up and rich, I'm gonna have pretty clothes just like you. I'm gonna have me a hat that sits back with flowers on it, and a charm bracelet, a dress that swings kind of when I walk, like a princess, like you." The incongruity of Jubie's idolatry of Maisie's personal style, of her likening of the impecunious and somewhat vulgar Maisie to a princess, is the source of the conversation's humor.

But while everything about Maisie's appearance — hair, dress, mannerisms — designated her as a low, comic other for middle-class audiences, the series was not for all that designed exclusively, or even primarily, for the middle-class spectator. Maisie is decidedly working class, and while that in itself does not destine her largely for popular consumption, the conditions of B production did. B movies, in the aesthetic poverty of their overall production values and the fact that they were developed primarily for subsequent-run theaters, reflect a deliberate exploitation of the popular market.

Maisie has a strong work ethic and won't take money for anything she hasn't earned through her own labor, making it a "point of honor" to refute the stereotyped image that the middle class has of members of the popular classes: the propensity for alcohol, sexual promiscuity, uncleanliness, and dishonesty (Bourdieu 440n8).[31] While her efforts to defend her honesty and integrity are in line both with the populist myth found in much of Hollywood cinema (Frank Capra's films coming readily to mind) and with a moralizing tendency that offers Maisie as exemplary of her class, the forces at work in any given Maisie movie tend less towards prohibition ("don't be like Maisie") and reform ("correct your conduct") than toward class solidarity for the biggest consumer of Maisie movies: the popular classes. In each film in the series there are moments similar to the conversation between Jubie and Maisie that slip in a certain ambiguity, and in this instance, about just how difficult of virtue Maisie is. She *has* accepted gifts from men, she makes clear, but only from those able to offer her quality goods, in other words, from middle-class men. Class difference and relations are at play in these movies. While Maisie may have a heart of gold, the narrative slips also let us know that she has been a bit of a gold-digger. The victim of the gold-digger and of this narrative is a man of means who can offer a girl the "genuine article," and this reversal of sexual relations translates necessarily into a reversal of power relations, of which the lower-class male spectator is the main beneficiary (Allen 212–14).

Marginalizing Maisie

The critiques of the Maisie movies echo the standard list of arguments against B-formula series films, all of which worked well to the series's advantage. Maltin's description of the series as characterized by "topical if trivial situations" and as reflecting the "changing role of American women in WW2 America," writes off the films, on the one hand, as nothing more than minor woman's films, and on the other, as nothing more than cultural and historical artifacts. Parish makes similar comments: "the *Maisie* series offers an interesting study of the changing role of the American woman between 1939–1946, during which time the war changed social values" (243).[32] And yet, Parish's comments on the A-class Thin Man series note the social impact on audiences of the portrayal of the very happily married Nick and Nora Charles. For him, the Thin Man movies "proved marriage could be just the beginning of an exciting relationship" (323). This is no small consideration since divorce rates had been increasing at an alarming rate since the turn of the century.[33] As for the Maisie movies, though, while Maisie represented "an emancipated gal who took no nonsense from men, and who could stand on her own feet in any given situation"—a potentially powerful model for young women—Parish states that the movies that featured her were surprisingly "non-controversial" to exhibitors (and, one understands, to discriminating viewers as well) (243). In other words, they felt that the Maisie movies mirrored but did not interface with social conditions in anything but a "non-controversial" fashion.

Genre, film series, and B movies are rarely perceived as controversial because of their relation to either the dissemination or a reflection of a conservative worldview. Robert C. Allen notes that "Because society is ordered in terms of power relations and structured in terms of registers of dominance and subordination, cultural production expresses these relations and these structures" (31). He qualifies the nature of these power relations as taking form less through actual dominance than through "ordination": those in power in a given society "attempt to regulate the arrangement of things in ranks and orders — what is high, what is low; what is us, what is them" (34). While regulation creates the means for distinguishing between groups, it also paradoxically attempts to reform and discipline, or in other words, to include the very groups that it excludes. The audience for B-genre movies and series was perceived as more lowbrow, and, according to Allen's description of ordination, one would expect them to reflect these power relations. Indeed, the imposition of ordination, even if merely at the level of formula, appears to be inherent in the nature of genre itself, since "the genre film, like all classical art, is conservative, both aesthetically and politically" (Sobchack 112). Its world is an orderly one where the law is generally victorious. As a consequence, the genre film, presenting a conflict in which the needs of the individual are opposed to those of the group, always opts for the group (Sobchack 109). The B-genre movie's vision of social order repeats the formulaic structure of hundreds of other films, a vision that by its very repetition appears natural and true, supposedly leading the potentially unruly low audience member back to the social order.

An explanation for the hardiness of the classic oppositional pattern (e.g., bad girl recognizes the error of her ways and becomes good girl at film's end) established by the genre film (B- or A-class) is that it encourages a catharsis that is played out purely in the imagination: "If spectators identify strongly with the figures of the drama, feeling pity and fear as drawn out by the activities going on before their eyes and ears, then, when properly concluded, given the appropriate ending, these emotions are dissipated, leaving viewers in a state of calm, a state of stasis in which they can think rationally and clearly" (Sobchack 109). The socially unacceptable behavior that is presented (e.g., the desire for individuation) is tolerated within a genre film by the status quo precisely because its power to attract is deemed to be defused in the resolution's reintegration of the protagonist into the community (Sobchack 110). The powers that be normally find no threat in these entertainments because this psychological release takes place within a "politically ineffectual space" (Allen 36).

When religious or reform groups make demands for the regulation of depicted behavior on the screen, as in the gangster or gold-digger films of the early 1930s, they are seeking through their quest for ordination at the very most outright elimination of portrayals of such comportment, and at the very least marginalization. Marginalization is a less aggressive, but no less effective, means of restricting access to any given entertainment. The gangster film is one example of the effectiveness of such marginalization. In response to pressure from religious groups, reformers, and the Hays Office, the producers of Howard Hawks's A-class *Scarface* (1932) "underwent constant revision both during and after production" (Balio 284). Accordingly, the heyday of the A-quality gangster film was short-lived, lasting but a year (Balio 284). The gangster film did not, for all that, die: it merely became a B movie relegated to subsequent run theaters and probably to the bottom half of a double bill. Its audience, too, became more lowbrow. Marginalization, therefore, served less to restrict the lowbrow spectator's access to these films — such films continued to be offered by minor producers/studios at third-, fourth-, and fifth-run theaters — than to protect the middle-class spectator.

Hence, a way to limit a film's appeal to the darker, immoral, or asocial side of human nature was to banish it physically and critically to the B and below production units whose films were destined almost exclusively to the subsequent-run market, and then to write it off as aesthetically inferior to A productions. This is a surprisingly effective means for circumscribing the presentation of perceived low behavior before discriminating audiences. As regards the Maisie movies, the critics' assessment of the "trivial," "non-controversial," and formulaic nature of the films' topics and representations served to reiterate the films' B status and to signal them as far from serious entertainment. This became increasingly important the more Maisie became popular with general audiences. That respectable critics took the trouble to review these films at all reflects the relative quality B productions coming from MGM.[34]

Maisie's sphere of influence, however, was kept in check by being relegated to subsequent-run theaters. However popular Maisie became as a character and a series, she was generally kept out of the nicer, more respectable, neighborhoods that her A-class sisters frequented. In addition, like Stella Dallas (*Stella Dallas* [King Vidor, 1937]), whose cheap behavior confines her within her class, Maisie's sphere of influence is checked by the distinctive markers of her class. Mary Anastasia O'Connor, a.k.a. Maisie Ravier, comes from Brooklyn, is of Irish descent (a group still considered by many at the time as an ethnic minority), and has the familiar alcoholic father. Equally in accordance with the stereotype, she has a deplorably vulgar, garish, and suggestive fashion sense. Each Maisie movie invariably involves some reference to her low background, her low profession, and/or her low-cut dress, offering Maisie to middle-class viewers as a harmless, ridiculous product of her class. Towards the end of the series, when the telltale markers of Maisie's class had been demonstrably toned down, the series formula continued to dictate that the villains would refer to Maisie's class. In *Up Goes Maisie*, duplicitous society maven, Barbara Nuboult, conspires to keep Maisie out of good society through her pending marriage to Joe Morton by pointing out the impropriety of the match. She draws upon ethnic stereotypes: "You're disgracing Joe.[...] They're all looking at you. All these people. They're saying you're drunk. Joe Morton's fiancée is drunk."[35]

Maisie's antics marked her as an object for middle-class ridicule — she clearly violates all rules of propriety and good taste — and her ability to upset social categories was circumscribed by spectator accessibility to her in subsequent-run theaters (marginalization), and by the formula's reintegration of her into the community at film's end. But, as Maisie became more popular, MGM offered Maisie movies in some first run theaters, where the audience composition was distinctly middle class. The *New York Times* reviewer of *Ringside Maisie* expresses such a sense of the impropriety of the mixing of the classes not only within the films themselves, but in the showcasing of Maisie films at more upscale venues:

> Ordinarily when Maisie comes to town she makes herself comfortable at one of the more modest showshops. But this time, in "Ringside Maisie," she is taking quarters at the Capitol which, as Maisie sometimes says, is "strictly a class joint." A little too classy, in fact, because Maisie is a sweet girl with a heart as big as a pumpkin, but her refinements are limited. Her voice has that honky-tonk inflection, a vocabulary to match, and she wears about two pounds too much costume jewelry [T. S.].

Series films of the B variety were unlikely fare in class joints like the Capitol anyway, which may account partially for the reviewer's sense of the incongruity of the match of a Maisie movie with this theater, but his specific reference to the marks of Maisie's class function as the first signs that Maisie was only seen as problematic once she appeared in fancier theaters. Because the series had become very popular, it was logical for MGM to increase its exposure, extending it to first-run theaters. The drawback, however, was that the traditional narrative devices that worked to contain Maisie visually began to lose much of their effectiveness. If the war hadn't come and worked its will on Maisie's fashion sense, stripping her of her frills and baubles, it is probable that her overall appearance and behavior would have undergone a similar transformation to accommodate her movement into more legitimate venues. Indeed, after the war, the humor in Maisie's appearance stemmed no longer from her class's stereotypical bad fashion decisions, but from the costumes she donned for the jobs in which she was employed (car hop flounces, dull secretary's outfit, millionairess's finery, etc.).

Perhaps most problematic for critics and reformers was *Maisie Was a Lady*. In this film, Maisie recalls the upwardly mobile woman of 1930s film in the anticipated marriage to the enormously wealthy Bob Rawlston/Lew Ayres. She feels a certain sense of the impropriety of the match Rawlston proposes and runs away. Yet, in the final scene of the film, Bob's insistence on marriage to her ends by winning her consent. The couple that is formed, however, allows for only a temporary sense of vicarious victory on the part of the lower-class spectator in Maisie's class rise since he knows that Maisie always begins each new film inexplicably unengaged: Rawlston will have disappeared without a trace in the follow-up film. Ironically, however, the only Maisie film matching her with a very well-off man is also the only film that a reviewer found problematic in terms of the continued life of the series's formula:

> "Maisie was a Lady" deviates from formula followed by its predecessors in that the South Brooklyn showgirl gets involved in a serious romance and is left at the finish engaged to Lew Ayres. Just how the scripters are going to untangle the affair to let Miss Sothern continue her escapades for further releases of the series is a writing problem in itself [Walt].

Marriage, however, was the expected outcome for all the previous Maisie movies, with the exception of *Gold Rush Maisie*, and continued to be so for all subsequent installments. As a general rule, the series's producers did not feel compelled to explain why Maisie reappeared unmarried in each new adventure.[36] Surprisingly then, just as it is customary for James Bond to bed a beautiful woman or for the Saint to follow a new woman at the end of each of their adventures, so, too, is it customary for Maisie to promise to tie the knot with the male protagonist at the end of each of her adventures. How ironic, therefore, that the only time the incongruity of these multiple engagements/partners jumped out at reviewers was when Maisie was moving up to a much higher social class. How relieved this reviewer must have been when *Ringside Maisie* came out and Maisie was once again single, dead broke, and out of a job.

The Maisie movies go even farther by chipping away at genre's efficacy in communicating the rightness of a conservative worldview. The spectator for the Maisie series is without doubt a repeat customer for whom repetition of the series formula is the main attraction. The Maisie fan would undoubtedly be most sensitive to any changes made to the formula, since a great deal of the pleasure in viewing series films is in anticipating certain types of situations: he expects the new situations to be both like the ones found in other Maisie movies (e.g., Maisie is out of money ... again ... and is sorely in need of a job; Maisie butts heads with someone, usually the male protagonist, and reads him the riot act), but unlike the others in that the situations are specific to the context of the new movie (e.g., dude ranch, Congolese jungle, Las

Vegas casino, Los Angeles police department). The one-time Maisie spectator will see only a movie that is entertaining in many respects, but which deviates little from the standard romance formula in which the heroine gets engaged to or marries the male protagonist at film's end. The one-time spectator who is a fan of the romance genre will be rewarded with the type of repetition that he seeks: the triumph of love. The spectator who views several installments in the Maisie series, however, will notice that one particular repeated situational element does not in itself allow for repetition. Indeed, the inversion of the generic series's formulaic end in which Maisie, who has been the source of the male protagonist's reintegration into the community, is herself reintegrated repeatedly into the community through a projected marriage to the protagonist, signals to this spectator that there are sites of resistance precisely in those aspects intended to communicate the greatest sense of a world in order. Of course, the Production Code would have required that Maisie, however incomprehensible it was for the continuity of the series, get engaged to the male protagonist.[37] The repetition of this action in all subsequent installments worked, however, against the code and generic conventions, since the only logical way of making sense of Maisie's repeated engagements (and relatively no further mention of them in subsequent episodes) is to assume that they hide the fact that Maisie sleeps with rather than marries each of these men. In other words, she either uses her body for social advancement like a gold-digger, or she is singularly sexually liberated. This last image of Maisie is in harmony with the heroine as she exists in Wilson Collison's novel and with the characterization of her spiritual sister Vantine in *Red Dust*. She is a New Woman — self-sufficient, morally driven (even though sexually uninhibited), in every respect a man's equal.

With the engagement ending remaining intact, Maisie's ability to work against the series formula's classic worldview continued during the war (*Swing Shift Maisie* and *Maisie Goes to Reno*) and into the last two films (*Up Goes Maisie* and *Undercover Maisie*), and this despite her increasingly more subdued and tasteful attire and appearance (the result of the war alone? Breen Office directives?[38] Sothern's efforts to distance herself from Maisie's hold?), and despite a new creative crew on these particular four films: a new producer, George Haight, came onto the series after the death of J. Walter Ruben, and his wife, Thelma Robinson, became the credited writer on the last two films.[39] It is certain that during World War II, Maisie's energies were harnessed for defense work just like millions of other American women. The regulation dress of the factory worker was stripped of all signs of femininity, and in conformity with the war effort Maisie sported fewer ruffled and lacy dresses, and even less baubles and make-up. Her signature black dress with white lace, which had become the very symbol of the series as it was introduced in the opening and the final credits, did not, for all that, disappear. In the initial Maisie films, the dress served as a distinctive, if ridiculous, marker of her class. But as the series became more firmly established, the dress became increasingly associated with Maisie's agency. So, even as Maisie was becoming more socially presentable during the war, doffing her silly frilly dress and dime store trinkets, the dress continued to empower its subsequent wearers. In *Swing Shift Maisie*, Maisie gives the dress to the black housekeeper, Myrtle, at the rooming house where she is living. This dress becomes for Myrtle a sign of the newfound social mobility afforded minority women by the war: she quits her job at the boarding house to do swing shift work.[40] Myrtle first calls her new job the "graveyard shift," referring to the least desirable hours to work — the hours, moreover, given to a significant number of women during the war — but is quick to rephrase it as the "swing shift," adding a new and positive connotation to the term by finishing off her comment with a little swish of her new lacy skirt.

Each film in the series examined individually seems to naturalize the ideology of the dominant class, much like those Classic Hollywood A films that reintegrate formerly empowered women back into the traditional community. Hildy Johnson in *His Girl Friday* (Howard Hawks, 1940) and Tess Harding in *Woman of the Year* (George Stevens, 1942) are reporters, and Amanda Donner in *Adam's Rib* (George Cukor, 1949) is an attorney, and they most threaten the status quo by working in traditionally male jobs. While these films' heroines spend the majority of their screen time in a man's world, they are either reintegrated into the patriarchal division of labor among the sexes (man as breadwinner, woman as homemaker and mother) or are outsmarted and tamed by a shrewd male protagonist by film's end, all of this taking place within their own class: the middle class. In the empowered woman series, however, the reintegration and the regulation of certain behavior are cancelled out by the incongruities that these reintegrations and regulations elicit by their very repetition. In considering the Maisie series along with other female empowerment series (e.g., Hildegarde Withers, Torchy Blane, Nancy Drew) of the Classic Hollywood era, it becomes evident that the generic repetition at the very heart of these series' structures wholly undermines the comforting resolutions that are offered in the individual installments. Hildegarde Withers does not stick exclusively to school teaching, but returns to solve other murders, simply because she is better at it than Inspector Oscar Piper. And despite all her efforts to get Lieutenant Steve McBride to show up on time at City Hall to get married, Torchy Blane, who claims to have ink for blood and a desire to hear the pitter patter of little typewriters at home, never makes it to the altar and continues to solve all of McBride's murders for him and beat every other male reporter in town to the scoops.[41] She has no intention of getting married whatsoever. As for Nancy Drew, the series proposes her as "wearing the pants," since she manages in each installment to get a man, usually her boyfriend, Ted Nickerson, into women's clothing. The trouble with Maisie is that she goes through men like James Bond goes through women.

Notes

1. I am using Thomas Sobchak's definition of the conservative nature of genre films, a category into which all film series fall: "The genre film is a structure that embodies the idea of form and the strict adherence to form that is opposed to experimentation, novelty, or tampering with the given order of things. The genre film, like all classical art, is basically conservative, both aesthetically and politically" (112).

2. Leslie Charteris, the author of the Saint novels, in many ways forced RKO to abandon the Saint as a film series source and take up the Falcon in its stead, starring George Sanders as a character remarkably similar to the one he portrayed in the Saint movies. One of Charteris's complaints about RKO's conceptualization of the Saint series was the "misrepresentation of the character," Simon Templar (Pitts, *Famous Movie Detectives*, 128). In addition, Charteris visualized Cary Grant in the title role (Gorman 16). Cary Grant was an A-movie actor at the time Sander's first Saint movie appeared (*The Saint Strikes Back* [John Farrow, 1939]). When Sanders left the Falcon series, it was because he was precisely "on his way out of B movies," into the A's (Gorman 16). William Powell, of the Thin Man series, was one of the few A movie stars to feature in a series, but then again, the Thin Man series departed from the norm by belonging to A-class productions.

3. While hardly dissident in either form or content, black and white Classic Hollywood films suffer ironically a similar fate to aesthetically dissident films. By the absence of color, they become stylistically inaccessible and aesthetically unappealing to young audiences that did not grow up watching them on television.

4. Other empowered women can be found in the Hildegarde Withers, Torchy Blane, and Nancy Drew series from the thirties.

5. *Time* magazine commented that "Cinemadicts know curvilinear Ann Sothern as a glamour girl, and as a glamour girl she has endured all the familiar permutations.... As Maisie, she is a healthier Jean Harlow, an untarnished Mae West. Whether she can keep her natural pewter is a question" (qtd. in Schultz 62).

6. J. Walter Ruben was the producer for the first six of the Maisie movies until his death in 1942. George Haight produced the last four.

7. Given the types of projects offered to Sothern by Columbia and RKO with whom she had had earlier contracts, and given the actors with whom she was most often paired, it is clear that Sothern was considered primarily B, not A, talent by the studios. For example, B movie *Three Hearts for Julia* (Richard Thorpe, 1943) starred Sothern and Melvyn Douglas, the latter who was considered a "second-rate William Powell" (Schatz 363). MGM tried to place Douglas, like Sothern, in a number of series (e.g., the Joel and Garda Sloane and the Bill and Sally Reardon series).

8. Don Miller preferred Joe and Ethel Turp to the Maisie series: "It proved far more felicitous artistically, but was doomed to last but for the one time" (192).

9. The relationship between Joan Blondell and Ann Sothern does not appear to have

been congenial, particularly on Blondell's part. As noted, Sothern performed roles similar to ones that had featured Blondell. Sothern had been offered the lead role opposite Bing Crosby in *East Side of Heaven* (David Butler, 1939), but had had to turn it down because of prior commitments. The role went to Blondell instead (Schultz 6). Both actresses co-starred in *Cry Havoc* (Richard Thorpe, 1943), a primarily female slant on the war experience. Critics had noted the physical and acting similarities between the two actresses. While Sothern strove to play down the resemblance, Blondell experienced it as a rivalry, seeing Sothern as patterning herself on her (Schultz 79).

10. Michael R. Pitts states that the Bill and Sally Reardon series was based on characters from "William Collison's magazine stories" (210). Pitts probably meant "Wilson" Collison, who coincidentally was the author who inspired both *Red Dust* and the Maisie movies.

11. As B movies go, however, MGM, the studio that produced the Maisie series, was known for producing B movies of much higher quality than the other studios. Tino Balio notes that, "MGM's low-budget entries looked like no other B films. 'When Metro goes out to make a Class B picture,' said *Variety*, 'they give it plenty of production, steady direction and a certain amount of class. It may not have big draw stars and the situation may be overdone, but it certainly will stand up on the second picture shelf in the theatres for which it was designed'" ("Feeding" 103).

12. Tino Balio's definition, while reflecting his concentration on the films of the 1930s, echoes Schatz's: "*Woman's film* is a term of convenience to describe a range of pictures commonly referred to as fallen-woman films, romantic drama, Cinderella romances, and gold-digger or working-girl stories.[...] The conflicts in the pictures involve interpersonal relationships that present the heroine with dilemmas the resolutions of which usually entail loss" (235).

13. All of the empowered women series featured this dynamic. The Nancy Drew series played the confrontation of the two formulas in a very visual fashion: in each film there invariably figured a man dressed in women's clothing, usually Nancy's boyfriend, Ted. The Torchy Blane series, as well, had gendered fun at the expense of Torchy's policeman fiancé, Steve McBride.

14. Hildegarde Withers is clearly Oscar Piper's equal:

> OSCAR PIPER: I got to admit, you can take it.
>
> HILDEGARDE WITHERS: Well, don't forget, when necessary I can dish it out, too.

15. According to Andrea Walsh, male-oriented cinema, which is said to represent the lion's share of Hollywood productions, typically involves specific genres (e.g., westerns, war movies, crime dramas, adventure, science fiction). Films for men are "often shot outdoors" and are characterized by "sparse dialogue, repressed feelings, and plenty of action (often violent)." Woman's pictures, on the contrary, fit less neatly into traditional genres, appeal to a greater range of emotions, are more verbally conceptualized (the exploration of relationships), and usually take place indoors (24).

16. This was also the case of *His Girl Friday* (1940), Howard Hawks' remake of *The Front Page* (Lewis Milestone, 1931). The Hecht-MacArthur source play was used two more times as *The Front Page* (Billy Wilder, 1974) and *Switching Channels* (Ted Kotcheff, 1988).

17. The written source for *Red Dust* was Wilson Collison's 1928 play, *Red Dust*. Collison's *Dark Dame* (1935) is credited as the source text for *Maisie*. Collison's novel, *Congo Landing* (1934) is the source for *Congo Maisie*. *Congo Landing* must be the novel version of the play *Red Dust*. Don Miller states that the source is the same for all three: "The credits of *Maisie* state that it is based on a story by Wilson Collison. That story, not identified, would seem to be *Congo Landing*, which MGM had turned into a box office bonanza in 1932 by casting Gable and Harlow in it and calling it *Red Dust*. Now the locale had been moved from the jungles to a dude ranch, but the essential plot was the same" (191).

As regards *Congo Maisie*, Miller comments that MGM "chang[ed] the players if not the plot, which occurred in the same location as *Red Dust*" (192). The formulaic similarities between the two films is not all MGM exploitation of a property, but is inherent in the source texts themselves: *Dark Dame* is the source for *Maisie*. Its heroine's name is Maisie, unlike *Congo Landing*'s Dolly, and the drama unfolds on a dude ranch. *Dark Dame*'s narrative structure is, nevertheless, strikingly similar to that of *Congo Landing*.

18. While it was economic prudence that dictated that B movie sets make use of sets used in A productions, there is no doubt that B movies relied on a maximum amount of familiar material (sets, dialogue, the narrative structure of earlier films, actor personas, etc.) to communicate information in a minimum amount of time and at a minimum expense. For example, as Ken Hanke notes, *The Vampire Bat* (Frank Strayer, 1933) has "a European village that comes straight from *Frankenstein* and an old dark house that *is* the genuine article from Whale's film of that title" (66–67). While the house was not used to its full potential by the film's director, it did nevertheless give the film "a sense of solidity it would otherwise not have" (67).

19. *Mr. Moto's Gamble*'s script was originally intended for the Charlie Chan series, but after the death of Warner Oland (the portrayer of Charlie Chan, who was succeeded by Sidney Toler for all subsequent installments) during the filming of *Charlie Chan at the Ringside*, Twentieth Century–Fox adapted it to the Mr. Moto series. This film also featured former boxer Max "Slapsie Maxie" Rosenbloom as boxer Knock-Out Wellington, who also played Chotsie the trainer in *Ringside Maisie*.

20. There were four Gold Diggers films: *Gold Diggers of 1933* (Mervyn LeRoy, 1933), *Gold Diggers of 1935* (Busby Berkeley, 1935), *Gold Diggers of 1937* (Lloyd Bacon and Busby Berkeley, 1936), and *Gold Diggers in Paris* (Ray Enright, 1938). *Dames* (Ray Enright and Busby Berkeley, 1934) featured Dick Powell, Joan Blondell, Ruby Keeler and a handful of character actors that appeared in at least one of the Gold Digger movies. This list is hardly exhaustive of the Broadway theatrical musical from this decade. Although the Gold Diggers movies possessed the same word in their titles, since there were no recurring characters, nor even consistently returning actors and actresses, these films do not qualify as a series.

21. Both films also shared some of the same creative team members. *Maisie Gets Her Man* was directed by Roy Del Ruth, who had partial, but uncredited, directorial duties on *Panama Hattie*. Norman Z. McLeod, the credited director of *Panama Hattie*, directed the next Maisie installment, *Swing Shift Maisie*. All three films shared the same screenwriter, Mary C. McCall, Jr., who had also worked on the scripts of all the previous Maisie movies.

22. Near the end of *Maisie Gets Her Man*, Maisie performs in a society benefit, "Bundles for Buddies," as the lead attraction of Frawley's Frolics. While there is no explicit explanation of who those "buddies" are, it becomes clear after Maisie grouses that they "get a very refined audience when it's for nothing," when she adds in patriotic spirit, "But these days you gotta do all you can." The movie ends with a performance for soldiers at an unidentified fort, the first direct reference to the war. This was also the first Maisie movie to advertise the buying of war bonds.

23. In 1960, a pilot for a sitcom starring Janis Paige as Maisie Ravier was not picked up by CBS. The plot summary on the Internet Movie Database introduces Maisie, "a Brooklyn born-and-bread [sic] showgirl," who "wins the coveted 'Miss Guided Missle [sic]' beauty contest and has to visit a backwater Army post to support their recruiting program." The series's popularity continued to rest on the association of Maisie with her trademark moxie of the war years.

24. Breezy: What does a dame like you know about defense work, anyhow?

> MAISIE: Listen, brother, I've been doing defense work of one kind or another all my life. I'll make out.
>
> BREEZY: (*sarcastically*) I don't doubt that. Eight hours a day, six days a week? Ha, ha!

MAISIE: Ha, ha! What do you think show business is, pray tell?

BREEZY: Well, throwing your hips around is no training for factory work. Why, you'd let a hot rivet drop while you repaired your paint job or regilded your hair.

MAISIE: Listen, I told you my....

BREEZY: I know, it's natural. No, Goldilocks, in an aircraft factory you'd be so much excess baggage. You're not the type.

MAISIE: Not the type, huh? Well, it's gonna take all types to win this war, from General MacArthur way on down to you. Well, I'll get in it and I don't need no introduction from you, nor none of your ilk. He's my Uncle Sam, too, you know. And as for how I'm dressed, I wear what suits the job I'm doing and make-up in proportion, and I'll handle myself in the factory just as good as on the stage. If you can fly planes, then brother, I can build 'em [*Swing Shift Maisie*].

25. Ann Sothern felt that Maisie hindered her career, but her arrangement with Louis B. Mayer to do at least one Maisie movie per year made it possible for her to play in some A pictures. In a 1975 interview she explained: "Every *Maisie* film cost under $500,000 and made two to three times that back. Sure, I felt she was a millstone around my neck at times. I'd tell Mr. Mayer to give me a musical and I'd do another *Maisie*. We'd bargain that way" (qtd. in Schultz 7).

26. Among the many factors that contributed to the perception of equal relations between men and women is the "relaxation of morals" that Norbert Elias perceived in what he terms the "civilizing process." He sites as two significant historical moments the freedoms women enjoyed in absolutist court societies during the seventeenth and eighteenth centuries, and the period following World War I. He attributes the "relaxation of morals" to the psychological internalization of social constraints that regulated social behavior (185–87). An extreme exploration of the perceived gains in equality in relations (and role reversals) between men and women is the 1933 film, *Female* (Michael Curtiz), featuring Ruth Chatterton as Alison Drake, a female business tycoon who sexually exploits her male labor. While the Production Code is generally credited with putting an end to such depictions of female license, it is probable that it is indicative of the type of fluctuation from a society of inner constraints to one of externally imposed constraints cited by Elias in this 1939 text: "But on closer examination it is not difficult to perceive that this is merely a very slight recession, one of the fluctuations that constantly arise from the complexity of the historical movement within each phase of the total process" (187).

27. The potential appeal of blond hair, natural or otherwise, to young, impressionable women was expressed in the early thirties by the film reviewer for the *New York Times* who commented on the influence of Jean Harlow in *Red Dust*: "Miss Harlow's presence in the picture apparently attracted a host of other platinum blondes, for on all sides there were in the seats girls with straw-colored hair" (Rev. of *Red Dust*). Blonde seems to function here almost as a code word for gold-digger, the implication being that Jean Harlow was the wrong kind of role model for impressionable young women.

28. Brian Taves distinguishes between programmers and B movies in his definition of B movies, with programmers belonging to the higher quality B output of the major studios. Programmers boasted higher budgets, slightly longer production and running times, and bigger stars than the average B film. Successful programmers "attracted major audiences and box-office grosses on a par with A's" (317). In this respect, the Maisie movies were more programmers than straight B's. Maisie's physical attributes, from her weight to her fashion tendencies, however, identify her with the working-class body and as such position those attributes in direct defiance of the dominant class's aesthetic values. In this sense, the Maisie movies were decidedly B's.

29. "I never had much schooling. I set a record for the mile running from the truant officer" (*Up Goes Maisie*).

30. Andrea Walsh notes of the relation between the prostitute and the gold-digger in Classic Hollywood films that, "Like prostitutes, golddiggers are cynically pragmatic about the relations between the sexes. For one heroine (*Golddiggers of 1933*), 'Either you work the men or the men work you'" (138). All of the men Maisie meet accuse her of "working" them. For example, Skeets Maguire accuses her of hatching a gold-digging scheme in *Ringside Maisie*, to which Maisie responds:

>MAISIE: How dare you!
>SKEETS: Oh, I dare. I'm brave.
>MAISIE: I never heard such vile talk in all my life, and I've been around some people who were pretty low.
>SKEETS: I'll bet, in your racket.
>MAISIE: You close your mouth! I've been earning my living since I was fourteen years old, and I never did a crooked thing or took one cent I didn't earn. If my own mother was to come back from her grave today I could look her right in the eye and never be ashamed of anything. Where do you get off talking about shakedowns and rackets?
>SKEETS: I know the type, sister. I've been around.
>MAISIE: Type! Type! Who's a type? I'm me! What are you trying to do, anyhow? Blame me for what every cheap girl ever did?

31. In *Maisie Was a Lady*, new maid Maisie is ridiculed by society girl Miss Abigail's guests:

>MISS ABBY: Bob was to see that you had employment for two months at $25 a week, wasn't that the arrangement?
>MAISIE: I had it coming to me after what he put me through, and that was the judge's idea, too.
>MISS ABBY: I think Judge Thatcher was perfectly right, but really I can't expect you to do this sort of thing. It isn't fair to you or to my guests, so perhaps we can solve everything by paying you now in advance. That'll leave you free to find something more suitable.
>MAISIE: Why don't you come out in plain English and say you want me out of here.
>MISS ABBY: Oh really, that wasn't...
>MAISIE: Listen, I told your brother it was a job or no dice. That happens to be the way I operate, lady, strange as it sounds. And when I put on this outfit, all I expected was $25 a week and halfway decent treatment in return for doing my best. But if that isn't good enough for you, just say so. I'll go, with exactly what I brought here: 2 dimes, a suitcase, and a talent for picking the jinxes!

32. Of course, the war changed women's overall social condition only temporarily. While many women worked during the war in elite jobs traditionally associated with men (women in war factories welded, riveted, assembled fighter planes and ships, etc.), after the war the majority of women returned to occupations typically associated with women. In addition, Michael Renov debunks the perception that the war effort was the cause for so many women being on the workforce. On the contrary, he explains, "A little known fact was that, even at the very height of the war, nearly two-thirds of the women employed began working well before the Pearl Harbor watershed" (39).

33. Walsh notes that "The wartime divorce rate for women over 15 rose — from 8.8 per 1,000 in 1940 to 14.4 per 1,000 by 1945" (67).

34. Critics didn't even bother to review the shoddy fare produced by the lesser studios in Hollywood. As regards the Maisie movies, the Variety review of *Congo Maisie* recommended that the "only requirement needed for continuance of the series is proper story material which is not stereotyped in plot structure" (Rev. of *Congo Maisie*). The *New York Times* called *Ringside Maisie* "a strictly routine little adventure" (T. S.). Of *Swing Shift Maisie*, the reviewer claimed that "Maisie isn't synthetic, but her latest adventure is" (T.

S.). The same paper wished that the screenwriters of *Maisie Goes to Reno* "would cook up something really worthy of Maisie" (T. M. P.).

35. B-movie regular Hillary Brooke played the part of Barbara Nuboult. Brooke was involved in the four filmed versions of the Pine-Thomas Big Town mystery series (previously a hit radio series) as police reporter Lorelei Kilbourne, who helps "Illustrated Press" newspaper editor Steve Wilson (Philip Reed) solve crimes: *Big Town* (Willaim C. Thomas, 1947); *Big Town After Dark* (William C. Thomas, 1947); *I Cover Big Town* (William C. Thomas, 1947); *Big Town Scandal* (William C. Thomas, 1948). She excelled in playing sneering sophisticated blondes who are capable of the worst actions, even murder.

36. The first Hildegarde Withers film, *The Penguin Pool Murder* (George Archainbaud, 1932) ends in her marriage to detective Oscar Piper. In all subsequent films in the series, however, the two are once again single, and they remain that way.

37. It is not certain that there was heavy PCA supervision of series films in general, and of the Maisie movies in particular, except perhaps for the fact that the latter were a higher class of B movie than those made at other studios. It is certain, however, that movie reviewers would not even bother to critique further installments in a film series if they felt that the films had become too formulaic.

38. Joseph Breen was director of the Production Code Administration from 1934 to 1954.

39. Mary C. McCall, Jr., had been credited with either story or screenplay for all the preceding Maisie features. Although Thelma Robinson is credited with the screenplay in the last two Maisie movies, it is likely that husband Haight, who had a significantly more substantial career in both writing and directing, contributed a great deal to the development of the scripts.

40. "One result of war and greater variety of job opportunity was a ten percent drop in the number of women employed in the lowest paying positions: domestic, personal and recreational services. Thousands of domestic workers found greater remuneration on the assembly line while their employers took up their own housekeeping chores for the duration" (Renov 40).

41. Torchy's efforts to get hitched to McBride may function like Maisie's repeated engagements: to deflect attention away from the fact that she really is ideally suited for crime detection.

Works Cited

Allen, Robert C. *Horrible Prettiness: Burlesque and American Culture*. Chapel Hill: University of North Carolina Press, 1991.
Balio, Tino. *Grand Design: Hollywood as a Modern Business Enterprise, 1930–1939*. Berkeley: University of California Press, 1995. Vol. 5 of *History of the American Cinema*.
Basinger, Jeanine. *A Woman's View: How Hollywood Spoke to Women, 1930–1960*. Hanover: Wesleyan University Press, 1993.
Bourdieu, Pierre. *La Distinction: critique sociale du jugement*. Paris: Editions de Minuit, 1979.
Elias, Norbert. *The Civilizing Process: The History of Manners*. Trans. Edmund Jephcott. Vol. 1. New York: Urizen, 1978.
Gorman, Ed. "Remembering the Saint." *Mystery Scene* 53 (1996): 16–18.
Grant, Barry Keith, ed. *Film Genre Reader II*. Austin: University of Texas Press, 1995.
Hanke, Ken. *A Critical Guide to Horror Film Series*. New York: Garland, 1991.
Maltin, Leonard. *2003 Movie and Video Guide*. New York: Signet, 2002.

Mead, Margaret. "The Women in the War." *While You Were Gone: A Report on Wartime Life in the United States.* Ed. Jack Goodman. New York: Simon and Schuster, 1946. 274–89.
Miller, Don. *"B" Movies: An Informal Survey of the American Low-Budget Film, 1933–1945.* New York: Curtis, 1973.
Monaco, Paul. *The Sixties: 1960–1969.* New York Scribners, 2001. Vol. 8 of *The History of the American Cinema.*
Naka. Rev. of *Maisie Gets Her Man*, dir. Roy Del Ruth. *Variety* May 1942.
Parish, James Robert, ed. *The Great Movie Series.* South Brunswick, NJ: A.S. Barnes, 1971.
Pitts, Michael R. *Famous Movie Detectives.* Metuchen, NJ: Scarecrow, 1979.
_____. *Famous Movie Detectives, II.* Metuchen, NJ: Scarecrow, 1991.
Ray, Robert A. *A Certain Tendency of the Hollywood Cinema, 1930–1980.* Princeton, NJ: Princeton University Press, 1985.
Renov, Michael. *Hollywood's Wartime Woman: Representation and Ideology.* Ann Arbor: UMI Research Press, 1988.
Rev. of *Congo Maisie*, dir. H. C. Potter. *Variety* 11 January 1940.
Rev. of *Red Dust*, dir. Victor Fleming. *New York Times* 5 November 1932
Russell, Sharon A. "Narrative Closure in Series and Serials." *Purdue University Seventh Annual Conference on Film.* Ed. Marshall Deutelbaum and Thomas P. Adler. West Lafayette, IN: Purdue University Press, 1983. 127–32.
Schatz, Thomas. *Boom and Bust: The American Cinema in the 1940s.* New York: Charles Scribner's Sons, 1997. Vol. 6 of *The History of the American Cinema.*
Schultz, Margie. *Ann Sothern: A Bio-Bibliography.* New York: Greenwood, 1990.
Sobchack, Thomas. "Genre Film: A Classical Experience." Grant 102–113.
Taves, Brian. "The B Film: Hollywood's Other Half." *Grand Design: Hollywood as a Modern Business Enterprise.* Ed. Balio, Tino. Berkeley: University of California Press, 1995. 313–50. Vol. 5 of the *History of the American Cinema.*
T. M. P. Rev. of *Maisie Goes to Reno*, dir. Harry Beaumont. *New York Times* 29 September 1944.
T. S. Rev. of *Maisie Gets Her Man*, dir. Roy Del Ruth. *New York Times* 16 July 1942.
_____. Rev. of *Ringside Maisie*, dir. Edwin L. Marin. *New York Times* 1 August 1941.
_____. Rev. of *Swing Shift Maisie*, dir. Norman Z. McLeod. *New York Times* 10 September 1943.
Walsh, Andrea. *Women's Film and Female Experience, 1940–1950.* New York: Praeger, 1984.
Walt. Rev. of *Maisie Was a Lady*, dir. Edwin L. Marin. *Variety* January 1941.

THE NEW HOLLYWOOD

6

The James Bond Films
JAMES CHAPMAN

The James Bond film cycle is the longest running and quantitatively the most popular series in the history of cinema. The first Bond film, *Dr. No*, was produced in 1962 and the series has remained in continuous production ever since.[1] It is widely claimed that over two billion people, or a quarter of the world's population, have seen a Bond film (Chu 68). Even allowing for the hyperbole of publicists, there is no question that the popular success of the Bond series has been genuinely international and that the Bond character has become part of "a shared global consciousness" (Albion 212). While critics have tended to disparage the Bond movies for their formulaic plotting and for their standardization of narrative and generic conventions — some of the later films in the series, especially, seem to represent little more than a form of filmmaking by numbers — the continuing popularity of the series suggests that critics are not representative of popular taste. Regardless of the perceived qualities of the films themselves, the longevity of the Bond series represents a remarkable production achievement that has still not received its due recognition from the film industry. How has the series persisted for so long, especially given that many critics felt it had passed its sell-by date at the end of the 1960s? The most frequent explanation, embedded in the publicity discourse of the films, is that they have reflected changes in western politics and society over the years during which they have been produced: the thawing of the Cold War, the rise of global terrorism, technological and scientific advances, the changing social and sexual mores that gave rise to the permissive society and the emergence of a modern consumer culture of conspicuous mass consumption. While this is undoubtedly correct, however, it still does not fully explain why the Bond series has remained at the forefront of popular action-adventure cinema for a period that spans over a third of the entire history of the film medium. This chapter argues that the unique place of the Bond series in cinema history is also due to its success both in negotiating changes in the political economy of the film industry and in responding to the unpredictable and often fickle nature of popular film culture. It considers the quantitative performance of the Bond films at the box office, analyses the relationship between the series and the film industry at large, discusses the professional ideologies of the films' producers, and finally examines the cultural politics of the films themselves.

Bond and the Box Office

In terms of its cumulative worldwide box-office gross, the Bond series is by some distance the most successful in cinema history. From a relatively modest start the grosses of the six films released during the 1960s followed a parabola: *Dr. No* ($59.5 million worldwide), *From Russia with Love* ($68.9 million), *Goldfinger* ($124.8 million), *Thunderball* ($141.2 million) *You Only Live Twice* ($111.6 million) and *On Her Majesty's Secret Service* ($64.5 million). *Thunderball* achieved the sixth biggest gross of the 1960s, and even the less successful Bond movies were amongst the top earners of their year. The first nine Bond films — from *Dr. No* in 1962 to *The Man with the Golden Gun* in 1974 — grossed a total $910.5 million (representing rental income to the distributor United Artists of $357.4 million), and the series passed the landmark $1 billion with the tenth film *The Spy Who Loved Me* in 1977. From the late 1970s the increased grosses of the films reflected the global inflation sparked by the oil crisis of 1974 before stabilizing again in the 1980s. The most successful Bond during this period was *Moonraker* ($202.7 million) and the least successful was *A View to a Kill* ($155.3 million). The cumulative total of the series passed $2 billion with the release of *The Living Daylights* in 1987, which also marked the twenty-fifth anniversary of the series and prompted *Variety* to declare that "no other celluloid concept has come close to a similar giga-take: i.e., hitting 10-digit sales twice over" (Watkins 57). When the series resumed in the 1990s following a six-year production hiatus, three films — *GoldenEye* ($331.3 million), *Tomorrow Never Dies* ($346.6 million) and *The World Is Not Enough* ($353.2 million) — added a third billion to the cumulative total. The highest-grossing of all Bond films to date is *Die Another Day* ($424.7 million), though when adjusted for inflation it is the films of the mid 1960s (*Goldfinger, Thunderball, You Only Live Twice*) that represent the height of Bond's success at the box office. In total the films' cumulative worldwide gross, unadjusted for inflation and not taking into account ancillary markets, currently stands at over $3.6 billion.[2]

As impressive as they may sound, box-office statistics alone do not prove anything: they need to be placed in context. It was only with *Goldfinger* and *Thunderball* that the Bond films set any real box-office benchmarks and could be regarded as extraordinary, rather than merely very successful, films. *Thunderball* was surpassed in the 1960s only by *The Sound of Music*, *Mary Poppins*, *Doctor Zhivago*, *The Graduate* and *Butch Cassidy and the Sundance Kid*: two family-oriented films, one epic romantic melodrama, and two films that reflected the social and cultural *zeitgeist* towards the end of the decade. The relative disappointment of the last Bond of the sixties, *On Her Majesty's Secret Service*, seemed to some to suggest that the series had run out of steam as its gross was only half that of the previous film, *You Only Live Twice*. And, although the Bond series came back strongly in the early 1970s with *Diamonds Are Forever* ($116 million) and *Live and Let Die* ($126.4 million), they now lagged behind films such as *The Godfather* ($245 million) and *The Exorcist* ($357 million). The inflated grosses since the later 1970s reflect a trend across the film industry as a whole and even the undoubted success of *The Spy Who Loved Me* and *Moonraker* does not compare with New Hollywood blockbusters such as *Jaws* ($470 million) or *Star Wars* ($514 million). Following the relative decline of the late 1980s — *Licence to Kill* is the least successful Bond movie when adjusted for inflation — the series came back strongly in the late 1990s. Even so this was, again, indicative of a general upward trend in the film industry at large. "In truth," as an editorial in *Screen International* remarked, "only a handful of self-declared cinematic milestones are of *Titanic*-scale significance; the rest should more properly be seen as symptoms of predictable economic growth curves, inevitable ticket inflation, breathless self-promotion or just fortuitous quirks that ought to remain historical footnotes" (Brown 8). None of the Bond films to date has made it into the top fifty all-time grossing films and even the most successful of them has returned less than competitors in the Star Wars, Harry Potter and Lord of the Rings series.[3]

The achievement of the Bond series, therefore, is less in the returns of the individual films and more in the consistency of its presence in the box-office charts for over forty years. While the Bonds may not be super-blockbusters in their own right, they still represent the sort of copper-bottomed success on which the film industry depends. The Bond "franchise" is far and away the most successful when placed alongside comparable action-adventure films such as the Lethal Weapon and Die Hard series (four films each) which threatened, but failed, to usurp Bond at the box office. The film series that have surpassed Bond (Star Wars, Harry Potter, The Lord of the Rings) are all fantasy adventures set in mythical worlds rather than contemporary action movies that, for all their unlikely scenarios, are rooted in the real world. Moreover, no other modern film franchise has extended to twenty-one films and none has been in almost continuous production for over forty years. The nearest rival in this regard is the Star Trek series: ten films over 24 years. To this extent the Bond series is an anomaly in contemporary cinema: one has to look back to the Hollywood series films of the 1930s and 1940s (Charlie Chan, Bulldog Drummond, The Saint, The Falcon, Sherlock Holmes, Tarzan, Blondie, Maisie et al.) to find cycles spanning more than a few films and all those (excepting MGM's six Johnny Weissmuller Tarzan films) were essentially supporting features. In 1963, indeed, the *Motion Picture Herald* greeted the U.S. release of *Dr. No* with the observation that it was "the first of what could become the most successful series of films of its kind since the happy days of the Charlie Chan pictures and the Thin Man films" ("Dr. No" 785).

Where the Bond series is also historically significant, furthermore, is that it demonstrates the importance of the international market. It has long been a rule of thumb in the film industry that the rental income of a major Hollywood studio release will usually be roughly the same from the "international" market (all territories outside North America) as from the "domestic" market (USA and Canada) (Maltby 69). The trend since the 1980s, however, has been towards a greater proportion of revenue coming from the international market (Schatz 26). To this extent *Screen International* observes that the success of the Bond series represents "the most visible signs of how far 'foreign' has emerged from the shadow of the North American box office" (Brown 8). Throughout their history, indeed, the Bond films have consistently taken more in the international market than in North America: it has not been unusual for their international earnings to be twice or even three times their domestic. This pattern was established from the beginning of the series with *Dr. No*, which earned 73 percent of its gross revenues from the international market.[4] Overall a pattern emerges whereby the most successful Bond films are less biased in favor of the international market (a ratio of around 55:45 or 60:40, roughly the norm for major studio releases) whereas the revenues of the less successful films in the series are heavily weighted in favor of the international market (sometimes a ratio in excess of 70:30, which is significantly more than the average). Thus the international market accounted for 59 percent of the total gross for *Goldfinger*, 54 percent for *Thunderball*, and 61 percent for *You Only Live Twice*, whereas *The Man with the Golden Gun* earned 75 percent of its revenue from the international market, *The Living Daylights* earned 73 percent, and *Licence to Kill* an extraordinary 78 percent. Overall the Bond series has taken approximately two thirds of its total revenues outside North America.

If *Goldfinger* and *Thunderball* represent the height of Bond's popularity in America, nevertheless the revival of the series since the mid 1990s has once again seen the Bond films establish themselves as a significant presence in the U.S. market. During the 1980s the gross revenues of the Bond films in the United States declined from $67.9 million for *Octopussy* to a mere $35.4 million for *Licence to Kill*. The disappointing performance of *Licence to Kill* is generally attributed to the fact that it faced stiffer-than-usual competition during the "blockbuster summer" of 1989 when three films — *Batman* ($251 million), *Indiana Jones and the Last Crusade* ($197.2 million) and *Lethal Weapon 2* ($147.3 million) — cleaned up in the action-adventure film market. *Batman*, indeed, took more on its opening weekend ($40.5 million) than *Licence to Kill* did throughout its entire run in U.S. cinemas. When Bond returned in the mid 1990s, furthermore, the bar had been raised to the extent that a domestic gross of $100 million had now become the industry's benchmark for a major box-office hit. To this extent the American grosses of the four Pierce Brosnan films — *GoldenEye* ($106.4 million), *Tomorrow Never Dies* ($125.3 million), *The World Is Not Enough* ($127 million), and *Die Another Day* ($160.9 million) — can be considered a significant success and compare favorably with other action-adventure films such as *Lethal Weapon 3* ($144.7 million), *True Lies* ($146.3 million), *Speed* ($121.2 million), *Clear and Present Danger* ($122.2 million), *Die Hard: With a Vengeance* ($100 million), *The Rock* ($134 million), *Con Air* ($101 million) and *Lethal Weapon 4* ($130.4 million). It was *Die Another Day* that most exceeded the industry's expectations when it took $47 million on the Thanksgiving Holiday weekend in 2002 — the highest opening weekend for a Bond film in the United States — and passed $100 million after only 10 days (*The World Is Not Enough*, in contrast, had taken 28 days to reach $100 million) ("The British are Coming" 37). Even so, and again demonstrating the rise in revenues across the board, even the highest-grossing Bond film in the United States did not earn a place in the year's top ten releases. In the international market, however, *Die Another Day* grossed a further $271.1 million and in most territories, particularly in Europe, was ranked at least in the top ten and usually in the top four or five releases ("James Bond" 39).

Which, then, are the significant markets for the Bond series? North America remains the largest single market, of course, but the Bond films are more than usually dependent upon European markets, with Britain and Germany the two largest national markets. This can be demonstrated when the international grosses for recent films in the series are broken down by territory.[5] The five Bonds between *Licence to Kill* in 1989 and *The World Is Not Enough* in 1999 grossed between them a total of $960.5 million in the international market, with Britain ($136.6 million) and Germany ($131.9 million) combined returning nearly 28 percent of the total, while France ($88.2 million) accounted for another 9 percent. In contrast Japan, which is usually one of the most lucrative foreign markets, returned only 8 percent ($80.1 million) despite its significantly higher population (twice that of Britain and France) and higher ticket prices. (In contrast, for example, Japan has accounted for almost 25 percent of the international gross of the Harry Potter films.) (Forde 11). It can reasonably be assumed that the "Britishness" of Bond is a major factor in the films' success in the British market, where the Bond film has usually been the number one box-office attraction of its year. Their popularity in Germany is more difficult to explain, however, especially given their tendency towards "Germanic" villains: Gert Frobe (*Goldfinger*), Curt Jurgens (*The Spy Who Loved Me*), Gottfried John (*GoldenEye*), and Götz Otto (*Tomorrow Never Dies*). The internationalism of the Bond films, nevertheless, is crucial to any understanding of their place in the film industry.

The Political Economy of Bond

The fact that the Bond series has been significantly more successful outside North America is one reason why the films tend to be regarded as non–American productions. For registration purposes the Bond films have been classed as British productions and the symbolic "home" of the series has always been at Pinewood Studios where the "007 Stage" (originally built for the production of *The Spy Who Loved Me*) is a permanent fixture. Yet the economic power behind the films is Hollywood in the form of first United Artists and then MGM (which took over United Artists in the early 1980s), which finances and distributes them. The Bond films, in fact, represent a unique combination of British cultural capital and American dollars that is rooted in the historical circumstances of their original production arrangements. For this it is necessary to consider the state of the British and American film industries in the 1950s.

The 1950s was a decade of transition for the U.S. film industry following the landmark decision by the Supreme Court in 1948 that vertical integration gave the major studios an unfair advantage in exhibiting their films and that consequently they should be required to divest themselves of their cinema holdings. One consequence of this decision, coupled with a decline in cinema audiences from the late 1940s, was a shift away from the bread-and-butter films on which the studios had hitherto relied and towards a "blockbuster mentality" in which the studios concentrated on producing fewer but bigger films (Schatz 12). At the same time the increasing recognition of the importance of the international market drove some film production abroad. Overseas production was attractive for a variety of reasons, primarily economic in that labor costs were lower in Europe and U.S. producers could benefit from subsidies from European government legislation designed to encourage investment in domestic production industries. Hollywood, through the machinations of its overseas trade organization, the Motion Picture Export Association, became highly adept at circumventing this legislation by having its films produced overseas by nominally British, Italian, or German companies. By the 1960s these "runaway productions' accounted for almost half of all American features (Maltby 70).

Britain became particularly attractive to American producers in the 1950s and 1960s: production costs were cheaper, there were tax breaks for overseas artistes who made their permanent home in Britain, and there was a pool of technicians without any of the language obstacles of other European countries. American producers also found that they could benefit from the Film Production Fund (commonly known as the Eady Levy), introduced in 1950 as a means of subsidizing film production through an additional tax on ticket sales that was paid to producers and distributors in proportion to the box-office receipts of their films. To qualify for the Eady Levy a film had to be produced by a British-registered company, shot in a studio in Britain or the Commonwealth, and with 75 percent of the labor costs paid to British workers (Harper and Porter 114). The Eady Levy, according to Bond producer Albert R. Broccoli, "was the carrot that induced American production to come here" ("Broccoli's Bond" 48). Broccoli and his partner Irving Allen had set up Warwick Pictures in Britain in 1952 and, backed by Columbia Pictures, produced eighteen films over the next nine years, specializing in war and action films such as *The Red Beret* (1953), *Hell Below Zero* (1954), *The Cockleshell Heroes* (1955), *Zarak* (1957), and *The Killers of Kilimanjaro* (1959). American investment in the British production sector continued into the 1960s, when United Artists led the way in backing films such as *Tom Jones* (1963), *A Hard Day's Night* (1964), and the Bond series.

It was in this context of U.S. involvement in the British film industry that the origins of the Bond series are to be found. Ian Fleming had published the first James Bond adventure, *Casino Royale*, in 1953 and the books followed at a rate of one a year until his death in 1964, with the last two (*The Man with the Golden Gun* and *Octopussy and the Living Daylights*) appearing posthumously. Fleming had tried to interest the British film industry in his books—Sir Alexander Korda read a proof of *Live and Let Die* and the Rank Organization took out an option on *Moonraker* (Lycett 250)—but the only adaptation had been an American television version of *Casino Royale* by CBS in 1954. In the late 1950s, however, the public visibility of the Bond character was increasing, due to the publication of paperback editions of the novels, a "James Bond" comic strip in the *Daily Express* from 1957, and the controversy that attended the publication of *Dr. No* in 1958 when Fleming was accused of peddling "sex, snobbery and sadism."[6] It was around this time that Broccoli, according to screenwriter Richard Maibaum, first took an interest in the Bond books:

> In 1956 or 1957, when I was in England writing for Cubby and Irving Allen, Cubby gave me two of the James Bond books to read. I read them and liked them enormously. Cubby was very excited, too, but Irving Allen didn't share his enthusiasm. So Cubby put them aside. It's my personal opinion now that that was a wise thing to do, because with the censorship of pictures that existed then, you couldn't have even the minimal sex and violence that we put into the pictures. They just wouldn't have been the same [McGilligan 284].

A few years later, following the end of his partnership with Allen, Broccoli looked again at the Bond books, only to discover that Fleming had sold an option to Canadian producer Harry Saltzman. Saltzman had previously been involved with Woodfall Films, a company set up by Tony Richardson and John Osborne that produced most of the key British "new wave" films of the early 1960s. Broccoli and Saltzman went into partnership, setting up Eon Productions to make the films and turning to United Artists when Columbia balked at the proposed $1 million budget for *Dr. No*. In July 1961 the trade press announced that Broccoli and Saltzman "have clinched a deal with United Artists for 100 per cent financial backing and distribution of seven stories which will be filmed here and on foreign locations" (*Kinematograph Weekly* 17).

The multiple-film deal suggests that both Broccoli-Saltzman, on the one hand, and United Artists, on the other, saw in Bond the potential for a series. In its review of *Dr. No* the *Monthly Film Bulletin* remarked that "the film is obviously destined to be the first of a James Bond series" (Dyer 136). It had originally been intended to make *Thunderball* as the first film—a logical choice as the story had started out as a screen treatment—but a legal wrangle over ownership of certain rights in the property meant that Broccoli and Saltzman turned to *Dr. No* instead. With location filming in Jamaica and studio sequences at Pinewood, the film qualified for a subsidy under the Eady Levy. Its negative cost was approximately $950,000 (a relatively modest amount given the large sets and pyrotechnics involved) and it was reported "to have recouped its negative cost in its initial engagements in England and on the Continent alone" ("Dr. No" 785). *Dr. No* eventually returned to United Artists rentals of $22.1 million, to which extent it may be adjudged to have made a healthy profit (the rental receipts represent the amount returned to the distributor after exhibitors have taken their percentage). A second film, *From Russia with Love*, began production before *Dr. No* was released in North America (May 1963) and evidence that the producers were now confident in the future of the series is to be found in the closing credits which declared: "The End.... Not Quite the End. James Bond will return in the next Ian Fleming thriller, *Goldfinger*." This tradition of naming the next film at the end of each installment in the series persisted until *A View to a Kill* in 1985, since when the declaration has simply been the promise that "James Bond Will Return."

The production history of the Bond series demonstrates perfectly the economic logic of the film industry: to spend money in order to make money. As the films became more and more successful, their production costs rose as the producers sought to make each film bigger and more spectacular than its predecessor. Thus *From Russia with Love*, at $1.9 million, was twice as expensive as *Dr. No*, while *Goldfinger*, at $3 million, cost as much as the first two films combined. In the early years the choice of which book to film next would also seem to have been economically determined to some extent: *From Russia with Love*, set entirely in Europe, was a way of shoring up Bond's popularity on the Continent, while *Goldfinger*, set mostly in the United States and with a conspiracy plot directed against American interests, can be seen as a calculated attempt to open up the American market that had hitherto proved resistant. The strategy was successful: *Goldfinger*'s North American rentals of $23 million were over twice the combined rentals of the previous two films. The budget rose to $5 million for *Thunderball* (returning worldwide rentals of $56.4 million) and up to $9 million for *You Only Live Twice* (worldwide rentals of $44.1 million) before stabilizing at between $6–7 million for the next four films. After nine films the partnership between Broccoli and Saltzman, which had become seriously strained by the early 1970s, was dissolved: Saltzman sold his stake to United Artists and Broccoli continued as sole producer of the series.

There is a sense in which the mid 1970s was time of crisis for the Bond series, which was faced with diminishing returns on the one hand (*The Man with the Golden Gun*, with worldwide rentals of $37.2 million, was significantly down on the two previous films) and increasing competition on the other hand from rivals such as Hong Kong martial arts films and the high-tech blockbusters of Steven Spielberg (*Jaws*) and George Lucas (*Star Wars*) that "recalibrated the profit potential of the Hollywood hit" (Schatz 17). This competition arrived at a time when production costs began to escalate at an alarming rate. The $13 million cost of *The Spy Who Loved Me* was twice the cost of previous entries in the series, representing as it did a return to the level of production values and sheer visual spectacle that had characterized *Goldfinger, Thunderball,* and *You Only Live Twice* but which some critics had felt lacking in the first two Roger Moore films, *Live and Let Die* and *The Man with the Golden Gun.* For his part Broccoli admitted that *The Spy Who Loved Me* was a make-or-break film for the series: "Hopefully, we'll reach that if the picture is successful. If it isn't, we've had it, that's all — you roll the dice and that's it" ("Cubby Counts the Cost" 11). The film was successful and United Artists were rewarded with worldwide rentals of $80 million. For the next film, *Moonraker,* the negative cost rose to $34 million, largely due to the effects of inflation, and with rentals of $87.7 million it was probably less profitable than *The Spy Who Loved Me. Moonraker* was the first Bond film produced outside Britain — its studio base was in France — where increases in taxation had made filming prohibitively expensive. The increased cost was partly offset by some of the most gratuitous product placement in the series: *Moonraker* includes numerous narratively unmotivated shots of advertising hoardings for 7-Up, Seiko watches, Marlboro cigarettes, and British Airways, while other products displayed prominently include Bollinger champagne, Christine Dior perfume, and Canon cameras.

The production costs of the Bond films stabilized in the 1980s at between $28 million (*Octopussy*) and $35 million (*Licence to Kill*), the latter film also made away from the usual Pinewood base (it was shot at the Churubusco Studios in Mexico) for economic reasons. The abolition of the Eady Levy in 1985 removed a major economic incentive to remain in Britain, though the technical expertise of the Bond production team built up over the years meant that it was practical to stay at Pinewood as long as costs permitted. It is almost certain that the increased production costs made the 1980s films less profitable as their rentals during this time did not match those of either *The Spy Who Loved Me* or *Moonraker.* Nevertheless the Bond "brand" was a commodity that held currency in the film industry and, moreover, at a time when sales to the ancillary markets of television, cable, and video were surpassing theatrical revenues, the Bond "back catalogue" represented a significant asset for MGM. One of the reasons for the production hiatus of the early 1990s was a dispute over the sale of the video and television rights for the Bond series (Hazelton 3). At this time the Bond films also became a pawn in an abortive take-over attempt of MGM by Pathé Communications. That the Bond franchise was viewed enviously by other companies is demonstrated in the attempt of Columbia Pictures (now owned by the Sony Corporation of Japan) in the late 1990s to launch a rival Bond series of its own. Bond was reportedly "one of several franchises now being developed by Sony to provide an annuity in sequels; others include *Men in Black, Jumanji, Bad Boys, Godzilla, Starship Troopers, Charlie's Angels,* and *Ghostbusters*" ("MGM's Bond Shaken" 3). The rival Bond series, based on the disputed rights of Kevin McClory to *Thunderball,* was forestalled in the courts. It is tempting to speculate, however, that Sony's acquisition of MGM in 2004 was motivated in some measure by its desire to acquire the Bond franchise.

The revival of the "official" Bond series in the mid 1990s represents another stage in the evolving political economy of the series. Michael G. Wilson, Broccoli's stepson who now produces the films in collaboration with Barbara Broccoli, has suggested a level of corporate instability at the studio that is difficult for the producers to negotiate:

> When you say MGM, you are talking about a group of people that changes a lot. Almost every time the creative team or the administrative team turns over between films. So we are always going to what is basically a new group of people who have not worked with us before and trying to form a working relationship. Sometimes it is bumpy and sometimes it is smooth. A lot of people do not like the idea that we have as much creative control as we do, but one wonders what would happen if we did not [Forde 12].

It is the Broccolis, for example, who have always resisted studio pressure to cast a leading Hollywood star as James Bond, preferring to cast British or at least Anglophone actors in the role. MGM, for its part, depends on the Bond series, partly because a greater proportion of its revenues come from film releases than other, more diversified entertainment conglomerates, and partly because the studio does not have any other film franchise such as Batman (Warner Bros.), Star Wars (Fox) or Star Trek (Paramount). As MGM vice-chairman Chris McGurk remarked in 2002: "Bond is the biggest and most important franchise in the history of the motion picture business. It is a huge asset for the company" (Galloway S1+).

The period since the mid 1990s has once again seen an escalation in production costs, which have risen faster than inflation and, moreover, by a much greater rate than the increase in their earnings. *GoldenEye,* at a negative cost of $50 million, was a relatively economical production, especially when compared to the reported $140 million cost of 1994's *True Lies,* the James Cameron-Arnold Schwarzenegger vehicle that promised a "Bond for the 90s," but since then the production costs of the Bonds have risen progressively: *Tomorrow Never Dies* ($80 million), *The World Is Not Enough* ($100 million), and *Die Another Day* ($140 million) (Galloway S1+). Again the increased costs are partly offset by product placement through which manufacturers provide goods and contribute towards promotional activities in return for screen time for their brands. *Die Another Day* "placed" about 20 different brands, ranging from Finlandia vodka and Norelco shavers (which both used Pierce Brosnan in advertising campaigns) to the Ford Motor Company which provided the cars used in the film, including several Aston Martins (Bond's car of choice), Thunderbirds (driven by heroine Jinx), Jaguars (for the villain Zao), and Range Rovers (used as utility vehicles on location). Wilson averred that "the value that we got far exceeded the cash they could give us" and the provision of cars saved millions in production costs (Chu 70). Eon's partners spent an estimated $120 million on advertising their products through tie-ins to *Die Another Day* and Eon's marketing branch oversaw a series of tie-in products using the "Bond" image. Licensed merchandising, further, is a means through which the cultural visibility of Bond is maintained in the gaps between films so that, even when a new Bond film is not on release, the figure of Bond remains "a dormant signifier" that is always capable of being reactivated (Bennett and Woollacott 38). In particular the sale of video and computer games based on the films represents a significant market as well as a means of raising "brand awareness" of the Bond character. In the words of MGM consultant Larry Gleason: "There's a whole generation of kids out there whose primary reference point isn't *Dr. No* or *The World Is Not Enough*. It's the *GoldenEye* game" (Chu 70). The gaming industry, indeed, is credited with having introduced an entirely new generation of fans to the pleasures of Bond who would not otherwise have seen any of the films.

The Production Ideology of Bond

The Bond series embodies a distinct production ideology: a set of professional practices and values that informs the making of the films. This production ideology also defines the nature of the Bonds as genre films by emphasizing their unique characteristics. The Bond producers use the term "Bondian" to refer to a set of expectations of what a Bond movie should be, what it should contain, and how it should be made. "Bondian," according to Janet Woollacott, who conducted a series of interviews for an Open University case study of the making of *The Spy Who Loved Me*, means "in the spirit of James Bond." It is also used "to describe the Bond films, which were seen as a distinctive formula, a specific genre of film" (Woollacott 210).

The Bond series formula has been described as "an unbeatable blend of conspicuous consumption, brand-name snobbery, technological gadgetry, colour supplement chic, exotic locations and comic-strip sex and violence" (Richards 193). The Bond films are genre films that combine action-adventure, suspense, melodrama, and romance. The narrative of each film is much the same: James Bond, secret agent "007" of the British Secret Service, is assigned to a mission that will take him to one or more foreign locations where he will discover a grand conspiracy by a diabolical criminal mastermind who threatens the security of the civilized world. Bond will have several narrow escapes from death before finally dispatching the villain and saving the day. Along the way he will meet and seduce a number of women, who may be either "good" or "bad," and one of whom will assist him in defeating the conspiracy. As important as the narrative conventions and archetypal characters is the visual style of the films which are characterized by glossy high-contrast cinematography and a *mise-en-scène* that foregrounds exotic foreign locales, material culture, and expensive consumerism. And the Bond films also have their unique signature trademarks, including the famous opening gun-barrel motif and their highly stylized title sequences featuring images of girls and guns and accompanied by a theme song performed by a leading recording artist.

The critical reception of the early Bond films suggests that they represented a new style of popular genre cinema. Critics were unsure precisely how to categorize *Dr. No*: the veteran British trade journalist Josh Billings, for example, described it as "a bizarre comedy melodrama" (5), while Bosley Crowther, senior film critic of the *New York Times*, called it "a tinseled action-thriller" and "a spoof of science-fiction and sex" (20). Broccoli felt that it was in *From Russia with Love* that "the Bond formula and style were perfected" (Broccoli 9). "The success of *Dr. No* has no doubt given the James Bond team added confidence, if that was necessary," wrote Penelope Houston, "and *From Russia with Love* is made by people who clearly know that they now have a gilt-edged formula to play with" (155). In fact *From Russia with Love*, which eschews the sleek modernist set design and science-fiction trappings of *Dr. No* in favor of a more Hitchcockian narrative of suspense and pursuit, represents a direction that the Bond series did not, in the event, take. It was *Goldfinger*, with its glossy visual excess and technological modernism (represented by Bond's extraordinarily equipped Aston Martin complete with passenger ejector seat), that set the standard for the rest of the series and which in the popular discourse is generally regarded as "the most perfectly realized of all the films" (Brosnan 75).

The first three films had not only established the Bond formula but also covered most of the narrative possibilities of that formula: later films in the series would simply represent variations of the same. If *Thunderball* marked the height of "Bondmania" as a phenomenon, it was also the point at which the films became more episodic in narrative construction as the set pieces became more standardized. The film critic of *The Times* felt that it showed "alarming signs that the series is going to seed" (12). The *Monthly Film Bulletin* found *You Only Live Twice* "rather less enjoyable mainly because the formula has become so completely mechanical." Like all genre films, the Bond series exemplifies a form of regulated difference: each new film in the series must be sufficiently different from its predecessors, but not too different so that it disappoints the expectations that audiences bring to it. It is significant in this regard that two of the least successful Bonds were those which departed most radically from the usual formula: *On Her Majesty's Secret Service* with its tragic ending in which Bond's new wife is killed and *Licence to Kill* with its non-secret service narrative in which Bond embarks upon a personal vendetta against the villain who has maimed his best friend. The Bond formula has itself become the main point of reference in critical responses to the films. As one critic remarked of *GoldenEye*: "We want to like most movies we pay to see but we already know the Bond formula — it has already earned our goodwill — so our pleasure revolves around seeing how the film-makers execute their turn" (Arroyo 40).

The early films were recognizably based on the Bond books, though Fleming's Cold War villains were replaced by the non-political criminal syndicate SPECTRE (the acronym stands for the Special Executive for Counter-Intelligence, Terrorism, Revenge, and Extortion) as part of a deliberate strategy to modernize the films in response to changing geopolitical circumstances (Black 93). *You Only Live Twice* was the first film to dispense entirely with Fleming's plot and use just the title and character names of the book, though this process was uneven as the next film, *On Her Majesty's Secret Service*, is the closest of all the films to the book both in narrative structure and in detail. By the 1970s, however, Fleming had been left far behind as the films continually refreshed the formula to remain abreast of geopolitical and technological developments. The promotional materials for *Moonraker* demonstrate how far the films had detached themselves from the books, asking rhetorically "who today would be satisfied with such an unambitious piece of villainy as a nuclear rocket hitting London?" ("The Book"). The film instead features a megalomaniac billionaire so obsessed with genetic purity that he intends to kill off the world's population with nerve gas. Its outer-space subject ("science fact rather than science fiction" the publicity asserted) was partly a response to the success of *Star Wars* and partly a means of maintaining the Bond films at the cutting edge of technology: the first orbital flight of the U.S. Space Shuttle *Columbia* was in 1981, but James Bond had got there two years earlier.

The case of *Moonraker*, probably the most visually spectacular of all the

Bond films, exemplifies the production strategy of a series in which size is indeed everything. This can be seen from the promotional discourse of the films which claim that each new film is either the "biggest" or the "best" yet: *Thunderball* ("Here Comes the Biggest Bond of All!"), *On Her Majesty's Secret Service* ("Far Up! Far Out! Far More!"), *The Spy Who Loved Me* ("It's the Biggest. It's the Best. It's BOND — and B-E-Y-O-N-D") and *Moonraker* ("Where all the other Bonds end ... this one begins"). Broccoli asserted the imperative to make each new installment more spectacular and exciting than the last:

> With each new Bond picture we *have* to be bigger, better, more spectacular, more exciting, more surprising than the previous ones. Dreaming up new stunts, new twists, original gimmicks, new ways to entertain and thrill audiences can take months of discussions and meetings with scriptwriters, stunt co-ordinators, production personnel and those who take care of the mounting costs of each new picture. Costs are a big headache. But all the James Bond films have been very profitable. So I guess you have to be philosophical about it and lay out money to make money [Noble 17].

Broccoli's policy to "lay out money to make money" is a typical statement of the commercial logic of the film industry. His emphasis on production values and spectacle locates Broccoli very much in the tradition of big-thinking "showmen" such as Cecil B. De Mille and David O. Selznick whose philosophy was always "to put the money on the screen." "The success of James Bond has always depended upon the values we put up there on the screen," he averred. "People may argue about the relative merits of the Bond films, but few would deny that they reveal the highest production values and technical skill" (Broccoli and Zec 308).

The Bondian production ideology therefore privileges spectacle over narrative: to this extent the films exemplify a sort of "cinema of attractions" and belong in the same historical lineage as the early "trick" films of Georges Méliès, the serial cliff-hangers of the silent era, the CinemaScope and Cinerama epics of the 1950s, and the high-tech special effects-driven blockbusters of Lucas, Spielberg, Cameron, and others in contemporary cinema. What is most memorable about the Bond series is not so much the plots of the individual films but rather their many outstanding set pieces, particularly the action sequences: examples would include, but are not limited to, the vicious fight on the Orient Express in *From Russia with Love*, the first of many pyrotechnic-driven car chases in *Goldfinger*, the epic battle inside the volcano in *You Only Live Twice*, the exhilarating ski chase of *On Her Majesty's Secret Service*, the breathtaking ski-parachute jump at the beginning of *The Spy Who Loved Me*, and the gripping struggle on the cargo net in *The Living Daylights*. Richard Maibaum, the most prolific Bond screenwriter, explained the approach to scripting Bond thus:

> Hitchcock once said to me, "If I have 13 'bumps' I know I have a picture." By "bumps," he meant, of course, shocks, highpoints, thrills, whatever you choose to call them. From the beginning ... [we] have not been content with 13 "bumps." We aim for 39. Our objective has been to make every foot of film pay off in terms of exciting entertainment [Maibaum 22].

This is another principle of the Bondian production ideology: the films are driven by incident and set pieces rather than by psychologically plausible characterization.

The Bondian ideology also emphasizes the role of the production team in making the films. The emergence of a core group of production personnel who have worked on several films in the series has institutionalized the same professional ideologies and practices over a period of time. It is significant, for example, that the first sixteen Bonds were made by only five directors: Terence Young (who directed three of the films), Guy Hamilton (four), Lewis Gilbert (three), Peter Hunt (one), and John Glen (five). Pierce Brosnan's tenure as Bond was unusual in that each of his four films had a different director: Martin Campbell (*GoldenEye*), Roger Spottiswoode (*Tomorrow Never Dies*), Michael Apted (*The World Is Not Enough*) and Lee Tamahori (*Die Another Day*). This consistency in the film-making process extends to other production personnel including title designer Maurice Binder (fourteen), screenwriter Richard Maibaum (thirteen), composer John Barry (twelve), stunt coordinator Bob Simmons (ten), production designers Ken Adam and Peter Lamont (seven each), and cinematographers Ted Moore (seven) and Arthur Wooster (six). The distinctive visual style of the Bond series is due in large measure to the innovative production design of Adam whose massive sets—the interior of Fort Knox (*Goldfinger*), the rocket launching silo inside a hollowed-out volcano (*You Only Live Twice*), and the submarine-swallowing supertanker (*The Spy Who Loved Me*)—combine motifs of modernism and expressionism to create a highly stylized world for Bond's fantastic adventures. Several of those involved with the films, moreover, have moved their way up through the production ranks: Lamont, for example, graduated from set dresser to production designer, while two Bond editors and second-unit directors, Peter Hunt and John Glen, became fully-fledged directors on the Bond series.

What of the role of the director in making the Bond films? The production discourse of the films suggests that the Bond series is essentially producer-led rather than director-led. Even the arch auteurist Andrew Sarris conceded that "it now seems reasonably certain that Broccoli had more influence on the origination and evolution of the Bond series than I, in my director-oriented predisposition, ever imagined" (Sarris S14). All the Bond directors would be categorized as *metteurs-en-scène* rather than *auteurs*; or, in the terms of the British film industry, as "journeymen." That said, however, there are certain stylistic differences between the films of the principal Bond directors. Thus Terence Young's films have a harder edge to the action sequences and a greater urgency of movement within the frame, Guy Hamilton's are notable for their visual gloss and sophistication, Lewis Gilbert is the undoubted master of handling the huge sets, and John Glen, as befits a former editor, is a crisp storyteller whose films are stronger on action than characterization. Young, as the first Bond director, liked to take credit for the style of the Bond films, averring that "above all I gave the picture [*Dr. No*] an enormous sense of tempo, in fact, it changed styles of filmmaking" (Schenkman 3). It was editor Peter Hunt, however, who developed a style of rapid, jarring editing that bore more resemblance to the comic strip than to the conventions of "invisible" classical narration. The early Bond films, especially, are characterized by their shorter-than-average shot lengths and by their close-ups of fists, feet, and guns thrust into the frame that resemble the panels of a comic strip. This editing style reached its fullest extent in the one Bond that Hunt directed, *On Her Majesty's Secret Service*, where the use of jump cuts and exaggerated sound effects enhances the sensation of violence in the bruising action sequences. More recently Lee Tamahori averred that he imposed his own style onto *Die Another Day*:

> It would be churlish for me to say I have reinvented the genre, but I think I have succeeded in some ways. I do think *Die Another Day* looks like a Bond movie and it does have some style and panache that was not evident in the last three. We are definitely modernising it in terms of the way it is cut and some of the way it is shot ["A View to a Thrill" 11].

In particular *Die Another Day* was notable for its more extensive use of computer-generated imaging (something which previous Bonds had largely avoided) and its elliptical editing. Yet the stylistic latitude extended to Tamahori is not typical of the series as a whole; nor did it bring about any significant change in terms of narrative structure and conventions. This is yet another indication of the extent to which the style of the Bond films is prescribed as much by the expectations of its audience as by the professional ideologies of its producers. The scope for an individual director to make any radical alteration to the formula is extremely limited.

The Cultural Politics of Bond

The status of the Bond series as genre films, with familiar narrative codes and conventions, makes them a ripe object for cultural and ideological analysis. It is surprising, however, that at a time when the agenda of film studies is shifting towards more critical engagement with popular genre cinema rather than merely privileging *auteurs* or traditions of art cinema, the Bond series, which represents popular cinema *par excellence*, has remained largely beyond the pale of academia. American film studies has focused, understandably enough, on genres such as the western, gangster film, musical, melodrama, and *film noir* that exhibit a particular relationship with American society and politics, but the Bond series has oddly been absent from the critical reclamation of popular film-making in British film studies that has recently seen once-despised forms as the Gainsborough costume melodramas and the Hammer horror films brought into the fold. One reason, perhaps, is that the Bond films do not obviously offer the scope for the transgressive pleasures that commentators have found in Gainsborough and Hammer. Another reason is simply that it is difficult to take Bond films seriously precisely because they are so formulaic and predictable. In his book *Hitchcock's Films*, for example, Robin Wood derided the "essential triviality" of the Bond films in comparison to the master of suspense, averring that *Goldfinger* was nothing more than "a collection of bits, carefully calculated with both eyes on the box office, put end to end with no deeper necessity for what happens next than mere plot" (Wood 96). In most histories of British cinema the Bond series usually merits only passing mention, a due acknowledgement of its popular appeal, but there is still considerable resistance to any serious critical engagement with the films themselves.

This neglect of the films is perhaps all the more surprising given that the Bond books have been subject to rigorous critical analysis. Umberto Eco's essay on the narrative structure of Fleming's novels has become, alongside Will Wright's analysis of the western, one of the two most oft-cited examples of the application of structuralist methods to popular cultural texts. Eco used the metaphor of a game of chess to explain the narrative construction of the Bond novels in which the characters are pieces that all move in pre-determined ways: Bond is given a mission by M (Head of the British Secret Service); Bond travels to a foreign location where he meets his secret service allies; Bond gives first check to the villain, usually beating him in a game that provides a ritualistic rattling of sabers (for example he beats Le Chiffre at baccarat in *Casino Royale*, Sir Hugo Drax at bridge in *Moonraker*, and Goldfinger at golf in *Goldfinger*); Bond meets "the girl" and either seduces her or begins the process of doing so; Bond and the girl are captured by the villain; the villain tortures Bond; Bond conquers the villain and possesses the heroine. It is the repetition of this narrative pattern that, Eco argues, explains the appeal of the books: "The reader's pleasure consists of finding himself immersed in a game of which he knows the pieces and the rules — and perhaps the outcome — drawing pleasure simply from the minimal variations by which the victor realises his objective" (Eco 58). Mapped onto this narrative, furthermore, are a set of overlapping structural oppositions: oppositions between characters (Bond/M, Bond/villain, Bond/girl), oppositions between ideologies (Soviet Union/Free World, England/non–Anglo-Saxon countries) and oppositions between values (duty/sacrifice, loyalty/disloyalty, luxury/discomfort, excess/moderation). The resolution of the narrative invariably represents the triumph of the ideologies that Bond represents (England, empire, duty, loyalty) over his enemies.[7]

Bennett and Woollacott, in their cultural studies analysis of the Bond phenomenon, argue that the Bond novels can be understood through three narrative codes that regulate the relationships between characters: the sexist code, the imperialist code, and the phallic code (93–142). The "sexist code" regulates Bond's relationship with the heroine who is usually out of place, either sexually, in the sense that she is initially resistant to Bond (such as Tiffany Case in *Diamonds Are Forever* and Pussy Galore in *Goldfinger*), or ideologically, in that she is in the service of the villain and needs to be "repositioned" (such as Solitaire in *Live and Let Die*, Tatiana Romanova in *From Russia, with Love*, and Domino Vitali in *Thunderball*). Bond succeeds in repositioning the girl, ideologically and sexually, by seducing and sleeping with her. The "imperialist code" regulates Bond's relations with his allies, who are usually loyal colonials (such as the Cayman Island fisherman Quarrel in *Live and Let Die* and *Dr. No*) or pro–British characters (Kerim Bey in *From Russia, with Love*, Tiger Tanaka in *You Only Live Twice*) who defer to Bond and are in a subordinate power relationship to him. The most frequent ally is CIA agent Felix Leiter who appears in six of the fourteen books but who, in a quaint reversal of the post-war Anglo-American power relationship, is very much the junior partner.[8] The "phallic code" regulates the relationship between Bond and M, the symbolic father who endows Bond with power and responsibility (his "license to kill"), and between Bond and the villain, who threatens Bond with symbolic castration through torture. In this reading two of the most important sequences in the books are Bond's ordeal at the hands of Le Chiffre in *Casino Royale* (almost a literal castration: the villain tortures Bond's genitals), and the early scene in *Dr. No* where M symbolically denudes Bond's phallic authority by ordering him to relinquish his gun for a more reliable model.

To what extent, then, are the ideological and cultural values of the books duplicated in the films? It would be disingenuous to expect the narrative ideologies of books written in the 1950s and early 1960s to be replicated exactly:

the films have been produced in different cultural and political climates. As previously mentioned, for example, the early films largely detached themselves from the Cold War narratives of the books in favor of the international criminal syndicate SPECTRE, though Cold War tensions still inform *From Russia with Love* (inevitably given the connotations of the title) and, to a lesser extent, *You Only Live Twice*. Two other areas in which the films modify to some extent the ideologies of the books are in their formulations of the imperialist and sexist codes. In their attitude towards British power, and in their representation of the relationship between Bond and women, the films perform ideological work that not only differs significantly from the novels but also demonstrates the strategies through which the series has responded to political and social change.

Fleming, of course, began writing the books at a time when Britain still had illusions of being a world power. David Cannadine points out that *Casino Royale* was published in the Coronation year 1953 ("a retrospectively unconvincing reaffirmation of Britain's continued great-power status"), whereas the last full novel, *The Man with the Golden Gun*, appeared in 1965, the year of Sir Winston Churchill's funeral ("self-consciously recognised as being a requiem for Britain as a great power") (46). In fact Fleming refers in the books to the decline of British power, most explicitly in *You Only Live Twice* where Bond's mission is to prove to the Japanese that "there is still an *élite* in Britain and this valuable [intelligence] material would be safe in their hands." The Bond films began production during the period of Britain's retreat from empire: the majority of Britain's remaining colonial outposts won their independence between 1957 and 1965. The choice of *Dr. No* as the first film was significant in this context. The narrative is set mostly in Jamaica, still a British colony in 1958 when the novel was written but achieving its independence in August 1962 between the shooting and release of the film. In the film, however, Bond still works as an agent of British colonialism, traversing locations such as Government House and the Queen's Club and assisted by dutiful, deferential West Indian policemen — "the Uncle Toms of Dock Green" (Durgnat 151). At the same time the film also alludes to the presence of American interests in the Caribbean by inserting the character of Felix Leiter (who does not appear in the book) into the narrative. Leiter's presence on British territory ("You limeys can be pretty touchy about trespassing") is explained by having the conspiracy directed against American interests — Dr. No is engaged in "toppling" rockets launched from Cape Canaveral — and it seems likely that the narrative of an island despot in America's back yard invested the film with a fortuitous topicality given that it was released in the same month as the Cuban Missiles Crisis (October 1962).

The colonial trappings of *Dr. No* are not apparent in later films in the series, where the references to Britain's imperial past tend to be ironic. In fact the films demonstrate an uneasy awareness of the decline of British power that is never fully resolved. In some films, such as *You Only Live Twice*, *The Spy Who Loved Me*, and *Tomorrow Never Dies*, Britain is presented as a great power of equal status with the United States and the Soviet Union. It is a British nuclear submarine that is the first to be hijacked in *The Spy Who Loved Me* and a British ship that is sunk to provoke a showdown with China in *Tomorrow Never Dies* ("We're sending the fleet to China," remarks M's secretary, Miss Moneypenny, in a line that irresistibly brings to mind the dispatch of the task force during the Falklands War of 1982). In other films, such as *For Your Eyes Only*, *The Living Daylights*, and *GoldenEye*, the conspiracy is directed against Britain. In *GoldenEye*, for example, renegade MI6 agent Trevelyan intends to use a hijacked Russian space weapon against London to avenge the deaths of his parents at the end of the Second World War ("England is about to learn the cost of betrayal — inflation-adjusted for 1945"). This contrasts markedly with *Diamonds Are Forever* in which Bond's arch-enemy Blofeld, in possession of a similar satellite weapon, is contemptuous of Britain ("Your pitiful little island hasn't even been threatened"). *Die Another Day* refers to the illusory nature of Britain's great power aspirations when Bond is captured on a mission to North Korea ("How pathetic that you British still believe you can police the world!") and to the legacy of imperial history when a Chinese agent is suspicious of Bond's presence in the former Crown Colony of Hong Kong ("Hong Kong's our turf now, Bond"; "Relax, I've not come to take back").

The films are similarly uneven in their representation of Bond's patriotic code and his sense of duty. This theme is strongest in *On Her Majesty's Secret Service* where both the title sequence (images of Britannia) and the *mise-en-scène* (the portrait of Queen Elizabeth II on the wall of Bond's office) provide visual signifiers of the nation and the institutions that Bond is sworn to defend. The motif of "For Queen and Country" recurs throughout the series. In some films it is used ironically, for example as Bond prepares to bed an enemy female in *You Only Live Twice* ("The things I do for England!") or when he is discovered *in flagrante delicto* with a beautiful Russian agent in *The Spy Who Loved Me* ("Bond, what do you think you're doing?"; "Keeping the British end up, sir!"), suggesting that the values of patriotism and duty are being mocked. Elsewhere, however, the assertion of Bond's code of duty is entirely unironic and is used to highlight ideological differences between Bond and the villain. In *The Man with the Golden Gun*, for example, the assassin Scaramanga mocks Bond's sense of duty without its due reward ("You work for peanuts — a hearty well-done from Her Majesty the Queen and a pittance of a pension. Apart from that, we are the same"), and in *GoldenEye* Trevelyan is contemptuous of his former friend ("James Bond, Her Majesty's loyal terrier, defender of the so-called faith"). In *Octopussy* Bond's patriotic code is mapped onto his relationship with the titular heroine, a jewel smuggler who attempts to persuade him to work for her ("A man of principle — naturally you do it for Queen and country!") and reacts angrily when he refuses ("I have no country, I have no price on my head. I don't have to apologize to you, a paid assassin, for what I am!"). The film that most problematizes Bond's sense of duty is *Licence to Kill* where he disobeys a direct order from M ("This personal vendetta of yours could easily compromise Her Majesty's Government") and becomes a rogue agent operating outside of official control. In this way *Licence to Kill* violates the code of professional ethics that Bond himself had asserted ("When I kill it's on the specific orders of my government," he told Scaramanga) and removes the ideological justification for his use of violence which is otherwise sanctioned by the state. This departure from the usual codes of the Bond movies may be one explanation for the film's relative failure at the box office.

While the films are, therefore, rather uneven in their attitude towards Britain, there is a greater consistency in their representation of Anglo-American relations. Britain is usually presented as a power of equal status with the United States and in several films (*Moonraker, Licence to Kill, Die Another Day*) this is reflected in the narrative strategy of having Bond pair up with a (female) American agent. The films promote common interests between Britain and America to the extent that Bond often acts to defend American security, for example preventing the destruction of Cape Canaveral (*Dr. No*), Fort Knox (*Goldfinger*), and Silicon Valley (*A View to a Kill*), and foiling plots to flood the United States with drugs (*Live and Let Die, Licence to Kill*). To a large extent, of course, this is a consequence of the political economy of the films and the imperative to sell the films in America. This strategy, however, has enjoyed only mixed success: while *Goldfinger* and *Diamonds Are Forever* were successful in the American market, *A View to a Kill* and *Licence to Kill* were rather less so. At the same time the films do not ignore tensions in the special relationship: thus *The Living Daylights* and *Die Another Day* both refer to American distrust of the integrity of the British intelligence services, while *Tomorrow Never Dies* allows the British to indulge in a little one-upmanship when they discover a stolen U.S. satellite encoder ("I wonder why the CIA will be more upset: that they stole it or we found it").

It is in their representation of and their attitude towards women, however, that the cultural politics of the Bond films are perhaps most revealing.

On one level, of course, Bond is fair game for feminist critics who aver that the films are at the best patronizing and at the worst downright sexist in their attitudes towards women. According to Janet Thumim:

> In line with other films popular at the sixties box office there are relatively few women to be seen on the screen in *Goldfinger*.... Even fewer have any significant narrative function.... Jill, Tilly and Pussy follow each other as "partners" to the central male character, James Bond.... The actions of all three are motivated by a very limited view of self interest and are highly susceptible to male influence, and they are all suggested to be incompetent in at least one narratively crucial skill. Jill is working for Goldfinger because, as she tells Bond, "he pays me" but is easily persuaded by Bond to change sides. Tilly is trying to avenge her sister's death but her incompetence with a gun leads to Bond's capture and her own death. Pussy is supposed to be a competent pilot and a trustworthy accomplice to Goldfinger, yet it is Bond who takes over at the end of the film when she panics as the punctured plane loses altitude [204].

Sue Harper similarly suggests that the Bond films represent "an essential femininity, which is submissive and dim" and characterizes the Bond girls as "Playboy Bunnies without the ears" (119). The relationship between the Bond films and *Playboy* was institutionalized in so far as several of the Bond starlets have posed for photo-spreads in the magazine. The notion of women in popular cinema functioning as mere objects of male desire has probably never been more prominent than in the Bond films which on a purely visual level represent nothing less than a form of institutionalized sexism.

Yet the perceived absence of female agency that feminist critics ascribe to the films can be questioned. For one thing, it runs counter to the production and publicity discourses of the films, which assert that they offer progressive and liberating roles for women. Claudine Auger (*Thunderball*) described her character as "the ultimate in modern, emancipated woman" and Barbara Bach (*The Spy Who Loved Me*) felt that her character was "really not one of Bond's girls so to speak. She's in the film doing her own bit" (qtd. in Bennett and Woollacott 231). It is probably fair to say that since the 1970s the films have extended greater narrative agency to their leading females. The key transitional film here is *The Spy Who Loved Me*. Unlike the previous film, *The Man with the Golden Gun*, in which the narrative focuses on the relationship between Bond and the villain and Bond's female sidekick Mary Goodnight is characterized as a feather-brained incompetent, *The Spy Who Loved Me* switches narrative interest to the relationship between Bond and the girl in that Major Anya Amasova is Bond's notional equal as the top agent of the KGB. The incompetences that Thumim identifies in *Goldfinger* are redressed in *Moonraker* where the heroine possesses a narratively crucial skill that Bond does not (she alone is able to pilot the space shuttle). Perhaps the most "liberated" Bond women are the action heroines of *Tomorrow Never Dies* and *Die Another Day* who are allowed to participate in the action sequences on an equal footing with Bond himself.

It is not so much the characterization and performance of women in the Bond films, however, as the ideological role they perform in the narrative that best demonstrate the social and sexual politics of the films. In particular the films challenge, and even subvert, the notion of the "repositioning" of women that Bennett identifies in the books. In *Thunderball*, for example, Domino knows that Bond has seduced her in order to convert her to his side and is complicit in the process ("So that is why you make love to me"). In the same film villainess Fiona Volpe refuses to be repositioned even when she has slept with Bond ("But of course I forgot your ego, Mr. Bond. James Bond, who only has to make love to a woman and she starts to hear heavenly choirs singing. She repents and then immediately returns to the side of right and virtue. But not this one!"). This character, indeed, is the first of several who challenge Bond's masculine supremacy, others including Helga Brandt (*You Only Live Twice*), Fatima Blush (in the *Thunderball* remake *Never Say Never Again*), May Day (*A View to a Kill*), and Xenia Onatop (*GoldenEye*). Where the sexist politics of the films remain in evidence is the fact that these women who challenge Bond's authority are too problematic to be allowed to live: their deaths are usually violent and spectacular. *The World Is Not Enough* subverts the usual process in so far as it is not the woman but Bond himself who is repositioned: Elektra King fools Bond into thinking she is the victim whereas in fact she has seduced the terrorist who kidnapped her and has induced him to murder her own father. *Die Another Day* features another cool villainess, treacherous MI6 agent Miranda Frost, who again resists repositioning by Bond ("I enjoyed last night, James, but this time it really is death for breakfast").

It would probably be fair to say that if the Bond films have responded to feminism, it is not by changing the attitude of Bond towards women but rather by changing the attitudes of the women around him to Bond himself. This is most apparent in the decision taken with *GoldenEye* to change the character of M to a woman: the symbolic father becomes a mother. The new M makes it clear that she regards Bond as "a sexist, misogynist dinosaur, a relic of the Cold War": to this extent she represents the series' strategy of responding to a legitimate criticism that could be made of Bond (that his attitude towards women was out of date in the 1990s) by voicing those very criticisms through the agency of a female authority figure. The decision to change M from a retired admiral to a middle-aged career woman can also be seen as one of the ways in which the Bond series has responded to and negotiated cultural change, reflecting as it did the real-life appointment of women such as

Stella Rimington and Judith Manningham-Butler to positions of authority in the intelligence services.

It is this responsiveness to social and cultural change, whilst being able to incorporate those changes into a relatively fixed narrative formula, that accounts in large measure for the longevity and enduring popularity of the James Bond film series. The "continuity and change" aspect of the Bond series was amply demonstrated with the production of *Casino Royale* in 2006. This much-publicized "reboot" of the series represented not only a back-to-basics but a back-to-Fleming Bond, adapting the first novel for the changing geopolitical climate of the early twenty-first century. Fleming's Cold War villainy is relocated in relation to the "War on Terror" and the antagonist, rather than being a Soviet spy paymaster in 1950s France, has become "private banker to the world's terrorists." Structurally, *Casino Royale* is really two films: an updated but reasonably faithful adaptation of Fleming's book in the middle section of the film, using his characters, some of his dialogue, and key incidents such as the card game and the torture sequence, with the big action set pieces expected of a Bond movie bolted on to the beginning and end. The film dramatizes Bond's first mission after gaining his "00" status. It documents how the raw, unrefined "blunt instrument" becomes "Bond-James Bond," the polished and sophisticated secret agent, acquiring such accoutrements as the vodka martini and the Aston Martin along the way. To this extent, therefore, it marks a break with the series's established continuity. At the same time, however, *Casino Royale* further develops one of the themes of the Brosnan Bonds in so far as it has Bond beleaguered by powerful figures of female agency, including not merely "M" (Judi Dench continuing in the role she had played opposite Brosnan) but also Treasury agent Vesper Lynd who controls the purse strings in Bond's epic poker duel with Le Chiffre.

Despite the controversial casting of Daniel Craig as the sixth James Bond, *Casino Royale* was both a critical and a popular success. Its nomination for a British Film and Television Academy Award for Best Picture suggests that, perhaps, the Bond film series was at last being recognized within the industry for the major production achievement that it is. For the time being, at least, it would seem that the character of "Bond — James Bond" is likely to remain an indelible part of popular film culture.

Notes

1. The "official" Bond series produced by Eon Productions and released through either United Artists, or latterly MGM, consists of *Dr. No* (Terence Young, 1962), *From Russia with Love* (Terence Young, 1963), *Goldfinger* (Guy Hamilton, 1964), *Thunderball* (Terence

Young, 1965), *You Only Live Twice* (Lewis Gilbert, 1967), *On Her Majesty's Secret Service* (Peter Hunt, 1969), *Diamonds Are Forever* (Guy Hamilton, 1971), *Live and Let Die* (Guy Hamilton, 1973), *The Man with the Golden Gun* (Guy Hamilton, 1974), *The Spy Who Loved Me* (Lewis Gilbert, 1977), *Moonraker* (Lewis Gilbert, 1979), *For Your Eyes Only* (John Glen, 1981), *Octopussy* (John Glen, 1983), *A View to a Kill* (John Glen, 1985), *The Living Daylights* (John Glen, 1987), *Licence to Kill* (John Glen, 1989), *GoldenEye* (Martin Campbell, 1995), *Tomorrow Never Dies* (Roger Spottiswoode, 1997), *The World Is Not Enough* (Michael Apted, 1999), *Die Another Day* (Lee Tamahori, 2002) and *Casino Royale* (Martin Campbell, 2006). At the time of writing *Quantum of Silence*, directed by Marc Foster, is to be released in November 2008. An earlier film of *Casino Royale* (John Huston, Ken Hughes, Val Guest, Robert Parrish & Joseph McGrath, 1967) and *Never Say Never Again* (Irvin Kershner, 1983) were produced outside the official Bond series.

2. The statistics in this paragraph are based on the tables appearing in "The James Bond Dossier" in *The Hollywood Reporter* 19 November 2002: S-14. See also "Bond Box Office Grosses" *Screen International* 5 December 1997: 21. Rental figures for the first fourteen films (up to *A View to a Kill*) can be found in the "James Bond 25th Anniversary" supplement of *The Hollywood Reporter* 14 July 1987. My source for the worldwide gross of *Die Another Day* is the Internet Movie Database (<http://www.imdb.com/title/tt0246460/business.html>).

3. At the time of writing (January 2006) the top ten biggest-grossing films worldwide are *Titanic* ($1,835 million), *The Lord of the Rings: The Return of the King* ($1,129 million), *Harry Potter and the Philosopher's Stone* ($969 million), *Star Wars: Episode I—The Phantom Menace* ($922 million), *The Lord of the Rings: The Two Towers* ($921 million), *Jurassic Park* ($919 million), *Shrek 2* ($880 million), *Harry Potter and the Chamber of Secrets* ($866 million), *Finding Nemo* ($865 million), and *The Lord of the Rings: The Fellowship of the Ring* ($861 million) (<http://www.imdb.com/alltimegross>, accessed 29 January 2006). The highest-ranked Bond film is *Die Another Day* in 62nd place with $424.7 million. Other Bonds in or around the top hundred are *The World Is Not Enough* (99th), *GoldenEye* (101st), and *Tomorrow Never Dies* (110th).

4. *Dr. No* grossed $43.5 million in the international market but only $16 million in North America.

5. These statistics refer to *The Living Daylights, Licence to Kill, GoldenEye, Tomorrow Never Dies,* and *The World Is Not Enough* and are based on statistics provided by the international distributor United International Pictures (UIP) and published in Forde. The international distribution of *Die Another Day* was handled by Twentieth Century–Fox, which has not published comparable data.

6. "Sex, Snobbery and Sadism" was the heading of Paul Johnson's vitriolic review of *Dr. No* for the *New Statesman* in which he declared it "without doubt the nastiest book I have ever read." "There are three basic ingredients in *Dr. No*," he went on, "all unhealthy, all thoroughly English: the sadism of a schoolboy bully, the mechanical, two-dimensional sex-longings of a frustrated adolescent, and the crude snob-cravings of a suburban adult" (Johnson 431).

7. Eco's work is open to the usual critique of structuralist analysis: that it becomes overly reductive as if suggesting that there is really only one basic narrative. In fact Eco's model is not equally applicable to all the Bond stories. It does not take account of *The Spy Who Loved Me*, for example, which is an unusual story written from the perspective of a female narrator in which Bond makes a belated, cameo appearance, nor of the short stories that comprise *For Your Eyes Only* and *Octopussy and the Living Daylights*. Eco suggests, rather disingenuously, that as these are not typical stories they can be ignored. Even in the books that he does include, however, Eco does not sufficiently recognize differences between stories. In *Moonraker*, for example, Bond does not get the girl, who leaves at the end to marry her fiancée, while *Casino Royale* and *On Her Majesty's Secret Service* both end with

the death of the girl. In *From Russia, with Love* and *Thunderball*, moreover, the conspiracy is known to the reader before Bond discovers it.

8. "The whole point of Felix Leiter, such a nonentity as a piece of characterization," wrote Kingsley Amis, "is that he, the American, takes orders from Bond, the Britisher, and that Bond is constantly doing better than he, showing himself, not braver or more devoted, but smarter, wittier, tougher, more resourceful, the incarnation of little old England with her quaint ways and shoe-string budget wiping the eye of great big global-tentacled multi-billion-dollar-appropriating America" (Amis 90).

Works Cited

Albion, Alexis. "Wanting to Be James Bond." *Ian Fleming and James Bond: The Cultural Politics of James Bond*. Ed. Edward P. Comentale, Stephen Watt, and Skip Willman. Bloomington: Indiana University Press, 2005. 202–20.
Amis, Kingsley. *The James Bond Dossier*. London: Jonathan Cape, 1965.
Arroyo, José. "GoldenEye." *Sight and Sound* New Series 6: 1 (January 1996): 40.
Bennett, Tony, and Janet Woollacott. *Bond and Beyond: The Political Career of a Popular Hero*. London: Macmillan, 1987.
Billings, R.H. "Three British Films Head the General Releases." *Kinematograph Weekly* 13 December 1962: 5.
Black, Jeremy. *The Politics of James Bond: From Fleming's Novels to the Big Screen*. Westport, CT: Praeger, 2001.
"The Book." Typed notes on the *Moonraker* microfiche at the National Library of the British Film Institute, London, n.d.
"The British Are Coming: Potter and Bond Take Thanksgiving." *Screen International* 6 December 2002: 37.
Broccoli, Albert R. "Introducing James Bond." Jay McInnerney, Nick Foulkes, Neil Norman, Nick Sullivan, Colin Woodhead. *Dressed to Kill: James Bond, the Suited Hero*. Paris: Flammarion, 1996.
_____ with Donald Zec. *When the Snow Melts: The Autobiography of Cubby Broccoli*. London: Boxtree, 1998.
"Broccoli's Bond." *Screen International* 27 September 1986: 48.
Brosnan, John. *James Bond in the Cinema*. London: Tantivy, 1981.
Brown, Colin. "James and the Giant Box Office." *Screen International* 29 November 2002: 8.
Cannadine, David. "James Bond and the Decline of England." *Encounter* 53: 3 (November 1979): 46–55.
Chu, Jeff. "The Man with the Golden Run." *Time* 11 November 2002: 68.
Crowther, Bosley. "Dr No." *New York Times* 30 May 1963: 20.
"Cubby Counts the Cost of Keeping 007 in the Manner..." *Screen International* 26 March 1977: 6.
"Dr No." *Motion Picture Herald* 3 April 1963: 785.
Durgnat, Raymond. *A Mirror for England: British Movies from Austerity to Affluence*. London: Faber and Faber, 1970.
Dyer, Peter John. "Dr No." *Monthly Film Bulletin* 29.345 (October 1962): 136.
Eco, Umberto. "Narrative Structure in Fleming." *The Bond Affair*. Ed. Oreste Del Buono and Umbert Eco. Trans. R.A. Downie. London: Macdonald, 1966. 35–75.
Forde, Leon. "The Man with the Midas Touch." *Screen International* 15 November 2002: 11.

Galloway, Stephen. "Forever Bond." *The Hollywood Reporter* 19 November 2002: S1+.
Harper, Sue. *Women in British Cinema: Mad, Bad and Dangerous to Know.* London: Continuum, 2000.
Harper, Sue, and Vincent Porter. *British Cinema of the 1950s: The Decline of Deference.* Oxford: Oxford University Press, 2003.
Hazelton, John. "Bond Case Springs into Action." *Screen International* 8 May 1992: 3.
Houston, Penelope. "From Russia with Love." *Monthly Film Bulletin* 30: 358 (November 1963): 155.
"James Bond: International Hit Man." *Screen International* 6 December 2002: 39.
Johnson, Paul. "Sex, Snobbery and Sadism." *New Statesman* 5 April 1958: 431.
Kinematograph Weekly 20 July 1961: 17.
Lycett, Andrew. *Ian Fleming.* London: Weidenfeld and Nicolson, 1995.
McGilligan, Pat, ed. *Backstory: Interviews with Screenwriters of Hollywood's Golden Age.* Berkeley: University of California Press, 1986.
Maibaum, Richard. "James Bond's 39 Bumps." *New York Times* 13 December 1964: 22.
Maltby, Richard. *Hollywood Cinema: An Introduction.* Oxford: Blackwell, 1995.
"MGM's Bond Shaken as Columbia's Rival 007 Stirs." *Screen International* 13 October 1997: 3.
Noble, Peter. "Broccoli Goes One Bigger and Better." *Screen International* 23 June 1979: 17.
Richards, Jeffrey. *Films and British National Identity: From Dickens to "Dad's Army."* Manchester: Manchester University Press, 1997.
Sarris, Andrew. "Cubby Broccoli & 007: A 25-Year Bond." *Hollywood Reporter* 14 July 1987: S12+.
Schatz, Thomas. "The New Hollywood." *Film Theory Goes to the Movies.* Ed. Jim Collins, Hilary Radner, and Ava Preacher Collins. London: Routledge, 1993. 8–36.
Schenkman, Richard. "The Terence Young Interview." *Bondage* 10 (1981): 2–7.
Thumim, Janet. *Celluloid Sisters: Women and Popular Cinema.* London: Macmillan, 1992.
The Times 29 December 1965: 12.
"A View to a Thrill ... Lee Tamahori." *Screen International* 15 November 2002: 11.
Watkins, Roger. "007 Sights $2-Bil in Ducats Overall." *Variety* 13 May 1987: 57–58.
Wood, Robin. *Hitchcock's Films.* London: Tantivy, 1977.
Woollacott, Janet. "The James Bond Films: Conditions of Production." *British Cinema History.* Ed. James Curran and Vincent Porter. London: Weidenfeld and Nicolson, 1983. 208–25.

7

Who's Your Daddy? Politics and Paternity in the Star Wars Saga

SUSAN ARONSTEIN *and* ROBERT TORRY

In June 2005 Lucasfilm ran a Father's Day promotion for its recently released *Revenge of the Sith*, distributing free posters that featured a masked and gloved Darth Vader gesturing towards the viewer, inquiring, "Who's your Daddy?" The poster, a saga in-joke that played off of what is arguably *Star Wars*' most famous (and certainly its most parodied) line "Luke, *I* am your father," marketed the film as the perfect Father's Day treat, the last installment of a series that had premiered when Dad was a boy, a natural link between father and son. It also, almost certainly inadvertently, identified both the saga's central theme and, with it, the political anxieties that inform its mythology: the problem of paternity. From 1977's *A New Hope* to 2005's *Revenge of the Sith*, the question "who's your daddy?" haunts the saga — not as a catchy marketing ploy but as an urgent query fraught with psychological complexities and political consequences.

This poster gives Vader, not Obi-Wan, the final word, an irony that plays into the peculiar chiasmus occasioned by the conflict between the six films' narrative trajectory and their chronological release. When viewed in narrative order, from *The Phantom Menace* to *The Return of the Jedi*, the Star Wars saga moves from pessimism to optimism, from the fall of Anakin and the decline of the Republic to the triumph of Luke and the reinstatement of democracy in a redemption of history that rewrites and suppresses the "imperial presidency" of Richard Nixon.[1] When viewed in chronological order, however, the feel-good story of the first trilogy — in spite of the invitation to return to that narrative issued at the end of *The Revenge of the Sith* — seems both dated and naïve. If in the 1970s and 1980s Lucas could offer his audiences a vision in which the 1960s offered a chance for the restoration of an

American ethos reflective of its revolutionary and democratic ideals, by the 2005 release of *The Revenge of the Sith,* it had become clear that such a restoration had not happened and was not going to happen; the political landscape depicted in the second trilogy pointedly references post 9/11 America — a culture of fear and attachment, the trade-off between liberty and security, another imperial presidency. When viewed in this order the saga gives us not historical progress but regression.

In this essay, we examine this conflict between narrative and history in the Star Wars saga, focusing on the saga's anxiety about America's political paternity, an anxiety that plays out across Anakin's and Luke's search for "Father." We begin by placing the original trilogy in the context of the nation's turn to optimism at the dawn of the Reagan era, paying special attention to the reinscription of American exceptionalism, with its myths of the nation's divine mission and privileged destiny, as exemplified in Stephen Spielberg's (Lucas' close friend and collaborator) *Close Encounters of the Third Kind.* Yet, we argue, while the original trilogy may have been hijacked by the Reagan/New Right agenda, Lucas's own vision — and the millennialism he offers — directly opposes that agenda; *A New Hope,*[2] *The Empire Strikes Back* and *The Return of the Jedi* may advocate a return to the values of World War II, but these films also depict the religious and political values of the 1960s counterculture as a necessary augmentation of traditional American ideals. However, if the original series inadvertently "made the world safe for Reagan," Lucas intends that the second not make the world safe for Bush. From *The Phantom Menace* to the *Revenge of the Sith,* the chronicle of Anakin's turn to the Dark Side and the fall of the Republic brings into question the very desires — for benevolent patriarchy, for millennial and messianic promise, for victorious militarism — that, in the first series made room for its hijacking by the New Right.

As what became known as the first example of Reaganite entertainment, the surprisingly successful *Star Wars,* as did Reagan himself, captured that nation at what Robin Wood has called "the ideological hesitation when the seventies became the eighties," arising on the screens, "like a breath of fresh air ... sweep[ing] away the cynicism that in ... recent years [had] obscured concepts of valor, dedication and honor" (Wood 108; Murphy). A "buoyant and exuberant film" "without a smudge of corrupt conscience in these corrupt times," Lucas's space opera offered the public what they didn't know they had been looking for — a "new hope" and a "new myth" — and a cultural legend was born (Krall 60).[3] Clearly, what American viewers wanted to see had changed: no more "downbeat films that ridicule the American Dream," no more "of the sad, the grubby, the corrupt.... They wanted protagonists they could cheer, people who succeed against incredible odds ... thus, proving the American dream, alive, well, and absolutely valid" (Bawer 14).

Peter Biskind has argued that, by tapping into and fostering the public's desire for optimism, heroism, and patriotism, the blockbuster films of the Reagan era, epitomized in the work of George Lucas and Steven Spielberg, "made the world safe for Reagan" (148). Or perhaps Reagan's election made the world safe for Lucas and Spielberg. As the New Right and the already-campaigning Reagan offered a politics of return to a receptive public, these directors offered audiences a return to the generic and ideological past and provided them with, in the words of Andrew Gordon, "a myth for our time." This myth played right into Reagan's politics. To a world where "the heroes [had] been cast down through such national catastrophes as Vietnam and Watergate" and in which "we desperately need[ed] a renewal of faith in ourselves as Americans, as the good guys on the world scene," Lucas and Spielberg offered conversion to the cynics of the 1960s and 1970s and faith to their children: "'I believe. I believe,' wrote a reviewer for the *Los Angeles Herald Tribune*, may be the only proper response to *Star Wars*. 'I believe in Tinkerbell and flying nuns, prissy robots and talking lions, munchkins and King Arthur's court'" (qtd. in Kramer; Gordon 324–325).

The film also encourages, however, another far more historically and nationally potent belief: American exceptionalism. This founding American myth originated with Puritan divines for whom the New World was destined by God to be the New Israel, a chosen nation meant ultimately to usher in the final, millennial chapter of divinely ordained history. As Sacvan Bercovitch observes, the Puritans believed themselves to be

> ... not only spiritual Israelites.... They were also, uniquely, American Israelites, the sole reliable exegetes of a new, last book of scripture. Since they had migrated to another "holy land," as Thomas Tillam hymned upon his first sight of Massachusetts—"the *Antitype* of what the Lord's people had of old...." [T]hey were a "second, more glorious Israel" ... [and] they inhabited the earth's millennial fourth quarter "to which that blessed promise truly's given" [113].

At the beginning of the Reagan era, the therapeutic revival of an American millennial faith—embodied in Ronald Reagan's own approving use of John Winthrop's famous description of the American "City on a Hill" serving as a beacon of righteousness and enlightenment to the world—sought to reinvigorate myths of national promise and privileged destiny for a post–Vietnam audience.

Steven Spielberg's 1977 *Close Encounters of the Third Kind* is a classic example *avant la lettre* of Reaganite entertainment's redemption of the historical past through a reinscription of America's divine destiny. As such, it marks the mid–1970s as a period of renewed interest in American millennialism. *Close Encounters* aims at delivering to its audience, in the year following the 1976 Bicentennial Celebration, a fourth of July designed to counter decisively the malaise of so significant a national birthday coming after the various traumas of the Vietnam/Nixon era. The therapeutic genius of the film lies in its use of science fiction to revive in a troubled time our oldest and most cherished religio-political myth: that of an American millennial destiny. Spielberg's narrative of election and apocalyptic revelation in which ordinary Americans like the protagonist Roy Neary are called by the benign aliens to their apocalyptic disclosure in Wyoming is replete with miraculous events produced by an advanced technology, yet suggestive of New Testament narrative and imagery. When, for example, Neary is converted to a belief in UFO's and enrolled among the elect invited to the glorious alien landing, he is blinded by a light as he sits in the road, reading a map, quite literally trying to find his way. We are invited in this sequence to recall Paul's blinding conversion experience on the road to Damascus in which he finds the way to Christian faith. The other characters called to the wonderful event in the heart of America reinforce the film's emphasis on conversion and election. Neary's friend Jillian and the others who travel to Wyoming are the beneficiaries of an experience with a UFO inviting them to the miraculous, revelatory landing. In proper biblical fashion, though, not all called are chosen. Neary and Jillian are the only pilgrims to achieve the goal. Some are persuaded by the government cover story to abandon the quest, and the other person who attempts the arduous climb of Devil's Tower succumbs to the sleeping agent sprayed by the army, an event recalling Paul's injunction in First Thessalonians 5.6 that those expecting salvation at the advent of the *parousia* must remain "awake."

Most dramatically, *Close Encounter*'s extended final sequence provides its audience and its awed pilgrims with a powerful apocalypse (which means, of course, a dramatic unveiling, a revelation) equally informed by traditional Christian imagery. We have, as elements in the enthusiastically awaited arrival of the god-like aliens, a symbolic "resurrection of the dead" in which persons previously taken by the aliens return, un-aged, to the earth. We have, as well, a version of St. Paul's promise in First Thessalonians 4.16 that the redeemed will "meet the Lord in the air" (a text that inspired in the 19th century the currently influential evangelical doctrine of the rapture), when, in the film's final image, Neary and the other Americans chosen to join the aliens, rise in the light-haloed mothership. Both the location of this apocalypse — Devil's Tower, America's first National Monument — and its cinematic unfolding — an extraordinary aerial light show that unfolds before an awe-struck audience gazing skyward — invite us to read the arrival of the mothership as a hyper-glorious Fourth of July celebration, a spectacular insistence upon the promise of American destiny.

If in *Close Encounters of the Third Kind,* Spielberg pre-figures a classic Reaganite renovation of our founding myth, George Lucas, Spielberg's friend and sometime collaborator, details in the Star Wars cycle a nearly fatal divergence from the course of millennial progress. At the same time, the cycle validates a "new hope" that is in fact a perennial hope in American spiritual and political promise as revealed in privileged historical eras, notably those of the Second World War and the 1960s. For Lucas the promise of America must always compete with the ultimately anti-democratic threats of greed, untrammeled ambition, and the excessive exercise of political, especially executive, power. If, the films suggest, the United States exemplified in World War II a commitment to fight on the behalf of democracy and human freedom, the Vietnam era posed a threat at home to precisely those values.

That attack is embodied in Darth Vader and the corrupt, power hungry Chancellor/Emperor Palpatine, who subvert the Republic and wage a murderous, highly technologized war against the Rebel Alliance, and are agents of error who decisively abandon the righteous path of democracy. Lucas, as we previously observed, based Palpatine on Richard Nixon, whose disastrous second term came to an abrupt end just four years prior to the release of *A New Hope*. The Vietnam War era, under both Lyndon Johnson and Richard Nixon, was a period in which what many viewed as the excessive use of executive power, especially in the prosecution and escalation of a war that was never officially declared by Congress, had become an issue of intense national debate. In 1973, Arthur Schlesinger, Jr.'s significantly titled book, *The Imperial Presidency,* a study of the threat of excessive presidential power in American history, included a chapter entitled, "The Presidency Rampant: Vietnam." Clearly, while the Watergate Scandal reflected a level of presidential corruption and threat to constitutional democracy egregious enough to inspire the Nixon/Palpatine parallel, the warfare waged against the Alliance by the Empire in the Star Wars films, and especially in the earliest, points toward the rampancy of the Nixon Administration's handling of the Vietnam conflict.

In *A New Hope*, the narrative focus on the need to destroy the lethal, planet-destroying Death Star suggests in historical context the widely condemned decision by Richard Nixon and Henry Kissinger to bomb transportation routes such as the "Ho Chi Minh Trail" and North Vietnamese Army command posts located across the Vietnamese border in neutral Cambodia. The carpet bombing of Cambodian targets began, without congressional consent, or even congressional knowledge, in February 1969, and would continue for fourteen months. Carpet bombing, the dropping of hundreds of bombs in a small area, was one of the most devastatingly destructive strategies in the American arsenal short of the use of nuclear weapons. The Nixon White House authorized over 3500 of these secret raids, resulting in an estimated 600,000 deaths. In the opening shots of the most dramatic sequence of *A New Hope*, the battle to destroy the Death Star before it can annihilate Yavin 4, and with it the Rebel base located there, there are several images of significant interest in this context. The most important is an establishing shot featuring a dense tropical forest out of which emerge the tips of two ancient temples. One of these is the Massassi Temple, used as a base of operations by the Alliance. Although the actual location for the temple shots is a Mayan ruin in Guatemala, the image of jungle and temples threatened by the destructive power of the Death Star — appearing only four years after the eventual secession of bombing in 1973 — powerfully suggests the Cambodian landscape ravaged by American B-52s. Indeed, in the combat sequence culminating in the destruction of the Death Star by Luke's Force-directed placing of a missile, *A New Hope* creates a visual spectacle pitting a mode of combat suggestive of Nixon's Cambodian campaign against one recalling the aerial combat of a far less morally and politically problematic war. Lucas, in storyboarding the attack of the Alliance fighters upon the Death Star, famously made use of air combat sequences from World War II movies. The film thus opposes — in a dramatic clash of references — the heroism of World War II as a struggle for the preservation of democracy against fascist aggression with the markedly condemnatory allusion to the Nixon Imperial Presidency's secret, massively destructive bombing of Cambodia borne by the Death Star.

This cinematic and ethical valorization of World War II encouraged critics to misread the trilogy as the founding example of Reaganite entertainment: a chronicle of the restoration of heroes and national authority that hinges on the Return of the Father, epitomized by Reagan himself, whom Gary Wills describes as "the rehabilitated parent par excellence" (qtd. in Kolker 237). However, to read Star Wars as a tale about the return of the fathers both misses the specificity of its historical context and requires us to read against the text. The fathers, Darth Vader and the Emperor — associated with Nixon, Vietnam, and Watergate — are hopelessly tainted, gone over to the Dark Side. The "grandfathers," Obi-Wan and Yoda, have wisdom, values, and purity to redeem the American vision for the rising generation.[4] By returning to the World War II generation, the original trilogy pits what Robert Bly calls "a poisoned patriarchy" against a benevolent one and exhorts its audience to "trust Grandfather" even if it cannot "trust Father." Furthermore, in this trilogy, Grandfather and his values have been re-envisioned through the mirror of the 1960s, and World War II heroes have become counter-culture Asian monks.

The original Star Wars trilogy's deep roots in its particular cultural moment shape its narrative. While the Rebel Alliance certainly echoes America's own birth in rebellion against authority, the Evil Empire in Star Wars is not foreign but domestic — the galaxy's initially democratic values have been sabotaged by the Rebel's own corrupted fathers. In order for the rebellion to be successful that past must be overcome — Luke must prove that he does not, as Uncle Owen worries, "have too much of his father" in him. This means a rejection of impatience, anger, and the temptation to grab at power, even in the service of an admirable cause. The attitudes and values that led to the political abuses of the Vietnam era must be avoided; future heroes must learn to embrace appropriate spiritual ideals through belief in the Force and place duty to friendship and community above all else. On the one hand, they must return to the forgotten values of World War II America and their culmination in the fifties' consensus of the center; on the other, they must also integrate the willingness to resist corrupt authority and rehabilitate abandoned spiritual beliefs. Thus, *Star Wars* advocates not, as is the traditional read on the film, a return to the Father, but a return to the Grandfather.[5] In *Star Wars*, grandfathers are the good guys; Obi-Wan is not Vader's contemporary — he was his mentor, not his peer. The script constantly emphasizes the Jedi's age; he is "a crazy old hermit" who has not heard his own name "for many years." White-haired and white-bearded, he is the last of the generation that battled to protect freedom and democracy. He must pass on his wisdom and values to Luke's "fatherless" generation if there is to be any hope for the future. The fact that grandfathers, not fathers, are the proper mentors for the rising generation is emphasized in the personnel of the Rebel Alliance and the Empire. In the Alliance, anyone over the age of thirty is also over the age of sixty. The empire is run by men in their forties and fifties.

Who, the trilogy asks, will the younger generation become? Will they listen to the Grandfathers and restore freedom to the galaxy, or will they become like their Fathers, self-serving and cynical, blinded and corrupted by power? The fate — and hope — of the galaxy lies in the answer to this question. If the Rebels are to succeed, they must persuade individuals to join the fight. The trilogy calls for a return to an earlier time; in this call it owes, as Lucas himself observed, a great debt to the films of Walt Disney, himself the great disseminator of America's post World War II vision of itself: one local boy, one evil parent, one mentor, two cute side-kicks, and wit, faith, optimism, and ingenuity winning the day in a world in which local boys and fledgling rebellions depend on each other and the triumph of the individual makes the triumph of the community possible. Luke is introduced as a classic Disney character. Hemmed into a humdrum future as a farm hand on the planet farthest "from the bright center of the universe," the boy in simple homespun clothes is a dreamer looking for the destiny he does not know he has. Seeming accident — the arrival of the robots, the malfunction of the R2 unit his uncle originally buys, the triggering of Leia's holographic message, Ben Kenobi's timely stroll through the desert — brings him to that destiny. In Ben's cave it becomes clear that Luke is "the Prince," as Leo Braudy has observed, "in disguise" (221). He learns that his father was a knight, a member of the Jedi order, and he receives his father's sword of power. Obi-Wan calls Luke to accept that sword and with it the responsibility to be a guardian of freedom and justice: "You must learn the ways of the Force. I need your help. She needs your help." Luke, however, resists this call: "I can't get involved. I've got work to do. It's not that I like the Empire. It's just that there's nothing I can do about it. It's so far away." However, the Empire is not far away; it's on Luke's doorstep, as he discovers when he goes home to find his aunt and uncle slaughtered. Their death spurs Luke to political action. "I want to come with you," he tells Obi-Wan, "I want to learn the ways of the Force and become a Jedi like my father."

Luke's desire to be "like [his] father," encapsulates the trilogy's central anxiety: will he listen to Obi-Wan and become a Jedi dedicated to justice or will he become a Jedi wed to power, like Darth Vader? Who will claim him as subject? What all the "grandfathers" in Star Wars fear is that it is already too late; that there is no younger generation capable of taking up the guardianship of galactic freedom and justice, that there is already too much of the bad Father in them. When Luke comes to the attention of Vader and the Emperor in the second film, the battle for his subjectivity begins: "If," the Emperor opines, "he could be turned, he would become a great ally." "He will join us or die," Vader answers.

The rest of the narrative of *The Empire Strikes Back* centers around the battle for Luke. Vader and the Emperor need Luke, because as a member of the Rebel Alliance, Luke's power constitutes a threat to their own authority. Yoda, the Jedi, and the Alliance also need Luke because he is their "last hope" (but one) of restoration. Keeping his promise to Obi-Wan to train as a Jedi, Luke travels to the Degoba system where he returns to his primordial roots in Yoda's pre-political swamp, to his true origins in a neutral world where he must confront both Light and Dark, Jedi knight and Vader. In many ways this visit is not a success; Luke fails to see past his pre-conceptions and recognize the Jedi master; in spite of his success in the physical part of his military training, he fails the test of belief. Unable to use his mind-powers to raise his ship from the swamp, he hotly declares, "I can't do it; it's impossible." When Yoda accomplishes the task with ease, Luke blurts, "I don't believe it!" "I know, Yoda replies, "that is why you failed." As Luke ignores Yoda's advice and leaves without completing his training, it seems as though Yoda's initial observation, "I cannot teach him. Boy has no patience. Much anger in him like his father," may indeed be correct. Luke still needs to "unlearn what [he] has learned" and substitute the patience and faith of the ancestors for the anger and self-interest of the fathers.

While Yoda offers Luke a selfless world of faith and duty, Vader offers him power. With Vader, they can "end this conflict and bring order to the galaxy" and "rule ... as father and son." "It," he promises, "is the only way." According to Vader, the younger generation's destiny is the one that Yoda fears: to become like their fathers — addicted to power and consumed by hatred. Luke, however, rejects Vader's definition of his future and chooses death over corruption. This act of self-sacrifice allows Luke to become a true Jedi and all but assures the victory of the alliance. When we next see Luke in the opening sequences of *The Return of the Jedi,* he is a mysterious cloaked figure, entering Jabba's corrupt world on a beam of light, in full possession of the quiet power that Obi-Wan once possessed. Throughout all of Jabba's ingenious tortures and plots, Luke never shows emotion — neither anger nor fear; he is clearly in control and triumphs with ease. The Emperor and Vader, contemplating the new Jedi conclude, "he has grown strong. It will take both of us to turn him now." And the dying Yoda, although the threat of the Dark Side still looms, passes the torch of the order to Luke: "Last of the Jedi you will be. Show what you have learned."

In the final sequences of the trilogy, Luke, indeed, shows what he has learned, comes into his full heritage, and achieves an end that even Obi-Wan and Yoda thought was unachievable: he redeems his father. By refusing to accept the Emperor's definition of his destiny ("take your father's place at my side") and refusing to misuse his power even in the service of his friends, Luke again chooses death before dishonor. In his dying agony, he turns to his father for aid, an act which shows that he still refuses to believe that "the good man who was once Anakin Skywalker is dead." Vader saves Luke, kills the Emperor, and both Anakin and, presumably, the Republic are reborn. The trilogy ends with a final vision of continuity and celebration: the Fathers — in an unbroken line from Yoda to Anakin — beam upon the worthy son as, in what Wood calls "a veritable Fourth of July of fathericity," fireworks — not fighters — light up the night sky (174). The past is not so much forgotten as it is redeemed and rehabilitated.

In spite of Lucas's own sense of himself as a 1960s liberal, *Star Wars'* new myth elevated national mythology to galactic status, echoing the move to the right and the revival of the populist consensus of the center at the heart of the Reagan Revolution.[6] Lucas's longing for the positive morality of his youth, as figured in the old genres, brought with it old values, values at the heart of Star Wars' reconstruction of heroes. Luke's becoming of a Jedi Knight reinstates American values and ideals traditionally associated with World War II, values that Reagan appropriated for the New Right. On the surface, his adventures seemed to call the audience also to accept those values and to believe — believe in submission to authority, in militarism as an effective instrument of positive change, and in the restoration of America as a way of ushering in a better and freer world, ruled by proto–American freedom fighters, in which the happy colonialism of the Ewoks replaces the decadent Orientalism of Mos Eisley and Jabba the Hutt.[7]

Such a response to the trilogy, however, results from a misalignment of "The Force"— the proper and skillful use of which leads to the eventual triumph of Luke and the other rebels over the imperial evil and for whom Vader is the most effective agent — with American Christian patriarchy. But the films never define the Force in such a way (or indeed in any detailed fashion), and the Force is a concept whose meaning should be approached not through traditional American values and ideals but through the clues provided by the Asian references running throughout the six episodes of the Star Wars cycle, references much more in tune with Lucas's own 1960s-inflected imagination than with the perspective of the Reaganite Christian Right. First, there is Obi-Wan Kenobe's obviously Japanesque name, creating an Asian resonance enhanced by his Zen monk-like robes, his use of the light saber, which recalls the samurai *katana*, and of course his membership in the order of Jedi knights. The term *Jedi*, is widely recognized to derive from *Jedai Geki*, the Japanese term for the film and television genre of historical romance typically involving samurai culture. Furthermore, Luke's (albeit incomplete) training by Yoda, the diminutive Jedi master dressed like Kenobe in monk-like attire, has its most obvious popular culture antecedent in the training of Kane, hero of the 1970s television series *Kung Fu*, by an ancient and benevolent master in the Shaolin Temple. There is also the proper name of Queen Amidala of Naboo: *Padme*, derived from the Tibetan Buddhist chant *Om Mani Padme Hum* ("the jewel is in the lotus"). These visual and aural references to Asian culture frame the saga's core Asian philosophies, which unfold in the protagonists' training in the Jedi arts, the core of which is of special significance in that it defines the proper attitude of a Jedi as a detached mode of action in which, ideally, the Force acts through the Jedi, an understanding of action suggestive of the Chinese Tao or Hindu Brahma as explained in *The Bhagavad Gita*.[8]

Indeed, the lessons provided by Krishna to the warrior Arjuna in the *Gita* are in several details strongly suggestive of the instruction received by both Anakin and Luke Skywalker in the course of their apprenticeships with Kenobe and Yoda. During his training on Degoba, as we have seen, Luke exasperates Yoda with his anger, which Yoda declared to be like that of his father, and he warns Luke that anger and aggression lead to the Dark Side. When in *Revenge of the Sith*, Anakin, plagued by presentiments of Padme's death, seeks the counsel of Yoda, explaining that he foresees "pain, suffering, death" for someone close to him, Yoda reminds him that "the fear of loss is the path to the Dark Side," and continues: "Attachment leads to jealousy; the shadow of greed that is.... Train yourself to let go of everything you fear to lose."

Yoda's advice in each instance as to the proper perspective of a Jedi Knight is remarkably similar to that given by Lord Krishna to Arjuna concerning the wisdom required of a warrior who properly understands the yoga of action. Note for example the following passages from *Bhagavad Gita*:

> He whose mind is untroubled by
> any misfortune, whose craving
> for pleasures has disappeared,
> who is free from greed, fear, anger,
>
> who is unattached to all things,
> who neither grieves or rejoices
> if good or bad things happen —
> that man is a man of firm wisdom....
>
> If a man keeps dwelling on sense-objects
> attachment to them arises;
> from attachment, desire flares up;
> from desire, anger is born [2.56–57, 62].

In the end, Luke internalizes Yoda/Krishna's lessons, rejecting greed, fear, anger, attachment and desire — his father's errors — and this rejection allows him to restore both father and democracy.

This emphatic approval of Asian mysticism in the Star Wars cycle suggests that Lucas's vision of a return to American redemptive promise derives from what is perhaps an initially curious blending of two historical periods. First, as we have seen, there is the celebration through the figure of Obi-Wan Kenobe of the generation who fought the good war on the side of democracy and freedom. Kenobe, the "grandfather" is contrasted to the "fathers," the functionaries of empire such as Darth Vader and the Emperor, whose misuse of executive power leads to the violent and anti-democratic Empire. These imperial executives, the film implies, subvert the promise of the Republic as the Nixon presidency subverted the American promise represented in the

World War II defeat of fascism. If the fear registered in the three initial films of the cycle is that Luke will follow the trajectory of his father, it is the pull of this anti-democratic militarized misuse of power, fueled by greed, attachment and anger that Luke must overcome. The approval throughout the films of a Buddhist/Hindu–inflected mode of spirituality, added to the need to resist the blandishments of the Dark Side as represented by Darth Vader, clearly marks a second period of American history as offering an alternative to the corrupt values of the Empire. Just as Luke will ultimately resist his father's path and embrace the mystical values and techniques of the Jedi Order, so the 1960s countercultural resistance to the Vietnam War often encouraged a renewed interest in what Aldous Huxley termed the "Perennial Philosophy," the supposed mystical core of all major religions largely undervalued in contemporary religious practice, especially in the Christian West. In the popular works of Huxley, Alan Watts, D.T. Suzuki, and the Beat Poets like Gary Snyder, Jack Kerouac, and especially Allen Ginsberg — the charismatic advocate of eastern religion and highly visible anti-war protestor — many young Americans found a spiritual discourse offering an alternative to what was often condemned as a comfortable middle-class Christianity too deeply embedded in "the establishment" to inspire or promote the aims of the anti-war counterculture.

That Darth Vader has been trained as a Jedi and has turned away from the path to embrace the Dark Side suggests that what the Jedi represent has always been a potent aspect of the Republic, one suppressed by the Empire but ultimately resurgent and victorious in the narrative order of the cycle. At the films' parabolic level, the implication is both the World War II era and the 1960s represent a perennial aspect of the American political and spiritual enterprise, one that if constantly threatened, is constantly renewable. If following the Allied victory in World War II, the United States emerged as the dominant world power, the following decades would bring about what the Star Wars cycle depicts as a moral and political decline. We are encouraged by the films' depiction of the Empire as an immense military/technological juggernaut to recall Dwight Eisenhower's warning against the rise of a "military/industrial complex," and, in Chancellor Palpatine's fear-mongering manipulation of relations between the Trade Alliance and the Republic, we are given a figure in whom is compressed decades of Cold War American politicians specializing in the exploitation of fear and paranoia. Yet, the films imply, if the moral heroism of World War II, the democratic virtues of the Republic, have been threatened in subsequent history, they remain available for articulation during the darkest hours of both the galactic Republic and the United States that Republic adumbrates.

Jedi values of selflessness and detached service, the opposition to greed, anger, and ambition, are imagined in the form of a 1960s Asian-inflected spirituality, but the films' continued reference not only to the United States, but to what was in many ways its model republic, Rome, suggests that Lucas's cycle is concerned with both the virtues of and dangers to all republics. Rome, of course lost the battle; the Roman republic, destroyed by men of immense political ambition and military resources, became irredeemably the Empire. Yet it was the virtues of the Roman Republic that inspired the founders of the United States. Robert Bellah, quoting Joseph Warren's 1772 commemoration of the Boston Massacre, reminds us how importantly both Rome's republican virtue and moral decline into empire animated American revolutionary thought: "It was *this* noble attachment to a free constitution, which raised Rome from the smallest beginnings to that bright summit of happiness and glory to which she arrived; and it was the loss of *this* which plunged her from *that* summit into the black gulph of infamy and slavery" (22; author's italics). If, like the Force, all republics contain a Dark Side empowered by greed and ambition, again like the Force, they also contain and inspire a countervailing aspect marked by selfless civic virtue and willing sacrifice.

Thus, the Asian spirituality adopted by the cycle to characterize the resistors of imperial force and corruption is, Lucas suggests, in its most important aspects, powerfully conducive of the virtues and ideals necessary to the creation and sustaining of a viable republic. If Steven Spielberg's therapeutic vision in the post–Vietnam era involved the re-inscription through science fiction of the Puritan founding myth and its millennial aspirations and promise, George Lucas offers a millennialism more suggestive of what Nathan O. Hatch has termed "Civil Millennialism," initially a product of the American Revolutionary era. As Hatch explains, this new version of American Millennialism interpreted the revolutionary struggle against Britain as inaugurating an American-inspired era of rapidly achieved historical progress promoting human liberty and democracy through the defeat of Old World tyranny and repression: "The Revolutionary millennialist ... based his apocalyptic hopes upon the civil and religious liberty that American victory over Britain would insure. His vision of the future inspired him to attempt to thwart the precipitous advance of power... (87)." It as this struggle against unjust power that defined America as the vanguard of millennial progress and enlightenment: "The spontaneous defense of liberty in America encouraged [civil millennialists] to interpret existing American society as the model upon which the millennial kingdom would be based (87)."

If in 1983 Lucas was able to offer his audiences this optimistic vision of American millennial promise, by the 2002 release of the *Attack of the Clones*, he had moved beyond such optimism. Richard Corliss and Jess Cagle report in a pre-release interview: "Lucas' own geopolitics can sound pretty bleak: 'All democracies turn into dictatorships — but not by coup. The people give their democracy to a dictator, whether it's Julius Caesar or Napoleon or Adolf Hitler. Ultimately, the general population goes along with the idea.... What kinds of things push people and institutions into this direction?'" While the original trilogy offered its audiences a therapeutic narrative of the defeat of the Dark Side and its imperial presidency, of the move from dictatorship to democracy, and the restoration of a proper political paternity, rooted in the recurring virtues of an Asian-inflected Roman/American Republic, the second trilogy — the last two films of which were released to a post–9/11 nation — tell the opposite tale. In 2005, history had proved to be not progressive but regressive and the intervention of history darkens the political and emotional affect of Lucas's saga — in spite of the films' narrative trajectory. In this second trilogy, Lucas interrogates political regression, urgently asking "what kinds of things push people and institutions" from democracy to dictatorship. Of course, this second trilogy, given its subject matter — the simultaneous fall of Anakin and the Republic — was always destined to be darker than the first. But, had history not intervened — had the millennial promise of an America guided by Jedi-like tenets seemed more obtainable — the saga's narrative order might not have been so unconvincing. However, given both *Attack of the Clones* and *The Revenge of the Sith*'s pointed references to contemporary America, it is impossible to take that narrative order seriously and the chronicle of Anakin and the Republic, like the original trilogy, becomes (with dismaying accuracy) "a myth for our time."

While 1999's *The Phantom Menace* does not directly participate in the political discourse of the final two films, it reflects Lucas's growing pessimism as it calls into doubt the entire idea of millennial promise — of reliance on the "chosen one." Qui Gon is misguided by the prophecy of one who is destined to "bring balance to the Force" and convinced that he has found his messiah in Anakin, a child for whom "there was no (human) father," with whom "the Force is especially strong," and about whom he concludes, "it's possible he was conceived by the mitochlorians ("microscopic life forms ... [that] talk to us, tell us the will of the Force)." But, what Qui Gon forgets in his desire for the Chosen One, is that the Force has two sides — the light and the Dark — and, even if Anakin was conceived by the Force, his paternity is in doubt. Whose Chosen One is he and what kind of balance will he bring? Will he become Jedi Master — child of Obi-Wan, Yoda and the Council — or Sith Lord, child of Palpatine? (As Palpatine suggests, Anakin may well have been conceived through manipulations of Darth Plagis, a notorious Sith lord.)

Yoda, always the wisest of the Jedi, foresees the danger, sensing in young Anakin the attachments that will ultimately corrupt him. "Your thoughts dwell on your Mother," Yoda observes, "Afraid to lose her. Fear is the path to the Dark Side ... anger, hate, and suffering." "Clouded," Yoda concludes, "This boy's future is." Qui Gon, however, refuses to heed Yoda, insisting with his dying breath that Anakin is indeed the Chosen One and extracting a promise from Obi-Wan that he will train the boy. The film ends — in spite of the requisite "Victory" tableaux — in ambiguity, as Yoda darkly predicts, "the Chosen One the boy may be. Nevertheless grave danger I fear in his training" and Palpatine (played by Ian McDiarmid and, therefore, immediately recognizable to all fans of the original trilogy as the Emperor), remarks "Young Skywalker. We will watch your career with great interest."

Just as the sequence from *A New Hope* to *The Return of the Jedi* chronicled Luke's quest for proper paternity in the choice between Jedi Knight and the Dark Side, this second sequence tells the tale of a son's search for the proper ideological father. And, as does Luke's quest, this search turns on Anakin's ability — or lack thereof — to practice the detachment required by Yoda and the Jedi. As Lucas comments, "He turns into Darth Vader because he gets attached to things.... He can't let go of his mother; he can't let go of his girlfriend. He can't let go of things. It makes you greedy. And when you're greedy, you are on the path to the dark side, because you fear you're going to lose things, that you're not going to have the power you need." It is this combination of attachment, fear, greed, and the ensuing desire for power that leads Anakin to turn from Obi-Wan, his "proper" father and mentor and become prey to the manipulation of Palpatine, a figure totally devoted to attachment of the most grievous sort. His journey begins as *Clones* opens, when, in spite of the fact that Anakin recognizes that Obi-Wan is "the closest thing I have to a Father," he chafes against both the restrictions Obi-Wan places on his power and the Jedi's prohibitions of attachment and possessions. Ignoring this prohibition, Anakin actively pursues a relationship with Padme and, when he senses his mother's plight, leaves for Tatooine, in direct dereliction of Jedi orders and duty. The results, for Anakin, are disastrous; his failure to save his mother unleashes a killing rage that sets him on the path to the Dark Side. When Padme tries to sooth him, "You're not all powerful," he retorts, "Well, I should be. Some day I will be. It's all Obi-Wan's fault. He's jealous. He's holding me back."

Anakin's secret marriage to Padme (ominously cross-cut with the Riefenstahl-inspired massing of the Clone army) and her pregnancy lead Anakin further down the path of attachment. His recurring dreams of Padme's death in childbirth exacerbate his fear, a fear of loss, which, Yoda reminds him, "is a path to the Dark Side." Anakin, however, cannot follow Yoda's advice; because of his attachment to Padme, he cannot accept the Jedi as his true ideological fathers; Palpatine, in his colloquy with Anakin in the Senate Chambers, offers his version of "wisdom." It is, he claims, no different from selfish power, and tempts Anakin toward the Dark Side by mentioning the power to keep those one loves from death. Palpatine thus manipulates Anakin, suggesting that attachment is a source of strength and that true power resides in the ability to protect oneself from all loss. When Palpatine offers him another way, a knowledge that can keep "the ones he cares about from dying," a power that cannot be learned "from a Jedi," Anakin snatches at it. "I want more," he tells Padme, "and I know I shouldn't. I found a way to save you from my nightmares."

Once Palpatine has convinced Anakin that Sith knowledge includes the power to defeat death, Anakin falls essentially under his influence, and will presently kill Mace Windu to save Palpatine's life — and thus his own access to the power Palpatine offers — and carry out the order to massacre the Jedi younglings. In this act, Anakin betrays the Jedi and his own immense positive potential, but more importantly, he acts to destroy the continuity represented by the Jedi in the history of the Republic. This attempt to eliminate the continuity of Jedi virtue and enlightenment seeks to prevent precisely what his own son, Luke, will come to represent in his ultimate defeat of his own anger and ambition, his turning from the path of his father and immersion in Jedi virtue and power. Luke, connecting with the virtuous past as represented by Obi-Wan will — in the narrative order of the films — reestablish the continuity Anakin/Vader hopes utterly to destroy.

In the historical order of the films, however, Anakin's choice of Palpatine as Father and subsequent turn to the Dark Side parallels the Republic's choice of Palpatine as political Father and Emperor so closely as to suggest that the fall of Anakin and the fall of the Republic stem from the same attachments, fears, and desire for power. In the context of George W. Bush's return to the politics of the imperial presidency, it also suggests a reconnection with a darker past, a continuity from Sith Lord to Sith Lord (or imperial president to imperial president). Not unlike the Bush administration, Palpatine preys upon fear and instability. He works behind the scenes, inventing threats to galactic security, stirring up war, and consolidating his power, invoking the very desires that, in the first trilogy, allowed the narrative to be hijacked by Reagan and the New Right: for benevolent patriarchy and exuberant militarism. In *The Phantom Menace,* Palpatine criticizes a moribund senate: "The Republic is not what it once was ... [the] bureaucrats are in charge now" and encourages Padme to "Push for the election of a stronger supreme

Chancellor." Padme follows his advice and Palpatine is duly elected Chancellor; the film ends with a triumphal procession and Palpatine's assurance that "together we shall bring peace and justice to the Republic." The *Attack of the Clones*—released the same year that *The Nation* published an editorial commentary on Bush's pre–Iraq policies entitled "The Imperial Presidency"—critiques this desire for the return of the patriarch, arguing that the appearance of benevolence merely masks ambitious tyranny.[9] *Clones*' opening crawl informs the viewer that "there is unrest in the Republic," an unrest that leads to the desire for strong leadership, someone to work things out. That this desire should be most explicitly expressed by Anakin, who complains that the democratic system does not work and muses that "someone wise" should decide "what's in the best interest of the people," signals the dangers of patriarchal desire, dangers that history has proved to be ever-present. The wise father might prove to be not Obi-Wan but Reagan — or Bush. He might evoke threats and unrest — he might even create them — in order to garner additional powers, all the while assuring the senate, as does Palpatine, that such powers are necessary "in response to a direct threat to the Republic" and that "the powers you give me I will lay down when the crisis has abated."

In addition to interrogating the first trilogy's seeming valorization of patriarchal desire, *Clones* casts doubt on the military exuberance invoked in that trilogy. When, near the end of the film, Yoda arrives leading the Clone army — just in time to save the vastly outnumbered Jedi — the initial effect is just such exuberance: Palpatine's "Grand Army of the Republic" seems to be a good thing, assuring peace and safety, but by the end of the film it is clear that the Sith lord has manipulated the whole scenario — "lies, deceit, and creating mistrust are his way"— that the appeal to militarism masks a grab for power. "Good news for you, my Lord," Count Dooku announces, "War has begun." As Mace Windu declares victory, Yoda corrects him, "Victory, you say. Not victory. The shroud of the Dark Side has fallen. Begun the Clone War has." The camera pans from Yoda to the marching Clone troops viewed, in a shot borrowed from Riefenstahl, from a balcony by the Chancellor and his advisors. If, in *A New Hope*, footage from *The Triumph of the Will* is quoted for a celebration of militarism, in *Attack of the Clones* similar footage functions darkly, an ominous portent of things to come.

By 2005 and *The Revenge of the Sith*, Lucas's fable of a political system giving into the Dark Side has become more pointed, as have his references to contemporary America. Beset by Separatists hiding on distant planets, the senate is determined to continue the war as long as the separatist/terrorist leader General Grievous is alive, even if such a war requires the steady erosion of the principals of democracy as it votes "more executive power to the Chancellor" in search of "less deliberation, more action." Finally, declaring even the Jedi enemies of the State, Chancellor Palpatine creates his imperial presidency. Calling on the rhetoric of fear, he announces "to ensure security and continuing stability, the Republic has been reorganized into the first Galactic Empire, for a safe and secure society." Palpatine's appeals to fear and his assurance that the erosion of liberty is necessary for security cannot help but call to mind debates about the Patriot Act and other extensions of executive power in response to "the terrorist threat;" Padme's contemptuous commentary, "so this is how liberty dies, to thunderous applause," applies equally to the narrative of the film and that of post 9/11 America. And when Darth Vader, paraphrasing George W. Bush, informs Obi-Wan "if you're not with me, you're my enemy," and Obi-Wan responds, "only a Sith deals in absolutes," the film makes explicit its vision of a nation turned to the Dark Side.

Even though *Revenge of the Sith* ends with baby Luke in the arms of Owen and Beru, setting the stage for a return to the "new hope" of the original trilogy, historical and political reality has made such a return impossible. The years between 1983 and 2005 did not fulfill — or even reach towards — the millennial promise of a redeemed American democracy, one that practiced the Jedi tenets of detachment and compassion, using its powers solely to serve as the guardian of peace and justice. Instead, those years, in Lucas's fable, had resulted in a culture of fear fueled by an attachment to power and privilege; Nixon may be gone, but a new "imperial president" sits in the White House, with Dick "Darth Vader" Cheney at his side (a Google search for George Bush/imperial presidency produces 1,210,000 results, one for Dick Cheney/Darth Vader, 163,000). For Lucas, anyway, contemporary America's political paternity is quite clear; the fears of the original trilogy have been realized; we do, indeed, have too much of our Father in us.

Notes

1. Lucas has, on several occasions, indicated that Nixon was his inspiration for the Emperor.
2. [Editor's note: *Star Wars* (George Lucas, 1977) was the original title for the first film in the trilogy. The addition of the prequel trilogy necessitated a repackaging of all the films in the series with an eye to boxed-set sales: *Star Wars* was given a new title that designates its place in the sequencing: *Star Wars: Episode IV — A New Hope*. The new order is as follows: *Star Wars: Episode I — Phantom Menace* (1999), *Star Wars: Episode II — Attack of the Clones* (2002), *Star Wars: Episode III — Revenge of the Sith* (2005), *Star Wars: Episode

IV—A New Hope (1977), *Star Wars: Episode V—The Empire Strikes Back* (1980), and *Star Wars: Episode VI—Return of the Jedi* (1983). George Lucas directed all the films in the series. References to *Star Wars* (italicized) indicate the 1977 film, also referred to as *A New Hope*; references to Star Wars (unitalicized) indicates either one of the trilogies according to the context or the series in general.]

   3. Star Wars has been the subject of numerous critical analyses all of which recognize the films' appeal to nostalgia through its presentation of what Robert Collins, has called "a past future" ("Pastiche"). Early critics focused on Star Wars' appeal as a "positive myth," put together out of bits and pieces of old genres and tales (including *Flash Gordon*, Arthurian legend, swashbucklers, Westerns, and Tolkien) and controlled by the use of the narrative structure of Joseph Campbell's monomyth (Gordon, "Myth" and "*Return of the Jedi*: The End of the Myth," *Film Criticism* 8 [1984]: 45–54; Lane Roth, "Raiders of the Lost Archetype: The Quest and the Shadow," *Studies in the Humanities* 10 [1983]: 13–21). Recently, John Lyden has argued that Lucas's controlling myth is Christian and apocalyptic ("The Apocalyptic Cosmology of *Star Wars*," *The Journal of Religion and Film* 4.1 (2000) <http://www.unomaha.edu/jrf/LydenStWars.htm>). Later critics read the film more explicitly through the lens of Reaganite entertainment, arguing that the movie enables its viewers to return to a pre-oedipal state, without responsibilities, and in which they can "trust father"—and Uncle George—to bring them safely home in the end (Wood, *Vietnam to Reagan*, Kolker, *Loneliness*). Other political approaches to the films include Anne Lancashire, *"Attack of the Clones* and the Politics of *Star Wars*"; Peter Lev, "Whose Future? *Star Wars, Alien*, and *Blade Runner*," *Literature/Film Quarterly* 26.1 (1998): 30–38; Kathleen Ellis "New World, Old Habits: Patriarchal Ideology in *Star Wars: A New Hope*" *Australian Screen Education* 31 (2003): 135–140, and John Rieder, "Embracing the Alien: Science Fiction in Mass Culture," *Science, Fiction Studies* 9.1 (1982): 26–37.

   4. We are aware, of course, that Nixon was a member of the generation that fought in World War II. Lucas employs here a generational shorthand to discriminate between the World War II and Vietnam eras, one in which the "Fathers," architects of the morally problematic Vietnam war, fail to evince the moral heroism of the "Grandfathers."

   5. The argument that Star Wars advocates a return to the father is heavily dependent on the work of Campbell and Jung. It argues that Obi-Wan and Vader represent two sides of an archetype—the light and dark father, a reading that Lucas himself has supported. However, details of the narrative, combined with casting decisions, undermine this interpretation of the relationship between the two men.

   6. As Lancashire notes, Luke and Han are "American archetypes," and the film's tale of a rebel alliance and an evil empire "worked with America's self-image as a freedom-loving nation which originally established itself by rebelling" (236–37).

   7. For a discussion of Spielberg's essential colonialism see Patricia Zimmerman, "Soldiers of Fortune: Lucas, Spielberg, Indiana Jones, and *Raiders of the Lost Ark*." *Wide Angle: A Film Quarterly of Theory, Criticism, and Practice* 6.2 (1984): 34–39; John Rieder, "Embracing the Alien: Science Fiction in Mass Culture," *Science Fiction Studies* 9.1 (1982): 26–37; and Peter Lev, "Whose Future? *Star Wars, Alien*, and *Blade Runner*," *Literature/ Film Quarterly* 26.1 (1998): 30–38.

   8. The Asian influence has been commonly recognized—see for example Kevin Wetmore, Jr: "The Tao of *Star Wars*, or, Cultural Appropriation in a Galaxy Far, Far, Away," *Studies in Popular Culture*, 23.1 (2000): 91–106. The Jedi's debt to the *Bhagavad Gita*, however, has not been previously noted.

   9. "The Imperial Presidency" *The Nation* 29 August 2002 <http://www.thenation.com/doc/20020916/editors>.

Works Cited

Bawer, Bruce. "Ronald Reagan as Indiana Jones." *Newsweek* August 27, 1984: 14.
The Bhagavad Gita. Trans. Stephen Mitchell. New York: Harmony, 2000.
Bellah, Robert. *The Broken Covenant: American Civil Religion in Time of Trial.* New York: Seabury, 1975.
Bercovitch, Sacvan. *The Puritan Origins of the American Self.* New Haven, CT: Yale University Press, 1975.
Biskind, Peter. "Blockbuster: The Last Crusade." *Seeing Through Movies.* Ed. Mark Crispin Miller. New York: Pantheon, 1990. 112–49.
Bly, Robert. *Iron John: A Book About Men.* New York: Addison-Wesley, 1990.
Braudy, Leo. "Genre and the Resurrection of the Past." *Native Informant: Essays on Film, Literature and Popular Culture.* New York: Oxford University Press, 1991: 214–24.
Collins, Robert C. "*Star Wars*: The Pastiche of Myth and the Yearning for a Past Future." *Journal of Popular Culture* XI.1 (Summer 1977): 1–10.
Corliss, Richard and Jess Cagle. "Dark Victory." *Time* 20 April 2002 <http://www.time.com/time/covers/1101020429/story.html >.
Fisher, Carrie. "The Arrival of the Jedi." *Time Magazine* 31 March 2003: 58–61.
Gordon, Andrew. "*Star Wars:* A Myth for Our Time.*" Literature/Film Quarterly* 6 (1978): 314–326.
Hatch, Nathan O. "The Origins of Civil Millennialism in America." *Reckoning with the Past: Historical Essays on American Evangelicalism from the Institute for the Study of American Evangelicals.* Ed. D.G. Hart. Grand Rapids, MI: Baker, 1995.
Kolker, Robert. *A Cinema of Loneliness.* Oxford: Oxford University Press, 1988.
Krall, Jack. *Newsweek.* 30 May 1977: 60–61.
Kramer, Peter. "'It's aimed at kids — the kid in everybody': George Lucas, *Star Wars* and Children's Entertainment," *Scope: An Online Journal of Film Studies* (December 2001) <http://www.scope.nottingham.ac.uk/article.php?-dec2001&id=278&section=article>.
Lancashire, Anne. "*Attack of the Clones* and the Politics of *Star Wars.*" *Dalhousie Review* 82.2 (2002): 235–53.
Murphy, A. D. Rev. of *Star Wars*, dir. George Lucas. *Variety* 25 May 1977. 14 March 2007 <http://www.variety.com/index.asp?layout=Variety100&reviewid=VE1117795168&content=jump&jump=review&category=1935&cs=1>.
Sklar, Robert. *Movie-Made America: A Cultural History of American Movies.* Rev. ed.. New York: Vintage, 1975, 1994.
Wood, Robin. *Hollywood: From Vietnam to Reagan.* New York: Columbia University Press, 1986.

EUROPE

8

The Transfiguration of Old Fritz: Münchhausen *and the* Fridericus *Series*

THOMAS L. COOKSEY

> "If only I had a brain!"
> "A heart!"
> "The nerve!"
> —from *The Wizard of Oz* (Victor Fleming, 1939)

Josef von Baky's 1943 *Münchhausen* was the Third Reich's answer to the *Wizard of Oz*. Commissioned as part of the twenty-fifth anniversary celebration of Ufa, Germany's most powerful commercial film studio, it premiered at the Ufa-Palast am Zoo on 5 March. The film represented a state-of-the-art extravaganza, only the fourth German feature movie produced in color. It included elaborate special effects, and a large cast, starring superstar Hans Albers as well as cameo appearances by many of the leading movie stars of the day. The screenplay was written by Erich Kästner and based on the tales of the infamous "lying Baron [Lügenbaron]," Karl Friedrich Hieronymus Freiherr von Münchhausen. These appeared most notably in *The Singular Travels, Campaigns, and Adventures of Baron Münchhausen*, by Rudolf Erich Raspe, *Wunderbare Reisen zu Wasser und zu Lande, Feldzüge und lustige Abenteurer des Freiherren von Münchhausen/Marvelous Travels on Water and Land: Campaigns and Comical Adventures of the Baron of Münchhausen* (1786), by Gottfried August Bürger, and *Münchhausen: Eine Geschichte in Arabesken/A Story in Arabesque* (1839–39), by Karl Leberecht Immermann. Kästner, who also did the book for *Emil und die Detektive/Emil and the Detectives* (Gerhard Lamprecht, 1931), and later *The Parent Trap* (1961, based on his 1950 novel

Das Doppelte Lottchen), was not on good terms with the party, so was identified on the screenplay by the pseudonym Berthold Bürger, a sly double allusion to both Gottfried Bürger and Bertolt Brecht.

At one level the fantastic adventures, with their opulent and exotic setting, their exuberant and carnivalesque pace, and their flamboyant performances, represented a diversion to a public weary of war and confronting a real possibility of defeat. On another level, *Münchhausen* was Berlin's answer to Hollywood, a symbol of German filmmaking and technological achievement. For these reasons Goebbels and the Ministry of Propaganda closely supervised its production. Given top priority, the production eventually cost nearly seven million RM, two million over its original budget. But what is *Münchhausen* beyond an extravagant diversion? The signs and symbol of the Third Reich are not overtly present. Only for a brief moment does a quick observer see a swastika on the radiator of an automobile in the frame narrative. Most of the action is set in the eighteenth century and does little to celebrate nationalism or war, aside from the Baron's sexually motivated acts of bravado. Similarly, only the Baron's exchanges with the magician Count Cagliostro (played by Ferdinand Marian of *Jud Süss/Jew Süss* infamy) hint indirectly at Nazi anti–Semitism. For these reasons, many contend that the film is not propaganda, that it is an aesthetic, technical, but essentially apolitical masterpiece.

The recent studies of Nazi cinema by Eric Rentschler and Linda Schulte-Sasse offer contrasting readings of the political character of *Münchhausen*. Rentschler sees in the movie "Nazism incarnate." Drawing on the theories of Theodor Adorno and Paul Virilio, he argues that "*Münchhausen* dramatizes [the] consonance between the machinery of cinema and the machinery of war" (202). The gun is equated with the camera, and the frenetic movement of the spectacle approaches the theme of total mobilization characteristic of Nazi ideology. In embodying a "self-reflexivity," an indulgence in sexual desire, and an unleashing of fantasy, the Baron becomes, in Rentschler's words, the Third Reich's "last action hero," the imaginary fulfillment of a male fantasy. Schulte-Sasse agrees that *Münchhausen* is about self-reflexivity, sexual desire, and fantasy, but argues that the movie continually overturns or at least threatens to overturn the ideology of Nazi cinema. The result, she suggests, is ultimately subversive. Schulte-Sasse deploys the theories of Lacan and Slavoj Zizek to describe the formation of a unified ideology. Where other "historical" films of the Nazi era attempt to construct a mirror reflecting the coherent embodiment of ideology, *Münchhausen* resists any unity. "If Frederick, like other historical models and Hitler himself, represents an anchor offering an imaginary reconciliation, Münchhausen is a more apocalyptic figure acknowledging its impossibility" (307).

I propose an alternate reading somewhere between those of Rentschler and Schulte-Sasse. Appearing in 1943 *Münchhausen* stands in succession with a series of historical movies, the Fridericus series, about the Prussian King, Frederick the Great, culminating in 1942 with the major movie *Der Grosse König/The Great King*. When *Münchhausen* is set against the horizon of the Fridericus series, it takes on an added historical and political significance, and by identity transforms the figure of Frederick into a fantasy figure. In other words, it is often the historical figure rather than the fantasy one that resists reconciliation with ideology. What is the need or significance of such a transformation?

From an early stage, the Nazi propaganda machine deliberately attempted to link the figure of the *Führer* and that of Old Fritz. To the end Hitler persisted in this identity, dying under Anton Graff's portrait of Frederick on the bedroom wall in his bunker. The historical Frederick the Great, however, was at best a problematic model for Nazi ideological unity despite his military victories. A Francophile inspired by the French Enlightenment who despised the German culture and language, a misogynist, a sarcastic and bitter cynic, a homosexual, and a leader whose political, economic, and even military achievements were hotly debated, Old Fritz required significant historical restoration to fit the Nazi ideal. Hilmar Hoffmann notes, "Goebbels used the techniques of propaganda to force Old Fritz and Hitler — two totally antithetical figures — into a symbiosis that would be accepted by the politically naive" (49). In turn, shifting political currents complicated historical parallels, undermining the image and authority of the *Führer* as a modern Frederick. It is exactly this failure as an historical model to provide an imaginary reconciliation that opened the need for a fantastic one that would suspend or redeem history. The figure of Münchhausen created by Hans Albers suggests a sort of idealized and fantastic Frederick the Great, a transfiguration of the Prussian king into the hero he ought to have been in the best of all possible worlds. In the context of German film this is evident when one places *Münchhausen* in the context of the Fridericus series, a popular series of movies that focused on the life and achievements of the Prussian king. Historically, *Münchhausen* appeared immediately after the *Der Grosse König/The Great King*, the last installment of the series to be produced, current events having exhausted the genre. As such the Fridericus series creates the horizon of expectations against which *Münchhausen* would have been viewed, resulting in a thick intertextuality. What seems apolitical fantasy in isolation, takes on historical and political significance when set against the films of the Frederick movies. It represents not so much a parody or satire on the material, but in Hegelian terms, an *Aufhebung*, a raising, canceling, and preserving, a transformation to the ideal. In a sense, the figure of Baron Münchhausen becomes the final apotheosis of Frederick.

The life, triumphs, and figure of the Prussian king had long been a favorite of literature from the satirical squib about *le roi des Bulgares* ("the king of the Bulgarians") in Voltaire's *Candide* (1759) and his off-stage presence in G.E. Lessing's comedy *Minna von Barnhelm* (1767), to a variety of historical novels such as those by Louise Mühlbach, Frederick Andreas, Bruno Frank, and Walter von Molo, and even a number of operettas. Not surprisingly then, the iconic Frederick also found his way into film from its earliest developments. The first of these was *Der Alte Fritz/Old Fritz* in 1896, subsequently remade in 1927 (Murray 76; see also Schoenberner 12). This was followed by *Friedrich der Grosse beim Flütenspiel/Frederick the Great Playing His Play*, a brief work directed by Oskar Messter, dating from 1898, which translates the image of Adolf Menzel's famous painting into the medium of film (Hoffmann 46, Thouart 106). Fed by a conservative nostalgia for the Hohenzollern monarchy in the wake of the First World War, the subject of Frederick the Great became an important staple of German cinema of the Weimar period and subsequently the Nazi era (Regel 124–134, Welch 174–75). Mining a variety of sources from the literary tradition as well as the historical record and the stuff of legend, the period from 1922 to 1942 produced some twelve films about Frederick (Petley 106, Thouart 107, Kracauer 265–7). These include:

> *Fridericus Rex (Ein Königsschicksal)/(The Fate of a King)* (Arzén von Cserépy, 1922, 23)
> *Die Mühle von Sanssouci/The Mill of Sanssouci* (Siegfried Philippi, 1925)
> *Der Alte Fritz/Old Fritz* (Gerhard Lamprecht, 1927)
> *Das Flötenkonzert von Sans-souci/The Flute Concert of Sans-Souci* (Gustav Ucicky, 1930)
> *Die Tänzerin von Sans Souci/Barberina* (Friedrich Zelnik, 1932)
> *Trenck* aka *Der Günstling des Königs/The King's Favorite* (Ernst Neubach, 1932)
> *Der Choral von Leuthen/The Anthem of Leuthen* (Carl Froelich, 1933)
> *Der Alte und der Junge König/The Old and the Young King* (Hans Steinhoff, 1935)
> *Heiteres und Ernstes um den großen König/Pleasant and Serious Things About the Great King* (Piel Jutzi, 1936)
> *Fridericus* (Johannes Meyer, 1936)
> *Das Schöne Fraulein Schragg/Pretty Miss Schragg* (Hans Deppe, 1937)
> *Der Grosse König/The Great King* (Veit Harlan, 1942)

The figure of Frederick also makes a brief appearance in *Das Fräulein von Barnhelm/Miss von Barnhelm* (1940), the Nazi reinterpretation of Lessing's famous play. With the exception of *Der Alte und der Junge König/The Old and the Young King,* which was about the traumatic relationship between the young prince Frederick and his father, Frederick William I, and *Trenck*, which was about the love between Frederick's sister Amalie and his rebellious and disobedient aide-de-camp Trenck, the series featured Otto Gebühr in the role of the Great King. Gebühr (1877–1954), who played King Luhois in *The Golem* (1921), had first developed the role of Frederick on the stage, bringing it to the silent screen. His near falsetto voice left something to be desired when the movies entered the sound era with the 1930 *Flötenkonzert/Flute Concert*. Nevertheless with his large twinkling eyes and bemused avuncular smile, he became so nearly identified with the figure of Old Fritz that when Veit Harlan wanted to cast Werner Krauss in the title role of *Der Grosse König/The Great King*, Gebühr was reinstated on Hitler's direct order (Hull 213). A joke ran during the height of his popularity that Gebühr was writing a memoir entitled, "How I Won the Seven Years' War" (Feld 72). The 1927 *Der Alte Fritz/Old Fritz*, directed by Gerhard Lamprecht, presented Gebühr's Frederick, "as an excellent military strategist, a cunning diplomat, a conscientious and hardworking public servant, and the peasants' guardian against the injustices of the wealthy," an idealized image characteristic of the Fridericus series of the Weimar Era (Murray 76).

Those Fridericus films produced in the Nazi era, including *Der Choral von Leuthen/The Anthem from Leuthen*, *Der Alte und der Junge König/The Old and the Young King*, *Fridericus*, and *Der Grosse König/The Great King*, develop Frederick's identity as the all knowing patriarch, the leader whose insight and sheer will allows him to lead Prussia to victory in the Seven Years' War, even though surrounded by its enemies and against terrible odds. In turn these films play on the role and cult of the *Führer*, his tragic genius and his sacrifices. But even earlier entries in the Fridericus cycle anticipate the rise of the Nazi party. *Das Flötenkonzert von Sans-souci/The Flute Concert of Sans-Souci*, directed by Gustav Ucicky, concludes with Frederick witnessing a parade of his goose stepping grenadiers, a scene shot with a deep focus that anticipates Leni Riefenstahl's *Triumph des Willens/Triumph of the Will* (1935) by three years.

With the exception of the early *Fridericus Rex* and the late *Der Grosse König/The Great King*, the productions were relatively low budget. With their flags flying, marching soldiers, and triumphant battle scenes, the series aimed largely at an audience of adolescent boys, with enough romance worked in to interest the adolescent girls in the audience. *Heiteres und Ernstes un den großen König/Pleasant and Serious Things About the Great King*, a short of about 20 minutes and aimed as filler between the main features, dramatizes two anecdotes about the king. These are held together in a frame narrative about two modern boys reading a biography of Frederick. The presence of these boys in the frame narrative suggest their role as the natural audience for these movies. Reports to Goebbels concerning audience response to *Der Grosse König/The Great King* were generally favorable, though it was added that the "unsophisticated couldn't follow the story," silently underlining the fact that the movie revised and scrambled history to make it fit the party line, often making the narrative line incoherent (qtd. in Leiser 161).

The reception of this image of Frederick was not without controversy, however. Siegfried Kracauer reports that the 1922 premier of *Fridericus Rex* raised strong condemnation in the press, complaining of its anti-democratic tendencies (116). *Das Flötenkonzert von Sans-souci/The Flute Concert of Sans-Souci* brought leftist demonstrations. Historian Werner Hegemann, looking at the general appropriation of Frederick by conservative and reactionary elements, tried to debunk the myth in his 1929 book *Frederick the Great*. "Erroneous political legends are dangerous," Hegemann declared, adding that "It seems to me that the Frederician legend is one of the most dangerous" (503). He challenged the view of Frederick as the enlightenment monarch, contending that his administration, foreign policy, and even military strategy had failed on all counts. He went so far as to suggest that Frederick's policies and wars had done much to retard German unity, adding ironically that the recently abdicated Kaiser, Wilhelm II, was more deserving of the title "the Great." Gerhard Lamprecht's *Der Alte Fritz/Old Fritz* seems cognizant of some of the ambiguity around Frederick. Instead of focusing on the Seven Years' War, as other films, he treats his reign from the end of the war in 1762 until his death in 1786. Helmut Regel argues that Lamprecht's inclusion of negative features such as Frederick's senility and misanthropy serve to undercut an idealization (127). Nevertheless, the film suggests the ideological position that a strong monarch or authoritarian figure might have avoided the chaos of the postwar period. As Bruce Murray writes, "*Old Fritz* communicated a very clear and relevant message to German moviegoers who had questioned the negotiation of the Versailles Treaty, protested the French occupation of the Ruhr, criticized the speculation of wealthy investors, suffered under inflation and unemployment, and contemplated the political right's caricature of the Soviets as 'Bolshevik terrorists.' The film asserted that just as the Prussians rejected their aging monarch while he continued to serve them, so also the German people had abandoned their kaiser prematurely" (Murray 79).

Frederick's sexuality represented another complication in the image (MacDonogh 106). Though historians hotly debated the issue, the evidence strongly points to his homosexuality. Indeed, a subtle awareness of this adds to the irony that Gustav von Aschenbach, the author hero of Thomas Mann's *Der Tod in Venedig/Death in Venice* (1912) was famous for his "prose epic" of the life of Frederick, even though his theme was ostensibly sacrifice and duty.

As a young prince, Frederick had attempted to flee Prussia with his friend and possible lover, Hermann von Katte. This failed plot led to Frederick's imprisonment by his father, and the execution of Katte before his eyes in 1730. Later, his marriage to Elizabeth Christine of Brunswick-Bevern produced no offspring, and a number of historians even suggest that it was never consummated. Voltaire coined the term "Potsdamite" as a synonym for sodomite, and indeed the famous designation of Frederick as "*le roi des Bulgares*," puns on *bougre*, making him the "king of the Buggers." From a strictly historical point of view, the exact nature of Frederick's sexuality remains uncertain, lost in the fog of history, and finally perhaps of limited importance. On the other hand, from the point of view of the mythic cult of the *Führer*, and the fantasy of the ideal masculine hero, such ambiguities are problematic. Otto Gebühr once reportedly cut the lace off the sleeves of his costume, complaining that such effeteness was contrary to the spirit and image of Frederick. Leni Riefenstahl perhaps came the closest in explicitly addressing Frederick's sexuality. For a brief period in the 1950s she collaborated with Jean Cocteau on the intriguing idea of a movie about the friendship between Frederick and Voltaire that was to feature Cocteau in both roles (Berg-Pan 184–85; Riefenstahl 403–404), although the project never found funding. Most of the film treatments of Frederick either avoided the issue of his sexuality, set up a diversion, or simply re-wrote inconvenient history.

Since Frederick's well-known and rabid misogyny offered little promising material to establish romantic interest, the films typically introduced a subplot featuring some young officer with a wife or girlfriend. In *Die Tanzerin von Sanssouci/Barberina*, Frederick invites the Venetian dancer to his court in Berlin. This turns out to be a ploy to make his enemies suppose he is distracted in a flirtation. In the end, he turns Barberina over to her real lover, affirming in Kracauer's words "the tragic solitude" of the leader. In the meantime, the audience, like Frederick's enemies, is also distracted with the image of the king as a charming lady's man. The 1942 *Der Grosse König/The Great King* transforms Frederick's historical nephew, Prince Heinrich (1747–1767), into his son. The young Prince, heeding the inner call of duty, disobeys his parents and risks danger to join his father on the eve of a desperate battle. Presented as a rouged fop, his image echoes something of the effeminate young Frederick, but here the rebellion of the son against the father is towards duty. Later in the movie, the young Prince dies of smallpox, as did the historical Prince, though in 1767, four years after the war was over, not in the middle of it. The symbolism is obvious, inferring that the king also knows the suffering of the people, having endured the sacrifice of his own son. Despite this loss, he stoically perseveres to perform his duty.

The ironies of history and current events had a way of further complicating the use of Frederick as a political ideal. In the actual Seven Years' War, Britain was Prussia's chief ally against France and Austria. (Frederick had been among the first European monarchs to recognize the independent United States, praising the greatness of George Washington when the latter chose to step down after his second term as president.) In the Second World War, of course, Austria was the ally of Germany (Hitler himself an Austrian), and Vichy France a collaborator against Britain. In the *Flötenkonzert/The Flute Concert*, the invading enemies necessarily remain France, Austria, Russia, and Saxony; nevertheless a subplot features Frederick using his charm to prevent the wife of one of his majors from committing adultery with an English merchant who is living near Potsdam. This merchant tries to seduce the woman with a combination of poetry and gifts of English china. He is largely a comic figure, portrayed as a cowardly and effeminate fop who obsessively powders his nose in front of a mirror. In one incongruous package, he embodies and ridicules the Englishman as a combination of sexual predator, effeminate fool, and capitalist speculator who threatens the burgeoning Prussian porcelain industry.

The last of the Fredericus films, *Der Grosse König/The Great King* was the most ambitious of the series, taking the theme of Frederick as the *Führer* to its literal apotheosis. The historical events depicted in this film were rewritten to emphasize contemporary parallels, and to strike, "a new note of heroic resistance and stoicism, and absolute faith" (Welch 175). One of the most expensive films made in the Third Reich, it was commissioned by the Ministry of Propaganda under the close personal supervision of Goebbels (Welch 176). Linda Schulte-Sasse discusses the multiple images of Frederick that present him as father, son, and spirit. The movie ends celebrating the final triumph over the Russians, French, and Austrians in the Seven Years' War. Frederick himself eschews the victory parade, letting an empty gilded coach of state pass before the queen and cheering crowds. (In a sense, he is a spiritual presence, even if bodily absent.) Instead he rides alone to the site of a mill that had been destroyed in the disastrous battle of Kunersdorf that began the movie. The mill has been rebuilt and life has started to return to normal. He then enters a church. Sitting alone while an organ plays variations on *Glorious Things of Thee are Spoken* in the background, he struggles to restrain his tears as he contemplates the losses of the war. The camera closes in on his eyes, and this image is then superimposed over the image of the mill, then over rolling fields of grain, finally rising into clouds, sky, and the image of the Prussian flag. Frederick becomes in Schulte-Sasse's words, "pure gaze," the omniscient deliverer of salvation and prosperity, the man whose personal tragedy and suffering has saved those who believed in him. "The scene," says Schulte-Sasse, "virtually fuses the two bodies of the King by eliminating all of his physical body but the part most conventionally associated with the 'soul'"(122). In short, he has been transfigured into something approaching God.

Shifting political currents complicated the initial release. When *Der Grosse König/The Great King* was completed, it was immediately banned without explanation by Goebbels. Only when Germany went to war with Russia was a revised version finally released. Because of the Stalin-Ribbentrop pact, the authorities objected to the episodes in which the Russian general Chernichev (played by Werner Krauss) turned over the Russian army at Thorn to Frederick. When director Veit Harlan complained about historical accuracy, Goebbels replied, "Never mind, we'll change history" (qtd. in Hull 213). In turn, the army general staff took exception to the implications of the thesis that Frederick stood out alone against the Prussian army and general staff, which had proved unreliable. Their concern was not unfounded. Commenting on the lessons of *Der Grosse König/The Great King* in an April 19, 1942, radio address, Goebbels argued that victory was the result of superior leadership and not economic or military resources, a not so subtle insinuation that failures on the battlefield were the result of a disaffected army staff, and that the only thing preserving Germany was the spiritual strength of the *Führer* (Welch 181). Only General Keitel's intervention with the general staff persuaded Hitler to finally release the movie.

In the end, Germany's declining military fortunes mitigated against further movies about Frederick. Otto Gebühr could only win the Seven Years' War so many times, and persistent defeats on the battlefield and relentless bombing of Berlin seemed to underline a lack of Frederician genius on the part of the current *Führer* to achieve a final victory. Veit Harlan's *Kolberg* (1945) opens with Napoleon's famous visit to the tomb of Frederick. "Hats off, gentleman," the Emperor tells his generals, "if he were still alive we should not be here," a remark that also signals the end of the Fridericus series.

If the 1942 *Der Grosse König/The Great King* eliminates any of Frederick's human failings by transfiguring him into God, the 1943 *Münchhausen* manifests the "real action hero" that Rentschler describes. Rather than rewriting history as *Der Grosse König/The Great King* or other of the Fredericus films, *Münchhausen* transforms Frederick's material/sexual body, suspending history altogether. The image and the adventures of Hans Albers's baron take as their intertext Frederick and the Fredericus films, while at the same time effacing the problematic to create an exuberant, athletic, heterosexual male ideal. He is suave and sophisticated, a lady's man whose very appearance is enough to seduce women with little additional effort. The opening credits of the movie run past a painted portrait of the baron. At the end of the credits, the image in the painting winks at the audience, symbolic of the movie's tone and treatment of its material.

It is relevant to note that Albers's handsome, clean shaven, athletic, and virile baron is contrary to the conventional image of Münchhausen, emerging from Gustave Doré's famous illustrations. Doré's Münchhausen is tall, gaunt, and wizened, resembling Don Quixote. He has a large aquiline nose adorned with great grenadier's mustachios. It is this image that informs most of the representations found in children's book art or in movies from Georges Méliès' *Les Hallucinations du baron de Munchhausen/Baron Munchhausen's Dream* (1911) and Piel Jutzi's *Münchhausens neuestes Abenteuer/Münchhausen's Latest Adventure* (1936) to the more recent incarnations by Karel Zeman (*Baron Prásil/The Fabulous Baron Munchausen*, 1961) and Terry Gilliam (*The Adventures of Baron Munchausen*, 1988).

Münchhausen plays on the theme of sexual identity from the beginning. The story commences in a rococo ballroom whose decor and features are strongly reminiscent of the rooms used to represent Sanssouci in the Fredericus films. Periwigged gentlemen and ladies dance the minuet in the silk and lace attire appropriate to Frederick's 18th-century court. Münchhausen, in the dress uniform of the image of the winking portrait, encounters the beautiful young Sophie in the billiard room. She indicates her sexual attraction to him, handing him a red billiard ball, a not so subtle allusion to Eve and the apple. Recognizing and playing on the Edenic imagery, the baron takes the ball, but resists playing Adam to her Eve. Angry at the rebuff, the young lady runs from the room and the house. At that moment a lace trimmed hand flicks a switch, turning on an electric porch light, as Sophie jumps into her automobile and drives away. Playing Genesis in reverse, the narrative begins with Adam, Eve, and the apple, and then moves to the creation of light. As the dance shifts from the minuet to the tango and a servant doffs his periwig, the light reveals that the scene is not a ball in the 18th century, but a costume party set in modern times (1940s), though there is no indication of the war, politics, or current events. The scene shifts to several days later. The monocled baron, supposedly the descendant of the famous adventurer, his wife, an aging baroness, the rebuffed Sophie, and her fiancé, aptly named Frederick, are all now in modern evening dress, enjoying cocktails on the terrace. Holding up a children's edition of Gottfried August Bürger, entitled *Münchhausen: Eine Geschichte in Arabesken/Münchhausen: A Story in Arabesque* (actually a conflation of Bürger and Immermann), the baron proceeds to recount the adventures of his famous ancestor, launching the movie viewers over the rainbow. Here the move is from the Kansas of the modern world of death and duty, through time, to the Oz of a fantastic 18th century of romance and adventure.

The film divides Münchhausen's adventures into five episodes, according to location and sexual adventure, and reinforced by careful color coordination. The first is set at the family estate at Bodenwerder, and centers on the relation between the baron and his father. This first episode is a sort of transition. He has just returned from Paris, and is soon called by Prince Anton Ulrich of Brunswick to join him in Russia. (The prince is pursing a mistress who is in the court of Catherine the Great.) The second episode centers around a cluster of adventures in Russia and Catherine's court. Here he seduces (or is seduced by) the Czarina, fights a duel with Prince Potemkin, and meets with the sinister magician Count Cagliostro, who gives the baron the gift of immortality, and a magic ring that will make him invisible for an hour. The adventures in Russia culminate in the famous ride on a giant cannon ball into the third episode. This is centered in the court and seraglio of Abdul-Hamid, the Sultan of the Ottoman Turks. Here Münchhausen, with the aid of Cagliostro's magic ring, liberates and escapes with the Venetian Princess Isabella d'Este, who had been given to the Sultan as part of a treaty with Venice. The fourth episode shifts to Venice, and the baron's conflict with Isabella's brother, the doge. Isabella is kidnapped by arrangement of her brother and put in a convent. When the baron learns that she can never be released, he bests her brother in a duel, finally escaping Venice in a balloon with his loyal servant, Christian. The balloon trip takes them to the moon in the fifth episode. In a surrealistic landscape, the baron learns that people's heads live separately from their bodies, and that reproduction is the result of growing children on trees. He also learns that time on the moon moves more swiftly. Each day is equivalent to a human year. With profound grief he watches Christian age rapidly and die before his eyes. Because of Count Cagliostro's gift of immortality, the baron himself is impervious to the effects of aging. At this point the scene dissolves, and the narrative returns to the frame story in the present. Here Münchhausen reveals that he is himself the actual baron and not merely his descendant. Shocked, the young couple hurry off. The baroness, recognizing her husband's sexual attraction to the flirtatious Sophie, offers him her permission to seek a liaison with this new Eve, since she after all is aging while he remains forever young and vigorous. Here Münchhausen declares that he will renounce the gift of immortality and remain loyal to his wife. "I demand everything!" he says, adding, "I also want the rest." Closing a circle that began with the modern baron turning on the electric lights, the film ends with the painted image of the original baron blowing out the candles of a candelabrum, echoing the closure of Revelation, returning the world to darkness. Like Dorothy, the baron chooses home in Kansas over Oz, despite the press of time and reality.

The cousins Freiherren von der Trenck suggest an important set of links between the Fredericus series and *Münchhausen*. Frederick of Trenck (1726–1794), an officer in the Prussian officer, earned the enmity of Old Fritz when he courted the king's sister Amalie. This story was explored in the 1932 movie *Trenck*, also known as *Der Günstling des Königs/The King's Favorite*, based on a novel by Bruno Frank (Kracauer 265). The king prefers for reasons of state that his sister marry the Crown Prince of Sweden. When she demurs in the name of happiness, he puts her into a convent, anticipating and echoing the fate of the relationship between Münchhausen and Isabella, when *her* brother the doge puts *her* into a convent for similar reasons. In turn Trenck disobeys Frederick's orders, is arrested and imprisoned, escapes, and settles in Russia where he becomes a favorite of the Empress, another striking echo of *Münchhausen*. After further misadventures, including ten years in the dungeon of Magdenburg, he is finally allowed after the death of the king to return to Prussia, a broken old man. Even more intriguing is the account he offers of his cousin Franz of Trenck (1711–1749) in his memoirs. *The Life of Baron Frederick Trenck* reads in many ways like a real-life version of the adventures of Münchhausen (see also Preradovich). Trenck's record of scandalous adventures and imprisonment also resonates with the more famous *Mémoires* of his contemporary Giovanni Casanova (1725–1798), adding another layer. During the Venetian sojourn in *Münchhausen*, Casanova appears as an old friend of the baron, marveling at his friend's perpetual youth and vitality. He also warns his friend of the sinister intentions of the doge.

At 6 feet 3 inches, Franz of Trenck was an adventurer and soldier of fortune, noted for his duels and love affairs. On one occasion he supposedly cut off the head of a man who had refused him money, subsequently ransoming his own release from prison with the price of four Turkish heads. In 1741 he formed a Croatian regiment, the Pandours (a type of Hungarian soldier), to fight for Maria Theresa against Prussia in the War of Austrian Succession, even plotting to kidnap the Prussian King. He was eventually imprisoned, committing suicide. Franz's adventures were captured in the 1940 movie *Trenck, der Pandur/Trenck the Pandour*, directed by Herbert Selpin and starring, aptly, Hans Albers in the title role. (Trenck's story was retold in a 1972 German television mini-series.) In some sense, the figure of Münchhausen created by Albers and Kästner is an amalgam of both Trenck cousins, suggesting elements of plot and character. Indeed, Albers even sports mustachios akin to those of the canonical image of Münchhausen. In both Trenck movies, the eponymous heroes are anti–Fredericks literally and symbolically. Willful, unruly, and careless, they put their own interests and ambitions above the state, resulting ultimately in an ignominious end. The figure of Münchhausen offers their romantic bravado, but mitigates the anti–Frederictheir dimensions.

Although Münchhausen is a soldier, the film plays very little with his military exploits, aside from the ride on the cannon ball. When he is shown in a military context, the movie hints at a resemblance between the image of the baron and Frederick the Great. The baron is shown riding near the battlefield in front of the Turkish fortress. He is dressed in a uniform and cocked hat, closely resembling the characteristic attire that was part of Frederick's trademark. And like Otto Gebühr's Frederick, he is shown dramatically on horseback, shot from the ground, with the camera looking up at the mounted rider to emphasize his stature. The image is conventional enough, but parodies ones used throughout the Fridericus series. On a similar note, the famous ride on a cannon ball ends with Münchhausen crashing into a tower in the Turkish fort. Unfazed by this, he doffs his hat and salutes the Sultan and other Ottoman officers in his midst, apologizing for his poor marksmanship. This conclusion offers some resemblance to the climax of *Der Choral von Leuthen/The Anthem from Leuthen* (based on a real historical incident). Having inadvertently gotten ahead of the advance guard after the decisive victory against the Austrians at Leuthen, Frederick goes walking into the former Austrian headquarters only to discover that the general staff of the enemy has not yet evacuated. One Austrian officer says incredulously, "But your Highness! You're in the Austrian camp!" To which Frederick replies, ""You mean this *was* the Austrian camp, sirs, it *was*" ("Gewesen, meine Herrschaften, gewesen!") (qtd. in Schulte-Sasse 92).

More curious and troubling are the scenes involving Münchhausen and the Count Cagliostro. These scenes are not part of the original tradition and have no prototypes in Raspe or Bürger. Historically, Alessandro di Cagliostro (1743–1795), born Giuseppe Balsamo, was a charlatan, claiming magical and alchemical powers. He was also a Freemason, founding a secret sect. Among his scams was the claim that he could prevent aging. Though ridiculed in Goethe's *Der Groß-Cophta/The Great Cophta* (1792), much of his reputation derives from the fictional accounts in Alexandre Dumas *père*'s novels, *Joseph Balsamo* (1846–48) and *Le Collier de la reine/The Queen's Necklace* (1849), in which he is the mastermind of a secret society. In *Die Tanzerin von Sans Souci/Barberina*, Cagliostro, played by Werner Krauss, appears as the head of an international conspiracy. In *Münchhausen*, he appears twice, framing the episodes in Catherine's court. The baron is dining at an inn, when the count's sleigh pulls up. The baron's servant Christian groans, "not him again!"

indicating that this is apparently not their first encounter. The count invites himself to join the baron over wine and tries to involve him in a plot to get control of the Duchy of Courland (Southern Latvia), part of a larger plot to partition Poland. The bemused baron declines: "You want to rule, I want to live. Adventure, foreign lands, beautiful women — I have use for all these things. But you misuse them!" The historical Cagliostro actually visited Courland in 1789 with the intention of founding a Masonic lodge. More subtly, this plot perhaps points to Frederick's role in the treaty of 1772 that began the partition of Polish land to Prussia, Russia, and Austria, culminating in the disappearance of Poland from the map until 1918, and the subsequent Nazi invasion in 1939.

The scenes with Cagliostro are the most explicitly political in the movie, though explicit by innuendo. The figure of Cagliostro presented in the movie is the Nazi archetype of the scheming Jew, even if he is not so identified. While the Cagliostro of history and legend was Catholic and not Jewish, his reputation contributed to myths about secret societies and international conspiracies that contributed to the anti–Semitic fiction of an international Jewish conspiracy. Nazi propaganda frequently alluded to the Jewish "lodges." Freemasonry as a whole was linked with political tendencies antithetical to the Nazi regime. Cagliostro's magic ring, allowing him to become literally invisible, resonates with the metaphor of "invisible" hands manipulating political and financial dealings. More to the point, he is here played by actor Ferdinand Marian, well known for his performance in the virulently anti–Semitic *Jud Süss/Jew Süss* (1940). Marian's portrayal of Cagliostro is essentially identical with that of the malevolent and unctuous Joseph Süss Oppenheimer in appearance, manner, and machinations. In this cameo appearance in *Münchhausen*, Süss/Cagliostro is up to mischief. More interesting, however, is the baron's bemused acceptance. He disapproves of him and what he stands for, but tolerates him, even warning him that Catherine's police are about to close in on him. Both are in some ways outsiders whose special identities put them on the margin of society. In her discussion of Frederick the Great movies, Schulte-Sasse develops the analogous thesis that "the cinematic Frederick the Great mirrors Nazism's 'Jew' as a 'positive' social fantasy, a vessel into whom reconciliation could be projected" (307).

While both the king and baron are shown to resemble each other in their heroic poses and bravado, it is the resemblances and parallels that cover over or transform differences that are more significant. It is with regard to the image of the king's sexual body that Hans Albers's representation of the baron most fully mediates the transfiguration of Frederick. Schulte-Sasse notes the obvious visual pun in the baron's famous ride across the sky holding onto a cannon ball between his legs (310). The image combines themes of the warrior with those of sexual potency. To underline the joke, Albers tips his hat to the movie audience, much as his image in the painting had winked in the opening credits, though he also nearly loses his grip on the cannon ball. The transformation of Frederick from a problematic sexual-material body into something more acceptable is manifest in three ways: first, the way in which the movie echoes and reconfigures the relationship between the Frederick and his father; second, the way in which it genders political relations; and third, the way in which it treats homoeroticism.

Both the narrative frame and the first episode of *Münchhausen* echo the conflict between Frederick and his father, Frederick William I, a trauma explored in *Der Alte und der Junge König/The Old and the Young King*. This movie starred Werner Hinz as the young Frederick and Emil Janings as his father, Frederick William I, and focused on the events around Hermann von Katte. Like the old king, Münchhausen's father wants to know when his son will settle down and establish a family. Here the relationship between father and son is less strained, but the son nevertheless demurs that he would rather have adventures. He has just returned to Bodenwerder from Paris. Hanging up the portrait of a recent Parisian conquest in his gallery of lovers and mistresses, he says that he can't make up his mind. The baron's decision in the end to remain loyal to his wife affirms the original wishes of his father. Like Frederick, Münchhausen has learned to sacrifice his personal gratification and cultivation to the duties of the family. This insertion of the theme of familial duty is the creation of Kästner's screenplay, and not found in either Raspe or Bürger. (Supposedly, the historical Münchhausen, the eponymous source of Raspe's stories, married a fortune hunter later in life, dying in 1797 "an unhappy man") (Carswell xxvii).

The execution of Katte in *Der Alte und der Junge König/The Old and the Young King* symbolizes a dramatic severing of the effeminate side of Frederick, expressed in his lace and embroidered clothes and cultivation of French culture (Schulte-Sasse 128). *Münchhausen* offers a farcical reading of this. While the baron's clothes from Paris are being unpacked, a rabid dog attacks them. Shortly thereafter, while father and son are talking about the future, the baron's armoire suddenly begins to howl and rock. The embroidered coats have gone mad because of the rabid dog bite, requiring the baron to shoot them on the spot. The premise of the mad coat derives from Raspe and Bürger, though there it was a fur coat and under very different circumstances. Set against *Der Alte und der Junge König/The Old and the Young King* as an intertext, and against the context of the discussion of the baron's future, this scene takes on a larger significance, hinting at the need to put aside some aspects of the past.

Politics and gender are an important theme in *Der Grosse König/The Great King*. The film suggests that much of the cause of the Seven Years' War is the result of machinations of three women: Madame de Pompadour in France, the Czarina Elizabeth I of Russia, and Maria Theresa, Archduchess of Austria and Queen of Hungary and Bohemia. At one level this is not entirely untrue. Frederick had tried to cultivate La Pompadour through various diplomatic channels in order to arrange peace (Asprey 460). Complaining about Catherine the Great's dealings in the Russo-Turkish War, he wrote to his brother Prince Henry, "that a woman is always a woman and that in a feminine government the cunt has more influence than a firm policy guided by straight reason" (qtd. in Asprey 602). The dome on the new palace in Potsdam is topped with the nude figures of La Pompadour, Maria Theresa, and Catherine the Great (who followed Elizabeth on the throne of Russia), supporting the Prussian crown. In one scene of *Fridericus* (1936), Maria Theresa receives the news of Austria's triumphs over Frederick and the Prussians. The scene shifts to France. La Pompadour is shown fanning herself with what turns out to be a map of Prussia. Meeting with her officers and diplomats, she draws a line across Prussia with her lipstick, partitioning it with Russia. Finally the scene shifts to Petersburg. A drunken Elizabeth staggers amid her priests and ministers, throwing back vodka, and cursing Frederick. *Münchhausen* also plays with this motif of gender and politics. Here however, his sexual charisma triumphs. Talking with his father, the baron indicates that Mme de Pompadour was one of his sexual conquests in Paris. Although Maria Theresa is not alluded to, Catherine the Great (played by actress Brigitte Horney) is among the baron's great loves. They vow their undying love to each other, "until one of us wishes to be free again." All of this suggests something of a satiric allusion to the complex diplomatic relations between the historical Catherine and Frederick. There might also be a coy allusion to the erstwhile pact between Germany and the Soviet Union, another union that lasted "until one of us wishes to be free again." Perhaps more than anything else, what saved Prussia and Frederick from final defeat in the Seven Years' War was the sudden death of Elizabeth. Her son Peter III, a supporter of Frederick, immediately changed sides in the conflict when he succeeded to his mother's throne, breaking Russia's alliance with Austria. His wife, Catherine II (the Great), continued this policy, if with some reservations, after Peter's overthrow and assassination. Frederick, like Münchhausen, owed much to his ability to charm Catherine, who was herself German. The movie's treatment of the relationship between the baron and Czarina greatly embroider the few suggestions of the original texts. In Raspe, the baron indicates only that (through a diplomat) Catherine offered him her bed and crown, "but as I never was ambitious of royal dignity, I declined her majesty's favor in the politest terms." He adds dryly, "What the sex see in me I cannot conceive, but the Empress is not the only female sovereign who has offered me her hand" (65).

Münchhausen provides another angle on the issue of gender and the sexual body. In the grand banquet scene one courtier quips to another that Catherine is more aptly addressed as "*der* Große" rather than "*die* Große," using the masculine form of the title "the Great." The point was not, of course, that she presents a masculine appearance: Brigitte Horney's Catherine projects a stunning beauty (contrary to the historical Catherine who was something of a *hausfrau*), owing much to the image created by Marlene Dietrich in Josef von Sternberg's gleefully cynical *Scarlet Empress* (1934). In the gender identity of the era, political and military greatness were associated with the masculine. According to the premise of this misogynist logic, the only sort of lover that would be truly appropriate would be another male, one who matched the virile code of the hero. To negotiate the implications of homoeroticism, however, the female lover is given a male valuation, allowing the baron to preserve his heterosexual identity. The movie, does, however, treat homoeroticism, if by suggestion and innuendo.

Both Schulte-Sasse and Rentschler note that Münchhausen shows more real affection to his servant Christian and to Count Cagliostro than to any of his female lovers. The case with Christian is most evident when the loyal servant dies of old age on the moon. The baron expresses profound grief at this loss, deciding to return to the earth and settle down thereafter. The baron also showed a curious affection for Cagliostro. After being wounded in a duel with Prince Potemkin, he goes to the Count for medical help. In turn, he warns the Count that he is about to be arrested by Catherine to prevent his mischief in her realm. In their conversation, they sit side by side at a piano playing music together and staring into each other's eyes. So that there is no ambiguity about sexual identity, however, both Christian and Cagliostro are shown to be explicitly heterosexual. In the first episode when the baron has returned with his servant from Paris, Christian takes an inventory of his wife and their numerous offspring, each one conceived during the brief periodic returns to Bodenwerder. Similarly, Cagliostro and Münchhausen admire the painting of a nude woman, posed from the back, somewhat in the spirit of Ingres's *Grande Odalisque*. Responding to Münchhausen's idle speculation about what she looked like from the front, Cagliostro magically causes the image in the painting to turn toward the beholder. He returns the nude to her original pose when the baron quips that he prefers the bare back to the exposed breast. As with the inversion and scrambling of the gender codes of "*der* Große" and "*die Große*" with regard to Catherine, this scene also plays with inversions and the scrambling of codes. The focus on the backside of the female nude becomes a sexual object hinting at sodomy. The female quality of her sexual identity is explicitly rejected. (In an analogous motif, Münchhausen dismissed the overtures of an old mistress in the first episode when she displays her ample bosom to him.) By this scrambling, the feminine can code for the masculine, and the masculine for the feminine. In this way, the ambiguous nature of Frederick's own sexual identity is erased.

In a December 1943 press conference, Veit Harlan addressed the issue of historical authenticity in historical films. *Film-Kurier* reported that he said that a film on a historical topic should not falsify history. He added, however, "But art, and film art in particular, consists to a great extent of omission. And so a historical film can only ever show a part, a small chapter of history that should nevertheless remind us of the great events" (qtd. in Welch 184). The history of the Fridericus series was a succession of omissions, revisions, and erasures that obscured or rewrote history. Given the pressures of that history, escape into an art that suspends history offers a strong allure. If Frederick the Great seemed to offer a natural model on which to model German identity, he also presented problems that even the best propagandist could not entirely ignore. *Münchhausen* like *The Wizard of Oz* presents parallel worlds over the rainbow. The threatening storm clouds of a real historical present, with its equivalent Miss Gulches and tornadoes, with its duty and mortality, is juxtaposed across time to a carnivalesque past of adventure, magic, and immortality. But at the same time, Münchhausen's magical past intersects with the historical past. The Catharines, Pompadours, and Cagliostros of history exist in the fantasy realm of Münchhausen's adventures, allowing him to redeem history. At the center of this rococo Oz, Münchhausen exists in the role corresponding to Frederick the Great. If the Old Fritz of the Fridericus series was not himself lacking in heart, brain, or nerve, Münchhausen leavened these qualities with grace, panache, and virility.

Works Cited

Asprey, Robert B. *Frederick the Great: The Magnificent Enigma.* New York: History Book Club, 1999.
Berg-Pan, Renata. *Leni Riefenstahl.* Boston: Twayne, 1980.
Bürger, Gottfried August. *Wunderbare Reisen zu Wasser und Lande, Feldzüge und lustige Abenteuer des Freiherrn von Münchhausen.* Stuttgart: Reclam, 1969.
Carswell, John. "Introduction." *Singular Travels, Campaigns, and Adventures of Baron Munchausen* by R.E. Raspe. New York: Dover, 1960. vii–xxxviii.
Feld, Hans. "Potsdam gegen Weimar oder wie Otto Gebühr den Siebenjährigen Krieg

gewann." *Preußen im Film. Eine Retrospektive der Stiftung deutsche Kinemathek.* Ed. Axel Marquardt and Heinz Rathsack, Hamburg: Reinbek, 1981. 68–73.
Hegemann, Werner. *Frederick the Great.* Trans. Winifred Ray. New York: Alfred A. Knopf, 1929.
Hoffmann, Hilmar. *The Triumph of Propaganda: Film and National Socialism, 1933–1945.* Providence, RI: Berghahn, 1996.
Hull, David Stewart. *Film in the Third Reich: A Study of the German Cinema, 1933–1945.* Berkeley: University of California Press, 1969.
Immermann, Karl Leberecht. *Münchhausen: Eine Geschichte in Arabesken.* Ed. Peter Hasubek. Munich: Hanser, 1977.
Kracauer, Siegfried. *From Caligari to Hitler: A Psychological History of the German Film.* Princeton: Princeton University Press, 1947.
Leiser, Erwin. *Nazi Cinema.* Trans. Gertrud Mander and David Wilson. New York: Macmillan, 1974.
MacDonogh, Giles. *Frederick the Great: A Life in Deed and Letters.* New York: St. Martin's, 1999.
Marquardt, Axel, and Heinz Rathsack, ed. *Preußen im Film: Eine Retrospektive der Stiftung Deutsche Kinemathek.* Hamburg: Reinbek, 1981
Murray, Bruce A. *Film and the German Left in the Weimar Republic: From Caligari to Kuhle Wampe.* Austin: University of Texas Press, 1990.
Petley, Julian. *Capital and Culture: German Cinema 1933–45.* London: British Film Institute, 1979.
Preradovich, Nikolaus von. *Das seltsam wilde Leiben des Pandurenoberst Franz von der Trenck.* Stuttgart: Stocken, 1980.
Raspe, Rudolph Erich. *The Travels and Surprising Adventures of Baron Munchausen.* Dadalus, 1988.
Regel, Helmut. "Die Fridericus-Filme der Weimarer Republic." *Preußen im Film: Eine Retrospektive der Stiftung Deutsche Kinemathek.* Ed. Axel Marquardt and Heinz Rathsack. Hamburg: Rowohlt, 1981. 124–134.
Rentschler, Eric. *The Ministry of Illusion: Nazi Cinema and Its Aftermath.* Cambridge, MA: Harvard University Press, 1996.
Riefenstahl, Leni. *Leni Riefenstahl: A Memoir.* New York: St. Martin's, 1992.
Schoenberner, Gerhard. "Das Preussenbild im deutschen Film: Geschichte und Ideologie." Marquardt and Rathsack 9–38.
Schulte-Sasse, Linda. *Entertaining the Third Reich: Illusions of Wholeness in Nazi Cinema.* Durham, NC: Duke University Press, 1996.
Thouart, Didier. "Quelques héros d'Europe centrale." *Historia* 507 (1989): 106–109.
Trenck, Friedrich. *The Life of Baron Frederick Trenck: Containing His Adventures and Also His Excessive Sufferings.* Whitefish, MT: Kessinger, 2005.
Welch, David. *Propaganda and the German Cinema: 1933–1945.* Oxford, England: Clarendon, 1983.

9

Caroline and Angélique: Seductresses of the French Screen

PIERRE SIVAN

The official history of the French cinema holds only a limited place for the two seductresses of the 1950s and 1960s that were the heroines of the Caroline series and the Angélique series. When they are not openly displaying their scorn regarding them, reference dictionaries devote to them only brief annotations. When they discuss *Dear Caroline/Caroline chérie* (Richard Pottier, 1951), the first episode in the Caroline series, it is often to show interest, first, in the success of Martine Carol, the performer of the principal role, and then, to turn to sociological reflections on the explanations for this success. However, the film had without doubt other merits: in 1951, at the time of its release, French audiences reserved a veritable triumph for the adventures of the young and innocent Caroline de Bièvre; as early as 1952, she returned to the screen in the first French film to take advantage of the American Technicolor process: *Caroline Cherie/Un Caprice de Caroline chérie* (Jean Devaivre, 1953). As for Angélique, the critical evaluations of film historians are hardly any more affectionate. *Angélique/Angélique, marquise des anges* (Bernard Borderie, 1964) was nevertheless one of the biggest public successes of 1965, followed a few months later by that of *Marvelous Angélique/Angélique merveilleuse* (Bernard Borderie, 1965).[1] The impact of these two series on audiences was undeniable. How many French teenage boys were marked by the fleeting vision of Martine Carol/Caroline's breast, bared by the sword of a noble *chouan*; a few years later, a similar emotion gripped their little

---

Translated by Jennifer Forrest.
This chapter is a reprint of "Caroline, Angélique, nos séductrices hexagonales," originally published in *Le Cinéma du sam'di soir*, ed. Gérard Desserre and Nicolas Schmidt (Condé-sur-Noireau, France: Corlet, 2000) 116–21.

brothers facing the cleverly exposed roundnesses of Michèle Mercier/Angélique and her romantic adventures.² It would certainly be rather useless to want to make "*auteurs*" of Richard Pottier, the director of *Dear Caroline/Caroline chérie*, and of Bernard Borderie, who put his signature, between 1964 and 1968, to the five episodes of the adventures of Angélique, in the sense that this term took in the 1960s. They were both respectable, indeed skillful directors. As for Jean Devaivre, the person in charge of *Caroline chérie/Un caprice de Caroline Chérie*, then for *The Son of Dear Caroline/Le Fils de Caroline chérie* (1955), he had shown himself to be much more inspired in some of his earlier works, whether it is a question of *The Eleven o'Clock Lady/La dame d'onze heures* (1948) or *The Farm of Seven Sins/La ferme des sept péchés* (1949). The fact remains that these films, above all concerned with pleasing wide audiences, succeeded in profoundly marking the imagination of their era.

In the Beginning There Was Hollywood

The project of *Dear Caroline/Caroline chérie*, just like that of *Angélique/Angélique, marquise des anges*, was undeniably governed by the concern to compete with Hollywood cinema, on its own favorite terrain — the spectacular adventure film. It was a question of offering to French audiences a cinema of entertainment combining the spectacular — reconstruction in the studio of a far away time, battles, horseback riding — and the charms of the romanesque, all of it in a very French setting. For Caroline, two American films seem to have particularly served as references: *Forever Amber*, directed by Otto Preminger in 1947, and *Gone with the Wind*, which, in 1950, at the moment when Gaumont decided to start working on *Dear Caroline/Caroline chérie*, was leading at the French box-office.³ It was a question in both cases of adaptations of controversial bestselling novels in the case of *Forever Amber*, giving star billing to strong, amoral or immoral women, ready for anything, even sometimes to offer themselves to achieve their ends, but both submissive to the law of love in the end. Preminger's Amber is thus in turns mistress of a soldier, companion of a brigand, wife of a great lord, and favorite of the king of England! But throughout the film, she remains attached to her first love, for whom she eventually sacrifices herself. A brief summary of Caroline's cinematic adventures will make it possible to assess the bonds that link the young French heroine to her American precursors.

The first episode of the series takes the Revolution as its historical setting; moreover, the action begins on the 14 July 1789. On that day, Caroline de Bièvre, a young aristocratic woman, falls in love with the nobleman

Gaston de Sallanches; but Gaston, libertine seducer, while particularly sensitive to Caroline's charm, is not disposed to marry her. Two years later, revolutionary events force the girl to go to Paris. Learning that Gaston has taken a mistress, Caroline, out of spite, marries Georges Berthier, a moderate revolutionary politician. The Revolution takes an increasingly tragic course; Georges Berthier, a *Girondin* deputy, is declared an outlaw at the moment when the Terror is established.[4] Caroline, with the help of Gaston, must hide. But, victim of a betrayal, she is arrested. Miraculously saved, she flees to Brittany, is captured by the *chouans*, and becomes the mistress of their leader Pont-Bellenger. The revolution having come to an end, Caroline, widowed opportunely by the death of Georges, can finally marry Gaston.

In the second episode, *Caroline Cherie/Un Caprice de Caroline Chérie*, we find the heroine a few years later in Italy. Her husband, Gaston de Sallanches, has become an officer in the Napoleonic army at the time of the Italian campaign. Caroline makes the acquaintance of a handsome dancer Livio, and a brief romance arises between the two young people. A rebellion breaks out. Forced to flee disguised as a man, Caroline leaves her husband in the arms of the Countess Clélia de Monteleone at whose home they found refuge. Jealous, seeking to avenge herself, Caroline sets off in search of Livio, who turns out to be in reality the leader of the rebels. Sallanches takes back control of the situation, is reassured about the conduct of his wife, and, magnanimous, pardons Livio, who goes back to Austria. As for the third episode, *The Son of Dear Caroline/Le Fils de Caroline chérie*, it uses the name of the heroine in its title, but she never appears in it.

At the origin of *Dear Caroline/Caroline chérie* (the film) is a bestseller by Cécil Saint-Laurent, constructed, the author admits with grace, according to the well-proven formulas of American bestsellers. Its success with readers, as phenomenal as they were unexpected, convinced the producers to undertake its cinematographic adaptation. With Caroline, France finally had, it was believed, a heroine capable of competing with Amber or with Scarlett O'Hara. Mimicking the method used by David O. Selznick for *Gone with the Wind*, the producers organized among spectators and cinema professionals a kind of referendum, which was supposed to designate the star best able to play the new national myth. To ensure the success of the project, they brought together prestige names intended to guarantee its quality. Jean Anouilh was thus put in charge of the writing of the script and the dialogue; he was at the same time one of the most famous French dramatic writers; as a scriptwriter, he had worked with renowned filmmakers like Julien Duvivier for *Anna Karenina* (1948) and Jean Grémillon for *White Paws/Pattes blanches* (1949). Georges Auric, who composed the score, was a respected musician who had already worked, as well, in the cinema. As for Richard Pottier, he was proving to be at the time an experienced director with recognized ability. The film's credits list, moreover, these famous names even before those of the actors.

A similar approach seems to have inspired the producers of the Angélique series. There again, it is a question of the adaptation of a bestselling novel series; there again, the main character is a woman caught in the ups and downs of historical events. The action, particularly rich in new developments, is spread out over five episodes: *Angélique/Angélique, marquise des anges, Marvelous Angélique/Angélique merveilleuse, Angélique and the King/Angélique et le roy* (1966), *Untamable Angélique/Indomptable Angélique* (1967), *Angélique and the Sultan/Angélique et le sultan* (1968). It takes place in the seventeenth century during the reign of Louis XIV. Angélique is, like Caroline, a young aristocratic woman who is the victim of destiny. Forced to marry Joffrey de Peyrac, a disfigured aristocrat said to be a sorcerer, she learns nevertheless to appreciate, then to love, this imposed spouse, who, for his part, is passionately in love with her. He is unfortunately arrested by the royal police for sorcery, condemned to death, and burned alive at the stake. He is in fact the victim of a political conspiracy and of the jealousy of the king, who is attracted to Angélique, and by the fabulous fortune of Joffrey. Afterwards, Angélique takes refuge among the beggars of the Court of Miracles,[5] gets mixed up in various political intrigues, once again frequents the court, and marries her cousin, the Marquis de Plessis-Bellières. Before long, the latter dies upon the field of battle, which gives the king of France Louis XIV the opportunity to court Angélique, once again a widow. But she puts up a fierce resistance to him. This doesn't stop the sovereign from assigning her a perilous — and amorous — diplomatic mission with the ambassador of the Shah of Persia. After having escaped various perils, Angélique acquires the certitude that Joffrey, whom she never stopped loving, did not die on the stake. And, indeed, Joffrey is still alive; he has even become captain of a pirate ship under the nickname of the "Rescator." Angélique leaves Paris, puts out to sea in pursuit of him, is captured by another French pirate, d'Escrainville, who sells her as a slave on the coast of North Africa. But Angélique's purchaser is none other than Joffrey. D'Escrainville, who has discovered everything, kidnaps Angélique again to sell her to the king of Miquenez, who is anxious to enrich his harem; Angélique succeeds, however, in fleeing into the desert, Joffrey saves her life, and the couple is finally reunited.

As in the case of *Dear Caroline/Caroline chérie*, the producers of the Angélique series had the intention of producing a spectacular work of prestige destined for a vast audience. The release of each of the episodes was preceded by great publicity campaigns. To film the naval battles, they had recourse to the sets of the Italian studios of Cinecittà, while the location shots were filmed at historical sites, beginning with the château at Versailles. The production was also set on calling on recognized talents for the conception and production of the film. Bernard Borderie, the director, was a specialist of action and historical films; he counted among his credits at the time an adaptation of *The Three Musketeers/Les Trois mousquetaires* (1961), adapted from Alexandre Dumas, and two adaptations of stories by Michel Zévaco[6]: *Clash of Steel/Le Chevalier de Pardaillan* (1962) and *The Gallant Musketeer/Hardi Pardaillan* (1963). The dialogue was entrusted to Daniel Boulanger, then to Pascal Jardin, two promising young screenwriters.

Note in the case of Angélique, as of Caroline as well, the intention of giving the title role, not to a recognizable star, but to an actress who, without being a beginner, did not enjoy immense prestige with audiences. Michèle Mercier was, for example, much more famous in Italy than in France; she was nevertheless preferred, it is said, to Catherine Deneuve and Claudia Cardinale. On the other hand, they made a point of surrounding these evolving stars with confirmed actors, capable of efficiently supporting them; Jacques Dacqmine, an experienced theater actor, played Gaston de Sallanches, the only true love of Caroline; Robert Hossein, who had already clearly established his presence in the French cinema, was Joffrey de Peyrac. The calculation proved to be shrewd: as had happened with Vivien Leigh, the two actresses became stars immediately, at least on a French scale. It is true that everything had been done to highlight them and point the projectors at them. The male characters, without being reduced to walk-on parts, had to be content with being supporting roles, sometimes more or less interchangeable, without benefiting from an aura comparable to that of the actresses. Moreover, the latter were both, moreover, more or less victims of an identification that audiences made between the actress and the role. The title of the three volumes of memoirs written by Michèle Mercier are in this way revealing: *Angélique with All Her Heart/Angélique à coeur perdu* (1987), *Yours, Angélique/Angélique vôtre* (1996), *I Am Not Angélique/Je ne suis pas Angélique* (2002). As for Martine Carol, even if she met with other successes, she was no less marked by the role of Caroline. Identified with a particular character, neither of the two actresses achieved the mythical dimension of a Brigitte Bardot. Michèle Mercier often did the covers of popular magazines, but she never became the object of a veritable cult.

History, Great and Small

The novels of Cécil Saint-Laurent, the creator of Caroline, just like those by Anne and Serge Golon, the inventors of Angélique, clearly reproduce the methods of the historical novel made famous in the nineteenth century by Alexandre Dumas. It is a matter of mixing fictitious characters and events with historical figures and events, of having history with a capital H interact with individual destinies. The novelists take delight in alcove stories or enigmatic episodes to which the fiction can bring the most unexpected solutions. They offer to the reader the pleasure of a change in scenery by plunging him into a universe that is different from his own, a universe that had been made familiar to him beforehand in school.

The cinematic adaptation of the adventures of the two heroines presents this pattern. The seventeenth century evoked in the adventures of Angélique thus draws on a series of clichés that have come straight out of a French schoolbook from the 1950s. Louis XIV is represented in them in accordance with the academic tradition in use at the time, like an authoritarian sovereign, proud, but equally concerned with the dignity of royal power and the grandeur of the State. His superintendent of finance, Colbert, is described by the king as "the most faithful of his ministers": and he sleeps "only five hours a night"; there again, we think that we are reading a history book for use by students. These details, without real importance for the course of the story, shows the screenwriters' concern for conforming to a traditional view; these details served to guarantee seriousness by sticking to what the spectator knows, or thinks he knows, of the seventeenth century. In the *salons* that she frequents, Angélique never fails to meet famous people; it is in this way that she meets La Fontaine, the author of the famous *Fables*, who, we are reminded, was particularly witty.[7] Angélique even becomes in *Angélique and the King/Angélique et le roy* the rival of the mistress, or favorite of Louis XIV, Madame de Montespan. This gets her mixed up in the famous Affair of the "Poisons."[8] The seventeenth century thus presents us with its historical figures, its prestigious (Versailles) or picturesque (the Court of Miracles) decors, its political conspiracies, or its court intrigues. In the same way, the unrest of the Revolution separates Caroline from Gaston de Sallanches and plunges the unfortunate girl into the darkest perils, making her come close to — and sometimes not only coming close to — dishonor and death.

The fact remains that the two series adopt quite different attitudes towards historical events. In *Dear Caroline/Caroline chérie*, the screenwriters, in accordance moreover with the spirit of the novel, do not hide their antipathy for the Revolution. Through the figure of the postilion who takes advantage of Caroline, the *sans-culottes* are depicted as stupid, uncouth, violent, lecherous fanatics.[9] Caroline's husband, a *Girondin* deputy, is a clumsy young man, incapable of satisfying her sexually; this coward doesn't hesitate to denounce Gaston de Sallanches to the revolutionary tribunal, whom he suspects of being Caroline's lover. His death is therefore a most satisfying script solution since it leaves Caroline to the handsome Gaston, noble yet faithful to his country, and, what is more, an excellent lover.

This reactionary view of the Revolution is rare enough in French cinema for it not to be noticed. It can be attributed largely to the author of the novel, Jacques Laurent, who used the pseudonym Cécil Saint-Laurent for the writing of the Caroline series, and did not hide his royalist sympathies, or rather flaunted them in a deliberately provocative manner just at the time when "leftist" thinking clearly dominated in the intellectual and artistic world of the 1950s. Provocative on a literary level, Jacques Laurent had thus become famous through his violent opposition to the Sartrian conception of the *roman engagé*.[10] There would be without a doubt in *Dear Caroline/Caroline chérie* the trace of a certain "dandyism," of an undisguised intention to show an aristocratic independence vis-à-vis the herd ready to follow the prevailing movement of democratic culture. In addition, if one considers that the film was produced in 1950, it seems difficult to not establish a parallel between that cruel revolution and a situation still rather fresh in people's memories. One is thus tempted to identify the period of the Terror as it is depicted in the film with that of the German Occupation. The *sans-culottes* easily take the place of the Nazis and the *chouans*, having taken refuge in the woods, can call to mind the *maquisards*.[11] The film presents us moreover with a submissive France, quick to denounce, where each person tries to extricate himself, even if it means switching camps as quickly as necessary in case of a reversal in the situation. How could one not think then about the France of the Occupation period, the one of anonymous letters, of the black market, of active or passive collaboration? How could one not think as well of the abrupt changes in opinion that accompanied the Liberation and that saw sympathizers of the Vichy Regime present themselves as sincere Resistance fighters?[12] The film's authors seem to cast a somewhat scornful look on this mediocre France; they prefer to reserve their admiration for some exceptional beings whose aristocratic temperament is dissociated from that of the plebeians. But, in this history, those who could appear like Resistance fighters are not really treated well: the *chouans* aren't much better, when it comes down to it, than their adversaries, and the two camps can be regarded with the same somewhat haughty distance.

With the Angélique series, the view of the seventeenth century is more in keeping with republican and democratic values. Aristocrats are by nature unbearably proud, indeed appallingly cruel: the king's brother doesn't hesitate (*Angélique and the King/Angélique et le roy*) to sadistically kill a young child. The rapes, of which Angélique is sometimes the victim, are characteristic of aristocrats. On the other hand, the heroine, in defiance of caste prejudices, willingly bestows her favors on attractive commoners. She seems even to feel a real partiality for marginals, whether it is a question of a penniless poet, or a big-hearted bandit, or of a political exile.... Exception to the rule: Joffrey de Peyrac, her husband, offers the face of an enlightened nobleman, precursor of the great thinkers of the Enlightenment, and herald of the ideals of 1789. A man of science, he devotes himself in his chateau to chemistry experiments which get him mistaken for a sorcerer; a victim of obscurantism, he is condemned to the stake; having become a pirate, he frees the prisoners condemned to row as slaves on the galleys of the king of France, an experience of which he equally takes advantage to invent and operate the first submarine.

This is typical of stereotyped, but not innocent, representations of History with a capital "H," in which the spectator, according to well-established patterns, easily finds his way. History is not only a backdrop. It offers a wealth of characters and situations that permits the narration to move forward. Its accidents or catastrophes play the role of an often-unjust destiny, separating the lovers who long to find each other again. The Revolution seems to have had for its main purpose in *Dear Caroline/Caroline chérie* to hinder the happiness of Gaston and Caroline, to raise between them, as in a melodrama, successive barriers to separate them better just when they were about to meet up again; but at the same time, its merit is to have allowed the heroes to feel the power of their mutual love. The Revolution also has the great merit of excusing the amorous adventures of Caroline, whether she is forced to give in to a postilion in order to save her life, or whether she gives herself out of the goodness of her heart to the nobleman Boismussy on the eve of an arrest that can only lead to the guillotine. The heroine manages then to be, as the film poster proclaimed, both "fickle and faithful" to present the spectator with the charms of libertinage without offending morality. In the same way, the supposed death of Joffrey de Peyrac authorizes Angélique to yield in all good conscience to the men who seduce her, and even to marry the Marquis de Plessis-Bellières.

The Eternal Feminine?

The easy virtues of the heroines obviously had something to do with the success of the films. It was an effective publicity stunt, and critics often privileged this feature, unaware that the screenwriters had also been able to present well-executed plots that were more often than not effective according to the *feuilletonesque* tradition that they had clearly adopted: there cinema rediscovered the romanesque vein of the nineteenth-century novel.[13] The novels of Alexandre Dumas, to cite the most significant example, were initially published in newspapers, in the form of serialized stories. The novelist could then lengthen the plot or shorten it according to audience responses, favor one character or another, expand one episode or another. The importance of this request by audiences is still felt in the Angélique movie series. Joffrey de Peyrac, considered dead at the conclusion of the first episode, came back to life in the third, that is to say, earlier than the screenwriters had anticipated: indeed, audiences had particularly liked the character and the performance of his interpreter Robert Hossein. They desired his return and manifested this desire by sending numerous letters to the producers of the film, who gave them satisfaction. So, the poster for *Angélique and the King/Angélique et le roy* was adorned with the inscription, "Joffrey returns," with Robert Hossein's face appearing in the background.

The fact remains that the two series undeniably owed a great part of their success to their erotic dimension. This eroticism, and the discrete forms that it takes, can obviously make people laugh today; let's recall, however, that in 1950, nudity was reserved for private movies. One understands then the shock that the sight, however fleeting, of Caroline's breast could represent in a film intended for general audiences. The two heroines are thus offered to male fantasies and desires. Angélique, in defiance sometimes of the most basic verisimilitude, constantly wears promising low-cut dresses. All pretexts are valid for undressing her, at least partially; the trailer for *Untamable Angélique/Indomptable Angélique* promises the spectator that the heroine "will be shown nude" on the slave market. In fact, the game consists in hiding until the last moment this breast that the enticed spectator will only glimpse (the breast of novice actress Michèle Mercier had been, however, fully unveiled some years earlier in a series of shots from *Shoot the Piano Player/Tirez sur le pianiste* [1960] in which François Truffaut poked fun at the hypocritical modesty of French films). The directors, Richard Pottier, Jean Devaivre, and Bernard Borderie, use and abuse shadow shows, revealing bathtubs, or cleverly torn costumes.... From there to being indignant about the woman-as-object fate reserved for these heroines, there is only one step. For Françoise Audé, these films are products of the tradition of a dominant, misogynist, and openly conservative cinema. One could relativize this condemnation. French cinema for general audiences in the 1950s was hardly in the habit of giving the leading role to a heroine, and even less to a heroine aspiring to relative independence, especially in the sexual domain. Similarly, it wasn't so common to suggest that a woman could give herself to a lover with the sole expectation of the pleasure that it could bring her. Such preoccupations are moreover products of *films à thèse* than entertainment films.[14] But in fact, neither Caroline nor Angélique seem like heroines with a disturbing sensuality likely to shock or offend Saturday evening or Sunday afternoon audiences. Despite their adventures, they long only to become faithful spouses and fulfilled mothers. Faithful to the old stereotypes weighing heavily on women, Caroline readily admits that she understands nothing about politics, a business, she explains, that should be left to men. On several occasions, the voice-off commentary of *Dear Caroline/Caroline chérie* lets mocking remarks about the weakness or "natural" duplicity of women filter through.

Angélique is hardly different on this point, even if the misogynistic stereotypes are a little less asserted in her case; fifteen years or so have gone by since *Dear Caroline/Caroline chérie* and new female figures burst onto screens. One thinks, of course, of Brigitte Bardot who played—an often-cited coincidence—a supporting role in *The Son of Dear Caroline/Le Fils de Caroline chérie*, the same Brigitte Bardot who was approached, it is said, to play Angélique. One thinks also of the female characters portrayed by films of the French New Wave. But French commercial cinema, of which the Angélique series is a good example, seems to have been on this point, as on so many others, quite closed to what was going on at its margins. Bold gestures, in whatever the domain, remain therefore rather timid or carefully controlled: never does one cross limits of decency, or of what it was assumed that family audiences would accept. At the very most, one can notice in episode after episode the relative increasing build-up in the ill-treatment of which Angélique is the victim. With *Indomitable Angélique/Indomptable Angélique* and *Angélique and the Sultan/Angélique et le sultan*, we nearly fall into sadism: just barely averted collective rape, torture, flagellation.... But such an inflation is explained above all by the logic of the *feuilleton*: it was necessary, from one episode to the next, to keep the attention of audiences who were beginning to grow weary of the adventures of Angélique.[15] The original script of the final episode, *Angélique and the Sultan/Angélique et le sultan*, on this point planned a last minute development: Angélique was once again separated from Joffrey, which left the possibility for shooting a new episode. In the end, the producers preferred adopting a happy ending that put an end to the series.[16] For the same reason, it became without a doubt unnecessary to transport the intrigue toward Barbary Coast lands and to offer spectators, perhaps tired of the court of Louis XIV, the charms of a conventional exoticism: burning deserts, slave markets, harems, oriental refinement.... The spectator then left historical imagery for a dream world straight out of a story told in picture books.

The most traditional formulas of the *roman-feuilleton* of the nineteenth century are therefore definitely at work here: narrative efficiency, concern for continually reviving the spectator's interest, for playing at the same time on the pleasure of the déjà-vu (recurring situation or characters), and the surprise of something new. The Angélique series was moreover conceived on the model of serial works: *Angélique/Angélique, marquise des anges* and *Marvelous Angélique/Merveilleuse Angélique*, released in theaters separately and a year apart, were, in fact, shot simultaneously; it was the same for *Untamable Angélique/Indomptable Angélique* and for *Angélique and the Sultan/Angélique et le sultan*. Each of these films is based moreover on the principle of alternation: passing from happiness to misfortune, from the province to Paris, from the slums to the court, from the West to the East....

The heroine is continually placed in an unstable situation that lends itself to *coups de théâtre* and to sudden accelerations of the story. This relative nervousness of the script is found even sometimes in a *mise-en-scène* capable, in its best moments, of effectively serving the story. Admittedly, there are no daring formal innovations, only the concern for putting a decor to good use, for setting off the beauty of the actress, for pleasing without every really surprising. There is in that all the craftsmanlike cautiousness of the cinema for general audiences. This balance owes without doubt a good portion of its success to both Caroline and Angélique, a success borne out today for Angélique by the televised broadcasting of films from the series as well as their release on VHS cassettes in the 1980s, and subsequently on DVD. Caroline did not have quite the same longevity. It should be noted that a remake was filmed in 1968, but it only met with the mocking of critics and the indifference of audiences. The main channel on French television, TF1, had envisaged in 2002 producing a new adaptation of the novel by Cécil Saint-Laurent, but this project did not materialize. Without a doubt Caroline suffers from several handicaps, which would explain her relative oblivion. For general audiences today, a film from 1951 is looked on as an antique, especially if, like *Dear Caroline/Caroline chérie*, it was shot in black and white. At the same time, the film does not have the status of a cinema classic, which would earn it a priori admiration and recognition.

Angélique had more luck. She benefited from color, an important asset for a televised broadcast at prime time, and she still calls up many memories in viewers over forty, even when it is not a question of nostalgia. Thus she still benefits from a sympathy, or a tenderness, which, without a doubt, goes beyond "popular" audiences. It is possible that Bernard Borderie's films are today regarded as products that are outdated, a little naive, and a little kitsch, but despite that they still retain an old-fashioned charm.

Notes

1. [Editor's note: The Internet Movie Data Base (IMDB) does not provide a U.S. title for *Angélique merveilleuse*. In the United Kingdom, however, it was called *Angélique: The Road to Versailles*. When there is no U.S. title for a film in these two series, I provide a literal translation from the French.]

2. *Chouans*: a term referring to the insurgents hostile to the French Revolution in the provinces of the west of France from 1791 onwards.

3. Gaumont was and remains one of the principal film production and distribution companies in France.

4. *Girondin* is a term referring to the moderate revolutionaries who were eliminated during Robespierre's Terror.

5. Neighborhood of Paris that constituted the landmark of beggars, thieves, and bandits of all sorts. Its most famous literary representation was given by Victor Hugo in his novel *The Hunchback of Notre Dame/Notre-Dame de Paris* (1831).

6. Prolific novelist from the end of the nineteenth and the beginning of the twentieth centuries; he is, among others, the creator of the character of Pardaillan, whose numerous adventures take place in the sixteenth century.

7. [Editor's note: A *salon* was a gathering of intellectuals, artists, philosophers, writers, noble persons, wealthy bourgeois, and in general, persons of quality, at the home of a refined host/hostess who could provide guests with stimulating conversation and contact with persons of talent.]

8. The Affair of the Poisons is one of the most famous judicial cases of the reign of Louis XIV. In 1675, an aristocrat, the Marquise de Brinvilliers, was arrested and indicted for poisoning. She had, for inheritance reasons, killed her father and two brothers. The inquest and the trial that followed made it seem that the marquise, with the help of an accomplice, Catherine Deshayes Monvoisin, or La Voisin, furnished high persons of the court with poison so that they, too, could get rid of their close relatives. These revelations provoked an immense scandal, all the more so since they implicated Madame de Montespan, the king's favorite. La Voisin did indeed practice witchcraft and Madame de Montespan was accused of having participated in some of these ceremonies in order to keep the love of the sovereign and to supplant one of her rivals. The Marquise de Brinvilliers and La Voisin were executed; the king saw to it that Madame de Montespan escaped legal proceedings.

9. [Editor's note: The *sans-culottes* were republicans from the poorer classes in Paris during the Revolution. The word initially referred to the long trousers (as opposed to the knee-breeches of the aristocracy) they wore, but came to refer more specifically to the holders of extreme revolutionary ideals.]

10. [Editor's note: The *roman engagé* is a novel of political and ideological commitment.]

11. [Editor's note: The *maquisards* were members of the French Resistance during the German Occupation in World War II.]

12. Jean Anouilh, in charge of the adaptation of the novel, had been sickened by the trials that, at the time of the Liberation, targeted writers and artists accused of having collaborated with the occupying forces.

13. [Editor's note: The *roman-feuilleton* was a serial novel published in newspapers during the nineteenth century. It is generally associated with popular genres considered to be of little literary quality. This critical assessment is misleading, however, since writers of the stature of Charles Dickens and Honoré de Balzac were *feuilletonistes*, ("serial writers").]

14. [Editor's note: A *film à thèse* is a film that sets forth a theory or treats a social problem.]

15. The week of its Parisian release, *Angélique/Angélique marquise des anges* sold 61,274 tickets, which put the film in the lead by the number of spectators. During the first five weeks of its run, it remained constantly among the top three films in box-office ratings. Results were almost comparable for the second episode, *Marvelous Angélique/Merveilleuse Angélique*. On the other hand, in the first week of Parisian exploitation, the last episode, *Angélique and the Sultan/Angélique et le sultan*, brought in no more than 41,000 spectators, which, while still a decent result, reveals the decline in interest on the part of audiences (figures provided by blog.lefilmfrancais.com).

16. As far as the novels are concerned, on the contrary, the adventures of Angélique continued for a much longer time to the point of taking the heroine to the New World.

Works Cited

Audé, Françoise. *Ciné-modèles, cinéma d'elles*. Paris: L'Age d'homme: 1981.

JAPAN, HONG KONG, AND INDIA

10

Through the Years with Godzilla and Tora-san: Film Series in Postwar Japan

WILLIAM M. TSUTSUI

Film series have been a staple of the Japanese movie industry since World War II. No comprehensive inventory has been compiled, but film series proliferated in Japan beginning in the 1950s and peaking in the 1960s, with a second wave of franchises appearing in the 1990s. The establishment of international records for film series longevity is notoriously contentious, but Japanese studios can credibly boast the world's longest ongoing film series (the Godzilla movies, launched in 1954) and the longest film series with the same leading actor (the *Otoko wa tsurai yo* franchise of 48 movies from 1969 to 1996). Successful series have spanned all the genres of postwar Japanese filmmaking, focusing on subjects as disparate as renegade samurai warriors, pencil-pushing office workers, dissolute mobsters, cute animated creatures, and all sorts of fantastical giant monsters. Some of these series have enjoyed international distribution and worldwide acclaim, notably the 25 *chambara* ("swordplay") films featuring the blind masseur Zatoichi, the various species of *kaijū eiga* ("monster movies") starring the radioactive reptile Godzilla, the gargantuan insect Mothra, and the flying turtle Gamera, and animated theatrical releases like the continuing Pokémon movie series. But most of the postwar series, even those boasting dozens of installments and faithful domestic followings, are completely unknown to audiences outside Japan. Thus, franchises like the thirty-title *shachō* ("company president") series of the 1950s and 1960s, a lighthearted look at the white-collar lives of Japanese salarymen, the eighteen-part *wakadaishō* ("young general") series of wholesome "big man on campus" pictures, and the nine-installment *wataridori* ("bird of passage") series of "angry young man" dramas, as well as seemingly endless strings of *yakuza* ("gangster") sagas and samurai epics, are landmarks of Japanese pop culture history generally ignored by film fans and critics abroad.

Despite their obvious appeal to Japanese audiences, postwar film series have not received significant scholarly attention in either the Japanese or English language literatures. Many of the standard academic works on Japanese cinema, focused as they traditionally have been on prominent director-*auteurs*, utterly ignore what are derisively labeled "popular series" (*ninki shirizu*) or else use them as deplorable examples of the "intellectual and aesthetic poverty" of Japanese filmmaking after the "golden age" of the 1950s (Anderson and Richie 427). Critics have generally been no kinder, disparaging long-running series as formulaic and unimaginative, or dismissing series, even those that regularly have attracted millions of moviegoers in Japan, as low-budget cult phenomena of minimal cinematic importance and marginal cultural relevance.

This essay will depart from the majority of previous appraisals and argue that due consideration of popular and financially successful series is essential to understanding postwar Japan's film culture and movie industry. The focus will be on the two leading Japanese series over the past half-century, the 28-film Godzilla franchise of Tōhō Studios and the *Otoko wa tsurai yo* series (better known in the West as the Tora-san movies, after the name of the main character) from rival Shōchiku. In addition to tracing the evolution of the two series, the themes they have addressed and the reasons for their deep and enduring popularity will be explored in the historical, cultural, and economic context of postwar Japan. Although the Godzilla and Tora-san series are often assumed to share little, except perhaps their sheer longevity and an alleged lack of intellectual and creative substance, this essay will consider the numerous similarities between the two franchises' formulas for success, as well as the reasons why Japanese monster movies are internationally celebrated while family comedies like the *Otoko wa tsurai yo* films have never attracted audiences abroad. Above all, this essay will reveal how the prevalence and durability of "popular series" like Godzilla and Tora-san reflected (and, in turn, shaped) the structure, strategy, and economics of the postwar Japanese film industry, the changing preferences and demographics of postwar moviegoers, and the ingenuity and adaptability of Japanese filmmakers.

The Making of a Global Icon: The Godzilla Series

In 1985, a *New York Times*/CBS News poll asked 1,500 Americans to name a well-known Japanese person. The top three responses were Emperor

Hirohito, Hong Kong martial arts star Bruce Lee, and Godzilla. This was, needless to say, a stinging indictment of American public knowledge of Japan. But it was also a testament to the impact that a Japanese movie monster has had on popular culture around the globe. More than five decades after the creature's cinematic premiere as a Jurassic survivor made monstrous by American H-bomb tests in the brooding 1954 classic *Gojira*, Godzilla stands as one of Japan's most enduring and pervasive cultural exports. The 28 Godzilla films produced in Japan by Tōhō, along with the 1998 Hollywood version, have been shown on every continent and in virtually every language; Godzilla today is an unmistakable icon of Japan in the world's popular imagination, parodied and paid homage to in art, literature, and film, and even inscribed in the English language with the ubiquitous "-zilla" suffix. Godzilla's legions of international admirers include North Korea dictator (and world-class film buff) Kim Jong-Il, who in 1985 commissioned his own giant monster film, a curious Marxist parable entitled *Pulgasari*, using a kidnapped South Korean director and the Japanese stunt man from inside Godzilla's latex suit (Tsutsui, *Godzilla on My Mind* 198–99). Godzilla must also be acknowledged as a pioneer of sorts, as the first creation of postwar Japanese mass culture to gain international exposure and acclaim. Godzilla paved the way in many respects for the other Japanese media products which have subsequently become ubiquitous in global pop culture, from Astroboy, Speed Racer, and the Mighty Morphin' Power Rangers, to Pokémon, *tamagotchi*, and Iron Chef.

Given Godzilla's status as one of the world's most recognizable and abiding movie stars, it is somewhat surprising how little scholarly attention this giant radiation-breathing reptile has received, either in Japan or in the West. Critics have generally judged the Godzilla films to be artistically lacking, intellectually vapid, and ideologically hollow. Donald Richie, the dean of American film critics of Japan, once characterized Japanese "cinema" as "a plethora of nudity, teenage heroes, science-fiction monsters, animated cartoons, and pictures about cute animals" (*Japanese Cinema* 80); one reviewer dismissed the somber lead of *Gojira* as "a miniature of a dinosaur made of gum-shoes and about $20 worth of toy buildings" (Crowther). Academics, long used to slighting popular culture and writing off *kaijū eiga* as cheesy preteen spectacles, have produced only a handful of significant studies of the Godzilla franchise. While Susan Sontag analyzed the appeal of Japanese creature features as early as 1965, writing unforgettably of "the aesthetics of destruction, ... the particular beauties to be found in wreaking havoc," no scholars followed her lead for more than two decades (41). Chon Noriega's 1987 essay "Godzilla and the Japanese Nightmare: When *Them!* is U.S." deployed Freudian analysis and rooted the series in Cold War nuclear anxieties; Susan Napier's influential overviews of Japanese popular culture, most notably her 1993 article "Panic Sites," placed Godzilla in a postwar Japanese tradition of dystopian science fiction. More recently, Yoshikuni Igarashi has examined the series in the context of war memory and postwar socio-economic change, William Tsutsui and Anne Allison have analyzed Godzilla's global popularity, and the contributors to a 2006 collection edited by William Tsutsui and Michiko Ito situated the king of the monsters in discourses of science, modernity, and empire, as well as in an intertextual constellation of contemporary pop culture forms from manga to professional wrestling. Japanese writings on Godzilla have been plentiful and varied, though largely superficial, the work of popular critics, media commentators, and obsessive *kaijū eiga* fanatics (*otaku*). Much like the existing English-language literature, "Japanese sources pose many important questions but only begin to provide much in the way of answers, the kind of scholarly building blocks necessary to understand the creation, meanings, and global reach of Godzilla" (Tsutsui, "Introduction" 3).

Godzilla was born of contentious Cold War politics, the fertile imaginations of Japanese moviemakers, and hardheaded movie-industry economics. The early 1950s were a boom time for giant monster films, both in Hollywood and around the world. The 1933 American classic *King Kong*, the prototype of the "monster on the loose" genre, was re-released internationally in 1952 and the new Warner Brothers film *The Beast from 20,000 Fathoms*, boasting the state-of-the-art stop-motion special effects of Ray Harryhausen, appeared in 1953. Both proved to be box-office hits in Japan and implanted the notion of giant monsters into the minds of Japanese film producers and directors, who have never been loathe to steal a good, bankable idea from Hollywood. But Godzilla's genesis was also conditioned by geopolitical tensions and atomic age anxieties. On March 1, 1954, the United States tested a hydrogen bomb, a weapon almost one thousand times more powerful than that dropped on Hiroshima, at Bikini Atoll in the central Pacific. A Japanese tuna trawler named the *Lucky Dragon No. 5/Dai-go Fukuryū Maru* had unknowingly strayed into the test zone and was subjected to radiation from the blast and its fallout. On returning to port, the fishermen were found to be suffering from radiation poisoning, the ship's contaminated tuna accidentally entered Japanese markets, and the media erupted in a frenzy of nuclear fear and anti–American resentment. With Hiroshima and Nagasaki still raw memories, the Tokyo tabloids proclaimed the "*Lucky Dragon* incident" as just the latest American atomic attack on Japan.

Godzilla, as the legendry has it, was the brainchild of Tanaka Tomoyuki, a producer for Japan's Tōhō Studios. Flying home in early 1954 from Indonesia, where the deal for a big-budget feature had just fallen through, Tanaka looked out over the expansive Pacific Ocean and agonized over a replacement for the cancelled blockbuster. His mind racing through the headlines of the day and recent trends in the film industry, Tanaka hit upon a notion. "The thesis was very simple," Tanaka later recalled. "What if a dinosaur sleeping in the Southern Hemisphere had been awakened and transformed into a giant by the Bomb? What if it attacked Tokyo?" (qtd. in Burgess).

Tanaka recruited top talent for the picture, since his monster film was intended to be serious fare with a substantive political message for an adult audience. Among the seasoned professionals on the crew were special effects expert Tsuburaya Eiji, whose use of elaborate miniatures in wartime propaganda films was celebrated in the industry, director Honda Ishirō, a friend and collaborator of legendary filmmaker Kurosawa Akira, and Ifukube Akira, one of the most distinguished composers of Western classical music (and film scores) in Japan. Tagged by one commentator "sophisticated men working in a highly unsophisticated genre," they all would have a long-term relationship with the Godzilla series, Tanaka producing 22 of the films, Honda directing eight, and Ifukube scoring a dozen (Galbraith 19).

Tōhō Studios made a substantial investment in *Gojira*: 60 million yen, about three times the budget of the average Japanese film at the time (although far less, one should note, than Hollywood would have spent on a run-of-the-mill B-movie in the 1950s). *Gojira* opened on November 3, 1954 and receipts were strong: the film recorded the best opening-day ticket sales ever in Tokyo and eventually grossed ¥152 million on 9.69 million paid admissions, though it was only the twelfth largest grossing film in Japan that year (well behind the leading Japanese film, the final installment of the sentimental *Kimi no na wa?* trilogy, and the leading import, *Roman Holiday*). Godzilla's success (and its export potential) was such, however, that a franchise was born and a new genre of giant monster movies launched in Japan.

Tōhō began shopping *Gojira* abroad from soon after its Japanese release. Hollywood distributors were interested, but they saw Godzilla as a classic exploitation picture, a mass-market horror flick, not a gloomy art-house release, heavy on subtitles and light on profits. As a result, the film was extensively edited, with twenty minutes of footage cut and new scenes spliced in, to produce the kind of faster-moving, linguistically accessible creature feature that would sell in American theaters. Raymond Burr was inserted as an American reporter narrating the attacks of Godzilla while virtually all the scenes from the original Japanese picture that could be interpreted as reflecting negatively on the United States, giving voice to Japanese resentments over World War II, or expressing anxiety over nuclear testing were edited out or neutralized so as not to offend American Cold War sensibilities. As Donald Richie once remarked, "all of the good stuff" in *Gojira* was "cut out to accommodate the gesticulations of Raymond Burr" in its transition to *Godzilla, King of the Monsters*, the made-for-America 1956 release (*A Hundred Years* 267).

The 1954 *Gojira* ended with the death of the monster, though the filmmakers were thinking ahead and the movie closes with one of the main characters wondering aloud that "if we keep on conducting nuclear tests, it's possible that another Godzilla might appear somewhere in the world, again." This transpired surprisingly quickly and the first sequel to *Gojira*, the rather slapdash effort *Godzilla Raids Again/Gojira no gyakushū* (1955), was in Japanese theaters within six months of the original. *Godzilla Raids Again* set the model for later installments in the franchise, with Godzilla matched up against another outlandish mutant creature (in this case a massive ankylosaurus of unknown origin called Angilas), but did not immediately spawn further sequels, despite a respectable showing at the box office. Indeed, the third entry in the series did not appear until 1962, when *King Kong vs. Godzilla/ Kingu Kongu tai Gojira* was released with great fanfare. In the interim, before Tōhō had settled on Godzilla as its monstrous leading man, the studio tested out a number of other rubber-suited protagonists, from the pteranodons in *Rodan/Radon* (1956) to the mammoth flying squirrel *Varan the Unbelievable/ Daikaijū Baran* (1958), to the colorful insect god *Mothra/Mosura* (1961), who would later appear in many of the Godzilla films and eventually star in a three-picture series of her own in the late 1990s.

The two Godzilla films produced in the 1950s, along with the thirteen that appeared on an almost annual basis between 1962 and 1975, are known collectively as the Shōwa series, after the reign name of Hirohito, Japan's Shōwa emperor. The franchise was discontinued after 1975, as box office returns had long been in decline, but was resurrected in 1984 after Tōhō recognized the continued popularity of Godzilla, especially among the young adult generations that had grown up watching the king of the monsters. Seven films were made between 1984 and 1995—known collectively as the Heisei series, after the reign name of the current emperor, who ascended the throne in 1989—ending with 1995's *Godzilla vs. Destroyer/Gojira vs. Desutoroia* in which Godzilla dies of an internal meltdown, a kind of radioactive heartburn. The latest run of Tōhō-produced films began with *Godzilla 2000: Millennium/Gojira nisen: Mireniamu* (1999), with a new feature released annually in the busy New Year's season. A blockbuster fiftieth-anniversary film, *Godzilla: Final Wars/Gojira: Fainaru uōsu*, heavily marketed as featuring, yet again, the death of Godzilla, premiered in Los Angeles in 2004 to mixed reviews and disappointing box office numbers. Tōhō has now placed Godzilla on an indefinite hiatus, stating that no further entries in the series will be made until at least 2009.

As even the most casual fans of Godzilla are aware, the serious tone and high production values of the original 1954 film were hardly representative of the larger series, and most notably the Shōwa films of the 1960s and 1970s. The serious anti-nuclear message of the first offering was rapidly replaced with more crowd-pleasing, politically palatable fare and the age of the movies' target audience declined steadily: the first film was specifically intended for adults, but by the 1970s, eight-year olds were the primary market Tōhō sought to capture. The films became more cynical money spinners for the studio, the quality of the special effects (never particularly high, according to many critics) plummeted, and the sober morals of *Gojira* were forgotten in the rush to serve up inexpensive, unprovocative entertainments to unsophisticated audiences. The series degenerated into big-time wrestling in rubber suits (a technique grandly christened "suitmation" by Tōhō) and the scripts and stunts were remarkably cheesy, although at the same time (at least in retrospect) quite appealingly and comically campy. The critics may have winced, but Japanese children giggled (and their parents continued to buy tickets) at the spectacle of the king of the monsters doing a little victory jig, flying on his tail, and playing volleyball (using a huge boulder) with a giant mutant lobster.

The Heisei series films of the 1980s and 1990s were intended to be more serious and to take Godzilla back for adult moviegoers. They generally boasted better special effects (though they were generally primitive by Hollywood standards of the day) as well as better overall production values, but most scripts were still weak and the acting was astonishingly poor at some points. The six films released since 2000, known to fans as the millennium or *shinsei* ("new generation") series, have generally garnered good reviews and solid financial returns — with significantly improved screenplays and some truly memorable monster fighting sequences — but many fans still criticize them for a lack of creativity and a continued pandering to preteen audiences. Although recent installments in the series have been infused creatively with the visual and narrative conventions of anime, and *Godzilla: Final Wars* (Ryuhei Kitamura, 2004) was an unabashed tribute to the Matrix films of Hollywood, "the basic character of the Godzilla oeuvre — a man in a rubber suit, pretending to be a mighty, giant lizard, drawn inexorably to the cities of Japan — and the movies' fundamental appeal — broad, unpretentious, and timeless — have always remained the same" (Tsutsui, *Godzilla on My Mind* 45–46).

Markets and Monsters

Godzilla debuted during Japan's "golden age" of cinema, the original *Gojira* appearing the same year as Kurosawa's epic *The Seven Samurai/Shichi-nin no samurai* and Kinoshita Keisuke's antiwar classic *The Twenty-Four Eyes/Niju-shi no hitomi*. The 1950s were good times for Japanese filmmakers and studios, both creatively and economically. The decade began with Kurosawa's *Rashōmon* (1950) taking the grand prize at the Venice Film Festival, a watershed event which propelled Japanese film into international prominence, and would bring not only a string of critically acclaimed pictures from the likes of Ozu Yasujirō and Mizoguchi Kenji, but also unprecedented commercial success. Box office receipts rose steadily over the course of the decade, topping ¥72 trillion in the banner year of 1958, when theater admissions reached an astounding 1.1 billion, the highest figure ever recorded, either before or since. The number of movie screens nationwide peaked in 1960 at almost 7,500, and Tokyo could boast more theaters than any other city in the world, a full two-and-a-half times what New York could claim. In 1958, the average Tokyoite went to the movies over twenty times a year, double the rate of the average American and 10 percent more than the typical Briton. The six Japanese studios that controlled the industry produced between 400 and 500 films annually over the decade, with a peak of 547 new features released in 1960, the same year that Japanese-produced films captured a dominant 78.3 percent share of the domestic market, a record never surpassed.

The glory days of the Japanese movie business were short lived, however. Suburbanization (that left many potential moviegoers far from downtown theaters), the proliferation of other leisure options (from golf to travel to American-style hobbies), and, above all, the rise of television, combined to drain audiences from Japan's movie theaters starting in the early 1960s. In 1953, when television broadcasting began in Japan, there were only 866 TV sets nationwide; by 1959, there were almost two million, with an additional 150,000 entering service every month; by the mid–1960s, 60 percent of Japanese homes had televisions, and by 1970 nearly total saturation of Japanese households (95 percent) had been reached (Anderson and Richie 254, 451). The effect on the movie industry of the television revolution was profound: by 1963, total admissions had slipped to less than half of their 1958 peak and by 1969 had withered to scarcely a quarter of that postwar record. The number of movie screens declined rapidly, falling to just over 3,000 at the end of the 1960s, and domestic movie production slumped, dipping below 400 films a year in the middle of the decade. The market share of the Japanese studios followed this downward trend until in 1975, for the first time since the end of the war, imports from Hollywood and Europe captured more than half of the Japanese movie market.

The collapse of the "golden age" led to a shakeout in the crowded Japanese movie industry. A first wave of rationalization in the early 1960s led to the failure of Shintōhō, a postwar offshoot of the venerable Tōhō, and financial reorganization of the other studios; in the early 1970s, Daiei and Nikkatsu both declared bankruptcy and had to be reorganized, while Shōchiku, Toei, and Tōhō only avoided that indignity by diversification into non-film businesses such as bowling alleys, supermarkets, and real estate. The belt-tightening also led to profound changes in how pictures were made and what pictures were made. Commercial concerns (admittedly always important) came to overshadow artistic ones and producers, with their eyes ever on the bottom line, took precedence over directors, deciding "what picture [was] to be made, who [was] to write and direct it and, more important, how it [was] to be written and directed" (Anderson and Richie 457). The studios also became less daring, as "the industry itself exacerbated its own problems by allowing only the safest of products, giving its writers and directors no freedom" and cutting production costs to the bone (Anderson and Richie 465).

One result of the dwindling audience for movies was an industry-wide adjustment in the kinds of films being made. As the critic Satō Tadao has observed, in the 1960s, "with the popularity of television, housewives [and] even the young unmarried women stopped going to movies." Consequently, "in movie theaters, where real women could not be found, erotic and violent stimuli escalated and aggressive and self-destructive impulses ran amok" (Satō 236). By 1969, *yakuza* films, aimed primarily at working-class, urban, male audiences, made up fully a third of all features released and by the 1970s, up to 75 percent of Japanese-made movies were "pink movies, *roman poruno* ["pornographic romances"], and other marginal sex exploitation pictures" (Anderson and Richie 454, 456). Another common strategy adopted by the struggling studios was to carve out exclusive niches, "staking off sections of the market as a company's private territory and fitting production plans to that particular audience" (Anderson and Richie 259). Thus, Tōhō aimed to cultivate a loyal audience among urbanites and salarymen, Shōchiku, in keeping with its corporate traditions, tried to monopolize the female audience with domestic melodramas, Daiei looked to teen moviegoers, Toei to children and rural audiences with a steady stream of thrillers, period pieces (*jidaigeki*), and *yakuza* films, and Nikkatsu to young men with its trademark action films and *roman poruno* offerings.

In this economic environment, with studios loathe to be adventurous and the market neatly segmented demographically, film series became a very attractive proposition for Japanese moviemakers. Not only did series films allow for "every kind of economy since sets, costumes, and actors remained the same," but they promised predictable revenues from niche audiences and had the potential to attract moviegoers to multiple serial features (Anderson and Richie 240). Especially in the cases of *roman poruno* and children's movies (a category that included the Godzilla films even from the early 1960s), where audiences were relatively unsophisticated and undemanding, the pressure to make high quality, creative pictures was minimal. Series films could thus be churned out "cheaply and unimaginatively" for narrowly defined and faithful audiences that welcomed the studios' formulaic offerings and tolerated corner-cutting in production values (Anderson and Richie 262).

The Shōwa series of Godzilla films very much focused on the youth demographic, which was one of the more reliable audiences for Japanese-made features in the 1960s and 1970s, as children found reading subtitles in foreign films to be difficult, if not impossible (Anderson and Richie 420). This youthful clientele explains many of the changes in the Godzilla films from the dark and political offerings of the 1950s to the more lighthearted, even comic fare of the next two decades: Tōhō catered to the short attention spans of its audience with bright, colorful, action-packed pictures, with plenty of monster-on-monster combat, humorously stylized violence, and storylines and characters that appealed to school-aged children. Godzilla was recast as a hero, a defender of Japan and a dependable force for good, and stern morals on nuclear testing were replaced by breezy treatments of schoolyard bullying and light parodies of James Bond, the Planet of the Apes films, and even Tōhō's own *shachō* series. Godzilla was even physically altered to meet the supposed demands of a younger audience: by the end of the Shōwa series, the king of the monsters had taken on a "friendlier, almost Muppetlike look," with a larger head, bigger eyes, a cute pug nose, and a long, comically snake-like tail (Lees and Cerasini 98).

Godzilla had more staying power than most series of the 1960s, which had run their courses and exhausted their markets by the early 1970s. None of the Shōwa features could match *King Kong vs. Godzilla*, which attracted more viewers—12.6 million—than any of the other 27 films in the franchise, and was the sixth biggest earner at the Japanese box office in 1962. Subsequent entries in the series performed well through the mid–1960s, with six of the features selling over 2.5 million tickets each, but receipts plummeted in the early 1970s, with *Godzilla vs. Mechagodzilla/Gojira tai Mekagojira* (1974) managing a gate of only 1.3 million and neither *Godzilla vs. Megalon/Gojira tai Megaro* (1973) nor *Terror of Mechagodzilla/Mekagojira no gyakushū* (1975) reaching even 1 million. Godzilla was thus sent on hiatus in 1975; as one commentator noted, "The mighty nuclear monster that once invoked Japan's greatest fears and faced an assembly line of worthy adversaries was powerless against the economic forces that were destroying the once proud Japanese movie business" (Ryfle 161).

When Godzilla returned to theaters in the 1980s with the Heisei series, the results were solid on the bottom line: each of the seven films, styled more as polished action pictures than juvenile diversions, attracted at least 2 million moviegoers and the movie featuring the king of the monsters' demise, *Godzilla vs. Destroyer*, sold 4 million tickets, the most of any Godzilla film in three decades. This second run of Godzilla films came to an end not because of poor financial results, but because Tōhō had dreams of attaining even greater economic returns by licensing Godzilla exclusively to Hollywood, dreams that were ultimately dashed when the 1998 TriStar *Godzilla* proved a critical and box office flop. By the time Godzilla was revived in Japan at the turn of the millennium, the Tōhō franchise became part of a new wave of series films in the Japanese movie industry. Though hardly rivaling the proliferation of film series in the 1960s, this latest surge in series has been driven not by financial exigency so much as by a modest but steady expansion in the market. The years since the late 1990s have witnessed a slight revival in the fortunes of the Japanese movie industry, driven in large part by the construction of suburban multiplexes and the only sustained increase in the number of movie screens in Japan since the 1950s. Needing more films for the mushrooming theaters, studios returned to the series model as a means of turning out predictable, marketable features with limited investments of creative staff and development resources. In addition to the Godzilla millennium series films, which performed respectably at the box office (three scoring in the annual top ten of Japanese-made pictures), recent developments have included a Mothra trilogy, a revived Gamera franchise (which had recorded eight features from 1965 to 1980, and added four more between 1995 and 2006), and entirely new series, from the sentimental *Tsuri baka nisshi* ("Diary of a Fishing Fool") films to the animated adventures of Pokémon, Doraemon, and Hamutarō. And although Tōhō has temporarily laid off the king of the monsters, Godzilla remains such an important and dependable property for the studio that his return to the screen after a brief retirement is all but assured.

Themes in the Godzilla Films

The 1954 *Gojira* clearly had a strong pacifist and anti-nuclear message which director Honda Ishirō sought to convey to audiences. Yet it is hard to conclude that the films have had a consistent message over time, especially as the series now has spanned a full fifty years. Over the decades, several of the Godzilla offerings have tried to tackle timely social issues — pollution, corporate greed, political corruption, even school bullying — but the majority of the movies have passed on social commentary in favor of escapist, crowd-pleasing entertainment value. Thus, with even the character (and appearance) of the monster himself evolving over time, there is no central premise or message that can be found to run through all of the Godzilla features, but instead, only a variety of themes and tendencies that seem to recur in the series. One might even conclude that the only constant about the Godzilla films is a deep ambivalence, a kind of moral and intellectual ambiguity that precludes drawing any firm, unitary conclusions. The message of Godzilla, if any, is complex and can be seen as reflecting a fundamental ambivalence on the part of postwar Japanese as they contend with challenging issues like modernity, technological change, science, nature, democratic politics, rearmament, and relations with the outside world.

Although many themes could be teased from the 28 Tōhō Godzilla films, five seem particularly relevant in understanding the king of the monsters' place in postwar Japanese culture and society. First, through the Godzilla series, we see a fairly consistent expression of anti–American sentiments and, at the same time, a strong sense of pride in Japan and Japanese accomplishments. The 1962 fan-favorite *King Kong vs. Godzilla*, which was marketed very overtly by Tōhō as a symbolic showdown between America and Japan, may be the most obvious example of this dynamic. Yet the prominence of this theme runs all the way back to the beginning of the franchise and the 1954 *Gojira*. The original movie seeks to evoke the audience's memories of World War II and makes explicit reference to both the atomic bombings and U.S. nuclear testing. Indeed, throughout *Gojira*, "memories of the past war and fears of a coming war are seamlessly intertwined," always with an unspoken sense of antagonism toward America (Tsutsui, *Godzilla on My Mind* 36). In one scene, set just before Godzilla's first raid on Tokyo, a group of commuters discuss the monster aboard a train. "It's terrible, huh?" one remarks. "Radioactive tuna, atomic fallout, and now this Godzilla to top it all off." "I guess I'll have to find a shelter soon," another sighs. "The shelters again?" one of their companions glumly notes, "That stinks!" Later, when the monster is pounding his way through the heart of the city, the camera falls on a woman crouched beside a building, holding her two children as the structures collapse around them. "We'll be joining your father soon," she cries, referring (one can safely assume) to a husband killed in the war. "Just a little longer, a little longer."

The 1954 *Gojira* also has the air of a morality play of sorts, ending with the victory of Japan and Japanese science over the monster. The moral dimension of Japan's triumph turns on the character of Dr. Serizawa, a scientist who creates the device — the oxygen destroyer — that ultimately destroys Godzilla, but who is tortured by the thought of his discovery falling into the wrong hands and being used as a super-weapon. At the climax of *Gojira*, Serizawa commits suicide, choosing to die in the depths of Tokyo Bay beside Godzilla, taking the formula for the oxygen destroyer with him to his watery grave. The apocalyptic fruits of Japanese science, the film thus bids us to conclude, would only be used for noble ends, for the preservation of humankind. This starkly contrasts, of course, with America's mastery of the atom and its inhumane use of atomic technology at Hiroshima and Nagasaki. "The moral here is obvious," as one commentator notes, "'good' Japanese science, which would never be used for aggressive or self-serving ends, triumphs over 'bad' American science, which bears responsibility, after all, for creating the scourge of Godzilla. Japanese audiences could thus leave *Gojira* confident in the knowledge that the monster was vanquished, that their nation had prevailed single-handedly, and that Japan was superior — technologically as well as morally — to atomic-age America" (Tsutsui, *Godzilla on My Mind* 36).

These themes come out particularly nicely in 1991's *Godzilla vs. King Ghidorah/Gojira vs. Kingu Gidora*, which posited a new genesis story for Godzilla, depicting the monster as having begun life on an remote Pacific island as a solitary surviving dinosaur, later rendered gigantic, radioactive, and implacable by American nuclear tests. During World War II, the dinosaur's isolated home was occupied by a company of Japanese marines and when U.S. troops storm the island in 1944, the proto–Godzilla emerges from the jungle to fight side-by-side with the Japanese to repel the American landing. Needless to say, this revisionist view of Godzilla's inception — with the king of the monsters cast as a patriotic Japanese soldier — was not received well in the United States: veterans groups protested, Hollywood distributors were chilly, and the movie was not released in America until 1998 (Tsutsui, *Godzilla on My Mind* 102).

Second, as most fans of the series will have noticed, Godzilla changes over time from being an enemy of Japan (which the monster clearly is in the first movie) to being a defender and champion of Japan against legions of other monsters, credulity-stretching aliens, and even residents of an Atlantis-like undersea civilization. Godzilla, in fact, seems to become "Japanese" over time, less an outsider than part of *wareware Nihonjin* ("we Japanese"). As historian Yoshikuni Igarashi has persuasively argued, Godzilla's transformation reflected larger transitions in Japanese society: "In 1960s Japan, a place overflowing with optimism inspired by economic growth, the monsters could not find a place other than as caricatures. The darkness that prevailed in the first two films of the mid–1950s had vanished from the screen and Japanese society" (121). In a reconstructed, increasingly self-confident and wealthy Japan, moviegoers were not interested in seeing a monster destroy Tokyo Tower, the Olympic stadium, or the budding skyline, the very symbols of Japan's postwar economic resurgence. Instead, Godzilla was "tamed and transformed" into a homegrown superhero, "a guardian of postwar Japan's prosperity" (Igarashi 121).

Yet really, and this is where the ambivalence comes in, Godzilla is never entirely friendly and protective: he always remains surprisingly hostile toward Japan and he never, of course, can become truly Japanese. Godzilla must always remain an alien himself, an unpredictable "other." Even if fresh from saving Japan from hostile invaders, "some deep genetic programming keeps even the benevolent Godzilla from taking the shortest, least populated route back to the sea; after a busy day of vanquishing outsized enemies, Godzilla always seems to have enough energy, before that long swim home to Monster Island, to drag his big scaly feet through the nearest urban area" (Tsutsui, *Godzilla on My Mind* 86–87).

Third, the vulnerability of Japan is a consistent theme in the Godzilla films, reflecting a similar strand in the Japanese popular imagination. Godzilla is portrayed, from the original 1954 feature on, as an unpredictable and uncontrollable force of nature, much like the earthquakes, volcanoes, typhoons, and tsunamis that batter a helpless Japan. Moreover, the Godzilla series also seems to reflect a sense of vulnerability to international political and economic forces beyond Japan's control: the Cold War, the oil shocks of the 1970s, economic protectionism, "Japan bashing," and so forth. Even in the 1980s and early 1990s, when Japan appeared headed for global economic dominance, the theme of Japanese vulnerability persisted in the Heisei Godzilla series, although the moral valence of this vulnerability gradually began to change. In the films made during the go-go "Bubble Economy" of the 1980s, Japan sometimes seemed less an innocent victim than a victim of its own success: "No longer compelling as radiation-made-flesh or a cinematic metaphor of wartime suffering, Godzilla was transformed in the Heisei series into a conscience for Japan, an uncontrollable natural force that popped the bubble of Japan's inflated national pride" (Tsutsui, *Godzilla on My Mind* 72). Producer Tanaka Tomoyuki insisted that Godzilla bring down the most ostentatious monuments of Japan's 1990s prosperity: the extravagant Tokyo civic complex in Shinjuku, the plethora of new waterfront developments, "the vain symbols of these abundant days," as Tanaka called them. "Japan is rich and people can buy whatever they want," he explained. "But what is behind that wealth? Nothing very spiritual. Everyone's so concerned with the material, and then

Godzilla comes and rips it all apart. I suspect that is good for us to see" (qtd. in Kalat 162)

Fourth, in common with most works of science fiction, whether Japanese or Western, the attitudes toward science and technology revealed in the Godzilla movies also appear quite ambivalent. There clearly is an anti-science theme in the films: Godzilla is the result of science gone wrong, anti-pollution and pro-environment messages appear in many movies, and there are plenty of mad, evil scientists on the scene. Godzilla himself often appears to be anti-progress and anti-technology: he levels cities, destroys industrial areas, and just about always manages to trample Japan's most modern and impressive real estate developments. Godzilla does occasionally devastate the repositories of Japanese tradition (including Kyoto, though never, one should note, the Imperial Palace in Tokyo) but he seems especially drawn to the flashy, modern, and industrial.

Although Godzilla may thus have the air of a Luddite about him, one cannot help but notice that the Godzilla films often revolve around scientists and scientific discovery, and it is often the heroic efforts of dedicated researchers that save Japan from Godzilla, as in the original 1954 offering. The movies also stress the humanity of scientists, especially Japanese ones: in *Gojira*, the paleontologist Dr. Yamane shows sympathy for the monster and yearns to study rather than destroy it, while Serizawa is tortured by the guilt of creating a super weapon. And so, as is typical in the genre of science fiction, the overall impression of science and scientists in the Godzilla series ends up being fundamentally ambiguous.

Fifth and finally, and again in common with the larger sci-fi genre, attitudes toward authority are highlighted in the Godzilla films. The movies consistently underline the weakness of traditional authority figures in times of crisis: in virtually every film, the military, the government, and intellectuals appear impotent in the face of Godzilla's threat: blustering, divided, and often incompetent. Thus the Godzilla films would seem to have a somewhat critical perspective on the establishment. But, at the same time, one could well argue that the films actually have a much more insidious subtext and that their message in fact reflects more conservative, even reactionary, undercurrents in postwar Japanese society.

Godzilla, for instance, doesn't really seem to be a great respecter of democratic values. In the 1954 *Gojira*, the king of the monsters makes a point of walking through the Diet Building, the home of Japan's parliament and the symbolic heart of Japan's postwar democracy. What's more, an earlier scene in the film features a rancorous debate in a Diet committee, with conservative representatives arguing that all information on Godzilla should be withheld from the public to prevent general panic, while left-wing opposition politicians stridently call for full disclosure, shouting "The truth is the truth.... The truth must be made public!" "But what is Godzilla's message in this deliberate destruction of the seat of Japan's democracy?" one scholar asks.

> Is there a message at all? Was the Diet, like the Empire State Building in *King Kong*, just a convenient landmark for the filmmakers to exploit? Or was Godzilla symbolically sticking one to the smarmy conservative politicians who tried — oh so unsuccessfully — to conceal his very existence? Or, most provocatively of all, might Godzilla have been rendering a judgment on democracy writ large, his actions a damning statement on the divisiveness, infighting, and ultimate impotence of democratic politics and, specifically, of Japan's fractured postwar political system? [Tsutsui, *Godzilla on My Mind* 92].

Provocatively, reports from the time suggested that Japanese audiences generally viewed *Gojira* in respectful, somber silence, some viewers even leaving the theaters in tears. The crowds were said to have broken into cheers, applause, and raucous laughter at only one point in the film, just when Godzilla expresses an apparently widely shared disgust with the political system by trampling the Diet Building into rubble.

The depiction of the military in the Godzilla films is also worth considering. Perhaps not surprisingly, the Japanese armed forces play a major recurring role in all the films in the *kaijū eiga* genre. Whenever Japan is threatened, either by Godzilla or any of his numerous monstrous adversaries, the Japanese military is there to provide admirable (but generally futile) defensive service with all manner of up-to-date (and sometimes purely fantastical) frigates, howitzers, jets, and laser cannons. Considering that the Godzilla series began less than a decade after Japan's defeat in World War II, this martial focus, which in some movies escalates to the full-scale glorification of the Japanese military, is curious. In the wake of the war, the Japanese public embraced pacifism and a commonly held vision was the idealistic reconstruction of the nation as a kind of Asian Switzerland. This was formalized in the 1946 constitution, drafted by Douglas MacArthur's occupation forces, that declared, in its famous Article 9, "Aspiring sincerely to an international peace based on justice and order, the Japanese people forever renounce war as a sovereign right of the nation and the threat or use of force as means of settling international disputes.... Land, sea, and air forces, as well as other war potential, will never be maintained." Japan would gradually remilitarize, though only under the banner of limited "Self Defense Forces," and public opinion would generally continue to resist Japan's reemergence as a military power.

It is in this light that the prevalence of Japanese armed forces in the Godzilla films, complete with plentiful military hardware and numerous rousing battle sequences, deserves comment. As Joseph Anderson and Donald

Richie wrote in 1959: "The temper of the Japanese populace in the mid–1950s was such that no film which in any way favored the Self Defense Forces and rearmament could have been successful at the box office; hence none was made. The few pictures which used Self Defense Forces for other than minor characters have shown the new military in an unfavorable manner" (269). Anderson and Richie must not have been watching monster movies very closely, because the Godzilla films (from the 1950s and beyond) regularly depicted Japan's postwar soldiers, sailors, and airmen and their tanks, destroyers, and bombers in a favorable, even heroic manner. By the late–1980s and 1990s, some of the taboos against celebrating the Japanese in popular culture had weakened, and Japanese society in general had drifted toward the political right, so many of the more recent Godzilla features — notably *Godzilla, Mothra, and King Ghidorah: Giant Monsters All-Out Attack/Gojira, Mosura, Kingu Gidora: Daikaijū sōkōgeki* (2001) — have been even more overt in exalting the honor, resolve, and sheer might of the Self Defense Forces.

It might be tempting to discount the impact of monster movies, especially those largely directed at children, on the postwar Japanese discourse of remilitarization, yet it is hard to ignore the positive portrayals of the military and the frequent battle scenes in the Godzilla series. As one scholar has concluded,

> Producers and directors, who could not, given the political sensitivities of the day, show the nation's troops engaging Americans, Russians, or Asians of any stripe were able to depict combat, showcase flashy new weapons, and gently stir nationalistic sentiments using Godzilla and other giant monsters as a foil. One of the great spectacles of modern cinema — the heroic battlefield — was thus rehabilitated for use in postwar Japan, with a fictional radioactive reptile installed as a legitimate and ideologically sound target for the nation's military might. One can only imagine, of course, what impact all this had on the viewers of the Godzilla films, and especially the impressionable preteens who have, over the decades, been the series' most devoted audience. We will never know for sure if a steady childhood diet of Godzilla pictures ... conditioned today's Japanese adults to favor a more assertive military policy or a less restrictive notion of pacifism.... Might we even regard the Godzilla films as a kind of military pornography, allowing the guilt-ridden, chastened, and disarmed Japanese public to indulge its illicit (and explicit) martial fantasies on the silver screen? [Tsutsui, *Godzilla on My Mind* 97].

With all this in mind, how, in the end, should Godzilla be characterized? Is Godzilla a subversive or a reactionary? Is Godzilla a rebel without a cause or a harsh social critic? An unpredictable natural disaster or the reptilian conscience of a materially wealthy but spiritually bankrupt Japan? Is Godzilla a harmless actor in rubber suit or a tool of right-wing indoctrination aimed at Japanese youth? The notions of ambivalence and ambiguity might well provide the answers here. Godzilla sends a mixed message: as both an enemy and a defender, both a force of nature and the product of high technology, as both an outsider and yet somehow truly Japanese, Godzilla was, in a way, like the larger processes of modernization and industrialization that postwar Japan was undergoing. Godzilla, like the modern world, could be both a curse and a blessing, both something alien and something Japanese. Perhaps above all, Godzilla, like the challenges of modern life, was inevitable and unavoidable, and Japan was forced to take the good with the bad in the decades after World War II.

Thus the Godzilla series, contrary to the assumptions of most critics, did not offer just the lighthearted pleasures of giant monsters wrestling or the escapist thrills of imaginative science fiction, though such rewards were no doubt sufficient for many a Japanese viewer. The Godzilla films also responded to deeper fears and fantasies, exploring unresolved tensions in Japanese society — from war memory and nuclear anxiety, to anti–American hostilities, to a pervasive sense of vulnerability, to the specters of a prosperous society, to the quandaries of nationalism and rearmament — in a format easily (and frequently) dismissed by critics as superficial and juvenile. One should not overlook the sensitivity of Tanaka Tomoyuki and the other men behind Godzilla to the changing moods of Japanese audiences, the ever-shifting eddies of Japan's politics, culture, and international relations, and the complex web of factors that kept the crowds buying tickets for Tōhō's creature feature fare. Considering that the king of the monsters' greatest battles may not have been against King Kong or Mothra, but against all the other competing leisure options available to Japanese consumers in the postwar era, the sustained popularity of Godzilla is a tribute to the series's ability to find audiences and consistently meet their demands for kinetic, creative, and relevant entertainment.

The World of Tora-san

Unlike the Godzilla franchise, the *Otoko wa tsurai yo* ("It's Tough Being a Man") films were not the standard film series fare. As critic Mark Shilling has observed, "The series lacked the usual elements of formula success: sex, action, special effects, and stud superstars" ("Into the Heartland" 245). Indeed, the films' central character, Kuruma Torajirō (or Tora-san as he was affectionately known) was "a squat, square-faced, middle-aged man who never finished junior high school, couldn't hold a steady job, and never got the girl" (Shilling, "Into the Heartland" 245). But this sentimental and nostalgic story of an itinerant peddler, his long-suffering Tokyo family, and the string of women he loved and lost was a veritable institution in Japan, a cinematic phenomenon spanning 27 years and 48 pictures from its feature-film debut in 1969 to the death of lead actor Atsumi Kiyoshi in 1996. Atsumi's alter ego Tora-san was said to be the second most recognizable personality, just behind the Emperor Hirohito, among the postwar Japanese public and the series enjoyed broad-based, enduring popularity, as well as consistent box-office success. Humorous and heartwarming family fare, invariably released at the start of the year or in the midst of the summer, the *Otoko wa tsurai yo* movies became part of the lives of the Japanese people, customary components of families' New Year celebrations and *o-bon* festival activities as much as greeting cards and seasonal delicacies. As the journalist Ian Buruma put it, the unlikely hero Tora-san became "an icon of Japanese popular culture like no other" (210).

The Tora-san films were the creation of Shōchiku's Yamada Yōji, who wrote all of the scripts and directed almost all of the installments of the franchise, and grew out of a short-lived (but popularly acclaimed) series on CX-TV (Fuji Television). The franchise was also born of longstanding traditions at Shōchiku, which had built its reputation before the war on *shomin geki*, what Satō Tadao calls "humanistic stories on the lives of average city dwellers," and above all *hōmu dorama* ("home dramas"), melodramatic tear-jerkers for female audiences (214). The champion of these genres was long-time studio head Kidō Shiro, tagged the "Louis B. Mayer of Shōchiku," whose faith in the Japanese family system and the values of "healthy family life" infused his company's product with a gentle humor and a characteristic weepy sentimentality (Anderson and Richie 321, 450–51). This strong "Ōfuna flavor" (named after the location of Shōchiku's studios in suburban Tokyo), distilled and perfected by Yamada, was the imaginative foundation of the *Otoko wa tsurai yo* pictures.

The basic story line of the series was deceptively simple: Tora-san was an eternally middle-aged good-for-nothing, who ran away from his home in the old *shitamachi* ("downtown") of Tokyo in his teens to become a *tekiya*, what Keiko McDonald translates as a "con-artist vendor," a kind of disreputable traveling huckster and low-level gangster (*yakuza*) (167). In the first film of the series, *Tora-san, Our Lovable Tramp/Otoko wa tsurai yo* (1969), Tora-san returns home for the first time in twenty years to see his remaining family, his half-sister Sakura and an aging uncle and aunt, who operate a decidedly old-fashioned *dango* ("rice dumpling") shop, the Toraya. In this, and each of the subsequent films, the same plot is invariably played out: Tora is welcomed home by his warm and thoroughly conventional family, only to quarrel with them over some trifle; he then meets a woman, either in his travels or in his family's neighborhood, who he immediately falls for; after a short courtship, in which Tora-san's love is always idealized and platonic (and almost never reciprocated), his heart is broken when the object of his affection marries another, runs off to pursue a dream or, in at least one case, dies; the disconsolate Tora then hits the road again and, reinvigorated by travel and peddling, is soon ready to start yet another adventure (and another film).

Almost all of the films begin with a pre-credit dream sequence, in which Tora-san, napping on a lonely railway platform or a farmer's haystack on one of his trips around Japan, imagines himself as "the hero in popular entertainments who inspires the admiration of the people back at the Toraya" (Torrance 237). Over the 48 pictures of the series, these light-hearted vignettes parodied virtually every genre of Japanese and Hollywood filmmaking, from swashbuckling samurai epics, to science fiction blockbusters, to pirate movies, to spaghetti westerns. In *Tora-san, The Matchmaker/Otoko wa tsurai yo: Tonderu Torajirō* (1979), for example, Tora is a mad scientist ardently striving to rid the world of constipation; in *Tora-san's Tropical Fever/Otoko wa tsurai yo: Torajirō haibisukasu no hana* (1980), he is a Tokugawa period (1600–1868) bandit, a kind of Japanese Robin Hood, who robs from the rich to help his impoverished family. The consistent subtext of these comedic sequences is Tora's desperate (and always unfulfilled) quest to prove himself worthy in the eyes of his saintly sister and his family back in Tokyo. The same yearning is addressed in the series's theme song, delivered with gusto by Atsumi Kiyoshi and addressed to Sakura: "You know, young sister, your brother's a *yakuza*. One day I'll become a brother you can be proud of" (trans. in Torrance 228). Such sentiments, usually played over scenes of very physical slapstick comedy as Tora-san returns home along the banks of the Edo River, underline the bittersweet nature of the *Otoko wa tsurai yo* films, fusing feelings of regret and disappointment with familial warmth and broad humor.

The quirky and distinctive personality of Tora-san, accurately described by journalist Ian Buruma as "arguably the most beloved character in the history of the Japanese cinema," is at the core of the films and their enduring popular appeal (209). Hot tempered yet tender hearted, easily offended yet also quick to fall in love, indolent and selfish yet surprisingly generous of spirit, Tora was a beguiling contradiction, thoroughly annoying but charming in his good-natured innocence. As Buruma put it, "with his golden heart, his quick temper, his easy sentimentality, his zest for life, his slyness, his failures, and his fast verbal humor, he [was] the mythical Everyman of urban Japan" (210). But Kuruma Torajirō was far from average. He was, of course, an "incurable romantic," yearning always for that elusive perfect someone and the stereotype of domestic bliss (Shilling, "Into the Heartland" 249). And he was also a true free spirit, a footloose vagabond, "the tiger who wanders on the wind" (*fūten no Tora*), never able to get the girl but, equally, never willing to settle down and accept a conventional, restricted life. Perhaps most noticeably, Tora-san was an anachronism in postwar "miracle economy" Japan, a throwback in appearance, profession, language, values, and lifestyle. Dressed for almost three decades in the same ridiculously unstylish clothing—a garish checkered suit, a woolen stomach warmer (*haramaki*), an undershirt, sandals, a good luck charm (*omamori*) around his neck, and a trademark tawny fedora—he was a singular individual in a society becoming ever more conformist. As Yamada Yōji described his protagonist, "He's really a sad character, a lonely character," yet Tora-san rose above the pathos with his sense of humor, his easygoing resilience, and his perpetual optimism (qtd. in Shilling, "Into the Heartland" 248).

Tora-san also relied on his family, and the portrait of life in an extended Japanese family, as anachronistic and romanticized in some ways as Tora himself, is another of the aspects of the *Otoko wa tsurai yo* series that captured the imagination of Japanese audiences. The modest Toraya was as familiar and comfortable a space to Japanese moviegoers as Archie Bunker's living room was to American television viewers at much the same time. Tora's uncle (Oichan) and aunt (Obachan) lived in the shop, with Tora's room upstairs, while nearby, just across the garden, a crowded printing shop, one of the myriad small enterprises that formed the base of the Japanese economy after World War II, was overseen by an intimate family friend, the bumbling company president (*shachō*) or, as he was nicknamed by Tora, Tako ("octopus"). Sakura, meanwhile, lived nearby with her husband, a foreman at the printing outfit named Hiroshi, who she married in the first film of the series, and a single son, Mitsuo. Like Tora-san, the family ensemble is thoroughly warm-hearted yet, unlike their wandering black sheep, they are thoroughly conventional: Oichan and Obachan are stereotypes of Japanese shopkeepers of an older generation, largely disapproving foils for Tora's antics; Hiroshi is a voice of probity and good common sense; Tako is a source of clumsy comic relief; and Sakura is "the ideal Japanese mother-figure," endlessly patient with Tora (who she familiarly calls Oniichan, "older brother") and always hoping that the wanderer will finally settle down (Buruma 214). The cast of the Toraya circle remained remarkably stable over the years (with the exception of the uncle, who was played by three actors, all of the other parts remained the same over the life of the series) and audiences could understandably feel like they had become part of the Kuruma family, watching Obachan grow elderly, following Mitsuo from crib to college, and standing by Sakura in her unfailing dedication to Tora. Home thus became a reassuring refuge, for the character Tora-san and the films' audiences alike, a place seemingly untouched by the vast changes in postwar Japanese society and always ready to welcome back, with affection and forbearance, that most wayward of sons.

While Tora-san and his family provided a strong element of continuity to the series, his love interests (numbering more than thirty over the years), provided a dose of novelty and variety in almost every installment of the franchise. These women, known as "madonnas," ended up being a virtual who's who of up-and-coming actresses in Japanese popular cinema, as a cameo in Tora's latest adventure was considered a sure way of helping a budding career. Despite the centrality of Tora-san to the *Otoko wa tsurai yo* movies, this constantly changing parade of female guest stars was an added appeal of the series and focused considerable attention on women and gender roles in postwar Japan. As Richard Torrance has detailed, the stories of the various madonnas highlight the changes in Japanese marriage customs, the prevalence of female business owners, the increasing choices available to educated women, and the vulnerability of Japanese wives widowed, divorced, or abandoned in the last decades of the Shōwa period (240–45). If Tora and his family were amiable and generally unchanging anachronisms, the madonnas were unmistakable reminders of contemporary, relevant, and ever-changing social issues.

In many ways, place was as important as character in establishing the distinctive flavor of the *Otoko wa tsurai yo* series. Tora-san's home, Shibamata in Katsushika ward of Tokyo, has long been something of an urban backwater and is depicted in the movies more as a cohesive, traditional village than as a part of Japan's greatest megalopolis. Life focuses on Shibamata's main thoroughfare, only wide enough for a single car to pass, crowded on both sides with myriad small shops (including the Toraya), the railway station at one end and the Taishakuten (Shibamata Daikyōji) temple at the other. Nearby are the grassy banks of the Edo River, always active with children, fishermen, and young couples, and usually the site of Tora's boisterous arrivals and tearful departures. The rhythms of life are marked by the regular toll of the temple bell, the horn of the passing tofu vendor, and the predictable procession of seasons, festivals, and holidays. The contrast is stark between the warm familiarity of Shibamata and the cold loneliness of the many towns around Japan where Tora-san travels to ply his trade (over the course of the series Tora-san visited every prefecture in the nation and one foreign country, Austria). As the critic Satō Tadao concluded, "The appeal of the series lies in [Tora's] free spirit and in [his] home, Katsushika Shibamata.... It is this idealization of the old neighborhood that captures the heart of modern Japanese audiences" (243).

Critics, and especially Western critics, have generally had few good words for the *Otoko wa tsurai yo* series as a whole. Mark Shilling, for example, characterizes the films as "formulaic, sentimental, not all that funny, little more than a cinematic soap opera with an unusually long run" (*Encylopedia* 269); Torrance bemoans "a formulaic plot of little interest ... and what can only be termed visually derivative images" (231); and Buruma labels Tora-san "a series that goes on for ever in endless variations of the same story" (*Encyclopedia* 269, 209, 231). Shilling, in fact, argues that unimaginative predictability and popularity went hand in hand: "A main appeal of the series was the very sameness that the critics attacked it for; Japanese who rarely went to the movies (the vast majority) would go to a Tora-san film because they knew exactly what they were getting. For them, it was like watching the latest episode of a television series" (*Encyclopedia* 252). But the series is hardly as uniform as many Western viewers would protest: while the films share a basic story line and are hardly action-packed by Hollywood standards, the 48 Tora-san features are far from the same and exhibit subtle differences and creative nuances that argue strongly for the sophistication of Japanese movie audiences, not their undiscriminating taste for ever more of the same. Torrance concedes this point, noting the "extraordinary complexity of the series, both formalistically and in terms of sociohistorical content" and concludes "it would be facile to dismiss [the movies] with the observation that they follow a formula. Each is different, each is constructed with extraordinary care" (227, 235).

One notable aspect of the creativity of the series is the language used by the characters, and specifically by Tora-san himself. What in part makes Tora such an appealing, amusing, and unforgettable individual (to madonnas and movie audiences alike) is his incredible verbal dexterity. He can tell a good story, crack an off-color joke, modulate his expression to meet every situation, pull off a wicked pun, and thrill with the distinctive and complex patter of the *tekiya*. For instance, one of his trademark lines, hilariously vulgar and almost poetic in its rhythms, delivered with spirit in virtually every one of the movies, was "Fine, that's fine, a cat's fine fur is covered with ash, and your ass is covered with shit" (*Kekkō kedarake, neko haidarake, oshiri no mawari wa kuso darake*) (trans. in Torrance 231). Torrance notes Tora's "comic eloquence" as well as the "literary quality of the screenplays" and, in fact, many of the scripts were published in Japan and Tora-san's most memorable one-liners anthologized in book collections (231). Linda Ehrlich has analyzed the roots of Tora's humor in the traditional Japanese theatrical form of *kyōgen* and numerous commentators have demonstrated its links to *rakugo*, a form of comic storytelling indigenous to Japan. But Tora-san's speech is also very much drawn from his locale, the lively and unpretentious world of Tokyo's old *shitamachi*, as well as from a specific socioeconomic milieu, the world of peddlers, small-time hoodlums, red-light districts, and working-class informality. In his language, as in his lifestyle and clothing, Tora-san was an unabashed anachronism in the "managed society" (*kanri shakai*) of postwar Japan, but in almost every word he spoke the cleverness and creativity of the character, the screenwriter (Yamada Yōji), and the actor (Atsumi Kiyoshi) shone through.

Moreover, although casual viewers may be struck by the sameness of the films, long-term viewers were no doubt aware of the many subtle and gradual (and thus quite realistic) changes in the lot of the Kuruma family and the world around them over the course of the series. As Ehrlich observes, "the content of the episodes in this series has adapted to the times, reflecting not stasis but considerable change, both within the microcosm of the central family and the macrocosm of the society at large" (102). So, in addition to seeing the members of the Toraya clan age and move through the life course, we also see them participate in the growing affluence, consumerism, and general social striving of their times: Sakura, when first married, lives in a tiny apartment and shares a hallway telephone, but later gets her own phone line and, later yet, moves with Hiroshi into a modest house of their own; Hiroshi progresses from being a laborer in the print shop to a foreman to finally, after 1983, a part owner of the operation; Mitsuo is the first in his family to successfully enter college; and the quotidian talismans of economic success — domestic appliances like televisions and rice cookers — keep multiplying in the dark old *dango* shop. As numerous scholars have observed, the Kurumas created a cinematic baseline for what it meant in Japan to be middle class, a crucial component in both individual and national identity in the wake of World War II's widespread destruction. Moreover, one can trace the passage of time and the marks of history in countless minor ways through the *Otoko wa tsurai yo* films, from the steadily inflating price of the sweets sold in the Toraya to the product mix that Tora-san hawks on his travels, what Torrance calls "a sort of museum of popular culture's junk" (249). In short, while Tora-san and his happy home may indeed have been idealized throwbacks, they did not inhabit an unchanging, fossilized world.

Nostalgia, Parody, and Popularity

One of the most striking aspects of the *Otoko wa tsurai yo* series was its remarkably consistent popularity over the decades. From 1971, when the eighth film in the franchise, *Tora-san's Love Call/Otoko wa tsurai yo: Torajirō koiuta*, attracted 1.48 million moviegoers and ranked number one at the box office, both for Japanese pictures and for all films including imports, every Tora-san offering sold at least 1.3 million tickets and finished in the top ten of Japanese movies for the year. Many of the films were seen by audiences in excess of two million people and, from 1975 through 1996, 31 of the 35 Tora-san pictures released grossed more than ¥1 billion, sure-fire hits by Japanese cinema standards. Unlike most other series (including the Godzilla films), Tora-san never really experienced a slump at the box office and the penultimate *Otoko wa tsurai yo* film, *Tora-san's Easy Advice/Otoko wa tsurai yo: Haikei, Tora-jirō-sama* (1994), sold 2.18 million tickets, earned ¥1.55 million, and was the third highest grossing Japanese film of the year. Although none of the films in the series were huge blockbusters (not approaching the results, for example, of *King Kong vs. Godzilla* in 1962 or some of the Heisei series entries of the 1990s), Tora-san was a steady performer and a crucial contributor to Shōchiku's bottom line. As Anderson and Richie have noted, the traveling salesman from Shibamata carried a whole studio on his back in the darkest days of the postwar movie industry: "desperate Shōchiku survived in the theatrical film market during the 1970s almost entirely on earnings from the semiannual releases in [the] home drama series, *It's Tough Being a Man*" (451).

The widespread popularity of Tora-san was further demonstrated in 1996 when over 100,000 people paid their respects to the late Atsumi Kiyoshi at Shōchiku's studios in Ōfuna; as Torrance reported, the crowd was a representative sample of Japanese society, "men and women, children, the elderly, young couples, and the middle-aged" (226). Indeed, Tora-san seems to have enjoyed a loyal audience and a diverse one: "He is not much liked by 'interi' [intelligentsia] film buffs," Ian Buruma observed, "but keeps drawing a huge popular audience. People who never go to the cinema will go and see the latest Tora-san movie" (209). In the early days of the series, however, the *Otoko wa tsurai yo* films were targeted at a more specific demographic, those "migrant workers and students from regional areas" who had come in large numbers to Tokyo and Japan's other major cities and who, isolated from home and family networks, were some of the most dependable customers for Japanese movie theaters in the 1960s and 1970s (Satō 236–37). As one Shōchiku publicist noted at the time, advertising for the series was "mainly aimed at shop-assistants, manual workers, and students leading lonely lives away from home" (qtd. in Buruma 212). The content of the films addressed the needs of these groups adeptly: in addition to romanticizing the warm and ever-welcoming home, the movies consistently focused on stories of young migrants and their struggles to find a place for themselves in the city, to negotiate relationships with families back home, and to discover love in an alienating environment. But if Tora-san began his cinematic career playing to the uprooted in Japan's mass postwar exodus of youth from the provinces to the cities, he ended up being a character of far broader resonance and demographic appeal; as film scholar Gregory Barrett has observed, the *Otoko wa tsurai yo* pictures were eventually "labeled *kokumin no eiga*, meaning films for the whole Japanese nation" ("Comic Targets" 222).

Scholars and film critics have struggled to explain the extraordinary popularity of Tora-san. As Richard Torrance has summarized the literature,

> Critics writing in a journalistic style tend to ascribe the popularity of the series to a single source: the formulaic quality of the plots, nostalgia, or the fact that the series came to perform a ceremonial function of celebration at New Year's, when one of the movies in the series was often released. These sources of appeal are commonly identified with a specific sociological characteristic of the Japanese, for example, the audience for these films as "cogs in the great Japanese export machine" or as the proverbial nails that have gotten hammered down. Nostalgia, or something like it, is one of the most frequently cited sources of the films' appeal for a mass audience by writers for an English-speaking readership [226–27].

Indeed, most Western observers identify the draw of the Tora-san films as a kind of nostalgic yearning for a simpler, gentler, less frenetic and impersonal Japanese past. "His films depict a nostalgic ideal," Mark Shilling argues. "Their Japan is not the country of conniving businessmen, lying politicians, and corrupt bureaucrats, but a warm heartland where even a wandering *tekiya* without the right diploma or business card can feel at home" ("Into the Heartland" 255). Tora-san, in other words, was an anachronistic alternative to the "work-obsessed, upwardly mobile, elite salaryman," a happy-go-lucky wanderer with little ambition but lots of heart and boundless optimism (Shilling, *Encyclopedia* 271). Tora, many observers have asserted, could thus be a refreshing tonic to all those Japanese who willingly joined the corporate rat-race after World War II, and yet who longingly looked backwards to a less standardized, competitive, and fragmented society.

Commentators have been divided over the question of whether Tora-san, in his role as a cinematic vehicle for nostalgic cravings, was seen by audiences as worthy of admiration or more as the object of pity. A number of critics have suggested that he was perceived as a hero, the ultimate free spirit or a kind of rebel drifter; as Barrett suggested, some "read an impeachment of modern, bureaucratized Japan in the free spirit of Tora-san" (*Archetypes* 91). Moreover, for all his faults, Tora-san could be (and in fact often was) held up as an ideal of worthy, albeit increasingly rare, Japanese values, the distinctive humanity, sensitivity, and genuineness that were apparently vanishing in "miracle economy" Japan. From the more cynical perspective of Ian Buruma, however, Tora was less inspiring role model and more reassuring loser, the failure whose misfortunes could make everyone else feel better about their lots in life: "Poor Tora-san, the lazy, unmarried failure: he is everything the average Japanese citizen is not. But he will always be loved for the same reason Edo townsmen loved prostitutes and actors and modern cinema audiences admire gangsters, *rōnin* [masterless samurai], and *nihirisutos* [nihilists]: the tragic fate of the outsider confirms how lucky we all are to lead such restricted, respectable, and in most cases, perfectly harmless lives" (218).

Other scholars, most notably Richard Torrance, have found the appeal of the *Otoko wa tsurai yo* series elsewhere, far removed from the psychic rewards to moviegoers of nostalgic reveries or the voyeuristic pleasures of failure. The compelling depiction of life as lived, Torrance argues, not a romanticized or ideal vision of life as it once may have been, is the core of Tora-san's attraction to Japanese audiences: "The appeal of the series, then, lies not so much in nostalgia as in the realistic portrayal of long-standing continuities in patterns of everyday life revealed through changing economic circumstances" (247). Japanese moviegoers, in short, have been enamored of Tora and the gang back at the Toraya because they can relate to them, far better, in fact, than they can relate to other icons in Japanese popular culture. This, Torrance suggests, is the other crucial aspect of the series's success: its ability to parody any and every other aspect of Japanese mass culture. The *Otoko wa tsurai yo* franchise "parodies from a common perspective (necessarily a class perspective) the representations of reality by other genres of the mass media and exposes as comical the stereotypes of popular entertainment" (246). The humor of the Tora-san films thus derive from the fun they poke (overtly and in more nuanced ways) at cinematic genres like *yakuza* films, samurai period pieces, and *hōmu dorama*, and the pointed (though always comic) barbs they shoot at intellectuals, big business, bureaucrats, the social elites, and state institutions like police and welfare agencies.

However Tora-san and his movies are interpreted, critics and moviegoers alike seem to agree that there is something distinctively Japanese about them. To Yamada Yōji, this was at least partially intentional, since he hoped to showcase the *yasashisa*, what one might translate as "warmth," of the Japanese people. The Japanese have long imagined themselves as having this heightened sense of warm-heartedness, what Buruma describes as being "gentle, meek, kindly," and Tora-san, as well as his family, are "blessed with those unique Japanese antennae, always sensitive to each other's feelings which never need to be spoken" (211). This cultural specificity is seemingly confirmed by the fact that, while Japanese audiences have flocked to the *Otoko wa tsurai yo* features, the series has never generated much interest abroad, and certainly not the kind of international attention and fandom that Godzilla and *kaijū eiga* have. Ehrlich politely observes that the films don't "translate well cross-culturally" (115), while Shilling states more bluntly that "foreigners never quite got the point" (268). The extreme *yasashisa* of the series might be partially responsible for this, but more of the blame is certainly due to the difficulty of rendering Tora-san's complex language in subtitles, the familiar pitfalls of translating humor across cultural boundaries, or the dense web of parodic references to Japanese mass culture in the films. For whatever reason, the Tora-san movies, that highest grossing, longest running, and most beloved of postwar film series in Japan, has apparently proven "too Japanese for foreign consumption," a dish too heavy on local flavor to meet Western tastes (Ehrlich 102).

Conclusions

On the surface, the Godzilla films and the Tora-san series could not have been more different. *Gojira* and its progeny were special effects blockbusters, marketed with publicity agents' superlatives, packed with action, and frequently aimed at children; the *Otoko wa tsurai yo* pictures were completely low-tech, lacking in frills and glitter, and conceived on an intimate (rather than an epic) scale. The hero of the Tōhō series was the ultimate strong and silent type, almost always victorious, while the loquacious protagonist of the Shōchiku franchise was an exceedingly fluent talker, yet also a perennial loser, especially when it came to the opposite sex. The Godzilla movies were violent, colorful, and flashy (*hade* in Japanese); Tora-san, though colorful enough in his own idiosyncratic way, was part of films that stressed subtlety, warm human emotions (*yasashisa*), and the reassuring embrace of the Japanese family. And while Tora was rooted in one continuous narrative (and one ensemble cast) stretching unbroken over almost three decades, the stories of the Godzilla features were fragmented, the casts of monstrous opponents were unpredictably varied, and even the headliner, Godzilla himself, died or was killed with unsettling regularity.

Perhaps the most noteworthy difference between the two series was their reception overseas. Godzilla was and is an international phenomenon, almost as well known and beloved in North America as in Japan, a pop icon recognized globally as a symbol, not just of Japan, but of size, power, and (for better or worse) the campy delights of less-than-perfect special effects and inelegant dubbing. Tora-san, meanwhile, despite his popular appeal in Japan (where there was even once a television quiz show based entirely on *Otoko wa tsurai yo* trivia), has never commanded sizeable audiences abroad, including in Asian markets where melodramatic Japanese serials have often performed well. The popular culture theorist Iwabuchi Kōichi has argued provocatively that the Japanese entertainment products that are most successfully internationally those that are "culturally odorless," that is, those that lack any strong cultural markers, any scent, of being "made in Japan." Thus, "neutral" Japanese technologies like Walkmen, karaoke, and video-game systems have won worldwide acclaim, as have those pop culture forms consciously or unconsciously rendered *mukokuseki* ("lacking in nationality") like anime or character goods (26–28). In Iwabuchi's framework, Tora-san, with his distinctive patois, Shibamata roots, and characteristic *yasashisa*, just smells too much of Japan to be readily accepted by audiences overseas. And although one might disagree about whether Godzilla is actually *mukokuseki*, the king of the monsters, with a less overt cultural odor of Japan, has clearly been able to the make the translation abroad with ease.

For all their differences, however, there are also a number of unexpected similarities between the Godzilla and *Otoko wa tsurai yo* series. Both, for example, featured a strong central character with a complex, contradictory personality, heroic in ways yet intriguingly flawed. Both engaged with some serious and timely social issues, from the fear of nuclear testing to anti–American resentments to social alienation, but generally in oblique ways; the two series, in other words, were engaged and relevant, but not preachy. They also intertwined humor and drama and, at their finest moments, could prove extremely moving to audiences (only the most cynical fans could not be touched by the monster's deaths in *Gojira* and *Godzilla vs. Destroyer*, or Tora-san's most crushing romantic rejections). Both made extensive use of physical comedy (using actors in latex monsters suits, in one of the series at least) and were sophisticated in their parodies of other genres and pop culture forms. Both, furthermore, affirmed Japanese identity in a complex postwar world: the Godzilla films celebrated Japan's moral superiority and national pride, while Tora-san upheld the cherished vision of Japan as the homeland of delicate interpersonal values. Nostalgia was an important component in the long-term success of both franchises: the *Otoko wa tsurai yo* cycle rejoiced in anachronism and a vanishing Japan; the Godzilla films, especially over the past couple decades, found their steadiest audience among middle-aged fans who fondly remembered growing up with *kaijū eiga* in the 1960s. And the two series can both claim fans in one prominent family: Kim Il-Sung once admitted to liking the Tora-san pictures, though perhaps not as much as his son Kim Jong-Il loved Godzilla, since he never kidnapped Yamada Yōji to make his own North Korean domestic comedies.

One should not, of course, lose sight of the fact that both the Godzilla and *Otoko wa tsurai yo* dynasties enjoyed astonishing and impressively consistent long-term success at the box office, the likes of which few (if indeed any) other film series in Japan or elsewhere around the world have been able to boast. The attachment of loyal audiences to the characters of Godzilla and Tora-san, and to the predictable but nuanced formulas of *kaijū eiga* and *hōmu dorama*, set the two franchises apart as the most successful series in Japanese (and perhaps global) film history. Although highbrow critics seldom had much good to say about either Japan's most famous radioactive creature or the voluble *tekiya* from Shibamata, both series show the remarkable creativity of Japanese filmmakers who, working with limited resources and a relatively narrow range of characters, plots, and locations, crafted movies of lasting popular appeal. The two series are also a testament to the remarkable tenacity of Japanese studios in holding on in a highly competitive, shrinking domestic market, locking in segments of a dwindling audience with relevant, consistent, and entertaining products. For if the heroic king of the monsters and the lovable vagabond Tora-san are recognized as two of the most enduring and beloved icons of world cinema, they must also be seen as valuable commercial properties, the bankable headliners of franchises rooted in the changing audience demographics, constant market fluctuations, and hard-nosed business plans of Japan's postwar movie industry. And, in the end, understanding Japanese film culture, both domestically and as a global product, means not just acknowledging the importance of often-overlooked mass-market darlings like Godzilla and Tora-san but also accepting the centrality of film series to the artistic and economic evolution of Japanese cinema.

Works Cited

Allison, Anne. *Millennial Monsters: Japanese Toys and the Global Imagination*. Berkeley: University of California Press, 2006.
Anderson, Joseph L., and Donald Richie. *The Japanese Film: Art and Industry*. Expanded ed. Princeton: Princeton University Press, 1982.
Barrett, Gregory. *Archetypes in Japanese Film*. Selinsgrove, PA: Susquehanna University Press, 1989.
_____. "Comic Targets and Comic Styles: An Introduction to Japanese Film Comedies." *Reframing Japanese Cinema: Authorship, Genre, History*. Ed. Arthur Noletti, Jr. and David Desser. Bloomington: Indiana University Press, 1992. 210–26.
Burgess. John. "Godzilla Rises Again." *Washington Post* 19 December 1984.
Buruma, Ian. *Behind the Mask*. New York: Pantheon, 1984.
Crowther, Bosley. Review of *Godzilla, King of the Monsters*. *New York Times* 28 April 1956.
Ehrlich, Linda. "Comic Traveller: Tora-san and the Interweavings of Japanese Popular Culture." *A Century of Popular Culture in Japan*. Ed. Douglas Slaymaker. Lewiston, NY: Edwin Mellen, 2000.
Galbraith IV, Stuart. *Monsters Are Attacking Tokyo!* Venice, CA: Feral House, 1998.
Igarashi, Yoshikuni. *Bodies of Memory: Narratives of War in Postwar Japanese Culture, 1945–1970*. Princeton: Princeton University Press, 2000.

Iwabuchi, Kōichi. *Recentering Globalization: Popular Culture and Japanese Transnationalism.* Durham, NC: Duke University Press, 2002.

Kalat, David. *A Critical History and Filmography of Tōhō's Godzilla Series.* Jefferson, NC: McFarland, 1997.

Lees, J.D., and Marc Cerasini. *The Official Godzilla Compendium.* New York: Random House, 1998.

McDonald, Keiko. "The *Yakuza* Film: An Introduction." *Reframing Japanese Cinema: Authorship, Genre, History.* Ed. Arthur Noletti, Jr., and David Desser. Bloomington: Indiana University Press, 1992.

Napier, Susan. "Panic Sites: The Japanese Imagination of Disaster from *Godzilla* to *Akira*." *Journal of Japanese Studies* 19:2 (Summer 1993): 327–51.

Noriega, Chon. "Godzilla and the Japanese Nightmare: When *Them!* Is U.S." (1987). *Hibakusha Cinema: Hiroshima, Nagasaki and the Nuclear Image in Japanese Film.* Ed. Mick Broderick. London: Kegan Paul, 1996.

Richie, Donald. *Japanese Cinema: An Introduction.* New York: Oxford University Press, 1990.

_____. *A Hundred Years of Japanese Film.* Tokyo: Kodansha International, 2001.

Ryfle, Steve. *Japan's Favorite Mon-Star: The Unauthorized Biography of "The Big G."* Toronto: ECW Press, 1998.

Satō, Tadao. *Currents in Japanese Cinema.* Trans. Gregory Barrett. Tokyo: Kodansha International, 1982.

Sengo, Nihon Eiga Kenkyūkai, ed. *Ninki shirīzu.* Nihon eiga sengo ōgon jidai, vol 25. Tokyo: Nihon Bukku Raiburarī, 1978.

Shilling, Mark. *The Encyclopedia of Japanese Pop Culture.* New York: Weatherhill, 1997.

_____. "Into the Heartland with Tora-san." *Japan Pop! Inside the World of Japanese Popular Culture.* Ed. Timothy Craig. Armonk, NY: M.E. Sharpe, 2000.

Sontag, Susan. "The Imagination of Disaster" (1965). *Hibakusha Cinema: Hiroshima, Nagasaki and the Nuclear Image in Japanese Film.* Ed. Mick Broderick. London: Kegan Paul, 1996.

Tora-san Kurabu, ed. *"Otoko wa tsurai yo" Tora-san tokuhon.* Tokyo: PHP, 1996.

Torrance, Richard. "*Otoko wa tsurai yo*: Nostalgia or Parodic Realism?" *Word and Image in Japanese Cinema.* Ed. Dennis Washburn and Carole Cavanaugh. Cambridge: Cambridge University Press, 2001.

Tsutsui, William. *Godzilla on My Mind: Fifty Years of the King of Monsters.* New York: Palgrave Macmillan, 2004.

_____. "Introduction." *In Godzilla's Footsteps: Japanese Pop Culture Icons on the Global Stage.* Ed. William Tsutsui and Michiko Ito. New York: Palgrave Macmillan, 2006.

Tsutsui, William, and Michiko Ito, ed. *In Godzilla's Footsteps: Japanese Pop Culture Icons on the Global Stage.* New York: Palgrave Macmillan, 2006.

11

Serial Brotherhood: The Better Tomorrow Films and Some Wuxia *and* Western Cousins

KENNETH E. HALL

John Woo's *A Better Tomorrow* (1986) was followed by a sequel, also directed by Woo, and a prequel, directed by his producer Tsui Hark. The three films feature continuing characters and, particularly in the case of the Woo films, a dynamic of brotherhood and family relationships which has both traditional and more modern elements. One important feature of the family relationships in terms of brotherhood relates particularly to a characteristic distinguished by criticism of certain American films, namely the motif of the prodigal son.[1] This feature is seen most sharply in Woo's 1986 film, in which the nub of the conflict between the two brothers is precisely the nature of the elder's prodigality. The question is further complicated by the presence of the Mark character (Chow Yun-fat), who is a figurative brother to the elder Ho (Ti Lung) and who also displays prodigal qualities. The thrust of the film militates towards the resolution of the family conflicts, by means of reintegration and by elimination of the outlying "problem" in the person of Mark. Despite featuring such charged dynamics, however, this series has recognizable serial qualities insofar as it employs inventive (perhaps implausible) strategies to "continue" the characters, for example the introduction of the now-dead Mark's twin brother Ken (also played by Chow) in the 1987 sequel.

In this respect as in others, most notably the highlighting of "heroic bloodshed" in the *wuxia* or martial tradition,[2] the Better Tomorrow series bears similarities to other series films such as the nearby One-Armed Swordsman films (themselves a clear influence on the Woo films) and films featuring the Western Zorro character,³ most recently represented in film by the two releases featuring Antonio Banderas and Catherine Zeta-Jones. Both the Swordsman films and the Zorro movies highlight familial relationships, including the prodigal son motif featured in the Better Tomorrow films. The other series films mentioned here also employ "serial" strategies such as the reintroduction or the reconfiguration of characters. The impetus towards familial reintegration or at least towards the restoration of an acceptable order of things, is a hallmark of these series films.⁴ A useful contrast to the generally positive trajectory of these films, particularly of the Zorro movies, is provided by the three Godfather films directed by Francis Ford Coppola, in which the bonds of family are gradually corrupted and dissolved by the poisonous influence of power.

A Better Tomorrow was a rather loose remake of a 1967 film by Cantonese director Lung Kong. This film, whose English title was *Story of a Discharged Prisoner*, actually had the same Chinese title as the remake (Cantonese, *Ying hung boon sik/True Colors of the Hero*).⁵ Woo collaborated with producer (and directorial colleague) Tsui Hark on scripting the remake. Despite Tsui's urging that the lead characters should be women, Woo insisted on male heroic leads. Woo and Tsui hired certain actors who would be crucial in the film's artistic and commercial success. One of these was Ti Lung, an erstwhile star of martial arts or *wuxia* films, especially those produced by the famous Shaw Brothers studio and directed by the legendary Chang Cheh (Woo's most important mentor). Ti Lung had been an iconic figure in many of these films. He often met a tragic end, in keeping with the pathos associated with the films' heroic ethos, and was frequently paired as hero with the equally iconic but distinctive David Chiang Dai-wei.⁶ Such pairings or "team" hero efforts were also to be found in Woo's films, beginning before *A Better Tomorrow* with works such as *Hui hap/Last Hurrah for Chivalry* (1978).

In this instance, Woo went to bat for the casting of another actor who was to become an icon of a rather different kind than Ti or Chiang. This *wuxia* film would not only update swords with guns, as Woo has remarked, but would bring the hero team up to date for a new generation of Hong Kong moviegoers, many of whom had become very accustomed to TV serials and melodramas. Woo's insistence on hiring Chow Yun-fat, an actor familiar to TV viewers, turned out to be a great stroke of inspiration. Despite studio objections because of the actor's status at the time as "box-office poison" (perhaps through TV overexposure), Woo was able to hire him. Chow became the "star" of the picture, although he was not really the lead: Ti Lung and the late pop star Leslie Cheung Kwok-wing were. In a story familiar to Hollywood studio lore, though, the supporting actor upstaged the leads and went on to a career with top billing: one is reminded of Bogart in *The Petrified Forest*, Alan Ladd in *This Gun for Hire* (Robert Preston was top-billed), Robert De Niro in *Godfather: Part II*. Leslie Cheung, already a major singing star, began a very successful film career although his life was tragically to end in suicide due to personal difficulties. Finally, in another nod to Hong Kong film tradition, the superb Tien Feng played the father of Ho (Ti Lung) and Kit (Leslie Cheung). Tien had often played patriarchal figures such as sword masters or local governors and could easily switch from benevolence to evildoing. One of his most famous roles, the *sifu* ("teacher") in Chang Cheh's 1967 hit *One-Armed Swordsman*, which launched Jimmy Wang Yu's career, was followed in the 1968 sequel *Return of the One-Armed Swordsman* by his portrayal of a mysterious and thoroughly malevolent leader of a gang of swordsmen running a fight club with coerced battles to the death.

A Better Tomorrow was not envisioned as the first part of a series, as is the case with some films which later become the first of a set, or which are self-consciously based on the serial tradition, such as the well-known example of George Lucas's Star Wars films.[7] Nevertheless, the concentration of cultural and mythic content within the major characters and in their relationships was of sufficient strength to imply a sequel. Tsui convinced Woo to direct *A Better Tomorrow II* in 1987, but the film was less successful artistically, although still a big draw at the box office. Tsui and Woo had begun to have creative differences by this time, and the relationship was strained still further by Tsui's insistence on directing a prequel himself. The Tsui-directed prequel, *A Better Tomorrow III* (1989), was set in Saigon during the Vietnam War and also in Hong Kong, and followed the career of Mark Gor before his days in the triads with Ho. (Woo's 1990 Vietnam film, *Bullet in the Head*, intersects the *Better Tomorrow* storyline at several points, working through similar themes of brotherhood and betrayal within triad or gang "families"). In all three Better Tomorrow films, notwithstanding the distinctions between them (especially between the first two and the third installment), the question of family dynamic is central.

The relationships within and between families in these films are of two general types. The first type concerns real, biological family units, such as Ho and Kit's family in *A Better Tomorrow*. The second concerns artificial or mock family units, namely triad organizations, which borrow terminology (such as *dai lo* ["elder brother"]) from real family entities: thus, in the first film, the relationship of "kinship" between triad members Mark, Ho, and Shing. Both types of kinship are merged in films like the Godfather series, in which the "family" is both biological and operational in terms of criminal activity.[8] In the case of Woo's and Tsui's Better Tomorrow films, the functions are separated — more clearly so in the first two films than in the third, chiefly because of the more explicit political and social concerns of Tsui's film.

The familial aspect of the films has been previously noted and to some extent discussed by Hall (*John Woo* Ch. 6) and Bordwell (101–02), but certain motifs important to the family dynamic in them have not been elucidated, and it is these motifs, particularly that of the prodigal son, which throw light on the powerful connections between Woo's films in particular and the film tradition of Hollywood. The prodigal son complex has been central to many Hollywood films, from Westerns to family melodramas, but William Marling has particularly emphasized its centrality to the *film noir* and thriller tradition. In the case of the Better Tomorrow films, the theme of prodigality (to borrow Marling's term) is most pronounced in the first installment. Here, the nub of the conflict between the two brothers Ho and Kit is precisely the nature of the elder's prodigality.[9] The question is further complicated by the presence of the Mark character (Chow Yun-fat), who is a figurative brother to the elder Ho (Ti Lung) and who also displays prodigal qualities (mainly, a tendency towards excess and lack of seriousness about one's role in society).[10] The thrust of the film militates towards the resolution of the biological family conflicts, by means of reintegration of Ho and Kit and by elimination of the outlying "problem" in the person of Mark. In the second film, the biological family is actually shifted into the background, since the father had died in the first film, and Kit is killed, so that the emphasis on loyalty and the concerns of prodigality are transposed onto the triad relationships, between Ho, Mark's brother Ken, and Lung, their mentor (that is, father figure), played by Dean Shek.[11]

Like the Better Tomorrow films, the three One-Armed Swordsman films directed by Chang Cheh employ serial strategies[12] and highlight familial relationships and prodigality. The early One-Armed Swordsman films (the original 1967 film and the first sequel, both starring Wang Yu and Chiao Chiao) concentrate most particularly on familial themes, but the relative emphasis given to different aspects of familial conceptualization varies between the two films. In the first film, the elements of prodigality and loyalty, as well as of filial piety, are highlighted; while the second film displaces the filial piety motif away from the Swordsman and locates it among the several sword families (some of them biological) involved against their will in the "fight club." The prodigality theme is muted in this sequel. The major concern of Fang Kang (the swordsman) is to stay at home farming with his wife (Hsiao Man, played by Chiao Chiao, his rescuer from the first film), but he is pulled back into the fighting life by the atrocities being committed by a criminal gang of fighters upon honorable swordsmen and their families. In fact, Fang's wife convinces him that he must intervene,[13] and so he leads a band of survivors of the savage attacks in a campaign that eventually destroys the evil clan.

The third film, also an important entry in the series, was directed by Chang Cheh but starred David Chiang as a new character, the swordsman Lei Li, and Ti Lung as Fung, a potential adversary who becomes his closest friend. This film, *The New One-Armed Swordsman* (1971), in fact takes the element of male friendship and figurative brotherhood one step further towards its eventual form in Chang Cheh films such as *Blood Brothers* (1973) and in Woo films such as *A Better Tomorrow*. Lei, who has actually inflicted his one-armed status on himself as part of an odd promise made to Lung (Ku Feng),[14] a rival to whom he loses a match, is morose and withdrawn through much of the film, having retired to work incognito as a waiter in a rural tavern. He is only roused from his reclusive life when befriended by the enigmatic Fung, who eventually dies trying to defeat Lung's forces.[15] Driven by motives of revenge, Lei displays his spectacular one-armed skills in defeating Lung and his men.

The two recent Zorro films, and their most important sound-era predecessor, *The Mark of Zorro* with Tyrone Power (Rouben Mamoulian, 1940), all engage the themes of familial loyalty and of prodigality (personified most importantly by the Zorro character in his public persona as foppish aristocrat and irresponsible son). Still, the latest film, *The Legend of Zorro* (Martin Campbell, 2005), dispenses with some of the apparatus of the earlier series (the son appearing to have no interest in social action, the concentration on his family of origin) in favor of a displacement of familial tension onto Zorro's own role as paterfamilias. Although not set in an Asian context, the recent Zorro series does provide a useful parallel to the Better Tomorrow series and the Swordsman films in its concentration on filial loyalty and familial duty.

The two Better Tomorrow films directed by Woo are centered upon the Sung family. This family is composed in the first film of Sung Tse Ho (Ti Lung), the elder brother, Sung Tse Kit (Leslie Cheung), the younger brother, their father (Tien Feng), and Kit's fiancée Jackie (Emily Chu). Ho is the first character introduced in the film, and he is soon paired with Mark (Chow Yun-fat), his colleague in the triads, and Shing (Waise Lee), an apprentice or junior "brother" to Ho and Mark. The early scenes of the film show the main characters as lighthearted, carefree, and most particularly, in the case of Mark, as prodigal in terms of excess—Mark lights up a large denomination bill in a display of insouciance. Soon, Ho meets up with Kit, who is about to enter the police force, and then Emily and the father are introduced to the narrative. The relationship between Ho and Kit at this point is also very lighthearted. In keeping with the conventions of melodramatic narrative, the sunny beginning of the film will soon undergo a violent and dark degeneration.[16] When Ho and Shing go to Taiwan to close a deal with another gang, they are ambushed by the gang, and then pursued by the police. Ho gives himself up to allow Shing to escape. Meanwhile, a henchman has been sent to threaten Ho's father against Ho's talking about the deal. When Ho's father resists, he is killed. Although Kit and Emily together dispatch the assassin, Kit blames Ho and his way of life for the father's death. This resentment will become a major plot element in the film, leading to unforeseen consequences.[17] Mark takes revenge on the gang leaders in Taiwan for the attack on Ho's family and on the obvious betrayal of Ho, killing the gang members but losing the use of a leg in the gunfight.

The conflict between Ho and Kit becomes central to the film. Not only does it affect the dynamic of the family, including the now pivotal Jackie, but it also leads to the necessity that Mark intervene to assist Ho in clearing his name. Ho has been framed by Shing, who had originally betrayed him and has now taken over the gang. The suspicion falling on Ho is exacerbated by Kit's resentful attitude and his unwillingness to believe Ho when he tries to point him in the right direction in the investigation of gang affairs. The Ho-Kit conflict is ostensibly about the blame attaching to Ho for the death of their father, but the disagreement has wider implications regarding the concepts of prodigality and of filial piety.

Early in the film, the father, in ill health, asks Ho to promise him that he will watch over Kit. As the elder brother, the filial duty of Ho is not only to obey the father, but also, in the event of the father's death, to assume his position in the family. In traditional Chinese society, this position of leader, or *chia-chang*, carried "power and authority ... not with force, but by reason of the single fact that he held superiority in age over other household members." The leader, normally the father in the family, was succeeded at death by other family members in a specific order: "first by the mother and then by the oldest brother, should both parents be deceased and the children decide to continue living together" (Traylor 36).[18] For Ho's father to urge him to take care of Kit, then, is perfectly reasonable, and Ho has no problem with this.

The difficulty between Kit and Ho arises because Kit blames Ho for the death of their father at the hands of the triad enforcer. When Ho returns from a three-year prison term in Taiwan, he goes to see Kit at his apartment. Kit arrives with Jackie; when he sees Ho waiting in the rain, he beats him and tells him he doesn't want to see him again. The balance of filial piety is endangered, because the younger brother no longer respects his elder, that is, the new *chia-chang* figure in the family. The inflexible Kit is not simply resentful towards Ho because of his putative role in the death of their father. Kit also blames Ho for his own failure to be promoted: his superior tells him that his career is being hampered by his relation to a man who is or has been involved in the triads. So, Kit's animus against Ho is personal and professional. The difficulty with his position is that, on the personal level at any rate, he presumes that Ho is still associated with the triads, and also that Ho was uncaring about their father's fate, when in fact Ho is trying his best to go straight (he works for Ken, a Pat O'Brien–like character [Kenneth Tsang][19] who runs a taxi company hiring ex-cons) and was also betrayed by Shing, who either set up the attack at the Sungs' house or was acquiescent in it. In short, Kit will not acknowledge the new reality of Ho's life and refuses to see that Ho has suffered at least as much as he has. Kit also refuses to play the role assigned to him by the traditional family code, that is, to honor his elder brother. Kit's fiancée Jackie plays an important role in the film by repeatedly trying to reason with him and even by bringing Kit and Ho together at the couple's apartment in an attempt at reconciliation.

Commentators have often implied or asserted that Woo's films are almost exclusively male-oriented. Such a critical position is overstated. While Woo does indeed privilege male characters, he does not thereby totally exclude or even necessarily condescend to female characters. Even a cursory examination of women characters in Woo films from *Hard-Boiled* (1992), with its assertive and prickly Teresa Mo cop character, to the frequently underappreciated *Hard Target* (1993), which features a strong heroine in Yancy Butler's character Natasha as well as a sympathetically portrayed and heroic cop in Kasi Lemmons's character Carmine, belies the notion that Woo has no interest in women characters.

In *A Better Tomorrow*, Jackie plays a role not unknown in Confucian tradition, and, in fact, common in Hong Kong popular culture: the "filial daughter-in-law" (see Tan 229–30). Although not as exaggerated as the pop culture stereotype of the long-suffering daughter-in-law familiar to Hong Kong soap opera viewers (Tan 226), Jackie's character certainly does her share of fretting and upbraiding in an attempt to bring the brothers together. In this role she fits well into the tradition of filial piety, which has long included examples of filial daughters-in-law. Although such roles for women were not addressed in the oldest texts of Confucianism, by the time of the Han dynasty, a need was perceived to address the status of women in societal ethics (Tan 226–27). Tan Sor-hoon describes the responsibilities of the filial daughter-in-law: "The daughter-in-law's role comes about by a woman's marriage and the relationship is formed through her husband. Her filiality is part of her responsibilities toward her husband.... The filial daughter-in-law's obedience ... also contributes to the husband's filiality, as she thereby avoids causing friction between her husband and his parents" (229–30).

Although Jackie is not yet married to Kit, she conducts herself in a filial manner towards Ho, the surrogate for the man who was to be her father-in-law.[20] She is unfailingly respectful of him, as is shown most notably by her appearance at the taxi company where he works. She comes to see him to make a difficult request of him, that he leave Hong Kong for a time so that the situation may be defused. Rather than intrude on his workspace, she waits outside for him and makes her request politely. When he declines, she does not upbraid him. Later, she invites him to the couple's apartment for her birthday celebration. She asks Kit not to be angry and then invites Ho inside. This is a clear example of the filial daughter-in-law attempting to reduce "friction" in the family. The attempt fails, however, and only at the end of the film are the brothers reconciled.

This reconciliation is accomplished not through the agency of Jackie but instead through the force of events and the moral suasion of Mark. During the final battle of the film, Ho and Kit are trapped by Shing and his henchmen. Mark, about to leave Hong Kong, turns his speedboat around and comes to their rescue. During a lull in the gunfight, Mark upbraids Kit for not helping the wounded Ho and for not appreciating his sacrifices. Mark is then killed by Shing and his men, and Ho and Kit retaliate. When the police arrive, the wounded Shing walks toward them, haughtily pointing out to Ho that he can be arrested and later released. Kit hands Ho his gun[21]; Ho shoots Shing and then turns toward Kit, handcuffing himself to him in a gesture of self-sacrifice and penitence. The film ends in a freeze-frame of the two walking off towards the police.

In the sequel, *A Better Tomorrow II*, a means was found of "reviving" the Mark character because of the unexpected popularity of Chow Yun-fat as Mark. In a move familiar to readers of comics, where methods are routinely devised for bringing back characters who had supposedly died in previous issues, a formerly unmentioned twin brother of Mark, Ken, appears in the sequel, also played by Chow. The reintroduction in this case is not of the character properly speaking but of the actor playing a clone of the original character and is an interesting example of one difference between print and film media. The star personality of Chow the actor here overrides narrative logic and plausibility. The viewer soon forgets, or puts aside, any awareness of Ken's difference from Mark. Ken even puts on Mark's trademark trench coat, filled with bullet holes, and wears identical shades.

Ken runs a Chinese restaurant in New York, where he tries to coach his younger colleagues into staying on the right side of the law. This situation changes drastically when another new character, Ken's mentor Lung, played by Dean Shek, comes to New York to plead with him for assistance back in Hong Kong. Lung's daughter Peggy is killed, and Ken and Ho eventually team with Lung to fight against the offending triad, whose leader Ko had also arranged for the death of Kit. The emphasis on prodigality is downplayed in this film, as is the focus on family conflict. Instead, the artificial brotherhood relationship between Ken and Ho, and their filial piety relationship to their surrogate father Lung, are highlighted. The role of male, not female, characters is paramount in this sequel. At the end of the film, after one of the most spectacular gunfights ever filmed, vengeance has been achieved, but all three heroes are at death's door. The only survivors from the carnage are Jackie, Ken the taxi-shop owner (Kenneth Tsang; a character continued from the first film), and Jackie and Kit's daughter Sung Ho Yin (whose given name Yin means "Spirit of Righteousness"). The biological and triad relationships are thus melded into one putative relationship, if we may presume that Ken will watch over Jackie and Yin.

This sequel treats the first film much like the premiere of a comic book series. Two brief scenes[22] feature a graphic artist with the walls of his studio bedecked with frames from a graphic novel or comic strip detailing the adventures of Mark, Ho, and Kit, and also with the beginning of a second installment showing the life of Mark's brother Ken up to that point in the film narrative. The artist has also kept memorabilia of Mark, such as his bullet-ridden trench coat, which he passes on to Ken. The missing material from the final cut probably would have expanded on and deepened this element of self-referentiality. The characters even seem to have some consciousness of living out a legend.[23] For example, when Lung becomes nearly catatonic following his betrayal and Peggy's death, Ken exhorts him to live up to his former reputation, as if Lung were not fulfilling the expectations of his "audience."

This consciousness of legendary qualities is heightened by clear references to Sam Peckinpah's *The Wild Bunch* (1969), which deals with questions such as the legendary status of Western heroes and outlaws.[24] During a peak in the mood of the Woo film, when Ken, Ho, Lung, and Ken the taxi man are planning their assault on Ko, Lung playfully tosses an orange to Ken (in a reference to the first thing Lung eats after refusing food), who tosses it in turn to everyone in the group. The other Ken, the taxi man, doesn't receive it, though, and dismissively says that he doesn't like oranges anyway. Instead of an orange, a similar pivotal scene in character mood and camaraderie took place in the Peckinpah film, with a tequila bottle passed around, and with Lyle Gorch (Warren Oates) receiving an empty bottle at the end of the scene, much to the amusement of his comrades. (The incident in the Peckinpah film is richer because Lyle and his brother have already been established as malcontents and complainers; so the comic mistreatment of Lyle underlines this point as, at the same time, Lyle and his brother are shown as reintegrated into the group because of the good-humored teasing given to Lyle.) In another clear reference to the Peckinpah film, the heroes at the end of *A Better Tomorrow II* walk abreast to confront the overwhelming odds at Ko's compound, much as the Bunch did at the end of their career.[25] Such references accentuate the self-consciousness of legendary or heroic status for the characters of the Woo film.

A similar, if less overt, strategy is used in the three Godfather films directed by Francis Ford Coppola and co-scripted by the late Mario Puzo. In the second film, several characters evince nostalgia for the "good old days" when the Corleones were strong and cohesive. The death of Pete Clemenza (Richard Castellano), one of the caporegimes (captains in the Family), is lamented[26] and is made rather mysterious by his henchman Willie Cicci's (Joe Spinell) comment that "That was no heart attack." And Johnny Ola, Hyman Roth's right-hand man[27] tells Michael sadly that "one by one, our old friends are gone. Death, natural or not, prison, deported."[28] Later in the film, during the Senate organized crime hearings (based on the famous Kefauver hearings), a chart is used by the committee members displaying the power relationships within the Corleone family. When carefully viewed, the chart seems like a character list for a comic book series, that is, the family members are treated within the film narrative rather like fictional characters, complete with photo and nicknames (and with their own "legends" in some cases). Additionally, several of the minor members are actually members of the production crew; although this practice of inserting crew names into film lists is not uncommon, in this case the quality of self-reflexivity is enhanced.[29] By the time of the third film in the series (Coppola, *The Godfather: Part III*), the mythologizing has become overt, even obtrusive: in one scene, Mary (Michael's daughter) asks Vincent (Sonny's illegitimate son [Andy Garcia]) about the old days, treating Michael and Sonny as legendary material. Mary (Sofia Coppola, the director's daughter) speaks of the family's past with an almost cloying reverence, and Vincent shows no awareness of the corrupting influence of Michael's power.[30]

The third film in the Better Tomorrow series is a prequel to the first film and includes only Mark as a character familiar to viewers of the other two films. Directed by Tsui Hark and set in Saigon and in Hong Kong, the film focuses on the efforts of two triad "brothers" (actually blood cousins) to make a living in Saigon and then to escape the chaos there. One of them, Mun

(Tony Leung Ka-fai), finally convinces his elderly father to leave Saigon with them. The familial concerns in this film center chiefly on filial piety and on the vengeance taken by Mun when his father is murdered. A subplot concerns the rivalry between Mark and Mun for the love of Kit (the late Anita Mui), who is actually the mistress of the villain of the piece. Her eventual death is substituted in the melodramatic trajectory of the film for the death of Mark in Woo's 1986 film.[31] The prominence accorded to her character as a tough, gun-wielding heroine differs essentially from Woo's treatments of his heroines, and the important role of government soldiers and of customs officials in this film stands in for the role of the police in Woo's two films.

The biological family of Tsui's film is supplemented by an informally adopted son, a Vietnamese orphan, Pat, who eventually joins the army forces fighting against the Viet Cong and is killed. Unlike the situation in Woo's 1986 film, though, there is no perceptible tension between the "brothers" in this family (other than the stress over the love triangle with Kit). The stressful relationship within the family is between the stubborn (but kindhearted) father and the cousins, because they have great difficulty in convincing him to leave Saigon and return to his native Hong Kong (where he will eventually be murdered by Kit's lover and boss Ho in a vengeance attack).

In all three films, the prodigal son motif is present, although more accentuated in some of the films than in others. Woo's first entry most clearly displays the prodigal son complex, even though its nature is rather complicated by the fact that Ho, the apparent prodigal, is in fact the elder son. The younger brother Kit, normally the prodigal in the traditional story, is in this case apparently not the prodigal son, because he is not a criminal and appears to follow his father's wishes by becoming a policeman, by marrying, and by staying at home. Perhaps the picture is not so clear, though. Despite Ho's criminality as far as society is concerned, he actually attempts to be a filial son by trying to protect his brother. He does fit the prodigal son matrix by returning home to Hong Kong and by attempting to live "straight," working at the taxi agency. His younger brother Kit, on the other hand, actually plays the part of the elder, stay-at-home brother in the traditional tale, because he resents Ho's very existence, blaming him for their father's death. Kit uses his police authority to prevent Ho's return to the family (by threatening him). A good case can be made for Kit's acting prodigally because he does not respect his father's wish for family unity, and he does not show filial respect towards Ho.

Kit is prodigal in some respects as is Michael Corleone in the Puzo novel *The Godfather* and in the first film of the Coppola series. Although Kit does not, as does Michael, leave home against his father's wishes, he is not a model son after the death of his father: like Michael, he is "rebellious" and keeps to himself.[32] As is often the case with Woo's films, however, the division between antagonists is not clear-cut; one often shares characteristics with the other, and each one will display positive and negative character qualities. So, to carry the analogy with Michael a little further, Kit displays some of his rebelliousness and withdrawn reserve, while Ho fits much better than does Kit the following description of Michael's trajectory (*pace* the remark about "assimilation"): "Michael, [Don Vito] Corleone's youngest son — his prodigal son — the Dartmouth graduate and war hero [in the Marines] who was intent upon assimilation into American society, returns to the family when a corrupt cop sets up his father to be murdered.... Michael realizes that legal justice is merely an illusion and returns to the fold to protect his father" (Chiampi 24).[33]

Michael Corleone acts in such a way because that is the template for the fictional Mafia member. As Alessandro Camon observes, familial dedication is central both to the Mafia "myth" and to the Coppola films: "The mutual loyalty of fathers and sons is the emotional core of the [Godfather] story: fathers 'do what they have to do' to grant their sons a better life; sons inherit the mantle to defend the achievements and the honor of their fathers. The affirmation of this bond is the ultimate value; profit and power are just means to an end. This fact is overlooked by many critics who consider the film a metaphor for capitalist business" (60).[34]

So, too, does Ho follow the familial ethic. He returns, although too late to protect his father. He is willing to risk his newfound job stability and his own life to keep Shing and his gang from harming Kit, even to the point of committing further criminal acts like concealing evidence and doing violence.

In Woo's sequel to *A Better Tomorrow*, the prodigal son elements, and the family conflicts generally, are not as sharply drawn or highlighted as in the first film. The conflict between Ho and Kit has been resolved, and Lung and Peggy seem to be a harmonious father-daughter pair. Tragedy ensues in both relationships, but this is not due to internal conflict; instead in both cases (of Kit and Peggy being killed) the violence comes from Mr. Ko's nefarious designs on Lung's position. Still, a case can be made for Ken (Mark's twin brother) to fill the position of prodigal son, in this instance a figurative or surrogate son for Lung, Ken's erstwhile triad mentor. Ken has been in New York, running a Chinese restaurant and not at all concerned with any triad activities in Hong Kong. He is presented, however, as a very tough customer who takes forceful action against some local wise guys who harass him and his staff (and who will later attempt revenge against him and Lung). After Lung is forced to leave Hong Kong, he ends up in New York, and Ken rescues, or revives him, from his near-catatonic state. Ken "returns to the fold," as it were, by involving himself once again in triad loyalties. He and Lung will return to Hong Kong to take vengeance on Mr. Ko for his actions against Lung, including the murder of Peggy. Ken acts very much the filial son in his strenuous efforts to revive Lung from his catatonia by trying to feed him, by cajoling him, and even by berating him. Lung only awakens from his cataleptic state when he sees Ken threatened with imminent death during the mob's revenge attack; he then regains his former fierceness, dispatching the rest of the wise guys while Ken laughs in relief. The little "family" has been restored and will be reunited with its former member Ho when Ken and Lung return to Hong Kong. Ho, Ken, and Lung will take vengeance on Ko's gang in an annihilating shootout reminiscent of the ending of *The Wild Bunch*. Although they will presumably die at the end (they are shown nearly dead but still conscious), they have maintained their triad's family honor and unity.

The protagonists of the Tsui Hark prequel are not as successful in maintaining unity within the biological family or within the triad. From the perspective of the biological father, Mun (Tony Leung Ka-fai) is the prodigal, because he consistently opposes his father's wishes to stay in Saigon and does not display the kind of submissive respect accorded the father by his adoptive Vietnamese "son." Mun is also involved in illegal activity, much like Ho in the first Woo film, and his loyalties are divided between his "brother" Mark and the relationship with his father. Tsui injects a component into this film that is absent from Woo's two works, a person of love interest who becomes the point of rivalry between Mun and Mark and who also is, at least at the beginning of the film, a female *wuxia* of more competence than the male heroes. Kit (Anita Mui) in fact fulfills some of the narrative function of Ho in the first film, because she is seen as a betrayer of family unity by tying herself to the fortunes of the corrupt boss; that is, she is divisive of the family in a way similar to (and just as unintended as) Ho. She also attempts to assume some of the role of filial daughter-in-law (although not officially so, not being married to Mun) by trying to attain unity within the biological family. Her secret loyalty to the corrupt boss Ho[35] leads to fatal consequences for her when she turns against him too late. The family in this film is fragmented, being reduced to Mark and Mun, who must come to terms with the loss of Kit.[36]

Unlike the Better Tomorrow series, the recent set of Zorro films works constantly towards family unity and towards the elimination of prodigality as a prominent element. The first of the two films, *The Mask of Zorro* (Martin Campbell, 1998), recasts the family dynamics of the most famous treatment of the Zorro material, *The Mark of Zorro* with Tyrone Power (itself a remake of the 1920 film starring Douglas Fairbanks). In the Tyrone Power version of the pulp legend, Don Diego Vega is the seemingly foppish son of a Mexican landowner, who is himself opposed to the unjust policies of the local governor but has feared opposing him directly. The young Vega openly courts the corrupt governor's daughter (Linda Darnell), while, as the fearless Zorro, secretly undermining his rule. He acquires as an ally the warrior-priest character (played lustily by the inimitable Eugene Pallette in a reprise of his Friar Tuck role in *The Adventures of Robin Hood* [Michael Curtiz, 1939]).[37] Eventually, justice is restored to the territory, with the bad governor leaving for Spain and the Vega family acquiring a daughter-in-law whose union with the young Zorro will presumably continue the line. The prodigality of the young scion is shown to have been only a pose, a ruse to cast suspicion away from Zorro's socially useful subversions of an abnormal state of affairs in the government.

In the new Zorro films, the focus shifts somewhat from the traditional story, although the elements of corrupt government and of covert opposition are maintained. Instead of the scion of a noble family, the new Zorro, Alejandro, is one of a pair of bandit brothers (the Murrieta brothers, based loosely on the Joaquín Murieta bandit legend). A true prodigal, the future Zorro is motivated in the early part of the film by greed and by a desire for vengeance on the men who killed his brother. He soon comes into contact in prison with an old man (Anthony Hopkins) who turns out to be the original Zorro (Diego de la Vega).[38] This man trains him (in a turn on the Phantom series, in which the "immortal" Phantom ["The Ghost Who Walks"] was actually a series of Phantoms who passed on the tradition)[39] as his successor, thus becoming a positive and firm father-figure who takes the rough edges off the prodigal orphan and socializes him to the point that he can actually play the fop when necessary. In effect, he is trained to fill the shoes of Tyrone Power's interpretation of the character, although he is only required to be especially dandified on one occasion in the film, when he and Diego (posing as his servant Bernardo) attend a formal dinner. As a father and son team, as it were, the two Zorros (with the assistance of the evil governor's daughter Elena [Catherine Zeta-Jones]) defeat the governor and his henchmen.[40] The elder Zorro dies at the end, leaving the field open for a new dynasty, again to be founded by the younger Zorro, who becomes Alejandro de la Vega, thus leaving behind his bandit heritage, and the daughter. Much the same dynamic is seen in the Better Tomorrow films and in the first Godfather film, in which the patriarch dies, clearing the way for a newer generation.

The Legend of Zorro, the sequel to the first Banderas/Zeta-Jones Zorro film, begins with the "Zorro" family intact, complete with a son who, the viewer presumes, may continue the Zorro tradition. The family is subject to stresses that reflect the contemporary strains in Western family dynamics, such as increased expectation that the father will participate in child rearing. Zorro's wife Elena wants him to stay retired, but he expresses his concerns about the current oppressive and corrupt political environment surrounding a propagandistic movement to restore California to Mexican ownership. The couple separates, and Alejandro engages briefly in prodigal activity, going out with the boys for a steam bath. He quickly becomes disenchanted with running around with the boys. Elena engages in an apparent relationship with the villain, a French count who has nefarious designs on the territory. This dalliance, which appears very serious at first, drives Alejandro to the expected fits of jealous temper. We discover later in the film, though, that her dalliance was merely a stratagem inspired by agents of the United States government. At film's end, with the villains dispatched, the family is not only reunited but regains its sense of purpose. The youngest Zorro presumably will inherit his father's mask. As in *The Mask of Zorro*, the impetus is towards the resolution of familial and ideological conflict and towards the reintegration of the family into the surrounding social milieu. The former prodigal has become a guardian of public values.

Unlike the Zorro films and the Swordsman series, the Better Tomorrow series and the Godfather films do not feature such a seamless reintegration of the jagged edges of familial disorder. The two Better Tomorrow films by Woo, which chronologically end the narrative of the trilogy, finally treat the major characters as ironic heroes who die with tongue in cheek; they are shown nearly dead, seated but sprawling, waiting for the police to arrest their corpses.[41] Coppola, on the other hand, deals with Michael Corleone in tragic, indeed, in operatic terms, as D'Acierno shows us (575–83).[42] As he had feared in *Godfather: Part II*,[43] he has lost his family and undergoes a solitary death, ending the trilogy with "a necessary closing with death" (Combs 44). Michael, the erstwhile prodigal son, has preserved, then perverted, and finally squandered his inheritance, which in this series is not material so much as emotional and spiritual. Unlike Michael Corleone, the *wuxia* characters of the Better Tomorrow films and the Swordsman films are shown to have preserved an inheritance of honor,[44] while the recent Zorro series, the most positive of all, depicts a seamless resolution in which the familial and social conflicts are subsumed to prevalent norms.[45] The corrosive ideology of Coppola's series finds little place in the more positive world of Mark, Kit, and Zorro. Woo's Better Tomorrow films attempt to maintain a mooring in traditional values of brotherhood, courage, and loyalty within an environment of uncertain allegiances (most particularly with the coming 1997 handover to China) and growing cultural and moral relativism. Unlike the recent Zorro films, which tend to retreat into a fantasy of an idealized heroic and familial ambiance, Woo's two films present a dual vision of an ideal world of tradition and an inescapably changing political and cultural environment, lending his series an especial poignancy.

Notes

1. My references to the prodigal son and to prodigality are inspired by the work of William Marling on American *noir* fiction and *film noir*.

2. In her recent book on *A Better Tomorrow*, Karen Fang notes that the local terminology for this film and similar movies which followed it was "*yingxiong pian*, or 'hero' films, [...]. The term refers to highly stylized and dynamic action/crime films which feature glamorized protagonists motivated and challenged by such traditional chivalric concerns as love, honor, and vengeance" (50).

3. The similarities discussed here between the Zorro films and Woo's Better Tomorrow films emphasize parallels rather than direct influence, although the possibility certainly exists that Woo was influenced either directly or indirectly (through his Hong Kong models like Chang Cheh) by films such as the Zorro movies starring Douglas Fairbanks (*The Mark of Zorro* [Fred Niblo, 1920] or Tyrone Power [*The Mark of Zorro*]). Perhaps, too, Woo's own work has had its impact on the recent Zorro films; many recent Hollywood action and adventure films betray stylistic influence from Hong Kong cinema.

4. Like Hollywood in recent years, Hong Kong has shown a clear predilection for series and sequels. In addition to the series already mentioned, Hong Kong viewers in the 1980s were treated to series such as Siu-Tung Ching's *A Chinese Ghost Story* (I, II, III, 1987–90). The 1990s were the decade of the Tsui Hark–directed Wong Feihong (Once Upon a Time in China) series, of which the best entries were the first three (1991–93). The Wong Feihong films, in particular, were later entries in a very long-running series of films and TV shows featuring the character: more than 100 entries since 1949 (see Ange Hwang, "The Irresistible: Hong Kong Movie *Once Upon a Time in China* Series — an Extensive Interview with Director/Producer Tsui Hark," *Asian Cinema* 1 [Fall 1998]: 10; see also Williams, "Kwan Tak-Hing and the New Generation," *Asian Cinema* 10.1 [Fall 1998]: 71–77). Hong Kong film has continued to follow the sequel star, with recent sets of films such as the Johnnie To-directed *Running Out of Time I, II* (1999, 2001) and the Infernal Affairs trilogy (2002–03), the first of which was remade as *The Departed* by Martin Scorsese (2006).

5. For details on the conceptual and the production history of Woo's film, see ch. 7 of Hall, *John Woo: The Films*. Unless otherwise noted, Chinese titles given in the text will be in Cantonese, the language of Hong Kong. Most films shot in the Hong Kong film industry are offered in Cantonese and in Mandarin versions (the Mandarin for marketing in Taiwan and on the mainland). Chinese personal names will follow the Chinese system, placing the surname first and the given name(s) following, except when the person is commonly known in a Westernized form like "John Woo."

6. A lapidary example of such pairing is the 1970 Chang Cheh film *Vengeance*, set in the warlord period of the early 20th century, in which Ti Lung's character, an opera performer, is viciously murdered in retaliation for his attack on a man who had insulted his wife. His brother, played by David Chiang, takes relentless and total vengeance on the triad gang who perpetrated the violence, dying himself in the process.

7. Although Woo's film was not originally intended as part of a series, it fits neatly into the general tendencies of Hong Kong film production at that time: Hong Kong films,

whether originally so intended or not, often spawned series or sequels, much as Hollywood products do today. The impetus, as in Hollywood, is the formula of box-office success, thought to be repeatable by producing new installments. One of the best-known series of the period, and artistically successful at least in some of its installments, was the Once Upon a Time in China series directed by Tsui Hark and starring, in most installments, Jet Li as martial arts folk figure Wong Feihong. This series, which began in 1991 and spawned a TV series as well, was itself modeled on the long-running series of Wong Feihong films starring Kwan Tak-hing from 1949–70 in more than seventy films (Hunt 8). Hong Kong films from the 1970s were frequently followed by sequels or featured continuing characters, as in the One-Armed Swordsman films directed by Chang Cheh, or the several films directed by Chu Yuan and scripted by Gu Long which starred Ti Lung as the recurring "Sentimental Swordsman" character, often under different names but with repeated characteristics. Other series or sequel sets of the period include the Chinese Ghost Story films, the three Swordsman films produced by Tsui Hark, and the Bride with White Hair series.

8. For remarks which amplify my observation regarding these films, see Cawelti 327–28; see also ch. 12 of Gaia Servadio, *Mafioso: A History of the Mafia from Its Origins to the Present Day* (New York: Stein and Day, 1976) and Franco Minganti, "The Hero with a Thousand and Three Faces. Michele, Mike, Michael Corleone," *Rivista di Studi Anglo-Americani: RSA* 3.4–5 (1984): 257–68. Note also the comments of Francis A. J. Ianni on crime "families" more generally:

> Italian-American criminal syndicates are rightly called families because the relationships established within them produce kinship-like ties among members, ties which become even stronger when they are legitimated through marriage or godparenthood. Every family member knows that every other member has some duties toward him and some claims on him. Whether the relationships are based on blood or marriage as they often are, or are fictive as in the intricate patterns of *compareggio* ("godparenthood"), it is also kinship which ties generations together and allies lineages and families [Ianni and Reuss-Ianni 169].

For "family" relationships in the triads, see Lau-fong Mak, "The Triads and the Underworld: Solidarity and Change," *Chinese Triads: Perspectives on Histories, Identities, and Spheres of Impact* (Singapore: Singapore History Museum, 2002) 33–46.

9. The elder son, usually the staid representative of homebound morality, in this case takes on the prodigal aspect of the younger son in the traditional parable. The case is not so simple, however, because Kit, the younger son, who loudly protests Ho's prodigality, is in fact the less responsible of the two: Ho goes to great lengths to respect his father's dying wishes by returning to the fold, as it were, and protecting his younger brother. Each brother, then, combines elements of prodigality and responsibility (Kit has stayed home but is immature and unrestrained; Ho has left home but returns and develops maturity and responsibility).

10. Mark might be said to actualize the darker, or less permissible, aspects of Ho's personality. For example, he lights his cigarette with money, he openly insults a Triad rival (Shing), and he talks about topics perhaps considered taboo, notably a tale about being forced to drink his own urine. The money-burning incident in particular highlights his prodigality, but the other incidents also position him as an extreme prodigal who does not respect social strictures. He is also noticeably frivolous (at the beginning of the film), as his money burning and his flirtation with a secretary demonstrate. Incidentally, the flirtation scene, which occurs in the outer office of a business concern (clearly a Triad front), is oddly reminiscent of James Bond's flirtation with Miss Moneypenny, a standard feature of the Bond films (to the point that, in *Goldfinger* [Guy Hamilton, 1964], M [Bernard Lee], Bond's superior, actually interrupts a dalliance with Moneypenny [Lois Maxwell] from inside his closed office, by calling on the intercom, asking her to "kindly omit the customary byplay with 007").

11. Shek, a producer in real life, here replicates in figurative form his role as one of the elders in Cinema City, the company in which he was involved.

12. The sets of films mentioned here (the Banderas–Zeta-Jones films, the One-Armed Swordsman films, and the Better Tomorrow films) are series, not serials, because each film ends without employing the well-known serial technique of withholding "closure," to use Roger Hagedorn's expression. (Here I follow Hagedorn's formulation of the distinction between the series and the serial. He distinguishes as follows between the strategies of Balzac and Sue: "Unlike Balzac's narration, which tended to end each installment of his novels at a point of *dénouement*, Sue's narrative strategy successfully exploited the inherent formal limitation of serial publication. His narrative purposely does not achieve closure; rather, he ended each installment at a point of unresolved narrative tension, precisely in order to leave his readers in suspense." Hagedorn draws the point that "The narrative break thus became the defining feature of what has come to be identified as the serial proper" (7). Note also the useful summation by Ileana Verzea in discussing TV shows, as she distinguishes between "the *serial* (a dramatized plot divided into episodes) and the *series* (a sequel of episodes whose unity is ensured by the presence of at least one and the same character) (4).

13. She had consistently opposed his involvement in fighting but changed her mind given the serious situation affecting the community. Consequently she prevails upon him to intervene.

14. Like the classical Hollywood studio system, the Shaw Brothers operation featured a "stable" of actors who appeared in many period films. Ku Feng was one of these. He was a versatile actor who usually played strong figures but who was equally proficient at playing heroic characters (for example, Fang Kang's father in *The One-Armed Swordsman*) and villains, as in this case.

15. Like Lei before the loss of his arm, Fung is a "twin-sword" specialist. Fung is thus a shadow or double of Lei, and his death at Lung's hands replicates the death of Lei's former self. Lei's vengeance on Lung is also serial, as he avenges the "death" of his own twin-sword self and the actual death of Fung, his "new" twin-sword self.

16. For a summary of some essential elements of melodramatic narrative, see Daniel Gerould, "Russian Formalist Theories of Melodrama," *Imitations of Life: A Reader on Film and Television Melodrama*, ed. Marcia Landy (Detroit: Wayne State University Press, 1991) 121–22, especially "element" 3 (121), on "reversals" and "twists" in the narrative.

17. The dynamic between Kit and Ho is quite similar to the tension between the two lead characters in *Cry of the City* (Robert Siodmak, 1948), figurative brothers from the same neighborhood, played respectively by Victor Mature and Richard Conte, who decide as adults to follow opposed courses. Candella (Mature) becomes a cop and makes Martin Rome (Conte), now a gangster, his chief adversary and target. Both share a close relationship with Rome's mother and are rivals for the loyalty of Rome's younger brother.

18. For Chinese family relations in a historical and cultural context, see also Paul Chao, *Chinese Kinship*, (London: Kegan Paul, 1983).

19. Tsang has played many roles in Hong Kong films and appeared recently as the villain in *The Replacement Killers* (Antoine Fuqua, 1998).

20. For a summary of traditional family roles in Chinese society, see Hugh D. R. Baker, *Chinese Family and Kinship* (New York: Columbia University Press, 1979) 12–21.

21. This gesture by Shing perhaps has influenced the very similar scene in *L. A. Confidential* (Curtis Hanson, 1997), when the corrupt police captain (James Cromwell) mocks his erstwhile protégé (Guy Pearce), walking away from the scene of a furious shootout and finally being shot by Pearce.

22. Woo told Kenneth E. Hall that material which would have bracketed these scenes was cut (Hall, *John Woo: The Films* 107n. 19).

23. Although there is almost certainly no direct influence here, the film does present an intriguing parallel with the second part of the masterwork by Miguel de Cervantes Saavedra, *El ingenioso caballero Don Quijote de la Mancha* (pt. 1, 1605; pt. 2, 1610), in which the two primary characters, Don Quijote and his squire Sancho Panza, comment ironically on a spurious account of their adventures and, by implication, go on further adventures in order to correct or improve the false record. (This spurious account was an actual novel written by Alonso Fernández de Avellaneda, which was actually published as Cervantes was writing the second part of his own work. See Thomas A. Lathrop, "Cervantes' Treatment of the False *Quixote*," *Kentucky Romance Quarterly* 32.2 [1985]: 214.) The consciousness by Don Quijote and Sancho of their own existence as literary characters, and as public figures thereby, is one of the great examples of self-referentiality in all literature.

24. The Hong Kong film audience might well have understood such references, due to the consistent presence of Hollywood product on Hong Kong screens. Like American audiences, the Hong Kong audience would have been composed of viewers of varying knowledge levels regarding film history. Still, a certain level of film culture, or at least of familiarity with American film stars, is presumed by the screenwriters: note the reference to Al Pacino in *A Better Tomorrow*, when Shing is told that he resembles Al Pacino.

25. Peckinpah had also used the "slow walk" of the heroic group in his great elegiac classic *Ride the High Country* (1961), but he developed it to iconic status in *The Wild Bunch*.

26. The character had to be written out of the script because negotiations between Castellano and the studio broke down. Details can be found in several sources, such as Harlan Lebo's *The Godfather Legacy* (New York: Fireside-Simon, 1997).

27. Ola is disparagingly called "his Sicilian messenger boy" by Frankie Pentangeli (Michael V. Gazzo), who had taken over for Clemenza.

28. The Hyman Roth character is a thinly disguised version of Meyer Lansky, the notorious Jewish gangster who was the crafty financial mind behind the scenes of much mob activity and who was never convicted of any serious offense, dying peacefully in "retirement" in Miami. According to Lansky biographer Robert Lacey, Johnny Ola is a fictional version of Lansky's friend Vincent "Jimmy Blue Eyes" Alo (Lacey 291). Incidentally, Ola was played by Dominic Chianese, familiar to viewers of *The Sopranos* as "Junior" Corrado Soprano, Tony's incredible uncle.

29. A good example of such playful name insertion can be found in Fred Zinnemann's *Day of the Jackal* (1973). When Inspector Lebel (Michael Lonsdale) studies the hotel register at the establishment where the Jackal (Edward Fox) had been staying, the names of several crew members appear on the register.

30. With regard to the concept of "family" in Puzo's source novel for the films, the comments of Cawelti are instructive: "Covertly, Puzo's novel is a celebration of the 'family.' ... The 'family' is a fantasy of collective, organized power that actually works to protect and support the individual as opposed to the coldness and indifference of the modern business or government bureaucracy" (354).

31. The three Godfather films follow a similar serial or sequel method of reflecting and commenting on earlier entries (see Anthony Ambrogio's article "'The Godfather, I and II': Patterns of Corruption," *Film Criticism* 3.1 (Fall 1978): 35–44). Coppola's films feature a more intricate set of reflections and parallels than do the three Better Tomorrow films.

32. In fact, Kit might be even more closely compared with Fredo (John Cazale), Michael's older brother who resents the bestowal of the title of Don on Michael (here Fredo and Michael fit the story's older brother who resents the prodigal) and who will betray Michael in the second film, thus becoming in a sense a prodigal himself. Of course Kit does not literally betray Ho, but he does resent his father's attentions toward him, and he does betray him emotionally by not forgiving him.

33. In fact, the cop (Capt. McCluskey, played in the film by Sterling Hayden) does

not "set up" Vito. He agrees to offer protection to the man who does the setting up, a sharp operator named Virgil Sollozzo (Al Lettieri).

34. On this topic and the family in the Godfather films (parts I and II), see also Robert Casillo, "Moments in Italian-American Cinema: From *Little Caesar* to Coppola and Scorsese," *From the Margin: Writings in Italian Americana*, ed. Anthony Julian Tamburri, Paolo A. Giordano, and Fred L. Gardaphé (West Lafayette, IN: Purdue University Press, 1991) 374–96.

35. Not to be confused with the Ho character from the Woo films.

36. The film's ending, which highlights the loss of the female lover, is strongly reminiscent (although most likely without any direct influence) of the customary *dénouements* of James Bond tales, particularly the Fleming novels, in which Bond always ends up alone after love relationships either break up, are terminated due to the death of the woman, or never come to fruition (see Eco 154–55). The sole exception is the final novel, *The Man with the Golden Gun* (1965); and had Fleming lived to write another novel, a similar result — a breakup — might have been expected. Clearly the strategy is to maintain Bond without ties and close affections; a parallel strategy may be at work here and is certainly to be seen in several instances in Woo's films, where the masculine relationships of "brotherhood" are much more important.

37. For more on Pallette, see Kenneth Hall, *Stonewall Jackson and Religious Faith in Military Command* (Jefferson, NC: McFarland, 2005) 161, 164–65.

38. Note the general name continuity with the Tyrone Power character. Additionally, the Zorro character has subtly acquired noble trappings with the addition of the 'de la,' the sign of hereditary land ownership.

39. *The Phantom* was a comic strip series created by Lee Falk (1911–99). Its first installment ran February 17, 1936, for King Features Syndicate. Falk continued creating the strip, as well as novelized versions of it, until his death ("Lee Falk: Father of the Phantom"). Some years ago a film based on the script was released, with Billy Zane in the title role.

40. In a further familial twist, Zeta-Jones is revealed as the daughter of the elder Zorro. She was stolen from him when the governor's men killed her mother and the governor then imprisoned the Zorro character. So, the new Zorro marries into the Zorro family.

41. Tony Williams sets this scene into Chinese portraiture tradition, specifically a portrait of the famed culture hero Kwan-Yu (from *Romance of the Three Kingdoms*) with the emperor and another figure (Williams, "Space, Place, and Spectacle: The Crisis Cinema of John Woo." *Cinema Journal* 36.2 [Winter 1997]: 77). Williams also notes the character continuity and symbolism (of the name of Kit's daughter) in *A Better Tomorrow II* (77).

42. For operatic references in *The Godfather: Part II*, see Deborah Anders Silverman, "Coppola, *Cavalleria*, and Connick: Musical Contributions to Epic in *The Godfather, Part II*," *Mid-Atlantic Almanack* 1 (1992): 26–40.

43. These fears are expressed in his final conversation with his mother.

44. Although Michael protests that he has tried all along to protect his family, he is clearly guilt-ridden and has certainly done things of which his father would never have approved (the most egregious being his murder of his elder brother). Thus he cannot be said to have preserved his father's legacy of Mafia "honor." See also Phoebe Poon, "The Tragedy of Michael Corleone in *The Godfather: Part III*," *Literature/Film Quarterly* 34.1 (2006): 64–70, and Poon, "The Corleone Chronicles: Revisiting the *Godfather* Films as Trilogy," *Journal of Popular Film and Television* 33.4 (Winter 2006): 187–95.

45. Some film information was obtained from the Internet Movie Database, at www.imdb.com. I would like to thank Dr. Win-chiat Lee, Department of Philosophy, Wake Forest University, for assistance with the concept of filial piety.

Works Cited

Bordwell, David. *Planet Hong Kong: Popular Cinema and the Art of Entertainment.* Cambridge: Harvard University Press, 2000.
Camon, Alessandro. "*The Godfather* and the Mythology of Mafia." *Francis Ford Coppola's Godfather Trilogy.* Ed. Nick Browne. Cambridge, England: Cambridge University Press, 2000. 57–75.
Campbell, Martin, dir. *The Legend of Zorro.* Perf. Antonio Banderas and Catherine Zeta-Jones. DVD. Columbia-Spyglass-Amblin-Sony, 2005.
_____. *The Mask of Zorro.* Perf. Antonio Banderas, Catherine Zeta-Jones, and Anthony Hopkins. DVD. Tri-Star-Amblin-Sony, 1998.
Cawelti, John G. "The New Mythology of Crime." *Boundary 2* 3.2 (Winter 1975): 324–57.
Chang, Cheh, dir. *Blood Brothers.* Perf. David Chiang, Ti Lung, and Kuan Tai Chen. DVD. Shaw Brothers-Celestial Pictures, 1973.
_____. *The New One-Armed Swordsman.* Perf. David Chiang, Ti Lung, and Li Ching. DVD. Shaw Brothers-Celestial Pictures, 1971.
_____. *One-Armed Swordsman.* 1967. Perf. Jimmy Wang Yu, Chiao Chiao, and Tien Feng. DVD. Shaw Brothers-Celestial Pictures, 1967.
_____. *Return of the One-Armed Swordsman.* Perf. Jimmy Wang Yu, Chiao Chiao, and Tien Feng. DVD. Shaw Brothers-Celestial Pictures, 1968.
_____. *Vengeance.* Perf. David Chiang and Ti Lung. DVD. Shaw Brothers-Celestial Pictures, 1970.
Chiampi, James Thomas. "Resurrecting *The Godfather.*" *MELUS* 5.4 (1978): 18–31.
Combs, Richard. "Coppola's Family Plot: The Godfather Variations." *Film Comment* 38.2 (Mar.-Apr 2002): 38–44.
Coppola, Francis Ford, dir. *The Godfather.* Perf. Marlon Brando, Al Pacino, Robert Duvall, Diane Keaton, and Richard Castellano. DVD. Paramount, 1972.
_____. *The Godfather: Part II.* Perf. Al Pacino, Robert De Niro, Robert Duvall, John Cazale, and Michael V. Gazzo. DVD. Paramount, 1974.
_____. *The Godfather Part III.* Perf. Al Pacino, Diane Keaton, Andy Garcia, Sofia Coppola, and Eli Wallach. DVD. Zoetrope-Paramount, 1990.
Curtiz, Michael, dir. *The Adventures of Robin Hood.* Perf. Errol Flynn, Olivia De Havilland, Basil Rathbone, and Claude Rains. DVD. Warner, 1938.
D'Acierno, Pellegrino. "Cinema Paradiso: The Italian American Presence in American Cinema." *The Italian American Heritage: A Companion to Literature and Arts.* Ed. Pellegrino D'Acierno. Garland Reference Library of the Humanities 1473. New York: Garland, 1999. 563–690.
Eco, Umberto. "Narrative Structures in Fleming." *The Role of the Reader.* Bloomington: Indiana University Press, 1984. 144–72. 1979.
Fang, Karen. *John Woo's A Better Tomorrow.* Hong Kong: Hong Kong University Press, 2004.
Fuqua, Antoine, dir. *The Replacement Killers.* Perf. Chow Yun-fat, Mira Sorvino, and Kenneth Tsang. DVD. Columbia, 1997.
Hagedorn, Roger. "Technology and Economic Exploitation: The Serial as a Form of Narrative Presentation." *Wide Angle* 10.4 (1988): 4–12.
Hall, Kenneth E. *John Woo: The Films.* Jefferson, NC: McFarland, 1999.
Hamilton, Guy, dir. *Goldfinger.* Perf. Sean Connery, Gert Frobe, Bernard Lee, and Lois Maxwell. Albert R. Broccoli-Harry Saltzman-MGM, 1964.
Hanson, Curtis, dir. *L.A. Confidential.* Perf. Kevin Spacey, Russell Crowe, Guy Pearce, Kim Basinger, and James Cromwell. DVD. Arnon Milchan-David L. Wolper/Regency-Warner, 1997.

Hunt, Leon. "Kung Fu Cult Masters: Stardom, Performance and 'Masculinity' in Hong Kong Martial Arts Films." *Defining Cult Movies: The Cultural Politics of Oppositional Taste*. Ed. Mark Jancovich, Antonio Lázaro Reboll, Julian Stringer, and Andy Willis. London: Manchester University Press, 2003. 157–71.

Ianni, Francis A. J., with Elizabeth Reuss-Ianni. *A Family Business: Kinship and Social Control in Organized Crime*. New York: Russell Sage, 1972.

Lacey, Robert. *Little Man : Meyer Lansky and the Gangster Life*. Boston: Little, Brown and Company, 1991.

"Lee Falk: Father of the Phantom." 2007 <http://www.deepwoods.org/lee_falk.html>.

Mamoulian, Rouben, dir. *The Mark of Zorro*. Perf. Tyrone Power, Linda Darnell, Basil Rathbone, and Eugene Pallette. DVD. Twentieth Century–Fox, 1940.

Marling, William. *The American Roman Noir: Hammett, Cain, and Chandler*. Athens: University of Georgia Press, 1995.

Mayo, Archie, dir. *The Petrified Forest*. Perf. Humphrey Bogart, Leslie Howard, and Bette Davis. Warner Bros., 1936.

Peckinpah, Sam, dir. *Ride the High Country*. Perf. Joel McCrea, Randolph Scott, and Mariette Hartley. DVD. GM/Turner Entertainment/Warner Bros., 1962.

_____. *The Wild Bunch*. 1969. Perf. William Holden, Ernest Borgnine, Warren Oates, Ben Johnson, and Edmond O'Brien. DVD. Warner Bros., 1969.

Puzo, Mario. *The Godfather*. New York: Putnam, 1969.

Siodmak, Robert, dir. *Cry of the City*. Perf. Victor Mature and Richard Conte. Sol C. Siegel, 1948.

Tan, Sor-hoon. "Filial Daughters-in-Law: Questioning Confucian Filiality." *Filial Piety in Chinese Thought and History*. Ed. Alan K. L. Chan and Sor-hoon Tan. London: RoutledgeCurzon, 2004. 226–40.

Traylor, Kenneth L. *Chinese Filial Piety*. Bloomington, IN: Eastern, 1988.

Tsui, Hark, dir. *A Better Tomorrow III: Love and Death in Saigon*. Perf. Chow Yun-fat, Tony Leung Ka-fai, Anita Mui, and Yam Shut Saam Long. DVD. Film Workshop, 1989.

Tuttle, Frank, dir. *This Gun for Hire*. 1942. Perf. Alan Ladd, Veronica Lake, Robert Preston, and Laird Cregar. DVD. Paramount-Universal, 1942.

Verzea, Ileana. "The Serial Novel and the TV Serial." *Synthesis (Bucharest)* 9 (1982): 1–6.

Woo, John, dir. *A Better Tomorrow*. Perf. Chow Yun-fat, Ti Lung, Leslie Cheung, Emily Chu, Tien Feng, Waise Lee, and Kenneth Tsang. John Woo, screenwriter. Film Workshop-Saerom, 1986.

_____. *A Better Tomorrow II*. 1988. Digital videodisc. With Chow Yun-fat, Ti Lung, Leslie Cheung, Emily Chu, and Kenneth Tsang. Screenwriter, John Woo. DVD. Cinema City-Anchor Bay, 2000.

_____. *Bullet in the Head*. Perf. Tony Leung, Jacky Cheung, and Waise Lee. Screenwriter, John Woo. DVD. Deltamac-Fortune Star, 1990.

_____. *Last Hurrah for Chivalry*. Perf. Damian Lau and Wei Pai. DVD. Fortune Star, 1979.

Zinnemann, Fred, dir. *The Day of the Jackal*. Perf. Edward Fox, Michel Lonsdale, and Cyril Cusack. DVD. Warwick Film Productions-Universal Productions France S. A./Universal, 1973.

12

The Allegorical Imagination in Hindi Film Series[1]

RASHMI DORAISWAMY

Introduction

In the Hindi cinema, genres lead more ambivalent and hybrid lives than their Hollywood counterparts do. Film series, as a consequence, maintain generic affiliations, but are linked equally firmly to stars, to *auteurs*, or thematic networks. Within the existing corpus of genres, the film series carves out a space for itself. The films in a series may partake of many genres, while being identified as a series because of the persona of characters/actors, or thematic networks that are repeated, or because it is a sequel.

A film series may or may not be intended when the first film is made; that it is the *first* film becomes evident *post facto* after the second film — when the same character, or theme, in a similar generic narrative — follows in a not too distant temporal framework. Actors or directors, particularly in the early stages of their career, are in a more fluid situation in terms of the screen persona they want to chart out. It is with the first box-office hit that the path of generic preferences is laid out. For some, the series is the pathway that leads to stardom.

In the studio and post-studio eras of the Hindi film, directors have played a crucial role in films that form a series. Raj Kapoor, who created one of the most important personae of post–Independence India, was not only the actor who played the role of Raj, but was also a director acknowledged as one of the masters of the Golden 1950s of the Hindi cinema. He owned the famous R.K. Studios, which produced many of the films in which the persona of Raj was forged. Manoj Kumar, who played the role of Bharat in the 1960s and 1970s, was also a director who fashioned his own distinct persona in film after film. (Bharat means "India"; it is also a common male name.) Both these directors were *auteurs*; they had marked styles of *mise-en-scène*. These styles were characterized by narrative density in the period of formation and stabilization and tended to degenerate with time. The "end" of an A-grade series is usually marked by a degeneration of form or a nonchalance towards matters of craft and thematic complexity.

The name of a protagonist in many ways is as important as the characterological traits he is known by. Many of the series are, in fact, identified by the actor's name, which is also the name of the lead protagonist. This involves a series of mediations as in the case of Raj Kapoor, who in playing Raj in his films, created the persona of a postcolonial subjectivity, who was marginal, an outsider, and a tramp, modeled on the image of Charlie Chaplin.

In a series of films from 1934 to 1969, when she retired from acting, the Fearless Nadia action and stunt films were inextricably linked to the name of the actress. Australian-born, blond, bold, and blue-eyed, she became known for the daring stunts she performed. Whether on horseback or on moving trains, she became the icon of a physically strong and assertive womanhood. That she was clearly "other," in no way detracted from her popularity. Nadia, by her very "foreignness," was beyond social inscribings. This was the liberating factor of her stunt films: she was a foreigner and was thus not inscribed in the social spaces that Indian women were, troubled equally by tradition and modernity. Nadia was untroubled modernity, alien and thus acceptable in social spaces and activities that her Indian counterparts could scarcely hope to be in.[2] She is best remembered for *Hunterwali/The Lady with the Whip* (Homi Wadia, 1935) and *Hunterwali ki Beti/Daughter of Hunterwali* (Batuk Bhatt, 1943). Her foreign origins gave her the license to tread where not many Indian women could.[3] This had significance in terms of genre formation as well as in terms of an engagement with realism as a mode of representation. The socials pitched their arguments within a mediated realist-melodramatic framework. The action film constantly transgresses these frameworks of realism.[4] A "realist" framework in the narrative of Nadia's films, however, is provided paradoxically by her being "alien," and by the public knowing that her stunts were "real," performed by Nadia herself, and not by a double.

In other cases, the relationship between actor and character is inverted. Whatever the name of the character in the film, the films carry the name of the actor in the title. Such is the case with the Johar and Johar-Mehmood series. In *Johar Mehmood in Goa* (I.S. Johar, 1965), for instance, the characters who are revolutionaries fighting for India's independence from the British are called Ram and Rahim. The other film of this series directed by I. S. Johar himself was *Johar in Kashmir* (1966). The later films were directed by others—*Johar in Bombay* (Shantilal Soni, 1967) and *Johar Mehmood in Hong Kong* (S.A. Akbar, 1971). These B-grade films were made on smaller budgets with lesser-known actors in formulaic narratives.[5] They were meant for specific distribution circuits and their engagement with the finer nuances of the craft of cinema was minimal, if not non-existent.

Names evoke larger cultural associations in B-grade film series as well. Tarzan inspired a whole series of films. Some of the earliest Tarzan films date from the 1930s: *Tarzan ki Beti/Tarzan's Daughter* (Roop K. Sheorey, 1938), and *Toofani Tarzan/Hurricane Tarzan* (Homi Wadia, 1937). The 1960s saw a spate of B-grade films featuring Tarzan in the title. Whether or not the protagonist had anything in common with the character honed in nature, untouched by the wiles of civilization, created by Edgar Rice Burroughs in 1912, is beside the point. It was a universally known icon of strength, of raw energy, that was being evoked. Several directors tried their hand at the Tarzan films.[6] While Azad played the lead role in most of these films, Dara Singh, the well-known wrestler, who became actor and director, played the lead in two of the films of this series: *Tarzan and King Kong* (A. Shamseer, 1965) and *Tarzan Comes to Delhi* (Kedar Kapoor, 1965).

Dara Singh remains one of the most interesting figures of the B-cinema. His performances centered on his physique and on action, rather than on acting. He was rustic, lacked any veneer of sophistication, and had a diction marked by his native Punjabi language. His off-screen persona of a wrestler was molded into four main film series (although he acted in many other films as well): the Tarzan films, the rural bandit films,[7] the films in which he was paired against strongman King Kong, a foreign wrestler, who was defeated time and again by this indigenous wrestler,[8] and the Rustam films. Rustam, a character from the *Shahnama*,[9] is a legendary hero, associated with bravery in the battlefield and immense physical strength. Hence the name stood for championship in fighting.[10]

The B-films also iconize their popular actors. Kedar Kapoor made a film entitled *Dara Singh* (1964), in which Singh played the lead role. *Mera Naam Johar/My Name is Johar* (Sarankant, 1967) was a thriller with Johar in the lead role.

National Allegory

Cinema in India developed alongside the nationalist movement for independence from British colonial rule. It developed several ways of representing the many concerns of this movement. In the postcolonial context, too, the nation as an imagined community is constantly evoked in direct and indirect ways. The ways in which popular cultural texts and high cultural texts construct allegories may differ greatly. In the popular cinema, the nation is often allegorized through hybrid modes that include realism and melodrama, among others. New Wave Indian films, for instance, deploy and debate with realism and modernism and draw on different registers of visual/performative arts to construct national allegories. This essay examines the film series in the context of national allegory because its varied forms become more apparent in the film series, in its repetitions.

According to Northrop Frye, "We have actual allegory when a poet explicitly indicates the relationship of his images to examples and precepts, and also tries to indicate how a commentary on him should proceed. A writer is being allegorical whenever it is clear that he is saying 'by this I also mean that.' If this seems to be done continuously, we may say, cautiously, that what he is writing 'is' an allegory.... Allegory, then, is a contrapuntal technique...." (54). Whether from Hollywood or Bollywood, these popular cultural texts are "allegories" because they are constructing contiguous, parallel symbolic narratives on changing notions of Good and Evil. They are "*national* allegories" because the exposition on Good and Evil is inscribed ideologically in an imagination of the nation. By saying *this* (the immanent narrative, the individual protagonist's narrative), they also mean *that* (the transcendent narrative, the narrative about the imagined nation).

We must here return to an old debate on Third World texts being *necessarily* national allegorical — a formulation put forth by Frederic Jameson and critiqued in a finely nuanced way by Aijaz Ahmad.[11] One can add to the debate by asking why First and Second World texts *too* cannot be read as national allegories of their nations as imagined communities. The Star Wars series of films, for example, are as much national allegories as any popular Third World text. The narrative that deals with the colonization of space, of traders fighting for routes and hegemony, a narrative that is supposedly set many years ago and many galaxies away, could only be possible in a nation that is the leading player in the myriad processes of globalization, in space research and voyages, with the corresponding technology and infrastructure to create and distribute convincing futuristic audio-visual imagery worldwide. All this calls for a state of development of the nation that is capable of producing this imagined narrative — a state that is characterized as late capitalist or post-industrial. Can we imagine this narrative being produced in Malaysia, Indonesia, Iran, or India? No. For the reason that we are, in the main, mixed economies in transition and our narratives correspond to our concerns *vis-à-vis* the communities we imagine ourselves to be part of. The play of temporalities in the Star Wars narrative ("long ago" and futuristic in the same breath) encompasses the "past" and "future" of Western civilization: it is a replay of the colonial enterprise when ships from Western Europe plied the seas all over the world, entering countries in other continents as traders and settling down as colonizers. Only now this old narrative is being played out in space, where the "natives" are all manner of creatures, robots, and mutants. It is the future colonization of space that is being represented as a past, a bygone era. We have here a narrative that is working on two levels as all allegories do: a literal story and a parallel narrative that represents a long-term political/colonizing agenda. It is an extended metaphor of the aspirations in space of the leading player in the politics of the colonization of space. As such, it binds a nation as it imagines its future in space. To this extent, it is possible to call Star Wars a national allegory. In his 1979 study of Wyndham Lewis, in particular the political and international nature of his works, Frederic Jameson writes that "national allegory should be understood as a formal attempt to bridge the increasing gap between the existential data of everyday life within a given nation-state and the structural tendency of monopoly capital to develop on a worldwide, essentially transnational scale" ("National Allegory" 313). In the context of films like Star Wars, one may add, not just on a transnational, but also on a galactic scale.

According to Jameson, one of the characteristics of national allegory in Third World narratives, the private and public are never split because "the story of the private individual destiny is always an allegory of the embattled situation of the public Third World culture and society" ("Third World" 320). It is not as if Jameson has not written of the possibility of a similar allegory in First World films. But here he defines allegory in a different, positive light, as a way of "figuring" the as-yet not fully manifested new relationships of class.[12] This concept of "figurability" is, in fact, useful in delineating the utopian moment of popular cultural texts of the Third World as well. Even when Jameson accepts that similar allegorical structures are possible in First World texts, he suggests that they are "unconscious": "they must be deciphered by interpretative mechanisms that necessarily entail a whole social and historical critique of our First World situation. The point here is that, in distinction to the unconscious allegories of our own cultural texts, Third World national allegories are conscious and overt: they imply a radically different and objective relation of politics to libidinal dynamics" ("Third World" 330). Implicit in this is the assumption that First World texts are more complex and therefore require more interpretative strategies to come into force because the allegories are unconscious. Third World texts, on the other hand, offer themselves easily to interpretation, because the allegories are overt and direct.

This distinction is open to question. The James Bond series, for instance, is one that is blatantly political, adapting to every new international hot spot from the West's point of view in the Cold War and post–Cold War eras. In the recent *The World is Not Enough* (Michael Apted, 1999) it is the West's emerging relationship with the strategically important geopolitics in Central Asia that receives what Jameson has called "figurability," in *Die Another Day* (Lee Tamahori, 2002)—North Korea. Moreover, in the Bond films too, the private and public domains collapse into each other—Bond remains the epitome of the all exterior, no interiority hero, collapsing most of the distinctions between the private individual destiny and public social destiny. The Bond films are national allegories on the West's foreign policy positions against whoever is construed as the current ideological enemy.

Third World societies are not homogenous ones, transiting smoothly—economically, politically and socially—from one historical period to another. Consequently, Third World cultural texts, too, are not a homogenous set of texts. There are high cultural articulations as there are popular ones. There is also a large area of interfacing between popular and high cultural texts, and the drawing of one into the other's ambit, playfully, dialogically, or critically. Both construct national allegories that are distinct from one another. Both Third and First World popular texts, particularly films, allegorize the nation in specifically historical ways. It is the specificity of the historical context that needs to be elaborated in the allegories of *both* the First and the Third World.

If the premise that Third World texts—like First or Second World texts—are national allegories is accepted, there is a need to examine just *when* Third World texts become *of necessity* national allegories: they become so at given moments of their history. National allegory is the dominant mode in cultural texts in periods of turmoil and transition, as, for instance, in the immediate pre- and post-independence-from-colonization contexts in the Third World.[13] In other less tumultuous periods, it may be to relinquish its position of eminence in the network of generic modes and become one of the many secondary genres of a given period. Its character, too, may undergo change, with the "national" moment of the allegory becoming subterranean in the text. Jameson's assertion that First World texts are national allegories at a more "unconscious" level, while Third World allegories are conscious and overt does not hold: while the Rambo and James Bond series on the one hand, display the allegories of the nation they espouse at an overt level, in the Third World Hindi film series, on the other, the allegory can be buried within the narrative, surfacing at given moments, and creating ripples of signification. The popular cultural text of the Third World can equally serve to "figure" the anxieties of a postcolonial situation, of double binds between tradition and modernity, of the street and home, of the village and the city, of agrarian and industrial economies, in much the same way as the First World texts figure the anxieties of late capitalist or post industrialist societies.

All sorts of popular cultural texts, whether they belong to the First or Third Worlds, can allegorize the nation as an imagined community. This representation of the imagined community may represent or refract dominant or contesting ideologies. It must be emphasized that this imagined community in India is almost always non-homogenous in terms of class, caste, and religion. The community is plural, and the plurality in Hindi film narratives is usually a vibrant one. Popular films allegorize the nation in different ways. Most of them personify Good and Evil in the characters of the Hero and Villain. This conflict connotes issues that have ideological relevance for a notion of the nation. Allegory is mainly realized through three agencies: the hero, the conflict between the hero and the villain, and the narrative in its entirety.

This essay focuses on the film series in the postcolonial period from the time India achieved independence from the British in 1947 to the present times. Three distinct periods can be charted in our postcolonial history that have given birth to corresponding subjectivities and narratives in the popular film.[14] The post-independence period of the 1950s saw the marginal, the underdog, addressing institutions in the making, making a plea for social justice. The 1970s were a transitional period once again, with unrest in the country: labor agitations, the spread of people's movements and ultra-left movements, the states questioning the authority of the Center, the crisis of institutions and the imposition of Emergency. In the post–Emergency period and the 1980s new trends were witnessed in the socio-political arena. Regional parties took center-stage, negotiating with "all–India" parties to govern not just their respective states, but also to create coalitions to govern from the center. There was also the spread of religious divisions with a new belligerence on the part of the majority community. In the 1990s globalization and the high profile and visibility of the diasporic community — the non-resident Indians — in turn exerted great influence on audio-visual fields in India. The national imaginary in cultural representations, which was an inclusive one despite the perceived inequities, in the 1950s, becomes increasingly exclusive and fragmented from the 1970s onwards.

This essay examines some of the ways in which the "organic" life of series films in the Hindi cinema represents and refracts dominant and contesting ideologies of social formations as "being," "becoming," or as "deterioration." Since it is not possible to cover all the types of series films that can be observed in the Hindi cinema in the framework of a single article,[15] the focus here will be on three significant types of series from the 1950s to the present time: the

"Name Series" (where the lead actor has a name that is repeated in many films), the "Title Series" (where the title or a part of it, is repeated in many films) and the "Character Series" (in which a character is repeated or a sequel ensues). Other than a character who appears in a new set of adventures in every new film of the series, the name of the character or the title of a film can also become the markers of a series because they begin to signify certain characterological and narratological traits that are repeated in film after film.

The Name Series

Two of the most important series in this category are the films of Raj Kapoor and Manoj Kumar, although there are several other actors who have repeated a name that clicked in film after film. Raj Kapoor and Manoj Kumar, however, created historically significant personae that went with the names they chose: Kapoor in the 1950s in the immediate postcolonial period and Manoj Kumar later, in the 1960s and 1970s. It is also of importance that both actors were directors and actively shaped their screen personae. Linked as this series is to the name of a character, played by the same actor, it plays an important role in the transformation of the actor to the status of a star. The name may be used by the same actor in other films, directed by other filmmakers, with or without the connotations ascribed to them. We will, however, only examine those films that constitute the series.

Raj Kapoor: Character, Actor, Star

Raj Kapoor's use of his own first name concretizes a specific kind of hero from *Awaara/Vagabond* (Raj Kapoor, 1951) onwards. Raj is a malleable name: the addition of a "u" to the end not only gives it the nuance of endearment, but also makes it more rustic, more indigenous. Raj, clipped and proper, is formal. This is what he is called in "westernized" settings like the club or the hotel. Coupled with Kumar, it means "Prince." "I am called Raj Kumar," says the unemployed pauper ironically to his landlady, Mrs. D'sa, in *Shri 420/ Mr. 420* (Raj Kapoor, 1955). Actor/character Raj is further molded in the Chaplinesque mode, one that comes into full "being" in *Shri 420/Mr. 420*, but is constantly evoked in all his films. Raj, singing "Mera joota hai Japaani, hai patloon Inglistani, sar pe lal topi Russi, phir bhi dil hai Hindustani" ("My shoes are Japanese, pants British, the red cap on my head is Russian, yet my heart is Indian") with his torn canvas shoes, is the graduate from the town, migrating to the big city, Bombay, in search of work, with a bundle of his belongings hung on a stick across his shoulder. The oft-repeated gesture of lifting up his cap, a very western one, is hardly in place here. This is a "composite character," unreal in the sense of realism. The composite nature of the image lies precisely in his bringing together the global referents of the Indian post-colonial scene with the specifically Indian.

The character of Raj/Raju cannot be fully comprehended without the context of postcoloniality. The character refers to western cultural signposts, but constantly emphasizes his Indian-ness. It explains Kapoor's popularity not just in the Soviet Union, but also in postcolonial, developing countries all over the world. Chaplin's evocation is particularly significant. Chaplin, an émigré to the United States, retained the image of an "outsider" despite his popularity worldwide. His romantic critique of industrialization and the machine age, his critique of fascism, and his well-known political views had a specific resonance in a country that was largely agrarian, industrialized in pockets, that had just won independence from the British, prided itself on being non-aligned, and was close to the Soviet Union in the Cold War scenario. All these significations worked at a subterranean level in the persona of Raj. What is made explicit is the lack of "fit" of this character in the newly independent nation, into which he *should* have "fitted." This is the tone of the narratives of three of the significant films that concretized the "misfit" persona: *Awaara/Vagabond* and *Shri 420/Mr. 420* directed by Raj Kapoor, and *Anari/The Unwise* (Hrishikesh Mukherjee, 1959). This character of the "small man" is extended further to that of Raju, the rustic bumpkin who becomes "accidental reformer" of dacoits in *Jis Desh Mein Ganga Behti Hai/The Country in Which the River Ganga Flows* (Radhu Karmakar, 1960), directed by Raj Kapoor's long-time cameraman. The character finally meets his end in Raj Kapoor's *Mera Naam Joker/My Name is Joker* (Raj Kapoor, 1970), where the composite character of Raj is eclipsed by the actor and aging star, who now tries to don the romantic-sentimental mask of one who makes the world laugh, while he himself cries. This was in stark contrast to, and an inversion of the persona he had built through the 1950s and 1960s of the character who keeps his chin up, no matter what the odds against him. The lead songs sung by Raj played an important role in positing him as a particular kind of subject, a subject whose mode of address changes: Raj Kapoor singing "Awaara hoon" ("I am a vagabond") shows streets that are benign: women who playfully throw him off the truck, children playing on the street. "Jeena isi ka naam hai" ("This is what living is all about") (*Anari/The Unwise*), "Hum us desh ke vasi hain, jis desh mein ganga behti ha" ("We are citizens of a country, in which the Ganga flows"), too, are characterized by a joyousness that is written *into* the premise of being a marginal. Compared to these songs "Kehta hai Joker, sara zamana, aadi haqeeqat, aadha fasana" ("The Joker says, the whole world is half real, half imagined") from *Mera Naam Joker/My Name is Joker*, in which he refers to himself in the third person, has a didactic edge to it.

The persona of Raj, holding binaries in balance — urbane/rustic, naïve/wise, western/Indian — is performative-pedagogic, but not overtly didactic.[16] Raj is inscribed in narratives of familial and social uprootment-resettlement. Societies in turmoil-filled transition from feudalism to capitalism, from colonization to postcolonization, employ the criminal character as a test case — it is against this character that the social background gets thrown into relief, that social values get judged. It is also in such periods that the debate of what creates the criminal — genes or social environment — gets inscribed in narratives. Shifting meanings of words spotlight a society in flux and serve to underline the disjunction between the subject/citizen and the state he is in. *Awaara/Vagabond*, *Shri 420/Mr. 420*, and *Anari/The Unwise* as titles highlight words whose signifieds represent different subjects to different enunciators. Just as in Dostoevsky's *The Idiot*, idiocy takes on many meanings, depending on *who* refers to Myshkin as an "idiot," in *Shri 420/Mr. 420* and *Anari/The Unwise*, the words are double-edged, telling us as much about the speaker as about Raj. When his beloved and his adopted family utter the words, it is an endearment, when the corrupt businessman says it, it shows the businessman up for what he is.

The three 1950s Kapoor films form a series also because they create topographies of the split city, the separate spaces of the rich and the poor in the period of immediate postcoloniality. Migration to the city, the slum, the moneyed class, their indifference to the plight of the poor but deserving citizens of the newly independent India, the corruption, the hypocrisy of the elite — these are the themes that are posited as oppositions.

Awaara/Vagabond remains a landmark film for the way it charts and links, for the first time, the figure of the father with law and that of the surrogate father with that of crime. Worked out by K. A. Abbas, this narrative schema was taken up later in the 1970s by Salim-Javed in the films they scripted for Amitabh Bachchan. The 1970s were another turning point of our postcolonial history. This, in fact, proved that this narrative structure was an analogon, resonating in times of turmoil.[17] *Awaara/Vagabond*, however, remains unsurpassed in the complexity of narrative, image, and realization. The social circumstances that pushed an individual into crime were meticulously dealt with. *Shri 420/Mr. 420* deals with a fraudulent housing scheme that cheats the poor of their hard earned money. *Anari/The Unwise*'s plot centers around unscrupulous pharmacists who adulterate medicines and cause the death of unsuspecting patients. *Anari/The Unwise* is also about secularism and the emotional adoption of the Hindu protagonist by a Christian woman, who happens to be his landlady.

The Raj Kapoor series debates issues of a nation-in-the-making — a nation that has just become independent and has to set its house in order. Even when the cognitive mapping is outwards (as in the song, "Mera joota hai japani"/"My Shoes Are Japanese"), the narrative address is inwards, defining post-independence subjectivity. All the great *auteurs* of the Hindi cinema in the 1950s never lost sight of this fact, despite the differences in styles. It is this engagement with national allegorical narratives that makes the 1950s the "Golden Period" of the Hindi cinema. The point of view adopted for these narratives was also of the small man who emerges victorious in the end, even though he may have fallen prey to temptation on the way. There is an aspiration, and a resolution, even if it is a utopian one, of an indigenous socialist order that will come into being, bridging the gap between the poor and the rich. *Shri 420/Mr. 420* remains the most explicit exposition of this parallel narrative, with its focus on housing for the poor and Raj's final appeal to the homeless who live on the footpath to never lose faith in their own power. It is a national allegory because written into the conflict between Good and Evil is a disquietude about the split in the imagined community that had fought for independence. Those who occupied seats of financial and political power are seen to be morally incapable of seeing the agenda of social justice through. This is the reason that the markers of Western lifestyle (bars, hotels, cabaret dancers, etc.) are always presented as the "other" life, contiguous with the new villains.

We must also address the distinction between traditional and modern/postmodern allegory.[18] These distinctions rarely work in postcolonial texts. In popular cinema, in particular, it is the palimpsestic mode that prevails.[19] Past, present and future, tradition, modernity and even postmodernity, exist not as consecutive developments but simultaneously, within the same time framework. *Awaara/Vagabond* is a good example of this coexistence. The allegory is modern (on the nation in the making). It also has epical references that are introduced in the song "Zulam sahe bhari janak dulari" ("King Janak's daughter, Sita, suffers the weight of injustice") when the wife is thrown out on the streets. The song is sung by street singers huddling in the rain who ask why the earth and sky did not split open at Sita's tragic fate. Thus the debate of "genes vs. environment" is inscribed in the larger mythological, cultural story of Sita who was also kept by Ravana (in *Awaara/Vagabond*, Jagga, the dacoit) and thrown out of the house by her husband, Lord Ram, on the issue of chastity. Unlike the queen in the epic, however, who retreats into the jungle and the lap of nature to give birth to and bring up her twin sons, this modern day narrative has the genteel woman travel to the city of Bombay and its slums to set up her new life. *Awaara/Vagabond* deconstructs a mythological story and critiques it. The allegorical discourse on the modern nation is thus simultaneously a critique of the mythical nation of the epic. If in the epic the children of Ram grow up away from him but in his image, in *Awaara/Vagabond*, the separated child is on the other side of the social divide and is everything the father is not. In this critique, the film partakes of the modernist impulse. One of the most interesting scenes in the film is when Raj's mother is on her way to the court to tell her estranged lawyer husband not to prosecute Raj for he is his son. The lawyer's car strikes her down. The lawyer visits her in the hospital, but she is fully covered with bandages, shrouded in an almost surrealist manner. Her face is not given to sight and the lawyer does not recognize his wife. He does not understand what she is mumbling beneath the bandages. Sight and comprehension are thus denied to the husband who has been unjust.

The series draws on realist and melodramatic modes of representation, and on other western cinematic traditions, that it bends to its own devices. German Expressionist aesthetics, which had influenced Hollywood *noir* with its externalizing of internal conflicts between Good and Evil in planar jutting lines of composition, chiaroscuro lighting, and brooding imagery, found its most cogent reflection in *Awaara/Vagabond*. These spatial configurations are all captured in images of high contrast, with several patterns of light and shade. The very materiality of architecture, or of the earth, creates a tortured atmosphere throughout the film. The bedroom Raj's mother lies in when in labor pain is one such example, where the patterns of the walls, ceilings, doors, curtains, upholstery—everything is so conflicting and disharmonious that it arouses a feeling of anxiety, quite apart from the tension between the husband and wife. The same is true even of the earth in scenes where it is shown: it is almost as if the ground is woven with snakes. The frames nearly always seem to be too full of disharmonious patterns. It is in this context that the first song in the film, "Hoshiyaar" ("Take Care"), sung by boatmen and dancers on land, assumes a new significance. The song is a metaphoric one about the boat of life, issuing a warning to be careful, but is shot on a panoramic scale, with nature—the sky and water—as dominant forces occupying the larger part of the frames. This is epic nature, with clean and clear lines, not yet corrupted by disharmonic patterns. The influence of Expressionism and of the director's fascination for deep focus cinematography have been combined to create a work that disturbs thematically *and* visually. Of interest in *Awaara/Vagabond* is the entire setting up of spatial oppositions: the countryside and city; the small town and the city of Bombay; the slums and high society of the city; the den of Jagga, the dacoit of the countryside and the den of Jagga the gangster in the city; the space of homes (Raj's and Rita's), and the space of institutions within the city — the prison, the hospital, the court, and the factory where Raj works for a short while. The *noir* aesthetics suited the representation of the small man on the mean streets of the city who could fall to temptation. The equivalent of the *femme fatale* of the American *noir* cinema was to be found in the precincts of the hotel/casino, with limited contribution to the hero's fall.

The three Raj Kapoor films discussed above, "figure" the utopian "bridge" between the two halves of the split city, with the narrative finale integrating the "haves" with the "have-nots," the footpath with the mansions and the high-rises.

Manoj Kumar: New Anxieties

The 1960s saw the retreat of films that referred overtly to imagined notions of the nation. With the advent of color in cinema and the rise to dominance of romance films, many of them shot in exotic locales, national allegory had to reinvent itself. In the entire matrix of genres in a given period, the actor tries out many garbs before finding a "fit." Manoj Kumar who had played romantic roles in the late 1950s and early 1960s molded himself into the persona of Bharat after the success of *Shaheed/Martyr* (Kewal Kashyap, 1965), based on the life of the revolutionary, Bhagat Singh, who had fought for independence from the British.[20] Bharat means India, and it is this name he donned in the films he directed, carving out a distinctive niche for himself as a "serious" character, as against the jumping, cavorting, romantic heroes of the day like Jeetendra, Shammi Kapoor, and Rajesh Khanna. Manoj Kumar retained the patriotic fervor of the persona of Bhagat Singh, but adopted a style of acting that was one of restraint, of internalized suffering, quite different from the volatile slogan-shouting revolutionary in *Shaheed/Martyr*.

Upkar/The Selfless Favor (1967), Manoj Kumar's directorial debut, deals with the rural vs. city divide, and the farmer who willingly stays back in the countryside. If *Upkar/The Selfless Favor* is about migration from the village to the city, *Purab aur Paschim/East and West* (Manoj Kumar, 1970) is about migration from India to a foreign land. His first two films are complex articulations within the commercial framework of this core anxiety of migration and those who choose to stay back. By the time he makes *Shor/Noise* (1972) and *Roti Kapda aur Makaan/Food, Clothing, and Shelter* (1974), he is firmly entrenched in the inequities of the city. The theme of treachery, of those who "sell" the ideals of the nation, is also central to the first two films. "Kasme, vaade, pyar wafa sab, baatein hain, baaton ka kya?" ("Promises of love and loyalty are mere talk, and how can mere talk be banked upon?") go the words of a popular song from the film. *Upkar/The Selfless Favor* is an ode to the tenacity and resilience of the Indian village although it does not match the epical scale of Mehboob's *Mother India* (1957). The most popular song of the film was an agrarian community song about the riches that could be harvested from this country's soil: "Mere desh ki dharti" ("The soil of my country"). *Upkar/The Selfless Favor* is the product of the new political milieu of a nation threatened at the borders. The rapid modernization the country is going through is leading to migrations to the city. The political slogan "Jai Jawan, Jai Kisan" ("Hail Soldier, Hail Peasant") is the core theme of this film. Lal Bahadur Shastri, who was Prime Minister of India for a brief period and led India in the Indo-Pak war against General Ayub Khan, formulated this slogan. This war, unlike the Indo-China war, under the leadership of Nehru, did not end in defeat, and the resulting resurgent nationalism under Shastri explains the visual importance Manoj Kumar accords him in his film. "Jai Jawan, Jai Kisan" was a slogan that emphasized the need for self-sufficiency in food[21] and in arms in order to be able to defend the country. The plough and the rifle are important visual symbols in the film and when Bharat is dispossessed of his land, it is the army that he enrolls in. The song pictured on the war cuts to the stepbrother who is engaged in adulterating food grains: "What kind of a merchant is it who buys corpses?" go the words of the song. *Upkar/The Selfless Favor* posits emphatically that the country has to be equally defended from outside attacks as it should be from the attacks of the corrupt within.

Purab aur Paschim/East and West addresses many of the political, cultural, and religious issues of the time. Social unrest over economic inequities had become more frequent, and conflicts over language and religious issues had come to the fore. This was also the time when the West turned to the East for its spiritual values and the time of "more equal," non-colonial cultural encounters of the West with the East (George Harrison and Ravi Shankar playing together, for example) and the spread of the Hare Rama Hare Krishna movement. It was the time of "brain drain," when highly qualified professionals from India went to the West for employment. Manoj Kumar's first two films very clearly deal with "internal" villainy. *Purab aur Paschim/East and West* begins with an act of treachery: Pran, the son of a saintly man, Guruji (played by Ashok Kumar), informs the British of the whereabouts of a freedom fighter who has returned for a short while to see his pregnant wife. The freedom fighter is shot down. Pran migrates abroad and takes his infant son with him, leaving behind his pregnant wife who subsequently gives birth to a girl. Bharat is born to the freedom fighter's wife. Guruji takes on the responsibility of looking after the boy and his mother. This splitting of a family into two — into those who side with the colonial power and go to live in England and those who stay back — is the background against which the main plot unfolds.

The adult Bharat, son of a freedom fighter who gave up his life, in a way carries on this nationalist struggle now on a new plane in the post–Indo-China and Indo-Pak wars context. It is the East that is the fountainhead of (spiritual) knowledge and the West that has scientific knowledge, says Bharat, playing on the words *gyan* and *vigyan* in Hindi. He goes to the West to study and finds that Indians who live abroad have lost their links with their traditions and values. Bharat, therefore, has to negotiate these internal divisive movements, as well as reiterate the pride of being Indian in a global scenario. The theme of a unified nation is reconstituted through narrative segments that deal with divisive forces and, more importantly, through songs. There are three such divisive issues Manoj Kumar singles out for attention: patriotism/treachery, conflicts among people of different religions, and tensions over the issue of a national language. The film begins with a song on India/Bharat and how it is the "heart of the East" having "been home" to the Gita, the Bible, the Koran, and Buddhism. The prologue to the film, too, stresses communal harmony. Set in Allahabad, 1942, it is impressively shot in black and white, in pouring rain. The rain has flooded the gully and even the inside of houses. The freedom fighter returns home under the camouflage of the cane basket that bobs up and down innocently in the water, unnoticed by the patrolling British soldiers. He enters his flooded home, with round, typically Indian vessels floating around in the water and meets his pregnant wife. (The vessels and water impart a feel of fertility and fecundity in this atmosphere of terror. It is also of interest that when the traitor Pran leaves the house with his son, the same street that had "wept" for the freedom fighter are now completely dry.) The husband is shot by the British before the eyes of his crying wife as he comes out of his house. A framed painting of the infant god Krishna being borne away, aloft on his father Vasudev's head, to safety (away from the treacherous maternal Uncle Kans), comes floating by in the water. The wife is led away by a Muslim and her child is born in their house. The Muslim comes out to the cries of the newborn infant and tells the soldiers that Allah will never forgive them. He is shot down as well and the floating painting is now picked up by Guruji, who will henceforth look after the mother and child. (The mythical palimpsestic reference to Uncle Kans is made in *Upkar/ The Selfless Favor* as well, pointing to the internal destructive forces within the family/nation.)

The other reference to the theme of harmony is when Bharat goes to Delhi to celebrate Republic Day. The announcement for the program refers to the language disputes in India: the announcer is forced to announce in English and Hindi simultaneously because sections of the audience have different demands. This theme of unity among religions is then repeated in the song, "Dulhan chali" ("The bride leaves for her new home") where the leaders Gandhi, Nehru, Shastri, and the spiritual savants of Hinduism and Christianity are visually shown. (Islam and Sikhism are evoked through architecture.) The country is seen as a young bride/sister who is adorned with all the attributes of the nation. "Whatever the state we come from, whatever the language we speak, we are first and foremost Indians," go the words of the song. The Republic Day signs are woven into the performance: the lit up Presidential Estate buildings and the tableaux representing the states, with the display of military might. The persona of Bharat had to seem to engage with the "real" in a more unmediated way than the heroes of other films where the "real" had been codified into generic modes.

While Raj Kapoor created the "composite character," Manoj Kumar created the character of "abstract essence" (India). Although the character is an identifiable social type, he is also allegorical. The character of Bharat, unlike Raj, is overburdened with familial relationships, many of which are disharmonic. He does not, like Raj, have to negotiate through the jungle of the city. The conflict between Good and Evil has a different set of topographical coordinates: not the rich and the poor city, but the village and city, or India and the West. The allegory in this series is *intrinsic* to narrative because the name itself carries the weight of allegory. Since the person stands for the country, the sufferings of the character, by metonymic extension, are the sufferings of the country. This metaphoric-metonymic sliding from person to nation is a device consistently employed by Manoj Kumar. "Bharat hi nahin sara desh tumhara hai" ("Not just Bharat, but the whole country is with you") says Manoj Kumar/Bharat to armyman David in *Upkar/The Selfless Favor*. "Bharat ka rehne wala hoon, Bharat ki baat sunata hoon" ("I am an inhabitant of Bharat and I will speak of Bharat,") he sings in *Purab aur Paschim/East and West*, the words of the song playing on his film name and the name of the country.

Manoj Kumar's off-screen persona also became merged with that of Bharat, and the dynamism of the character remained until a whole range of extra-textual factors caused its collapse. Prominent among these was the fact that from the 1970s onwards, India ceased to lend itself to a unitary/unified signified. The splintering of the very notion of "India," and the contesting relationships between center and periphery, led to the recognition of many

"Indias." The scaffolding for the allegorical Bharat could, therefore, no longer hold. In *Roti Kapda aur Makaan/Bread, Clothes, and House*, Bharat, in an inversion of his own image of the upright citizen resorts to corruption, to provide for his family. He has two brothers, one in the army and the other a policeman, who support him in various ways. This splintering of the allegorical subjectivity of those who will uphold the Law and Bharat himself, who is not above breaking the Law, points to the new social conjuncture the protagonist of the Hindi film narrative is now placed in. Manoj Kumar's alignment with the rightist Hindu-chauvinist Bharatiya Janta Party (BJP) in the late 1980s, was the final nail in Bharat's coffin, since the pan-political, pan-religious persona of Bharat — the man and actor — no longer rang true.[22]

In the late 1970s and 1980s, Manoj Kumar's didactic cinema could not stand up to the overwhelming presence of the revenge/vigilante narrative, with Amitabh Bachchan as its leading executor. The Bharat figure gets enmeshed in mild revenge narratives as in *Dus Numbri/The Ultimate Trickster* (Madan Mohla, 1976), or in a fable-historical drama as in *Kranti/Revolution* (Manoj Kumar, 1981), and is unable to achieve the pitch of didacticism evident in the earlier films.

The Title Series

The Khiladi Series

To Akshay Kumar goes the credit of acting in the most sustained series through the 1990s, although he has never occupied the top slot either in terms of stardom, or in terms of box-office record: *Khiladi/Gamester* (Abbas-Mastan, 1992); *Main Khiladi Tu Anari/I Am a Gamester, You Are a Fool* (Sameer Malkan, 1994); *Sab Se Bada Khiladi/The Biggest Gamester of All* (Umesh Mehra, 1995); *Khiladiyon ka Khiladi/The Biggest Gamester Among Gamesters* (Umesh Mehra, 1996); *Mr. and Mrs. Khiladi* (David Dhawan, 1997); *International Khiladi* (Umesh Mehra, 1999); *Khiladi 420* (Neeraj Vora, 2000). The series, however, has had its hits.

The persona of the *khiladi* referred to in the titles is built up in film after film on the basis of daredevil stunts that Akshay Kumar performs himself. Jumping from a bicycle on to a helicopter, or from a helicopter on to a car top (*Sab Se Bada Khiladi/The Biggest Gamester of All*) or jumping off a moving interstate bus (*Khiladiyon ka Khiladi/The Biggest Gamester Among Gamesters*) are just some of the stunts he has done. He has also built up a reputation as a martial arts expert trained in southeast Asia. This is played upon in *Khiladiyon ka Khiladi/The Biggest Gamester Among Gamesters*, in which he fights against the Undertaker as well as a sumo expert. The actor himself has stated that these films are inspired by the James Bond series. But the national allegory on foreign policy, central to the Bond films, is absent. For the most part the series is very hybrid, with several genres, in their diluted form, flowing through it. The only link it has with the Bond films is the action (sans the state-of-the-art technological gadgetry that is part of Bond's spy-kit) and the exotic locales, where action unfolds.[23]

The series began with Abbas-Mastan's *Khiladi/Gamester*. Since it began with Abbas-Mastan, it was colored by the thematic preoccupations of the directorial duo. The negative hero and the murder story are precariously perched between the genres of thriller and horror. This combination that received its most explicit representation in *Baazigar/Gambler* (1993), is first seen here. In fact, the Khiladi series inaugurated by them, with the protagonist having shades of dark grey in his character make-up, outlasted the psychotic hero they put forth in *Baazigar/Gambler*. This character trait is retained even in the humorous film of the series, *Mr. and Mrs. Khiladi*, directed by David Dhawan, in which the protagonist thinks he can become rich without doing any work.

In *Khiladi/Gamester*, the protagonist likes to bet. The betting becomes increasingly diabolical and the hero enters the grey area where "play" and "real" kidnapping become indistinguishable. The murder that takes place makes their "game" go completely awry and become macabre. The corpse that poses problems in being buried — in death it seems possessed of a weird will of its own — is then repeated in many of the other films of this series directed by other directors. Barbara Creed says of the corpse in the horror film that, "It represents the body at its most abject. It is body evacuated by 'self' — but worse still, it is a body which has become a 'waste'" (146). In the Khiladi films and the Abbas-Mastan films, the body is not fully evacuated of self, nor does it become waste: it becomes heavy meat, dead weight that poses problems in being disposed of. In *Khiladi/Gamester*, the friend who has been murdered by an unknown assailant proves difficult to get rid of, from the dickey of one car, she is laboriously shifted to another, her uncovered face causing uneasiness to her friends; the gamester husband's body in *Sab Se Bada Khiladi/The Biggest Gamester of All* disappears uncannily from the deep freeze, and then "refuses" to be buried, etc. It is in these moments that a greater horror than that of murder is invoked: the horror of the persistence of the corpse.

Main Khiladi Tu Anari/I Am a Gamester, You Are a Fool touches upon an actor's fascination with the "real, raw" life "out there." The *khiladi* of the title is Akshay Kumar, a police officer and the *anari*, the unwise one, is Saif Ali

Khan, an actor. The film also plays on the notion of male bonding, a staple of many, many films in the Hindi cinema. While the police officer rejects the actor for the better part of the film, he accepts him towards the end. In *Sab Se Bada Khiladi/The Biggest Gamester of All*, a complicated history of migration is charted. Akshay Kumar, once again a police officer, doubles up as a rustic fool, who gets married to the rich industrialist's daughter, to catch the blackmailers and murderers. This is revealed only at the end of the film. What we witness is the cuckolding and "murder" of the husband. There is a strange modernization of the horror genre usually associated with feudal imagery and old, crumbling mansions in the Hindi cinema. The *khiladi*'s body is hidden in the deep freeze in the kitchen. This icy coffin is a mutation of the graveyard in the cemetery. This is another corpse that is difficult to bury. *Khiladiyon ka Khiladi/The Biggest Gamester Among Gamesters* has Akshay Kumar split between two women: one who is older, conversant with the ways of the world, and the other, her young, innocent sister. The older woman is Maya, who is a don of the underworld in Canada. Among other things she has the WWF heroes at her beck and call. In *Khiladi 420*, Akshay Kumar plays twins, a Good and Evil brother. The Evil brother hatches a diabolical plot to marry a rich industrialist's daughter and kill her on their wedding night. The girl gets the better of him and has to rely on the Good brother to get her out of the jam she is in. The Khiladi series, as it developed, went westwards, setting the action in foreign countries. This was not a case of cognitive mapping, which films dealing with non-resident Indians do (*Dilwale Dulhaniya Le Jaayenge/The One Who Loves Will Take the Bride Away* [Aditya Chopra, 1995] or *Pardes/Foreign Country* [Subhash Ghai, 1997], for instance), with part of the narrative set in India and the other abroad. The "globalization" of the *khiladi* image had very little thematic function; it just served as an excuse to show exotic locales in touristy display. This attempt to "over-familiarize" the familiar or the unfamiliar (as opposed to what the Russian Formalists called defamiliarization), reaches ludicrous limits in the song "Mera pagal dil hua bekarar" ("My crazy heart is restless") in *Khiladiyon ka Khiladi/The Biggest Gamester Among Gamesters*, where the hero and heroine with a troupe of dancers dance on and below the wings of an Aeroflot airplane that is parked at an airport.

What the series brings to the fore is a renovation of the horror genre. Horror, which in its previous incarnation had led a B-grade existence in the films of Ramsay Brothers, is here woven into several other narratives.[24] The iconography of horror and the world of the dead is present almost constantly through *Sab Se Bada Khiladi/The Biggest Gamester of All*: the blue make-up beneath the eyes not just of the corpse, but also of the police officer played by Gulshan Grover. There are also references to a diluted version of the vampire myth: an image repeated through several films of the series is that of a blood splattered jaw. In *Sabse Bada Khiladi/The Biggest Gamester of All* the heroine says that Akshay Kumar bites her lower lip like an animal. There is even a song dedicated to this theme: "Zahar hai ki pyar hai, tera chuma" ("Is it poison or love, your kiss?"). This vampire myth is amalgamated with the *Mata Sherawali* ("Mother Goddess astride a tiger") imagery, for both have tasted blood and have it over their mouths, as in *Khiladiyon ka Khiladi/The Biggest Gamester Among Gamesters*. In this film, at a masquerade ball, Akshay wears the mask and sings a song in which the refrain asks the question, "Who are you?" The actor, in a coming together of the diegetic narrative and reality replies, "I am a devotee of the Mother Goddess, I am the simpleton Akshay." This invocation of the name of the actor is a characteristic feature of the series films. The Undertaker and some of the other villains are vanquished in the temple dedicated to the Mother Goddess. Alok Bhalla, writing on commentators who have compared the goddess with the vampire image in literature, says:

> Kali is, as opposed to the vampire, an affirmative principle; she is part of a sacred ritual of creation, destruction and renewal of the world.... Even in her terrifying and destructive aspect she is a manifestation of the divine energy. The vampire, on the contrary, is the personification of all the pestilential powers in the psyche of man, as well as in the actual and social world he inhabits. The vampire is the anguish which disrupts composure, it is the desecration of the body; the consciousness of derangement of meaning; the helpless recognition that the social space is a site of torture and disintegration [5–6].

This difference between the goddess and the "diluted" vampire is however wiped out in the film: both bloodthirstily vanquish evil.

The No. 1 Series

The No. 1 series — *Coolie No. 1/Luggage-Carrier No. 1* (David Dhawan, 1995), *Hero No. 1* (David Dhawan, 1997), *Anari No. 1/The Unwise No.1* (1999), *Biwi No. 1/Wife No. 1* (David Dhawan, 1999), *Aunty No. 1* (Kirti Kumar, 1998), *Jodi No. 1/Pair No. 1* (David Dhawan, 2001) — belongs, in the main, to the actor Govinda and the director David Dhawan. *Biwi No.1* stars the actor Salman Khan and was directed not by Dhawan but by Kirti Kumar. The Dhawan-Govinda team also has actor and dialogue-writer Kader Khan as an integral member. According to Govinda, the No.1 label is lucky for him at the box-office. Be that as it may, the series, that has run from the 1990s to the present, would not be what it is without the persona of Govinda himself. The gossip magazines call him *Virar ka chokra*, the boy from Virar (a suburb of

Bombay). This pet name is an indicator of the very distinctive persona and niche Govinda has carved out for himself. Many actors come from smaller towns and suburbs to be absorbed into the Bombay film industry. This process of absorption is a homogenizing one: it molds each actor into a dominant image, which, for the past several years has meant an image based on a gym-perfect body and designer clothes and accessories. Govinda's image has been tangential to this dominant type. His outrageous sense of color combination, his non-designer induced flamboyance, his very different body-type, his immense capacity for mimicking and humor, and his sense of rhythm and dance have made him one of the most enduring subcultural icons. "The communication of a significant *difference*, ... (and the parallel communication of a group *identity*), is the 'point' behind the style of all spectacular subcultures," says Dick Hebdige (102). Govinda's thick muscularity, stocky frame, and chubby cheeks are distinct from the lean, mean muscularity of other contemporary male stars, in tune with a global body type. His body language causes even designer suits to sit on him differently. The very notion of being "No. 1," that is, being on top, coming first, bespeaks a character who perceives himself as having a negative marking somewhere, but has the self-esteem and bravado to emerge the winner.

It is David Dhawan's films (both the No. 1 series and non–No. 1 films) that have tapped Govinda's talent to the fullest. In Dhawan's films, no pretence is made to follow the rules of space-time continuities. From around the mid–1990s onwards, Dhawan gave up any simulation of realism in the diegetic worlds he created, working with a specific group of actors in sets of similar-looking opulent, nouveau-riche houses, with narratives that were more in the nature of propositions. For the songs he often unabashedly cuts from Indian settings to locations abroad, to come back again when the narrative resumes. Although he is not the only director to employ this non-continuity method of song picturization, in his films there is a consistent irreverence towards realism as a mode of representation. This mass production includes several films in which he hits rock bottom in terms of crudity, although there are moments when a genuinely carnivalesque atmosphere prevails.

Govinda/Dhawan still take up the old problematic of the construction of a subjectivity that draws on the opposition between provincial and modern India. This persona, however, is very different from the protagonists of the post-independence period, who were made of better moral fiber. Even when they gave in to temptation, they had a consciousness of what was right. Govinda's persona of the "small man" suffers from no moral trepidation. In *Coolie No. 1/Luggage-Carrier No. 1*, the protagonist falls for the daughter of a rich man. He doesn't balk at lying in order to marry the girl. The business of making money in Dhawan's and Govinda's films, more often than not, has to do with lying, even small time thieving, all done with supreme ethical nonchalance. There are no melodramatic scenes where the protagonist realizes his mistakes. The moment of redemption passes by lightly. These moral blind spots exist even in the protagonist's libidinal life, where he thinks nothing of two-timing. Govinda is also adept at cross-dressing, exploited to the hilt in *Aunty No. 1*. The No. 1 films are threshold films; they tap the world of the B-movie, but make the A-grade because of the star status of the actors and the veneer of the A-movie achieved through higher budgets.

Some of the films quote the narratives of earlier films: *Jodi No. 1/Pair No. 1* quotes *Sholay/Flames* (Ramesh Sippy, 1975), one of the biggest blockbusters of Hindi cinema, for instance, and *Hero No. 1* reminds one of superstar Rajesh Khanna's middle cinema hit *Bawarchi/The Cook* (Hrishikesh Mukherjee, 1972).[25] These quotations are, however, not deep allusions: they work at a surface level. Jameson, writing of acting in the postmodern age says: "The latest generation of starring actors continues to assure the conventional functions of stardom (most notably, sexuality) but in the utter absence of 'personality' in the older sense, and with something of the anonymity of character acting.... This 'death of the subject' in the institution of the star, however, opens up the possibility of a play of historical allusions to much older roles ... so that the very style of acting can now also serve as a 'connotator' of the past" ("Postmodernism" 205). This is also true of the filmic and non-filmic characters Govinda mimics with great rapidity. These nuanced linguistic registers do not lend themselves easily to global assimilation. In *Jodi No. 1/Pair No. 1*, for instance, he plays a small-time crook, who runs into big-time trouble with his accomplice. He mimics a non-sophisticated Punjabi accent, and achieves a certain typical timber in the pronunciation of equally typical phrases.[26]

The Character Series

The repetition of a character in different situations and narrative frameworks occurs in three kinds of recent films: (1) Rajkumar Hirani's Munna Bhai series, Priyadarshan's Hera Pheri series, and Sanjay Gadhvi's Dhoom series; (2) remakes of hits of the seventies and eighties: *Don* (Chandra Barot, 1978) and *Don—The Chase Begins Again* (Farhan Akhtar, 2006), *Umrao Jaan* (Muzaffar Ali, 1981) and the remake of the same directed by J.P. Dutta in 2006, *Sholay/Flames* (Ramesh Sippy, 1975), remade as *Ram Gopal Verma Ki Aag* (Ram Gopal Verma, 2007); and (3) sequel films: *Koi Mil Gaya/I Found Someone* (2003) and

Krrish (2006) both directed by Rakesh Roshan.[27] In Rajkumar Hirani's *Munna Bhai MBBS* (2003) and *Lage Raho Munna Bhai/Munnabhai Meets Mahatma Gandhi* (2006), Munna Bhai and his sidekick Circuit (played by Sunjay Dutt and Arshad Warsi), are small-time underworld dons, who return with a new love interest in the latest installment in the series. The comedy derives from the face-to-face encounter of two worlds and worldviews: underworld values and middle-class morality. *Hera Pheri* (2000) has three down-and-out city dwellers, Raju (Akshay Kumar), Shyam (Sunil Shetty), and Babu Rao (Paresh Rawal) get rich without too many qualms through foul means; *Phir Hera Pheri* (2006) has the trio enjoying this money, losing it, and embarking on another plan to make money. *Dhoom/Blast* and *Dhoom 2* have cop Jai Dixit and his side-kick Ali (Abhishek Bachchan and Uday Chopra) chase new-age, high-flying robbers. Of the remakes, *Don—The Chase Begins Again* has been the most successful and has introduced several twists into the tale, replete with an international setting to warrant viewing it as a *variation*, rather than a remake of the 1978 *Don*. *Krrish* is a sequel to the Hindi cinema's first attempt at interplanetary science fiction with *Koi Mil Gaya/I Found Someone*, in which an extra-terrestrial grants super-intelligence to the protagonist, Rohit, who is somewhat retarded. Rohit's son is the hero of *Krrish*. Brought up in the hills, far away from civilization, Krrish (short for Krishna, the name of a Hindu god), has supernatural physical powers and is a cross between Tarzan, Batman, and Superman.

In the era of globalization, the nation is itself a vexed category. The neo-liberal agenda of a state that has given up all forms of protectionism creates an ideological horizon that is oriented towards the outside, rather than an introspective, inclusive one about nation-building. The dominant narrative of the popular cinema now is oriented towards the West and the diasporas settled there. It is significant that the diasporas being called forth are in the white First World (the USA, Canada, and Australia): the large Indian diaspora living in Africa is non-existent in this imagining. This is the virtual global neighborhood towards which the cultural ideological horizon is now oriented for which we have given up the real neighborhood of the Indian village and countryside.[28] Rarely nowadays do we see protagonists who are struggling to make it in the world ethically; no more do we see migrants, or the dispossessed from the hinterlands, trying to make it in the big city without becoming part of the underworld. Even a film that evokes Gandhi such as *Lage Raho Munna Bhai/Munnabhai Meets Mahatma Gandhi* serves us an ideologically emaciated Gandhi. This is a strange coming together of the local and the global, in which the local suffers dilution and "thinning." In the imagined world of this film, it is not communalism, the upliftment of the poor and the untouchables, a simple, non-consumerist lifestyle, or rural India, that were so close to Gandhi's heart, and are burning issues in India even today, that receive representation. The film (or should we say, the sitcom, for it lacks the dynamic mobility of cinema, that was very much evident in the first film) shows instead urban themes, not very close to the Gandhian agenda: a non-violent agitation to save property (for an old people's home), the importance of honesty (when one gambles and loses all at the stock market), the body language and behavior a girl should opt for in a life-partner, and the way to deal with corrupt, petty clerks who will not release an old man's pension.

Action films are increasingly being set abroad (*Dhoom 2*, *Krish*, and *Don—The Chase Begins Again*), probably for reasons of the availability of professional skill (especially in the field of real and virtual action scenes), the topography of world-class cities (particularly important in chase, thrills, and fight scenes), and better financial deals.[29] As Toby Miller points out, the New International Division of Cultural Labour (NICL) with competitive prices for professional skills, highly developed technology and communication that allow quick and efficient transportation of products, has led to the splintering and fragmentation of culturally productive skills across the globe (499–500).

Conclusion

National allegory in the Hindi film series has been dealt with in this essay within the framework of the postcolonial period. In both the A and B film series, the lead protagonist and the narrative encapsulating the conflict between Good and Evil are the agencies through which postcolonial anxieties are expressed. The Raj Kapoor film series in the post-independence period constructs an imagined community of the nation as a consistent allegory, running parallel to the literal tale. The individual destiny bespeaks the destiny of the nation. Raj Kapoor in the role of Raj, created a postcolonial subject who was not rich or powerful but had a stake in the nation-in-the-making. In the 1970s, the Manoj Kumar film series posit a subjectivity that becomes the beleaguered nation. Bharat is the postcolonial subject who wants to assert his country's place in the world, while overcoming internal divisive forces. From the 1980s onwards, the perceived collapse of the institutions that make up the state bring forth new series in which the man from the margins wishes to be part of the mainstream, and is not too bothered by the ethics of the road he takes. There is the shift from the constructive energies of the protagonist to negative ones. The spectrum ranges from those whose moral vision is blurred (some of the Khiladi and No. 1 films) to psychotic behavior. There has been a shift in the recent series films in the vision of the nation and hence its allegorization. The allegorical moment now features the local or the global, rather than the national. It is probably this de-saturation of the plural significations of what constitutes the nation that has led to the rush of remakes of films from an era when narratives were "more dense." The focus is now on the fragmented city and its underbelly, the underworld: there is also an insertion into global cultural and production processes.

The mode of allegorizing the nation varies from series to series. While some create a continuous parallel allegorical narrative (the films of Raj Kapoor and Manoj Kumar), others call it forth in flashes. Yet others employ the metonymic mode. These references open out the narrative onto a larger set surpassing those of the unfolding individual destinies. This larger whole onto which the narrative periodically opens refers to the nation, creating a frame of reference of a different order. Even when the allegory is not a contrapuntal narrative, the references do not allow the narrative to remain on the unilinear plane of individual destinies.

Some films allegorize anxieties about the split times of the nation — tradition/modernity and rural/urban. Legends, myths, and epics are called forth and critiqued, even as the modern nation is envisioned. There exists simultaneity of many time frames, both uncanny and palimpsestic, within the allegory of the nation. Constituting this allegory, in the more significant films, is a dual temporal framework: on the one hand, a heady contemporaneity, on the other, mythical or epical references. The allegory can be a critical one too, as in *Awaara/Vagabond*, where the epical story is replayed, but from the point of view of modernity. This results in the replay not being true to the original, but diverging from it in its significant moments. A shadow narrative structure is thus set up *vis-à-vis* the epical reference: another set of narrative coordinates are set up that function as the national allegory, coordinates which intersect at many moments of the narrative. The refiguration of myth in plots that deal with contemporary life is a device employed by many kinds of narratives. In the film series, as part of a larger allegory, it creates a multilayered temporal mode, serving to critique some of the premises of the allegory itself.

Notes

1. Parts of this essay are excerpts from my project "Changing Narrative Strategies in Hindi Cinema," written under the Mumbai-based NGO, MAJLIS' Research Fellowship Programme, January–December, 1999.

2. Often social issues such as the emancipation of women in *Diamond Queen* (Homi Wadia, 1940), the plight of the lower castes in *Hurricane Hansa* (R.N. Vaidya, 1937), and Hindu-Muslim unity in *Lutaru Lalna* (Homi Wadia, 1938), were inscribed into the action narrative.

3. Films such as *Deccan Queen* (Mehboob, 1936), did feature Indian women in action and stunt roles. It was only Nadia, however, who could carry a series on her shoulders for such a long period.

4. For a discussion on realism and the action film see my "The Spectacle of Action: John Woo's *Face/Off*," *Cinemaya* 39–40 (1998): 17–19.

5. Many of these actors also acted in A-grade films and became stars. I.S. Johar and Mehmood were well-known comedians in A-grade films; Sonia Sahni and Simi, too, acted in A-grade films. Mumtaz, who acted in several B-films with Dara Singh, went on to become a star, featuring as the lead heroine in many of the films of the late 1960s and 1970s. The A and B categories are very fluid in the Hindi cinema. Music directors who composed music for A-films sometimes gave music for the B-films. Once in a while songs from these films became as popular as songs from the A-movies. There are also instances of big stars and big budgets featuring in B-grade presentations, because the director lacked the vision to produce an A-grade work.

6. A select list of Tarzan films in Hindi: *Rocket Tarzan* (B. J. Patel, 1963), *Tarzan and Gorilla* (Pyarelal, 1963), *Tarzan aur Jadugar/Tarzan and the Magician* (Radhakant, 1963), *Tarzan and Delilah* (A. Shamseer, 1964), *Tarzan aur Jalpari/Tarzan and the Waterfairy* (Radhakant, 1964), *Tarzan and Circus* (Shiv Kumar, 1965), *Tarzan Comes to Delhi* (Kedar Kapoor, 1965), *Tarzan and King Kong* (A. Shamseer, 1965), *Tarzan and Hercules* (Mehmood, 1966), *Tarzan aur Jadui Chirag/Tarzan and the Magic Lamp* (Babubhai Bhanji, 1966), *Tarzan Paristan Mein/Tarzan in Fairyland* (Sushil Gupta, 1968), *Tarzan ki Mehbooba/Tarzan's Beloved* (Ram Rasila, 1966), *Tarzan 303* (Chandrakant, 1970), *Tarzan Mera Saathi/Tarzan Goes to India* (John Guillermin, 1962), *Tarzan and Cobra* (Bhagwant Chowdhary, 1988).

7. *Daku Mangal Singh* (Chand, 1966), *Daku Mansingh* (Babubhai Mistri, 1971), and *Sultana Daku* (Mohammad Hussein, 1972).

8. *King Kong* (Babubhai Mistri, 1962), *King of Carnival* (T. Prasad, 1963), *Samson* (Nanabhai Bhatt, 1964), and *Sangram* (Babubhai Mistri, 1965).

9. [Editor's note: The Shahnama is an epic poem written by the Persian Ferdowsi around 1000 CE.]

10. *Rustam-e-Baghdad/Rustam of Baghdad* (B. J. Patel, 1963), *Rustam-e-Rome/Rustam of Rome* (Radhakant, 1964), *Rustam-e-Hind/Rustam of India* (Kedar Kapoor, 1965). Dara Singh directed himself in the last of these films, *Rustam/Champion* (1982).

11. "All third-world cultural productions seem to have in common and what distinguishes them radically from analogous cultural forms in the First World. All third-world texts are necessarily, I want to argue, allegorical, and in a very specific way: they are to be read as what I will call *national allegories*, even when, or perhaps I should say, particularly when their forms develop out of predominantly western machineries of representation, such as the novel" (Jameson, "Third World" 319).

Aijaz Ahmad's reply to this essay questions the very validity of Jameson's use of terms like First, Second, and Third Worlds, and his "overvalorization" of nationalist ideology born of the Third World's experience of colonialism and nationalism and their inadequacy in understanding the multifaceted narratives of this World. He also points out that colonized nations have several nationalisms of varying progressive and regressive tendencies. Ahmad states that while the First World is seen as the subject/maker of history, the Third World is a mere object of the history of colonization, a distinction that prompts him to ask "if only the First World is capitalist and the Second World socialist, how does one understand the Third World? Is it pre-capitalist? Transitional?" (100).

12. "The relationship between class consciousness and figurability ... demands something more basic than abstract knowledge, and implies a mode of experience that is more visceral and existential than the abstract certainties of economics and Marxian social science.... To become figurable — that is to say, visible in the first place, accessible to our imaginations — the classes have to be able to become in some sense characters in their own right" ("Class" 291).

13. Films on saint-poets of the Bhakti movement, for instance, constitute an important thematic series of the pre-Independence era. The calls to reform and the protests against religious orthodoxy that formed the basis of the Bhakti movement in medieval India, were seen as corresponding to the concerns of the nationalist movement. The saint-poet films, *Chandidas* (Debaki Bose, 1932, remade by Nitin Bose in 1934), *Sant Tulsidas/Saint Tulsidas* (N.G. Deware, 1934, remade by Jayant Desai in 1939), *Sant Tukaram* (Fattelal-Damle, 1936), *Sant Dnyaneshwar* (Fattelal-Damle, 1940), *Sant Sakhu* (Fattelal-Damle, 1941), *Bhakta Kabir/Kabir, The Devotee* (Rameshwar Sharma, 1942), *Bhakta Surdas* (Chaturbhuj Doshi, 1942), and *Meera* (Ellis Duncan, 1945) were made in different Indian languages and allegorized the nationalist movement in various ways.

14. For a discussion of the phases of "history" in post-Independence India and the corresponding narratives engendered in the Hindi cinema, see Madan Gopal Singh's 'If Music Be the Food of Love: Jottings on the Indian Film Song," *Cinemaya* 39-40 (1998): 6.

15. The focus is on Hindi cinema. There are no doubt other series in the many vibrant cinemas of India, particularly in the south.

16. The pedagogic and the performative are concepts developed by Homi Bhabha to designate the borders of the nation, the liminality of the people, and the impossibility of conceiving of the nation as an expressive totality aligning a plural, plenitudinous present (with the people as performative subjects) with a visible past (people as pedagogical objects): "The pedagogical founds its narrative authority in a tradition of the people ... as a moment of becoming designated by *itself*, encapsulated in a succession of historical moments that represents an eternity produced by self-generation. The performative intervenes in the nation's self-generation by casting a shadow between the people as 'image' and its signification as a differentiating sign of Self, distinct from the Other or the Outside" (299).

17. Drawing on Sartre's concept from his *Psychology of Imagination*, Jameson defines the analogon as "that structural nexus in our reading or viewing experience, in our operations of decoding or aesthetic reception which can then do double duty and stand as the substitute and the representative within the aesthetic object of a phenomenon on the outside which cannot in the very nature of things be 'rendered' directly" ("Class" 305).

18. "This modernist notion of allegory is, of course, opposed to the traditional one: within the traditional narrative space, the diegetic content functions as an allegory of some transcendent entity (flesh-and-blood individuals personify transcendent principles: Love, Temptation, Betrayal, etc.; they procure external clothing for suprasensible Ideas), whereas in the modern space, the diegetic content is posited and conceived as the allegory of its own process of enunciation" (Zizek 218).

19. "The characteristic of the palimpsest is that, despite such erasures, there are always traces of previous inscriptions that have been 'overwritten.' Hence the term has become particularly valuable for suggesting the ways in which the traces of earlier 'inscriptions' remain as a continual feature of the text of culture, giving it its particular density and character" (Ashcroft et al. 174).

20. Kewal Kashyap's *Shaheed/Martyr* was preceded by K. N. Bansal's *Shaheed Bhagat Singh* in 1963. This "series" was resurrected in 2002 with two more films on him: Raj Kumar Santoshi's *The Legend of Bhagat Singh* and Guddu Dhanoa's *23rd March, 1931, Shaheed*.

21. This was the time when India was receiving wheat from the USA under the PL 480 scheme.

22. An entry on Manoj Kumar in the *Encyclopaedia of Indian Cinema* states that he "Indulges in national chauvinism, contrasting son-of-the-soil goodness with Western evil, providing moral lessons together with the commercially attractive scenes of the abhorred debauchery (e.g. *Purab aur Paschim*)" (124).

From *Roti Kapda aur Makaan/Food, Clothing, and Shelter* onwards it is possible to classify Manoj Kumar's patriotism as kitsch nationalism. The series of four films directed by him, mentioned above, cannot be condemned as "national chauvinism" as the entry, quoted above, does. It is unfair to trash his brand of nationalism as it is manifested in his early cinema, retrospectively, on the basis of his espousing BJP ideals later in his life, as this encyclopedia entry does. The history of creative practice abounds with examples of conservative artists producing liberal, or even progressive works, antithetical to their political beliefs.

23. His high profile off-screen romances with his leading ladies, prior to his marriage, also nurtured his *Khiladi* image.

24. The Ramsay family, consisting of father F.U. Ramsay and sons, Tulsi, Shyam, and Kiran have since the 1970s been producing and directing B-grade horror films. Their first entry into the world of horror, *Do Gaz Zameen ke Neeche/Two Yards Under the Ground* (1972), was a hit. In the early 1990s they moved to television with the serial Zee Horror Show.

25. "Middle cinema" refers to the cinema that came into being between the commercial cinema and the Indian New Wave in the 1970s made on smaller budgets and less formulaic narratives, but working within the commercial industry's star system and performative mode.

26. This is equally true of the timber and tone of voice he achieves as the thief in the doubles film, *Bade Miyan Chote Miyan/Big Brother, Small Brother* (David Dhawan, 1998).

27. [Editor's note: *Krrish 2*, also directed by Rakesh Roshan, is scheduled to be released in 2009. It is not yet clear whether this film is a true sequel or an entry in what will be a series.]

28. The next film in the Munna Bhai series is reported to be *Munna Bhai Chale Amerika/Munna Bhai Sets off for America*.

29. The production unit for *Krrish*, for instance, included Tony Ching Siu Tung (action director, Hong Kong), Verite Productions (line producer, Singapore), Paul Pirola (Sound-firm, Australia — this firm also figures in the credits of *Don—The Chase Begins Again*), Marc Kolbe and Craig Mumma (visual effects supervisors, USA); for *Dhoom 2*, A.B. Moussa (line producer, South Africa).

Works Cited

Ahmad, Aijaz. *In Theory: Classes, Nations, Literatures*. Delhi: Oxford University Press, 1995.

Ashcroft, Bill, Gareth Griffiths, and Helen Tiffin. *Post-Colonial Studies: The Key Concepts*. London: Routledge, 2002.

Bhabha, Homi, "DissemiNation: Time, Narrative, and the Margins of the Modern Nation." *Nation and Narration*. Ed. Homi Bhabha. London: Routledge, 1991. 291–322.

Bhalla, Alok. *Politics of Atrocity and Lust: The Vampire Tale as a Nightmare History of England in the Nineteenth Century*. New Delhi: Sterling Publishers, 1990.

Creed, Barbara. "Horror and the Carnivalesque: The Body-Monstrous." *Fields of Vision: Essays in Film Studies, Visual Anthropology, and Photography*. Ed. Leslie Devereaux and Roger Hillman. London: University of California Press, 1995. 127–59.

Frye, Northrop. *The Anatomy of Criticism*. Princeton, NJ: Princeton University Press, 1957.
Hardt, Michael, and Kathi Weeks, eds. *The Jameson Reader*. Oxford: Blackwell, 2000.
Hebdige, Dick. *Subculture: The Meaning of Style*. New York: Methuen, 1979.
Jameson, Frederic. "Class and Allegory in Contemporary Mass Culture: *Dog Day Afternoon* as a Political Film." Hardt and Weeks 288–307.
_____. "National Allegory in Wyndham Lewis." Hardt and Weeks 308–14.
_____. "Postmodernism, or the Cultural Logic of Late Capitalism." Hardt and Weeks 188–232.
_____. "Third World Literature in the Era of Multinational Capitalism." Hardt and Weeks 315–39.
Miller, Toby. "Globalization and Culture." *A Companion to Cultural Studies*. Ed. Toby Miller Oxford: Blackwell, 2006: 490–509.
Rajadhyaksha, Ashish, and Paul Willeman, eds. *Encyclopaedia of Indian Cinema*. (New Delhi: Oxford University Press, 1995).
Zizek, Slavoi. "In His Bold Gaze My Ruin Is Writ Large." *Everything You Wanted to Know About Lacan but Were Afraid to Ask Hitchcock*. Ed. Slavoi Zizek. London: Verso, 1992. 211–72.

About the Contributors

SUSAN ARONSTEIN is professor of English at the University of Wyoming. She has published essays on medieval French and Welsh Arthurian romances, medievalism and popular culture, Disney, and Arthurian Film. She is the author of *Hollywood Knights: Arthurian Cinema and the Politics of Nostalgia* (Palgrave 2005). She is co-authoring a book on Steven Spielberg with Robert Torry.

JAMES CHAPMAN is professor of film at the University of Leicester. He has published widely on British cinema and television history, including *Licence to Thrill: A Cultural History of the James Bond Films* (Columbia University Press, 1999; rev. ed. 2007), *Saints and Avengers: British Adventure Series of the 1960s* (I.B. Tauris, 2002), *Past and Present: National Identity and the British Historical Film* (I.B. Tauris, 2005) and *Inside the Tardis: A Cultural History of "Doctor Who"* (I.B. Tauris, 2006).

THOMAS L. COOKSEY is professor of English and philosophy at Armstrong Atlantic State University in Savannah, Georgia, where he has taught since 1987, with courses in world literature, general philosophy, ethics, world religions, and comparative literature. He received a Ph.D. from the University of Oregon. His interests are diverse, ranging from Dante to the trickster, and with the intersections of philosophy, religion, and literature. He has also done work on film adaptations of the Faustian tradition and of Proust, and on world cinema. He has published the books *Masterpieces of Philosophical Literature* (2006) and *Masterpieces of Non-Western World Literature* (2007), both with Greenwood Press.

RASHMI DORAISWAMY studied Russian language and literature at Jawaharlal Nehru University, New Delhi. Her doctoral thesis was on Mikhail Bakhtin. She is professor (Central Asia) at the Academy of Third World Studies, Jamia Millia Islamia, New Delhi. Her writings on literature and cinema have been published in several Indian and foreign publications. She was awarded the National Award for the Best Film Critic in 1995, and the MAJLIS research fellowship in 1999 for a project entitled "Changing Narrative Strategies of Hindi Cinema." She has participated in international seminars on cultural issues, has served on several film festival juries in India and abroad and been on selection committees of films for international film festivals. She is co-editor of the book *Being and Becoming: The Cinemas of Asia* (Macmillan, 2002) and author of *The Post-Soviet Condition: Chingiz Aitmatov in the '90s* (Aakar, 2005).

JENNIFER FORREST is professor of French at Texas State University–San Marcos. She is co-editor with Leonard R. Koos of *Dead Ringers: The Remake in Theory and Practice* (SUNY, 2002). She is the author of articles on late-nineteenth-century French literature and popular culture. She is working on a book-length study of the late-nineteenth-century circus in French literature, visual arts, and popular culture.

TOM GUNNING is the Edwin A. and Betty L. Bergman Distinguished Service Professor at the University of Chicago. He works on problems of film style and interpretation, film history and film culture. His published work (about 100 publications) has concentrated on early cinema. Notable publications include *D. W. Griffith and the Origins of American Narrative Film: The Early Years at Biograph* (University of Illinois Press, 1991); "Tracing the Individual Body AKA Photography, Detectives, Early Cinema and the Body of Modernity," in *Cinema and the Invention of Modern Life*, ed. Vanessa R. Schwartz and Leo Charney (University of California Press, 1995); "The Horror of Opacity: The Melodrama of Sensation in the Plays of André de Lorde" in *Melodrama—Stage, Picture, Screen*, ed. J.S. Bratton, Jim Cook and Christine Gledhill (BFI, 1994); and "The Cinema of Attractions: Early Film, Its Spectator and the Avant-Garde," in *Early Film*, ed. Thomas Elsaesser and Adam Barker (British Film Institute, 1989).

KENNETH E. HALL is professor and chair of the Department of Foreign Languages at East Tennessee State University. His recent books include the forthcoming *John Woo's "The Killer"* (Hong Kong University Press, 2008), *Stonewall Jackson and Religious Faith in Military Command* (McFarland, 2005) and *John Woo: The Films* (McFarland, 1999). His recent articles on cinema include: "*Blind Swordsman: Zatoichi* by Kitano Takeshi: Not a Mere 'Entertainment'" (*Asian Cinema*, 2005); "Gangsters in the New Eden: The Mythification of Criminality in Works by Agustín Yáñez, Mario Puzo and Francis Coppola, and Gustavo Alvarez Gardeazábal" (*South Eastern Latin Americanist*, 2001); "Life with the Silver Screen: *Cine o sardina*," and "Movies and Mock Encomia," in Ardis L. Nelson, ed., *Guillermo Cabrera Infante: Assays, Essays, and Other Arts* (Twayne, 1999), as well as 14 entries on filmmakers and films for the *Encyclopedia of Chinese Film* (Routledge, 1998).

MICHAEL HARNEY is associate professor at the University of Texas at Austin in the Spanish and Portuguese Department and Comparative Literature Program. Recent publications include a book on kinship and marriage in chivalric romances, and articles on social stratification in French and Spanish epic, legal and political mentalities in early chivalric romances, American remakes of French films (in *Dead Ringers: The Remake in Theory and Practice*, SUNY 2002), medieval travel narratives, and violence in chivalric romances. He is writing a book about tourism and ethnography in early modern Spanish travel literature.

CAROLE MARTIN is associate professor of French at Texas State University–San Marcos and author of *Imposture utopique et procès colonial: Denis Veras—Robert Challe* (Early Modern France Critiques, 2000), on early modern French utopias and reform projects. She has published and has forthcoming articles in *Studies on Voltaire and the Eighteenth Century*, *The French Review*, *Dix-Huitième Siècle*, *Eighteenth-Century Fiction*, *Yale French Studies*, *Studies in Early Modern France*, *Studies in Eighteenth-Century Culture*, and *Dix-Septième Siècle*. A student of film theorist Raymond Bellour, she teaches film in the Department of Modern Languages and the Mitte Honors Program. Under the auspices of the French American Cultural Exchange, she is the organizer of the 2008 Tournées French Film Festival and Symposium at Texas State University–San Marcos.

PIERRE SIVAN is professeur en classes préparatoires aux grandes écoles at the Académie de Créteil in Les Pavillons-sous-Bois, France. Among his publications are "Caroline, Angélique, nos séductrices hexagonales [Caroline and Angélique, Our National Seductresses]," which was published in *CinémAction* (2000), and "Le Dernier Acte est sanglant ... *Lancelot du Lac* de Robert Bresson [The Last Act is Bloody ... Robert Bresson's *Lancelot du Lac*]" in *Lancelot* (Editions Autrement, 1996). Since 1990 he has been a regular contributor to the review *Télévision française, la saison* [*French Television, the Season*].

ROBERT TORRY is associate professor of English at the University of Wyoming. He has published articles on *The Wild Bunch*, *Jaws*, *Close Encounters of the Third Kind*, *The Ten Commandments*, *The Day the Earth Stood Still*, *Alien*, and *King Kong* (among others) and is co-author (with Paul V.M. Flesher) of *An Introduction to Film and Religion* (Abingdon Press, 2007). He is co-authoring a book on Steven Spielberg with Susan Aronstein.

WILLIAM M. TSUTSUI is professor of history at the University of Kansas. A specialist in the business, economic, and cultural history of Japan, he is the author of *Banking Policy in Japan: American Efforts at Reform During the Occupation* (Routledge, 1988), *Manufacturing Ideology: Scientific Management in Twentieth-Century Japan* (Princeton University Press, 1998), and *Godzilla on My Mind: Fifty Years of the King of Monsters* (Palgrave, 2004). He is the editor of *Banking in Japan* (Routledge, 1999), *A Companion to Japanese History* (Blackwell, 2006), and (with Michiko Ito) *In Godzilla's Footsteps: Japanese Pop Culture Icons on the Global Stage* (Palgrave, 2006). He received the 1997 Newcomen Society Award for Excellence in Business History Research and Writing, the 2000 John Whitney Hall Prize (for best book on Japan or Korea published in 1998) of the Association for Asian Studies, and the 2005 William Rockhill Nelson Award for non-fiction.

Index

A movies 11, 12, 16nn.6, 12; 106, 107, 108, 109, 110, 111, 116, 117, 118, 123nn.2, 7; 125n.18, 126n.28; *see also* production practices
Abbas 279, 280; *see also* Mastan
Abbas, K.A. 272
Abel, Richard 15, 36n.5, 47, 56nn.17, 20
Adam, Ken 145
Adam's Rib (1949) 122
adaptation (and readaptation) 3, 4, 5, 6, 8, 9, 10, 11, 39, 41, 42, 43, 46, 47, 54, 56n.17, 57, 84, 87, 92, 98, 137, 154, 158, 201, 207, 208n.12, 259n.24
Adorno, Theodor 179
The Adventures of Robin Hood (1938) 254
Affair of the Poisons 202, 208n.8
Affleck, Ben 3
Africans (description of) 64, 66, 73, 75
Ahmad Aijaz 266, 288n.11
Akbar, S.A. 265
Akhtar, Farhan 284
Albers, Hans 178, 180, 186, 187, 189, 191, 192
Ali, Muzaffar 284
Alien series (film) 36
Alkmene (play) 84
Allain, Marcel, and Pierre Souvestre 43, 45, 46, 51
allegory 14, 266–69, 273, 274, 278–80, 28–87, 288nn.11, 289nn.13, 18
Allen, Irving 136, 137
Allen, Robert C. 116, 117
Allenby, Edmund (General) 67
Allison, Anne 213
Almodóvar, Pedro 16n.11
Alo, Vincent "Jimmy Blue Eyes" 259n.28
Alphaville (1965) 18n.21
Alphaville, une étrange aventure de Lemmy Caution see *Alphaville*
Altman, Rick 6
Amadís de Gaula 61, 62, 64, 68, 69, 72, 76
Ambrogio, Anthony 259n.31
American Mutoscope and Biograph Company 39, 40, 41, 42, 55nn.2, 8, 9
Amis, Kingsley 155n.7

Amphitruo (Plautus play) 84, 85, 86, 92
Amphitryon (Kleist play) 87
Amphitryon (Molière play) 98
Amphitryon 38 (play) 103n.23
The Analysis of Film (book) 82
Anderson, Joseph 225–26, 234
Andreas, Frederick 181
androgyny 99
Andy Hardy series (film) 7
Angélique à coeur perdu see *Angélique with All Her Heart*
Angélique series (film) (France) 13, 197–98, 200–7, 208n.16; *Angélique and the King/Angélique et le roy* (1966) 200, 203; *Angélique and the Sultan/Angélique et le sultan* (1968) 200, 205, 207, 209n.15; *Angélique/Angélique, marquise des anges* (1964) 197, 198, 200, 207, 209n.15; *Marvelous Angélique/Angélique merveilleuse* (1965) 197, 207, 208n.1, 209n.15; *Untamable Angélique/Indomptable Angélique* (1967) 200, 205, 207
Angélique vôtre see *Yours, Angélique*
Angélique with All Her Heart (book) 201
Anna Karenina (1935) 199
Anouilh, Jean 199, 208n.12
anti-semitism 179, 191
Apocalypse films 17n.19; *Apocalypse: Caught in the Eye of the Storm* (1988) 17n.19; *Apocalypse II: Revelation* (1999) 17n.19; *Apocalypse III: Tribulation* (2000) 17n.19; *Apocalypse IV: Judgment* (2001) 17n.19
Apted, Michael 145, 268
Archainbaud, George 109, 110, 128n.36
Arlen, Michael 32
Aronstein, Susan 12
art (high vs. low) 27, 33; *see also* culture
art cinema (vs. commercial cinema) 23, 147
Artamène, ou le Grand Cyrus (novel) 30
Astaire, Fred 8
L'astrée (novel) 30
Astro Boy (Japanese manga series) 212
Atsumi Kiyoshi 228, 229, 233, 234
Audé, Françoise 205

audience 5, 6, 7, 10, 14, 23, 24, 25, 28, 29, 34, 35, 42, 46, 47, 48, 50, 51, 60, 75, 82, 85, 88, 105, 106, 109, 110, 115, 116, 118, 123n.3, 146, 161, 198, 218, 219, 227, 228, 236, 237, 247, 249, 250
Auger, Claudine 152
Auric, Georges 199
Austen, Jane 5
Austin Powers series (film) 3
Austrian Succession (war of) 189
auteur 6, 145–46, 147, 211, 263, 264, 273
authorship (and authorial control) 10, 24, 25, 26, 27, 31, 32, 33, 34, 35, 37n.18, 39
Ayres, Lew 119
Azad 265

B movies 1, 11, 16n.12, 17n.17, 106, 107, 108, 109, 110, 111, 115, 116, 117, 118, 119, 123nn.2, 7; 124n.11, 125n.18, 126n.28; *see also* production practices
Baazigar see *Gambler*
Bacall, Lauren 97, 98, 99, 101n.1
Bach, Barbara 152
Bachchan, Amitabh 272, 279, 285
Bacon, Lloyd 125n.20
Bad Boys (1995) 140
Bagehot, Walter 65
Baker, Chesney 72
Baker, Hugh D.R. 258n.20
Bakhtin, Mikhail 25
Baky, Joseph von 13, 178
Baldwin, Alec 3
Balio, Tino 15nn.3, 12; 124n.12
Balsamo, Giuseppe *see* di Cagliostro, Alessandro
Balzac, Honoré de 28, 29, 37n.11, 43, 258n.12
La Bande à Bonnot 56n.17
Banderas, Antonio 241, 254, 258n.12
Bansal, K.N. 289n.20
Barbershop 2: Back in Business (2004) 7
Bardot, Brigitte 201, 205
Barker, Lex 60
Barney, Matthew 8
Barot, Chandra 284
Barrett, Gregory 235
Barry, John 145
Basinger, Jeanine 108
Batman (superhero) 63, 285
Batman series (film) 140; *Batman* (1989) 134
The Beast from 20,000 Fathoms (1953) 213
Beat Generation poets 169
Beaumont, Harry 111
Bébé series (film) (France) 49
Bee Movie (2007) 15n.2
Before Sunrise (1995) 7
Before Sunset (2004) 7
Bellah, Robert 170
Belloï, Livio 56n.19
Bellour, Raymond 11, 81, 82, 93
Ben Hur (1907) 40
Bennett, Bruce *see* Brix, Herman

Bennett, Tony 148
Benson, Mildred Wirt 102n.9
Bercovitch, Sacvan 160
Berglund, Jeff 70
Berkeley, Busby 8, 108, 125n.20
Bertillon method 47–48, 56n.18
Better Tomorrow series (film) (Hong Kong) 14, 26, 241–53, 255, 256, 256nn.2, 3, 7; 258n.11, 259n.31; *A Better Tomorrow* (1986) 241, 242, 243, 245, 247, 249, 251, 252, 253, 255; *A Better Tomorrow II* (1987) 243, 245, 248, 249, 250, 251, 255, 260n.41; *A Better Tomorrow III* (1989) 243, 250, 251
Bhaba, Homi K. 70, 289n.16
Bhagat Singh series (film) (India) 289n.20; *The Legend of Bhagat Singh* (2002) 289n.20; *Martyr/Shaheed* (1965) 275, 289n.20; *Shaheed Bhagat Singh* (1963) 289n.20; *23rd March 1931, Shaheed* (2002) 289n.20
The Bhagavad Gita (Sanskrit text) 167, 168
Bhakti Movement 288n.13
Bhalla, Alok 282
Bhanji, Babubhai 288n.6
Bharat series *see* Manoj Kumar series
Bharatiya Janta Party (BJP) 279
Bhatt, Batuk 264
Bhatt, Nanabhai 288n.8
The Big Sleep (1945, 1946) 12, 83, 97–99, 101n.1
Big Town series (film) 128n.35; *Big Town* (1947) 128n.35; *Big Town After Dark* (1947) 128n.35; *Big Town Scandal* (1948) 128n.35; *I Cover Big Town* (1947) 128n.35
Bikini Atoll 213
Bill and Sally Reardon series (film) 108, 123n.7, 124n.10
Billings, Josh 142
Binder, Maurice 145
Biograph *see* American Mutoscope and Biograph Company
Bird, Brad 103n.26
"Bird of Passage" (*wataridori*) series (film) (Japan) 210
The Birth of a Nation (1915) 61, 62, 63
Biskind, Peter 160
Black Mask series (stories) 110
Bleiler, Everett 60, 71
Blondell, Joan 108, 123n.9, 125n.20
Blondie series (film) 109, 133
Blood Brothers (1973) 245
Bly, Robert 163
Bogart, Humphrey 97, 98, 101n.1, 243
Bollywood 266, 283
Bolt, Robert 67
Bombay film industry *see* Bollywood
Bond series *see* James Bond series
Bongie, Chris 68
Bonnafé, Marie 89, 101n.3
Boone, Daniel 64
Borderie, Bernard 18n.21, 197, 198, 201, 205, 207
Bordwell, David 15, 18n.25, 26

Boruchoff, David 69
Bose, Debaki 289n.13
Bose, Nitin 289n.13
Boulanger, Daniel 201
Bowman, Lee 114
Bram Stoker's Dracula (1992) 8
Braudy, Leo 165
Brecht, Bertolt 179
Breen, Joseph 128n.38; *see also* Hays Office, Production Code
Bréon 46, 48
Bride with White Hair series (film) (Hong Kong) 257n.7
Bridget Jones: The Edge of Reason (2004) 17n.17
Brill, Steven 3
Brinvilliers, Marquise de 208n.8
Brix, Herman 58
Broccoli, Albert R. 136, 137, 138, 139, 140, 142, 144, 145
Broccoli, Barbara 140
Bronski, Michael 102n.9
Brooke, Hillary 128n.35
Brosnan, Pierce 141, 145
Buck, Chris 59
Buck Rogers serial 60
"Buffy the Vampire Slayer" series (television) 63
Bulldog Drummond series (film) 133
Bullet in the Head (1990) 243
Bürger, Berthold (pseudonym) *see* Kästner, Erich
Bürger, Gottfried August 178, 179, 187, 192
Burr, Raymond 214
Burroughs, Edgar Rice 11, 57–62, 65, 67–72, 74, 76–78, 265
Buruma, Ian 228, 229, 232, 234, 235, 236
Bush, George W. 173, 174, 175, 176n.3
Butch Cassidy and the Sundance Kid (1969) 132
Butler, David 124n.9
Butler, Yancy 247
Buzzell, Edward 108

Caesar, Julius 171
Cagle, Jess 171
Cagliostro, Alessandro di 190, 191, 195
Calvert, John 37n.16
Cameron, James 144
Camon, Alessandro 252
Campbell, Joseph 176n.3
Campbell, Martin 145, 155n.1, 245, 253
Candide (novel) 181
Cannadine, David 149
Cantinflas 9, 18n.22
Capra, Frank 3, 115
Cardinale, Claudia 201
Carol, Martine 197, 201
Caroline series (film) (France) 13, 197–207; *Caroline Cherie/Un Caprice de Caroline* (1953) 197, 198, 199; *Dear Caroline/Caroline chérie* (1951) 197, 198, 199, 200, 202, 203, 205, 207; *The Son of Dear Caroline/Le Fils de Caroline chérie* (1955) 199, 205
Carroll, John 114
Carson, Kit 64
Casablanca (1942) 106
Casanova, Giacomo 189
Casillo, Robert 260n.34
"Casino Royale" series (television) 137
Castellano, Richard 250, 259n.26
The Catalogue of Women (poem) 101n.4
Catherine ("the Great") II (empress of Russia) 193, 195
Catsoulis, Jeannette 4, 5
Cawelti, John G. 257n.8, 259n.30
Cazale, John 259n.32
CBS (Central Broadcasting Station) 125n.23
Cervantes, Miguel de 259n.33; *Don Quixote* (novel) 187
Champreux, Jacques 46, 56n.17
Chand 288n.7
Chandler, Raymond 97, 101n.1
Chandrakant 288n.6
Chang Cheh 242, 243, 244, 245, 256nn.3, 6; 257n.7
chanson de geste (epic poetry) 30, 31
Chao, Paul 258n.18
Chaplin, Charlie 111, 264, 270, 271
Chapman, James 12, 15
Charlie Chan series (film) 9, 35, 36, 125n.19, 133; *Charlie Chan at the Ringside* 125n.19; *Charlie Chan in Reno* (1939) 111
Charlie's Angels (2000) 140
Charteris, Leslie 32, 36, 123n.2
Chatterton, Ruth 126n.26
Cheatwood, Derral 58
Chechik, Jeremiah S. 5
Cheney, Dick 175
Chernichev, Ivan (General) 186
Cheung Kwok-wing, Leslie 242, 243, 245
Le Chevalier de Pardaillon see Clash of Steel
Cheyfitz, Eric 64
Cheyney, Peter 9, 18n.21
Chianese, Dominic 259n.28
Chiang Dai-wei, David 242, 245, 256n.6
Chiao Chiao 244
China Seas (1935) 110
Chinese Ghost Story series (film) (Hong Kong) 256n.4, 257n.7
Ching Siu Tung, Tony 290n.29
Chopra, Aditya 281
Chopra, Uday 285
chouans 197, 203, 208n.2
Chow Yun-fat 241, 242, 244, 245, 248
Chowdhary, Bhagwant 288n.6
Chu, Emily 245
Chu Yuan 257n.7
Churchill, Sir Winston 149
Churubusco Studios (Mexico) 139
The Ciné Goes to Town (book) 47
Cinecittà (Italian film studio) 200
Cinema City (Hong Kong film studio) 258n.11

Index

"cinema of attractions" 52, 144
cinemascope 144
Cinématographe 39
Cinerama epics 144
"civilizing process" 126n.26
Clancy, Tom 3
Clash of Steel (1962) 201
class relations 86, 87, 114, 115, 117, 118, 119, 120, 122, 126n.28
Clear and Present Danger (1994) 3
Clemens, William 83, 88, 89, 100
Close Encounters of the Third Kind (1977) 159, 160, 161, 162
Clouzot, Henri-Georges 5
Coates, Paul 76
The Cockleshell Heroes (1955) 136
Cocteau, Jean 184
Colbert, Jean-Baptiste 202
Cold War 12, 130, 143, 149, 153, 154, 169, 213, 215, 223, 268, 271
Collins, Robert 176n.3
Collins, Wilkie 47
Collison, Wilson 121, 124nn.10, 17
colonialism 149, 150, 167, 176n.7, 265, 288n.11
colonization 27, 65, 267, 268
Columbia Pictures 108, 123n.7, 136, 137, 139
comic strips 249, 250, 260n.39
commedia dell'arte 31, 32, 37n.14
Con Air (1997) 134
Conan Doyle, Sir Arthur 32, 33, 43, 66
Confucianism 247
Congo Landing (book) 124n.17
Conrad, Joseph 77
Congrès de Paris 40
Congrès International des Éditeurs du Film (CIDEF) 40, 55n.4
Constantine, Eddie 9, 18n.21
consumer (of culture, markets, texts, etc.) 27, 28, 29, 34, 130
Conte, Richard 258n.17
Conway, Tom 37n.16
The Cook/Bawarchi (1972) 284
Cook, David 1, 5, 15n.1
Cooksey, Thomas L. 13
Cooper, James Fenimore 64
Coppola, Francis Ford 8, 242, 250, 252, 255, 259n.31
Coppola, Sofia 250
copyright 33, 39, 40, 54nn.1, 2
Corliss, Richard 171
Crabbe, Buster 58
Craig, Daniel 36, 154
Creed, Barbara 280
Cremaster movies 8
Crockett, Davy 64
Cromwell, James 258n.21
Crosby, Bing 9, 26, 124n.9
cross-dressing *see* transvestism
cross-gender(ing) and identification 87, 88, 89, 90, 96, 101

Crowther, Bosley 142
Cry Havoc (1943) 124n.9
Cry of the City (1948) 258n.17
Cserépy, Arzén von 181
Cuarón, Alfonso 16n.11
Cuban Missiles Crisis 149
Cukor, George 111, 122
culture (high vs. low) 25, 27, 29, 30, 31; *see also* art
Curtiz, Michael 7, 106, 126n.26, 254

Dacqmine, Jacques 201
Daiei (Japanese film studio) 218
Dalton, Timothey 36
La Dame d'onze heures see *The Eleven o'Clock Lady*
Damle, Vishnupant Govind 289n.13
Dara Singh (1964) 265
Dark Dame (novel) 124n.17
Darnell, Linda 254
Darwinism (social) 65, 71
The Day of the Jackal (1973) 259n.29
Death in Venice (novel) 183
Deccan Queen (1936) 288n.3
dédoublement see doubling
Delgado, Miguel M. 18n.22
Del Ruth, Roy 108, 111, 125n.21
De Mille, Cecil B. 144
Demme, Jonathan 3, 17n.16
Dench, Dame Judi 154
Deneuve, Catherine 201
De Niro, Robert 243
The Departed (2006) 256n.4
Deppe, Hans 181
Dergarabedian, Paul 4
Desai, Jayant 289n.13
desire (object of) 87, 92
desire (of the other) 84, 86, 93, 94, 95, 98, 99, 100, 101
desire (subject of) 93
deus ex machina 84, 92, 93, 94
Devaivre, Jean 197, 198, 205
Deware, N.G. 289n.13
Dhanoa, Guddu 289n.20
Dhawan, David 279, 280, 282, 283, 284, 290n.26
Dhoom series (film) (India) 284, 285, 286; *Blast/Dhoom* (2004) 285; *Dhoom 2* (2006) 285, 286, 2990n.29
Diabolique (1955) 5
Les Diaboliques see *Diabolique*
Diamond Queen (1940) 288n.2
"Diary of a Fishing Fool" series (film) (Japan) 220
Diaz del Castillo, Bernal 69
Dickens, Charles 29; *The Pickwick Papers* (novel) 29
Die Hard series (film) 132; *Die Hard with a Vengeance* (1995) 134; *Live Free or Die Hard* (2007) 5
Dietrich, Marlene 194

le dieu de la machine 92
difference (sexual) 82, 83, 87, 88, 89, 97, 101
dime novels 29, 54
disguise 45, 46, 47, 48, 49, 50, 51, 52, 53, 54
Disney Studios 57, 59, 73, 165
dissidence 105, 106, 107
Dmytryk, Edward 37n.16
Dr. Kildare series (film) 35
Doctor Zhivago (1965) 132
Don (1978) 284
Don—The Chase Begins Again (2006) 284, 285, 290n.29
Doniger, Wendy 81
Donner, Richard 17nn.17, 18
Das Doppelle Lottchen (novel) 179
Doraemon series (anime) (Japan) 220
Doraiswamy, Rashmi 14
Doré, Gustave 186
Dostoevsky, Fyodor 272; *The Idiot* (novel) 272
doubling 83, 84, 85, 86, 91, 92, 93, 95, 99; *see also* narcissistic doubling
Douglas, Melvyn 108, 123n.7
Dracula series (film) 8, 9, 31
Duel Scene from Macbeth (1905) 55n.8
Dumas, Alexandre 37n.11, 190, 201, 202, 205; *The Countess Salisbury/La Comtesse de Salisbury* (novel) 37n.11; *The Queen's Necklace/L'Affaire du collier de la Reine* (novel) 190
Duncan, Ellis 289n.13
Dutt, Sunjay 285
Dutta, J.P. 284
Duvivier, Julien 199
Dyer, Richard 60–61

Eady Levy 136, 137, 139
East Side of Heaven (1939) 124n.9
Eastwood, Clint 63
Éclair (French film studio) 49, 50, 51
Éclipse (French film studio) 50
Eco, Umberto 10, 22, 23, 24, 25, 26, 27, 36n.7, 63–64, 147–48, 155n.7
Edison Manufacturing Company 39, 40, 41
Edwardian era 61, 65, 66, 71, 72, 76
The Egg and I (1947) 9
Ehrlich, Linda 232, 233, 236
Eisenhower, Dwight 169
The Eleven o'Clock Lady (1948) 198
Elias, Norbert 126n.26
Elizabeth (empress of Russia) 193
Elizabeth Christine of Brunswick-Bevern 184
Elizabethan era 62
Emergency Period (India) 269
Emil and the Detectives (1931) 178
Emil und die Detektive see *Emil and the Detectives*
Emma (novel) 5
Enlightenment (French) 180
Enright, Ray 125n.20
entertainment industry 57, 61, 64, 76

Eon Productions 137, 141, 154n.1
Erskine, Chester 9
escapism 24
Esslin, Martin 24, 25, 26, 27, 30, 37n.9
Euripides 84, 85, 87
The Exorcist (1973) 132
exoticism 206

Fables (poems) 202
fabula 45, 47, 55n.13
Fairbanks, Douglas 253, 256n.3
Falcon series (film) 32, 36, 37n.16, 123n.2, 133; *The Falcon Takes Over* (1942) 32
Falk, Lee 260n.39
A Family Affair (1937) 7
Fang, Karen 256n.2
Fantômas series (film) (France) 10, 11, 22–24, 46–53, 55nn.12, 14
Fantômas series (novels) 11, 43, 44, 45, 46, 51, 52, 55n.12, 56n.17
The Farm of Seven Sins (1949) 198
Farrell, Glenda 36
The Fast Runner (2001) 16n.11
Fattelal, Sheikh 289n.13
Faust (play) 41
Faust and Marguerite (1904) 41
Fearless Nadia series (film) (India) 264; *Daughter of Hunterwali/Hunterwali ki Beti* (1943) 264; *The Lady with the Whip/Hunterwali* (1935) 264
Female (1933) 126n.26
feminist criticism 11, 81, 87, 107, 152, 153, 205–6
Ferdowsi 288n.9
La Ferme des sept péchés see *The Farm of Seven Sins*
Fernández de Avellaneda, Alonso 259n.23
Feuillade, Louis 11, 22, 43, 46, 47, 50, 51, 52, 53
feuilleton-roman see roman-feuilleton
feuilletonesque see roman-feuilleton
"figurability" 267, 268, 289n.12
filial piety 246, 247, 248, 249, 251, 252, 260n.45
film à thèse 206, 208n.14
film criticism (magazine, newspaper, and trade paper) 2, 4, 5, 212, 213
film noir 99, 147, 244, 256n.1, 275
Film Production Fund see Eady Levy
films d'art 10, 42, 48, 55n.11
Finding Nemo (2003) 155n.3
First World (culture, society, texts) 266, 268, 269, 285, 288n.11; *see also* Third World
Fiske, John 25, 26, 27
Flames (1975) 284
Flash Gordon serial 60, 176n.3
Fleming, Ian 22, 25, 27, 137, 143, 147, 149, 154, 260n.36
Fleming, Victor 13, 63, 110, 178
Folies Bergere (1935) 108
folk hero 64

Ford, Harrison 3, 16n.6
Ford, John 111
Ford Motor Company 141
Foreign Country (1997) 218
Forever Amber (1947) 13, 198
Formalism (Russian) 55n.13, 281
Foster, Marc 155n.1
Foster, Norman 111
Four Daughters (1938) 7
The Four Feathers (2002) 3
Four Wives (1939) 7
Fox, Edward 259n.29
Foxy Grandpa and Polly in a Little Hilarity (1902) 42
franchising 4, 16n.10, 58, 132, 133, 140, 210, 211, 212, 214, 220, 228, 236, 239
Francis, Kay 113
Frank, Bruno 181, 189
Frankenheimer, John 17n.17
Frankenstein (1931) 125n.18
Frankenstein, or the Modern Prometheus (novel) 8
Frankenstein series (film) 8, 9
Das Fraulein von Barnhelm see von Barnhelm, Minna
Frederick ("the Great") II (of Prussia) 13, 179–86, 189–93, 195
Frederick I (of Prussia) 192
Frederick the Great (book) 183
Frederick the Great Playing His Play (1898) 181
The French Connection (1971) 17n.17
French Resistance 203, 208n.11
French Revolution 13, 198, 199, 202, 203, 208n.8
Freud, Sigmund 101n.3
Fridericus series (film) (Germany) 13, 180–87, 189–95; *The Anthem of Leuthen/Der Choral von Leuthen* (1933) 181, 182, 190; *Barberina/Die Tänzerin von Sans Souci* (1932) 181, 184, 190; *The Fate of a King/Fridericus Rex* (1922, 23) 181, 182, 183; *The Flute Concert of Sans-Souci/Das Flötenkonzert von Sans-souci* (1930) 181, 182, 183; *Fridericus* (1936) 181, 182, 193; *The Great King/Der Grosse König* (1942) 180, 181, 182, 183, 184, 185, 186, 193; *The Mill of Sanssouci/Die Mühle von Sanssouci* (1925) 181; *The Old and the Young King/Der Alte und der Junge König* (1935) 181, 182, 192; *Old Fritz/Der Alte Fritz* (1896) 181, 183; *Old Fritz/Der Alte Fritz* (1927) 182; *Pleasant and Serious Things About the Great King/Heiteres und Ernstes um den großen König* (1936) 181, 182; *Pretty Miss Schragg/Das Schöne Fraulein Schragg* (1937) 181; *Trenck* (1932) 181, 189
Friedkin, William 5
Friedrich der Grosse beim Flütenspiel see *Frederick the Great Playing His Play*
Frobe, Gert 135
Froelich, Carl 181
The Front Page (1940) 110, 124n.16

The Front Page (1974) 124n.16
Frye, Northrup 266
Fuqua, Antoine 258n.19

Gable, Clark 124n.17
Gadhvi, Sanjay 284
Gainsborough costume melodrama 147
The Gallant Musketeer (1964) 201
Gambler (1993) 280
Gamera series (film) (Japan) 220
Gandhi, Mahatma 278, 285, 286
Garcia, Andy 250
Gardner, Erle Stanley 9
Gargan, William 108
Garnett, Tay 108, 110
Gaudreault, André 55n.2
Gaumont (French film studio) 46, 48, 49, 56n.17, 198, 208n.3
Gauthier-Garguille 31
"The Gay Falcon" (short story) 32
Gazzo, Michael V. 259n.27
Gebühr, Otto 182, 184, 186, 190
gender identification 11, 81, 82, 84, 97, 98, 99
gender politics 87, 88, 96
Genette, Gérard 56n.15
genre 2, 3, 4, 5, 6, 8, 9, 10, 14, 17n.15, 23, 24, 27, 29, 35, 36n.3, 43, 49, 50, 51, 52, 53, 54, 86, 106, 107, 109, 110, 112, 116, 117, 120, 121, 122, 123n.1, 124n.15, 130, 141, 142, 143, 146, 147, 167, 180, 210, 211, 213, 214, 218, 228, 229, 236, 238, 263, 275, 280; action 10, 17n.17, 37n.20, 130, 132, 133, 141, 201, 256n.3, 280, 288nn.2, 3, 4; adventure 10, 12, 17n.17, 37n.20, 50, 65, 69, 71, 109, 124n.15, 130, 132, 133, 141; "angry young man" (Japan) 211; anime (Japan) 238; biopics 109; children's 219; chivalric romance 11, 60, 61, 62, 64, 65, 71, 72, 73; comedy 50, 85, 86, 109, 111; "company president" (*shachō*) (Japan) 210, 219; crime 6, 47, 50, 52, 56n.17, 124n.15 (see also detective, mystery); detective 9, 10–12, 42, 45, 49, 50, 53, 54, 98, 109, 110; domestic comedy 109; empowered woman 12, 21, 107, 109, 113, 122, 123n.4, 124n.13; espionage 10, 12; fairy tale 73; family 10, 132; folk epic 24; gangster 118, 147 (see also yakuza); "hero" (*yingxiong pian*) (Hong Kong) 256n.2; "heroic bloodshed" (*wuxia*) (Hong Kong) 14, 241, 242, 253, 255; historical 10, 201; "home drama" (*hōmu dorama*) (Japan) 228, 236, 239; horror 3, 6, 37n.20, 109, 214, 280, 281; "humanistic stories on the lives of average city dwellers" (*shomin geki*) 228; magic see genre, trick; manga (Japan) 212; martial arts 10, 14; melodrama 42, 132, 142, 147, 218, 228, 237, 242, 244, 245, 251, 266, 274; monster (*kaijū eiga*) (Japan) 210, 212, 213, 214, 215, 216, 225, 236, 238, 239; musical 109, 125n.20, 147; mystery 10, 43, 47, 51, 52, 54, 89, 90, 91, 99, 101, 108, 142 (see also detec-

tive); period piece (*jidaigeki*) (Japan) 218; pirate 229; pornographic romance (*roman poruno*) (Japan) 218, 219; romance 10, 73, 107, 109, 121, 132, 142, 167; samurai warrior films 210, 229, 236; science-fiction 9, 10, 12, 37n.20, 60, 109, 124n.15, 142, 143, 161, 213, 224, 229; soap opera 247; spaghetti westerns 229; suspense *see* mystery; swashbuckler 17n.17, 176n.3; "swordplay" (*chambara*) 210; thriller 10, 50, 99, 218, 244, 265, 280; tragedy 85, 86; tragicomedy 85; trick 40, 51, 144; war 109, 124n.15; westerns 9, 17n.17, 25, 26, 27, 42, 75, 109, 110, 124n.15, 147, 176n.3, 249; woman's 3, 12, 107, 109, 110, 116, 124nn.12, 15 (*see also* genre; empowered woman); yakuza 211, 218, 236
German Expressionism 274
Gerould, Daniel 258n.16
Gerretsen, Peter 17n.19
Ghai, Subhash 281
Ghostbusters (1984) 140
Gibbons, Cedric 73
Gibson, Mel 17n.17, 23
Gilbert, Lewis 145, 146, 155n.1
Gilliam, Terry 187
Ginsberg, Allen 169
Girardin, Émile 28
Giraudoux, Jean 103n.23
Girouard, Mark 64, 74
Gleason, James 109
Gleason, Larry 141
Gleason, William 70
Gledhill, Christine 76–77
Glen, John 145, 146, 155n.1
Glover, Danny 17n.17
Godard, Jean-Luc 18n.21
The Godfather (novel) 250
Godfather series (film) 14, 242, 243, 250, 251, 252, 254, 255, 259n.31, 260nn.34, 44; *The Godfather* (1972) 106, 132, 251, 254; *The Godfather: Part II* (1974) 255, 260n.42; *The Godfather: Part III* (1990) 250
Godzilla series (film) (Japan) 13–14, 210–17, 219–27, 234, 236–39; *Godzilla* (1998) 140, 220; *Godzilla: Final Wars/Gojira: Fainaru uōsu* (2004) 215, 216; *Godzilla, King of the Monsters!* (1956) 215; *Godzilla, Mothra, and King Ghidorah: Giant Monsters All-Out Attack/Gojira, Mosura, Kingu Gidora: Daikaijū sokogeki* (2001) 226; *Godzilla Raids Again/Gojira no gyakush* (1955) 215; *Godzilla 2000: Millennium/Gojira nisen: Mireniamu* (1999) 215; *Godzilla vs. Destroyer/Gojira vs. Desutoroia* (1995) 215, 220, 238; *Godzilla vs. Mechagodzilla/Gojira tai Mekagojira* (1974) 219; *Godzilla vs. Megalon/Gojira tai Megaro* (1973) 219; *Gojira* (1954) 212, 214, 215, 216, 220, 221, 222, 224, 225, 237, 238; *King Kong vs. Godzilla/Kingu Kongu tai Gojira* (1962) 215, 219, 221, 234; *Terror of Mechagodzilla/Mekagojira no*

gyakush (1975) 219; *see also* Heisei, "new generation, Shōwa
Goebbels, Joseph 179, 180, 183, 185, 186
Goethe, Johann Wolfgang von 190
Gold Diggers movies 8, 111, 125n.20; *Gold Diggers of 1933* (1933) 125n.20, 127n.30; *Gold Diggers of 1935* (1935) 125n.20; *Gold Diggers of 1937* (1936) 125n.20; *Gold Diggers in Paris* (1938) 125n.20
The Gold Rush (1925) 111
golddiggers 114, 116, 117, 121, 124n.12, 127n.30; *see also* woman
The Golden Boy (1939) 111
Golden 1950s (Hindi cinema) 263, 273
"GoldenEye" (James Bond game) 141
The Golem (1921) 182
Golon, Anne 201
Golon, Serge 201
Gone with the Wind (1939) 13, 63, 198, 199
Gontran series (film) (France) 49
Gordon, Andrew 160
Gosnell, Raja 4
Govinda 282, 283, 284
The Graduate (1967) 132
Graff, Anton 180
Le Grand Cyrus see *Artamène, ou le Grand Cyrus*
Grande odalisque (painting) 194
Grant, Cary 123n.2
The Grapes of Wrath (1940) 111
The Great Cophta (comedy) 190
Green, Martin 69
Greengrass, Paul 5
Grémillon, Jean 199
Greystoke: The Legend of Tarzan, Lord of the Apes (1984) 59
Griffith, D.W. 61, 62, 63
Gros-Guillaume 31
Der Groß-Cophta see *The Great Cophta*
Grover, Gulsan 281
Gu Long 257n.7
Guérin, Robert *see* Gros-Guillaume
Guéru, Hugues *see* Gauthier-Garguille
Guillermin, John 59, 288n.6
Gunning, Tom 10
Gupta, Sushil 288n.6

Haas, Charles F. 59
Hagedorn, Roger 28, 29, 30, 34, 37n.10, 258n.12
Haggard, H. Rider 61, 62, 65, 66
Haight, George 121, 123n.6, 128n.39
Hall, Kenneth E. 14, 244, 256n.5, 258n.22, 260n.37
Halloween series (film) 3
Hamilton, Guy 145, 146, 154n.1, 155n.1, 257n.10
Hamlet (early silent film adaptations) 41
Hamlet (play) 41
Hammer films 8, 147
Hammett, Dashiell 9

Index

"Hamutarō" series (television) (Japan) 220
Han dynasty 247
Hanke, Ken 125n.18
Hannibal Lecter series (film) 3, 4; *Hannibal* (2001) 3; *Hannibal Rising* (2007) 3; *Manhunter* (1986) 3, 6; *Red Dragon* (2002) 3; *Silence of the Lambs* (1991) 3, 6, 17n.16
Hanson, Curtis 258n.21
Hard-Boiled (1992) 247
A Hard Day's Night (1964) 136
Hard Target (1993) 247
Hardi Pardaillan! see *The Gallant Musketeer*
Hare Rama Hare Krishna movement 276
Harlan, Veit 181, 182, 186, 195
Harlow, Jean 107, 108, 123n.5, 124n.17, 126n.27
Harmon, Gary L. 64
Harney, Michael 11
Harper, Sue 152
Harrison, George 276
Harry Potter series (film) 4, 132, 133, 135; *Harry Potter and the Chamber of Secrets* (2002) 155n.3; *Harry Potter and the Order of the Phoenix* (2007) 5; *Harry Potter and the Philosopher's Stone* (2001) 155n.3
Harry Potter series (novels) 33, 37n.18
Harryhausen, Ray 213
Hart, Joseph 42
Hatch, Nathan O. 170
Hawks, Howard 12, 83, 118, 122, 124n.16
Hayden, Sterling 259n.33
Hays Office 118; see also Breen, Joseph, Production Code
Heart of Darkness (novel) 77
Hebdige, Dick 283
Hecht, Ben 124n.16
Heerden, André van 17n.19
Hegel, Georg Wilhelm Friedrich 180
Hegemann, Werner 183
Heilbrun, Carolyn 101
Heinrich (prince of Prussia) 184, 193
Heisei (Godzilla) series (film) 216, 219, 223, 234; see also Godzilla series
Hell Below Zero (1954) 136
Herapheri series (film) (India) 284; *Hera Pheri* (2000) 284, 285; *Phir Hera Pheri* (2006) 285
Hercules series (film) 59
Hesiod 83
Higgins, Jonna 72
Hildegarde Withers series (film) 109, 110, 122, 123n.4, 124n.14, 128n.36; *Murder on the Blackboard* (1934) 109; *The Penguin Pool Murder* (1932) 109, 128n.36
Hinz, Werner 192
Hirani, Rajkumar 284, 285
Hirohito (emperor of Japan) 211–12, 215, 228
Hiroshima 213, 222
His Girl Friday (1940) 122, 124n.16
Hitchcock, Alfred 142, 145
Hitchcock's Films (book) 147

Hitler, Adolf 171, 179, 180, 182, 185, 186
Hively, Jack 32
Hodiak, John 114
Hoffmann, Hilmar 180
Holiday (1938) 111
Hollywood cinema 2, 8, 11, 15n.3, 16n.12, 25, 29, 75, 82, 83, 95, 96, 105, 106, 107, 108, 122, 123n.3, 133, 138, 198, 214, 244, 256nn.3, 4; 258n.14
Holson, Laura M. 4, 7
Homer 62
Honda Ishirō 214, 220
Hope, Bob 9, 26
Hopkins, Anthony 254
Horney, Brigitte 193, 194
Hossein, Robert 201, 205
Houston, Penelope 142
Hover, K.S. 55n.3
How a French Nobleman Found a Wife Through the New York Herald Personal Columns (1904) 40
Howard, Sandy 58
Huang Feihong series (film) (Hong Kong) 31, 36, 256n.4, 257n.7
Hughes, Ken 155n.1
Hugo, Victor 208n.5
Humberstone, H. Bruce 58, 59, 75
The Hunchback of Notre Dame (novel) 208n.5
Hunt, Peter 145, 146, 155n.1
Hurricane Hansa (1937) 288n.2
Hussein, Mohammad 288n.7
Huston, John 155n.1
Huxley, Aldous 169
Hwang, Ange 256n.4

I Am Not Angélique (book) 201
Ianni, Francis A.J. 257n.8
identity (assumed) see disguise
Ifukube Akira 214
The Iliad (epic poem) 30, 37n.9, 83
imagined communities 266, 269, 273, 286
Immermann, Karl Leberecht 178, 187
imperial presidency 159, 163, 168, 173
"The Imperial Presidency" (article) 174, 176n.9
The Imperial Presidency (book) 162
imperialism 25, 26, 36n.6, 63, 68, 69, 72, 78, 149
"imperialist code" (Bennett and Woollacott) 148–49
The Incredibles (2004) 103n.26
Indiana Jones series (film) 16n.6, 17n.17, 18, 36; *Indiana Jones and the Last Crusade* (1989) 134
Infernal Affairs series (film) (Hong Kong) 256n.4
Ingenioso caballero Don Quijote de la Mancha, El (novel) 259n.23
Ingres, Jean-Auguste-Dominique 194
Inspector Tahar series (film) (Algeria) 26
insubordination 24, 107

"Iron Chef" series (television) (Japan) 212
Isma'il Yasin series (film) (Egypt) 24, 26
Ito, Michiko 213
Iwabuchi Kōichi 237, 238
Iwerks, Daniel 69

Jack Ryan series (film) 3, 4, 16n.5; *Clear and Present Danger* 134; *The Hunt for Red October* (1990) 3
Jackass: The Movie (2002) 4
James Bond" (comic strip) 137
James Bond series (film) 3, 10, 12, 22, 35, 36, 120, 123, 130–54, 155n.1, 219, 257n.10, 260n.36, 268, 280; *Casino Royale* (1967) 149, 155n.1; *Casino Royale* (2006) 154, 155n.1; *Diamonds Are Forever* (1971) 132, 150, 151, 155n.1; *Die Another Day* (2002) 131, 134, 140, 141, 145, 146, 150, 151, 153, 155nn.1, 2, 3, 5; *Dr. No* (1962) 130, 131, 133, 137, 138, 141, 142, 146, 149, 150, 151, 154n.1, 155n.4; *For Your Eyes Only* (1981) 150, 155n.1; *From Russia With Love* (1963) 22, 131, 138, 142, 144, 149, 154n.1; *GoldenEye* (1995) 131, 134, 135, 140, 143, 145, 150, 151, 153, 155nn.1, 3, 5; *Goldfinger* (1964) 22, 131, 132, 133, 134, 135, 138, 139, 142, 144, 145, 147, 151, 152, 154n.1, 257n.10; *Licence to Kill* (1989) 132, 133, 134, 135, 139, 143, 151, 155nn.1, 5; *Live and Let Die* (1973) 132, 137, 138, 151, 155n.1; *The Living Daylights* (1987) 131, 133, 144, 150, 151, 155nn.1, 5; *The Man with the Golden Gun* (1974) 131, 133, 138, 139, 149, 150, 152, 155n.1; *Moonraker* (1979) 131, 132, 137, 139, 143, 144, 151, 552, 155n.1; *Never Say Never Again* (1983) 153, 155n.1; *Octopussy* (1983) 134, 139, 151, 155n.1; *On Her Majesty's Secret Service* (1969) 131, 132, 143, 144, 146, 150, 155n.1; *Quantum of Silence* 155n.1; *The Spy Who Loved Me* (1977) 131, 132, 135, 139, 141, 144, 145, 150, 152, 155n.1; *Thunderball* (1965) 131, 132, 133, 134, 137, 138, 139, 142, 144, 152, 153, 154n.1; *Tomorrow Never Dies* (1997) 131, 134, 135, 145, 150, 151, 152, 155nn.1, 3, 5; *A View to a Kill* (1985) 131, 138, 151, 153, 155nn.1, 2; *The World Is Not Enough* (1999) 131, 134, 135, 140, 141, 145, 153, 155nn.1, 3, 5, 268; *You Only Live Twice* (1967) 131, 132, 133, 138, 139, 143, 144, 145, 149, 150, 153, 155n.1
James Bond series (novel) 25, 27, 136, 137, 143, 147, 148; *Casino Royale* 136, 147, 148, 154, 155n.7; *Diamonds Are Forever* 148; *Dr. No* 137, 148, 155n.6; *For Your Eyes Only* 155n.7; *From Russia With Love* 148, 156n.7; *Goldfinger* 147, 148; *Live and Let Die* 148; *The Man with the Golden Gun* 136, 260n.36; *Moonraker* 147, 155n.7; *Octopussy and the Living Daylights* 136, 155n.7; *On Her Majesty's Secret Service* 155n.7; *The Spy Who Loved Me* 155n.7; *Thunderball* 140, 148, 156n.7; *You Only Live Twice* 148

Jameson, Frederic 266, 267, 268, 284
Jancovich, Mark 6
Janings, Emil 192
Jardin, Pascal 201
Jason Bourne series (film) 5; *The Bourne Ultimatum* (2007) 5
Jasset, Victorin 52
Jaws (1975) 132, 138
Je ne suis pas Angélique see *I Am Not Angélique*
Jefferson, Joseph 55n.9
Jenkins, Henry 37n.19
Jesse James series (dime novels) 29
"Jesse Stone" series (television) 8
Jet Li 257n.7
Jew Süss (1940) 179, 191
Jewison, Norman 3
Joe and Ethel Turp Call on the President (1939) 108, 123n.8
Joel and Garda Sloane series (film) 108, 123n.7; *Fast and Furious* (1939) 108; *Fast Company* (1938) 108
Johar series (film) (India) 264; *Johar in Bombay* (1967) 265; *Johar in Kashmir* (1966) 264; *My Name Is Johar/Mera Naam Johar* (1967) 265
Johar, I.S. 264, 288n.5
Johar-Mehmood series (film) 264; *Johar Mehmood in Goa* (1965) 265; *Johar Mehmood in Hong Kong* (1971) 265
John, Gottfried 135
Johnson, Lyndon Baines 162
Johnson, Paul 155n.6
Jones, James 97, 103nn.27, 28
Joseph Balsamo (novel) 190
Jud Süss see *Jew Süss*
Jumanji (1995) 140
Jurca, Catherine 72
Jurgens, Curt 135
Jutzi, Piel 181, 187
Juve Contre Fantômas (1913) 46, 50, 52, 54

Kakutani, Michiko 2, 3, 4, 16n.11
Kalem Company 40
Kaplan, Amy 61–62
Kapoor, Kedar 265, 288nn.6, 10
Kapoor, Raj 263, 264, 270, 271, 278, 286, 287
Kapur, Shekhar 3
Karmakar, Radhu 271
Kashyap, Kewal 275, 289n.20
Kästner, Erich 178, 189, 192
Katte, Hermann von 184, 192
Keeler, Ruby 125n.20
Keene, Carolyn 32
Kefauver hearings 250
Keighley, William 110
Keitel, Wilhelm (General) 186
Kerouac, Jack 169
Kershner, Irvin 155n.1
Khan, Ayub (General) 276

Khan, Kader 282
Khan, Mehboob *see* Mehboob
Khan, Saif Ali 280–81
Khan, Salman 282
Khanna, Rajesh 284
Khiladi series (film) (India) 279, 280, 281, 287; *The Biggest Gamester Among Gamesters/Khiladiyon ka Khiladi* (1996) 279, 280, 281, 282; *The Biggest Gamester of All/Sab Se Bada Khiladi* (1995) 279, 280, 281, 282; *Gamester/Khiladi* (1992) 279, 280; *I Am a Gamester, You Are a Fool/Main Khiladi Tu Anari* (1994) 279, 280; *International Khiladi* (1999) 279; *Khiladi 420* (2000) 279; *Mr. and Mrs. Khiladi* (1997) 279, 280
Kidō Shiro 228
Kidron, Beeban 17n.17
Kieslowski, Krzysztof 8
The Killers of Kilimanjaro (1959) 136
Kim Il-Sung 238
Kim Jong-Il 212, 238
Kimi no na wa? trilogy 214
King Features Syndicate 260n.39
King Kong (1933) 213, 225
King Kong (1962) 288n.8
King of Carnival (1963) 288n.8
King Solomon's Mines (novel) 65, 66
Kinoshita Keisuke 217
kinship 14, 243, 257n.8, 258nn.18, 20
Kipling, Rudyard 65
Kissinger, Henry 162
Kleist, Heinrich 87
knight errant 11, 62, 63, 64, 72
Kolbe, Marc 290n.29
Kolberg (1945) 186
Korda, Alexander 137
Korda, Zoltan 3
Kosminsky, Peter 4
Kotcheff, Ted 124n.16
Kracauer, Siegfried 183, 184
Krauss, Werner 186, 190
Krrish series (film) (India) 17n.17, 284–85, 286, 290nn.27, 29; *I Found Someone/Koi Mil Gaya* (2003) 17n.17, 284, 285; *Krrish 2* 17n.17, 285, 290n.27; *There's No One Like You/Koi Mil Gaya 2: Krrish* (2006) 17n.17, 284–85, 286, 290n.29
Krymko-Bleton, Irène 23
Ku Feng 245, 258n.14
Kumar, Akshay 279, 280, 281, 282, 285, 290n.23
Kumar, Ashok 276
Kumar, Kirti 282
Kumar, Manoj 263, 270, 275, 276, 278, 279, 286, 287, 290n.22; *see also* Manoj Kumar series
Kumar, Shiv 288n.6
Kunersdorf, (battle of) 185
"Kung Fu" series (television) 167
Kunuk, Zacharias 16n.11
Kurosawa Akira 214, 217

Kwan Tak-hing 31, 36
Kwan-yu 260n.41

L.A. Confidential (1997) 258n.21
labor relations 86, 87, 89, 90, 100
LaBute, Neil 4
Lacan, Jacques 179
La Cava, Gregory 111
Lacey, Robert 259n.28
Ladd, Alan 243
La Fontaine, Jean de 202
Lamont, Peter 145
Lamprecht, Gerhard 178, 181, 182, 183
Lancashire, Anne 176nn.3, 6
Lansky, Meyer 259n.28
Last Hurrah for Chivalry/Hui hap (1979) 242
The Last of the Mohicans (1992) 17n.16
Lathrop, Thomas A. 258n.23
Lau-fong Mak 257n.8
Laurent, Jacques *see* Saint-Laurent, Cécil
Lawrence, T.E. 66–67
Lean, David 67
Lebo, Harlan 259n.26
lecture féminine 81
Lee, Bernard 257n.10
Lee, Bruce 212
Legrand, Henri *see* Turlupin
Leigh, Vivien 201
Leitch, Thomas 8
Lem, Stanislaw 17n.14
Lemmon, Kasi 247
Lemmy Caution series (film) (France) 9, 18n.21
LeRoy, Mervyn 125n.20
Lesser, Sol 58, 59
Lessing, G.E. 181, 182
Lethal Weapon series (film) 17nn.17, 18, 23, 132; *Lethal Weapon* (1987) 17n.17; *Lethal Weapon 2* (1989) 17n.17; *Lethal Weapon 3* (1992) 17n.17; *Lethal Weapon 4* (1998) 17n.17
Lettieri, Al 260n.33
Leung Ka-fai, Tony 250, 253
Lev, Peter 176nn.3, 7
Lewis, Jerry 24, 26
Lewis, Wyndham 267
Liberation (France) 203, 208n.12
The Library (anthology of myths) 84
The Life of Baron Friedrich Trenck (book) 189
Lima, Kevin 59
Lincoln, Elmo 57, 58
Linder, Max *see* Max series
Linklater, Richard 7
literacy 28
Lonsdale, Michael 259n.29
Lord of the Rings trilogy 3, 4, 7, 16n.7, 132, 133; *The Lord of the Rings: The Fellowship of the Ring* (2001) 155n.3; *The Lord of the Rings: The Return of the King* (2003) 155n.3; *The Lord of the Rings: The Two Towers* (2002) 155n.3

Lo's Diary/Diario di Lo (novel) 33
The Lost World (novel) 66
Louis XIV (king of France) 13, 200, 202, 202, 206, 208n.8
Lucas, George 12, 138, 144, 158, 159, 160, 162, 167, 168, 170, 171, 172, 174, 175, 175nn.1, 2; 176nn.3, 4, 5; 243
Lucasfilm 158, 160
Lugosi, Bela 31
Lumière Company 39
Lung Kong 242
Lutaru Lalna (1938) 288n.2
Lyden, John 176n.3

Ma and Pa Kettle series (film) 9, 24
MacArthur, Charles 124n.16
MacArthur, Douglas (General) 225
Macbeth (early silent film adaptations) 41
Macbeth (play) 41
MacDonald, Betty 9
Mafia 252
Maibaum, Richard 137, 144–45
Maid in Manhattan (2002) 3
Maisie series (film) 12, 22, 31, 36, 107–16, 118–123, 123nn.5, 6, 8; 124nn.10, 11, 17; 125nn.21, 22, 24; 126n.25, 28, 29; 127nn.30, 31, 34; 128nn.37, 39, 41; 133; *Congo Maisie* (1940) 110, 114, 124n.17, 125n.17, 127n.34; *Gold Rush Maisie* (1940) 111, 114–15, 120; *Maisie* (1939) 107, 110, 114, 124n.17; *Maisie Gets Her Man* (1942) 111, 125nn.21, 22; *Maisie Goes to Reno* (1944) 111, 114, 121, 128n.34; *Maisie Was a Lady* (1941) 111, 119, 127n.31; *Ringside Maisie* (1941) 111, 114, 119, 120, 125n.19, 127nn.30, 34; *Swing Shift Maisie* (1943) 111, 121, 125n.21, 127n.34; *Undercover Maisie* (1947) 111, 121; *Up Goes Maisie* (1946) 111, 112, 119, 121
Malkan, Sameer 279
Maltin, Leonard 98, 108, 109, 112, 116
Mamoulian, Rouben 111
Mann, Michael 3, 17n.16
Mann, Thomas 183
Manoj Kumar series (film) (India) 275, 276, 286, 287, 290n.22; *East and West/Purab aur Paschim* (1970) 275, 276, 278, 290n.22; *Food, Clothing, and Shelter/Roti Kapda aur Makaan* (1974) 275, 279, 290n.22; *Noise/Shor* (1972) 275; *The Selfless Favor/Upkar* (1967) 275, 276, 277, 278
maquisards see French Resistance
Maria Theresa (empress of Prussia) 189, 193
Marian, Ferdinand 179, 191
Marin, Edward L. 110, 111
Marin, Louis 60
markets (international vs. domestic) 133
Markham, Monte 16n.8
Marling, William 244, 256n.1
Mars series (novels) 60, 62, 67, 71, 72; *The God of Mars* (novel) 67
Marshall, Garry 4

Martin, Carole 11
Marvelous Travels on Water and Land: Campaigns and Comical Adventures of the Baron of Münchhausen (book) 178
Marx Brothers 9
Mary Poppins (1964) 132
Mason, Bobbie Ann 101, 103n.31
Mastan (also Abbas) 279, 280
master-slave relationship 86, 87, 88, 90, 91, 97
Matrix trilogy 7, 216
Mature, Victor 258n.17
Max series (film) 50
Maxwell, Lois 257n.10
Mayer, Louis B. 126n.25, 228
Mayer, Ruth 65
McCall, Mary C., Jr. 125n.21, 128n.39
McCarey, Raymond 21
McClory, Kevin 140
McDiarmid, Ian 172
McDonald, Keiko 228
McGrath, Joseph 155n.1
McGurk, Chris 140
McLeod, Norman Z. 111, 125n.21
McTiernan, John 3
Mead, Margaret 112
Mehboob 276, 288nn.3, 5, 6
Mehra, Umesh 279
Méliès, Georges 41, 51, 56n.24, 144, 187
Men in Black (1997) 140
Mercier, Michèle 198, 201, 205
Merrily We Live (1938) 111
Messter, Oskar 181
Meyer, Johannes 181
MGM (Metro-Goldwyn-Mayer) 58, 59, 73, 107, 108, 112, 118, 119, 123n.7, 124n.11, 125n.17, 133, 135, 139, 140, 141, 154n.1
middle cinema (India) 290n.25
"Mighty Morphin' Power Rangers" series (television) (Japan) 212
Mildred Pierce (1945) 58
Milestone, Lewis 6, 110, 124n.16
millennialism 159–62, 170
Miller, Don 110, 123n.8, 124n.17
Miller, Toby 286
Mills, C. Wright 62
Minganti, Franco 257n.8
Ministry of Propaganda (Third Reich) 179, 185
Minna von Barnhelm (1940) 181
mirror image 82, 86, 95, 98, 100
Miss Jane Marple series (film) 109
Mr. Deeds (2002) 3
Mr. Deeds Goes to Town (1936) 3
"Mr. Deeds Goes to Town" series (television) 16n.8
Mr. Moto's Gamble (1938) 111, 125n.19
Mistri, Babubhai 288nn.7, 8
Mizoguchi Kenji 217
Mo, Teresa 247
Mohla, Madan 279

Molière 92, 95, 102n.18
Molo, Walter von 181
Montespan, Madame de 202, 208n.8
Monvoisin, Catherine Deshayes 208n.8
Moore, Roger 139
Moore, Ted 145
Morris, Glen 58
Morton, Walt 58, 76
Mother India (1957) 276
Mothra series (film) 220; *Mothra/Mosura* (1961) 215
Motion Picture Export Association 136
Motion Picture Patents Company 40, 55n.4
Mühlbach, Louise 181
Mui, Anita 251, 253
Mukherjee, Hrishikesh 271, 284
Mumma, Craig 290n.29
Mumtaz 288n.5
Münchhausen films 13, 178, 179, 180, 186–95; *The Adventures of Baron Munchausen* (1988) 187; *Baron Munchhausen's Dream/ Les Hallucinations du baron de Munchhausen* (1911) 187; *The Fabulous Baron Munchausen/Baron Prášil* (1961) 187; *Münchhausen* (1943) 13, 178, 179, 180, 186–95; *Münchhausen's Latest Adventure/Münchhausens neuestes Abenteuer* (1936) 187
Münchhausen, Karl Friedrich Hieronymus Freiherr von 178, 192, 193
Münchhausen: Eine Geschichte in Arabesken see *A Story in Arabesque*
Munna Bhai series (film) (India) 284, 285; *Munna Bhai MBBS* (2003) 285; *Munna Bhai Meets Mahatma Gandhi/Lage Raho Munna Bhai* (2006) 285; *Munna Bhai Sets Off for America* 290n.28
Murder My Sweet (1944) 37n.16
Murieta, Joaquín 254
Murphy, George 111, 114
Murray, Bruce 183
Musser, Charles 41, 55nn.2, 5, 7
My Man Godfrey (1936) 111
myth (and mythology) 60, 61, 63, 64, 67, 69, 72, 83, 101n.3, 115, 176n.3, 159, 160, 162, 167, 287

Nabokov, Dmitri 33
Nabokov, Vladimir 33
Nagasaki 222
Nancy Drew series (film) 11, 36, 88–92, 96, 97, 102n.9, 109, 110, 123, 123n.4, 124n.13; *Nancy Drew and the Hidden Staircase* (1939) 89, 101n.2, 102nn.11, 14, 15; *Nancy Drew-Detective* (1938) 88, 89, 91, 101n.2; *Nancy Drew-Reporter* (1939) 88, 89, 101n.2; *Nancy Drew-Troubleshooter* (1939) 100, 101n.2
Nancy Drew series (novels) 11, 32, 89; *The Clue in the Diary* 97; *The Hidden Staircase* 102n.17; *The Message in the Hollow Oak* 103n.28; *Nancy Drew, Detective* 101n.2; *Nancy Drew Mystery Stories* 102n.8

Napier, Susan 213
Napoleon 28, 171, 186
narcissistic doubling 11–12, 82–90, 94–98, 101
narrative (closure, open-endedness) 22, 23, 24, 50, 82, 107
national identity 14
Nat Pinkerton series (film) 11, 49, 50; *L'emmuré* (1911) 50
Navarre, René 46, 48, 49, 53
Nazism (and nazis) 13, 111, 112, 179, 180, 181, 182, 191, 203
Neale, Steve 62, 69
Nehru, Jawaharlal 276, 278
Neill, Roy William 32
Neubach, Ernst 181
Neumann, Kurt 74
"new generation" (*shinsei*) (Godzilla) series 216; *see also* Godzilla series
New International Division of Cultural Labour (NICL) 286
New Right 159, 160, 173
New Testament 161
"new wave" (British) 137
New Wave (French) 206
New Wave Cinema (India) 266, 290n.25
newspaper serialization 28
Niblo, Fred 256n.3
Nichols, Mike 4
Nick Carter series (dime novels) 29, 33
Nick Carter series (film) 11, 49, 50
Nick Winter series (film) 11, 49
nickelodeon 40
Nikkatsu (Japanese film studio) 218
9/11 America 159, 171, 175
Nixon, Richard 158, 161, 162, 163, 168, 175n.1, 176n.4
noir (fiction) 256n.1
No. 1 series (film) (India) 282, 283, 287; *Aunty No. 1* (1998) 282, 284; *Hero No. 1* (1997) 282, 284; *Luggage Carrier No. 1/Coolie No. 1* (1995) 282, 283; *Pair No. 1/Jodi No. 1* (2001) 282, 284; *The Unwise No. 1/Anari No. 1* (1999) 282; *Wife No. 1/Biwi No. 1* (1999) 282
Noriega, Chon 212
Notre-Dame de Paris see *The Hunchback of Notre Dame*
Noyce, Phillip 3
Nye, Robert A. 56n.18

Occupation (German, of France) 203, 208n.11
Oates, Warren 249
Ocean's Eleven series (film) 5, 6; *Ocean's Eleven* (2001) 6; *Ocean's Thirteen* (2007) 5
Odyssey (epic poem) 30, 37n.9, 83
Oedipus complex 89
Oland, Warner 125n.19
Oliver, Edna May 109
Oltean, Tudor 30, 34, 36
Once Upon a Time in China series (film) (Hong Kong) 26, 256n.4

One-Armed Swordsman series (film) (Hong Kong) 26, 241–45, 255, 257n.7, 258nn.11, 14; *The New One-Armed Swordsman* (1971) 243; *The One-Armed Swordsman* (1967) 243; *The Return of the One-Armed Swordsman* (1969) 243
One Who Loves Will Take the Bride Away/*Dilwale Dulhaniya Le Jaayenge* (1995) 281
Onésime series (film) (France) 49
ordination 117; *see also* subordination
originals (and originality) 4, 5, 8, 9, 17n.17, 23, 27, 33, 34, 42, 54, 57, 59, 86
Osborne, John 137
Otto, Götz 135
The Outlaw Josey Wales (1976) 63
Ozu Yasujirō 217

Pacino, Al 259n.24
palimpsestic mode 273, 289n.19
Pallette, Eugene 254, 260n.37
Panama Hattie (1942) 111, 125n.21
Paramount Studios 140
Pardes see *Foreign Country*
The Parent Trap (1961) 178
Parish, James Robert 9, 109, 112, 116
parody 31, 35, 86, 88, 90, 110, 229, 236, 238
parousia 161
Parrish, Robert 155n.1
Patel, B.J. 288nn.6, 10
paternity 159, 163
Pathé (French film studio) 49
Pathé Communications 139
patriarchy 12, 72, 73, 81, 88, 122, 159, 163, 164, 165, 167, 173, 176nn.4, 5
Patriot Games (1992) 3
Pattes blanches see *White Paws*
Pearce, Guy 258n.21
Pearson, Roberta 42
Peckinpah, Sam 249, 250, 259n.25
"pedagogic" mode 272, 289n.16
Pellucidar series (novels) 60, 71
penny dreadfuls 29
Pera, Pia 33
"performative" mode 272, 289n.16
peritext 56n.15
Perret, Léonce 47
Perry Mason series (film) 9
Personal (1904) 40
Peter III (tsar of Russia) 193
The Petrified Forest (1936) 243
"phallic code" 148–149
Phantom series (comic strip) 254, 260n.39
Phéline, Christian 56n.18
Pherecydes of Leros 101n.5
The Philadelphia Story (1940) 111
Philippi, Siegfried 181
Philo Vance series (film) 16n.6
Pinewood Studios 135, 137, 139
Pirola, Paul 290n.29
Pitts, Michael R. 9, 124n.10
Planet of the Apes series (film) 219

Plautus 84, 85, 86, 87, 90, 92, 93, 94, 100
Pokémon series (film) (Japan) 210, 212, 220
Pompadour, Madame de 193, 195
Poon, Phoebe 260n.44
popular culture 31, 32, 33, 34, 35, 42, 57, 58, 63, 130, 131, 147, 211, 212, 213, 226, 228, 236, 237, 238, 247, 266, 267, 268, 269
popular entertainments 39, 41, 42, 236
popular film 13–15, 26, 130, 131, 147, 152, 211, 273, 285
Possession (2002) 4
postcolonial period (India) 265, 268, 269, 270, 271, 283, 286
postcolonial subjectivity 264, 286
postmodernism 274
Potter, H.C. 110
Pottier, Richard 197, 198, 200, 205
Powell, Dick 125n.20
Powell, William 16n.6, 123nn.2, 7
Power, Tyrone 253, 254, 256n.3, 260n.38
Prasad, T. 288n.8
Preminger, Otto 13, 198
La Presse (Paris) 28
Preston, Robert 243
Pretty Woman (1990) 4
Pride and Prejudice (novel) 5
Priestman, Martin 30
Priyadarshan 284
prodigality 14, 241–46, 251–55, 257n.9, 259n.32
product placement 139, 140, 141
Production Code 121, 126n.26, 128nn.37, 38; *see also* Breen, Joseph; Hays Office
production practices (film) 1, 2, 3, 4, 6, 7, 8, 12, 13–14, 40, 49, 106, 108, 115, 118, 124n.11, 131, 135, 136, 144, 145, 200
programmers 126n.28
The Psychology of Imagination (book) 289n.17
Pulgasari (1985) 212
Puzo, Mario 250, 251, 259n.30
Pyarelal 288n.6

race 65, 66–68, 72, 75, 76
racial stereotypes 97
Radhakant 288nn.6, 10
Ragland, Rags 111
Raimi, Sam 4, 5
Raj Kapoor series (film) (India) 270–75, 286, 287; *The Country in Which the River Ganga Flows/Jis Desh Mein Ganga Behti Hai* (1960) 271; *Mr. 420/Shri 420* (1955) 270, 271, 272, 273; *My Name Is Joker/Mera Naam Joker* (1970) 271, 272; *The Unwise/Anari* (1959) 271, 272; *Vagabond/Awaara* (1951) 270, 272, 273, 275, 287
Ram Gopal Verma Ki Aag (2007) 284
Rambo series (film) 268
Ramsay, F.U. 290n.24
Ramsay, Kiram 290n.24
Ramsay, Shyam 290n.24
Ramsay, Tulsi 290n.24

Index

Ramsay Bros. (Hindi film production company) 281, 290n.24
Rank Organization 137
Rashōmon (1950) 217
Rasila, Ram 288n.6
Raspe, Rudolf Erich 178, 192, 193
Rathbone, Basil 31
Ratner, Brett 3
Rawal, Paresh 285
Ray, Robert B. 105–106
readaptation *see* adaptation
reader response criticism 81
readers (and reading strategies) 25–27, 34, 36n.8, 46, 51, 81, 82, 95, 147, 202
Reagan, Ronald 159, 160, 173, 174
Reagan era 12, 159, 160, 162, 163, 167
realism 265, 274
"reception shift" 42
"recycling" (of film material) 2, 3, 4, 16nn.5, 11, 30
The Red Beret (1953) 136
Red Dust (1932) 110, 121, 124nn.10, 17; 126n.27
Reeves, Steve 59
Regel, Helmut 183
relation homosexuée 98
remakes 2, 3, 4, 5, 8, 9, 15n.4, 37n.16, 124n.16, 242, 284, 287
Rentschler, Eric 179, 180, 186, 194
repetition compulsion 23, 24
The Replacement Killers (1998) 258n.19
resistance (as a strategy) 81
Rice, Florence 108
Richardson, Tony 137
Richie, Donald 212, 215, 225–26, 234
Ride the High Country (1962) 259n.25
Rieder, John 176nn.3, 7
Riefenstahl, Leni 172, 174, 182, 184
Rigadin series (film) (France) 49, 50
"Rip Van Winkle" (story) 41
Rip Van Winkle (early silent film scenes) (1896) 41; *Awakening of Rip* 55n.9; *Rip and the Dwarf* 55n.9; *Rip Leaving Sleepy Hollow* 55n.9; *Rip Meeting the Dwarf* 55n.9; *Rip Passing Over the Hill* 55n.9; *Rip's Toast* 55n.9; *Rip's Toast to Hudson and Crew* 55n.9; *Rip's Twenty Years' Sleep* 55n.9
RKO Radio Pictures 32, 37n.16, 123nn.2, 7
Road to ... series (film) 9, 26
Robinson, Phil Alden 3
Robinson, Thelma 121, 128n.39
Robinson Crusoe (novel) 41
The Rock (1996) 134
Rodan/Radon (1956) 215
Rogers, Ginger 8
Rollerball (2002) 3
roman breton ("courtly romance") 30–31
Le Roman de Renart (tales) 31, 37n.13
roman engagé 203, 208n.10
roman-feuilleton 29, 37nn.11, 12; 51, 205, 206, 207, 208n.13
Roman Holiday (1953) 214
Romantic era 62
Rooney, Mickey 7
Rosalie series (film) (France) 49, 50
Rosenbloom, Max "Slapsie Maxie" 125n.19
Roshan, Rakesh 17n.17, 285, 290n.27
Roth, Lane 176n.3
Rowling, J.K. 33, 37n.18
Ruben, J. Walter 108, 121, 123n.6
"runaway" productions 136
Running Out of Time (1999) 256n.4
Running Out of Time 2 (2001) 256n.4
Rural bandit series (film) (India) 265, 288n.7; *Daku Mangal Singh* (1966) 288n.7; *Daku Mansingh* (1971) 288n.7; *Sultana Daku* (1972) 288n.7
Russo-Turkish war 192
Rustan series (film) (India) 265, 288n.10; *Champion/Rustam* (1982) 288n.10; *Rustam of Baghdad/Rustam-e-Baghdad* (1963) 288n.10; *Rustam of India/Rustam-e-Hind* (1965) 288n.10; *Rustam of Rome/Rustam-e-Rome* (1964) 288n.10
Ryuhei Kitamura 216

Sadoul, Georges 55nn.4, 11
Sahni, Sonia 288n.5
Saint series (film) 32, 37n.15, 37n.16, 120, 133; *The Saint Strikes Back* (1939) 123n.2; *The Saint Takes Over* (1940) 32, 37n.16, 123n.2
Saint-Laurent, Cécil 199, 201, 203, 207
saint-poet movies 289n.13; *Chandidas* (1932, 1934) 289n.13; *Kabir, the Devotee/Bhakta Kabir* (1942) 289n.13; *Meera* (1945) 289n.13; *Saint Dnyaneshwar/Sant Dnyaneshwar* (1940) 289n.13; *Saint Sakhu/Sant Sakhu* (1941) 289n.13; *Saint Tukaram/Sant Tukaram* (1936) 289n.13; *Saint Tulsidas/Sant Tulsidas* (1934, 1939) 289n.13; *Surdas, the Devotee/Bhakta Surdas* (1942) 289n.13
Le Salaire de la peur see The Wages of Fear
Salim-Javed 272
Saltzman, Harry 137, 138
Samson (1964) 288n.8
Sanders, George 32, 37n.16, 123n.2
Sangram (1965) 288n.8
sans-culottes 202, 203, 208n.8
Santoshi, Raj Kumar 289n.20
Sarankant 265
Sarris, Andrew 145
Sartre, Jean-Paul 203, 289n.17
Satō Tadao 218, 220
Sazie, Léon 51
Scarface (1932) 118
The Scarlet Empress (1934) 194
Scary Movie series (film) 37n.20
Schatz, Thomas 109, 124n.12
Schlesinger, Arthur, Jr. 162
Schulte-Sasse, Linda 179, 180, 185, 186, 191, 194
Schultz, Margie 108

Schuster, Harold D. 58
Scooby-Doo (2002) 4, 16n.9
Scorsese, Martin 256n.4
Scott, Gordon 59, 60
Scott, Ridley 3
Scott, Sir Walter 62
Scream series (film) 37n.20
Second World (culture, society, texts, etc.) 266, 288n.11
Seinfeld, Jerry 15n.2
Seitz, George B. 7
Self Defense Forces 225–26
Selleck, Tom 8
Selpin, Herbert 189
Selznick, David O. 144, 199
sequels 1–9, 17n.17, 29, 33, 50, 63, 107, 241, 243, 244, 249, 254, 257n.7, 263, 290n.27
serial production 28, 83, 219
seriality 10, 28, 30, 34, 37n.9, 85, 86, 241, 242, 243, 244; *see also* seriesicity
serialized novel 28, 29, 37n.12
serials 3, 16n.7, 17n.17, 22–23, 28, 34, 35, 37n.10, 50, 53, 63, 86, 144, 237, 242, 258n.12
series 1–15, 17n.17, 21–36, 37nn.10, 11; 49, 50, 53, 57, 63, 82, 86, 88, 95, 96, 97, 106–110, 112, 116, 118–120, 128n.37, 210, 219, 220, 250, 257n.7, 258n.12, 263, 264, 269, 270, 279, 287, 289n.15, 290n.27; *see also specific series*
seriesicity 10, 30; *see also* seriality
Servado, Gaia 257n.8
The Seven Samurai/Shichi-nin no samurai (1954) 217
Seven Years' War 182, 183, 185, 186, 193
Sévigny, Madame de 30
"sexist code" 148–49
Shahnama (epic poem) 265, 288n.9
Shamseer, A. 265, 288n.6
Shankar, Ravi 276
Sharma, Rameshwar 289n.13
Shastri, Lal Bahadur (prime minister of India) 276, 278
Shaw Brothers Studio 242, 258n.14
Shek, Dean 244, 249, 258n.11
Shelley, Mary Wollstonecraft 8
Sheorey, Roop K. 265
Sherlock Holmes series (film) 31, 32, 133; *Sherlock Holmes in Washington* (1943) 32
Sherlock Holmes series (novels) 24, 32, 33, 43
Shetty, Sunil 285
The Shield of Herakles (poem) 83, 101n.4
Shilling, Mark 227, 231, 232, 235, 237
Shintōhō (Japanese film studio) 218
Shochiku (Japanese film studio) 211, 218, 228, 234, 237
Sholay see *Flames*
Shoot the Piano Player (1960) 205, 208n.4
Shōwa (Godzilla series) 215, 216, 219; *see also* Godzilla series

Shrek 2 (2004) 155n.3
Silverman, Deborah Anders 260n.42
Simi 288n.5
Simmons, Bob 145
Simonet, Thomas 2, 15n.1
Sinclair, Robert B. 108
Singh, Bhagat 275
Singh, Dara 265, 288nn.5, 10
Singh, Madan Gopal 289n.14
Singular Travels, Campaigns, and Adventures of Baron Münchhausen (book) 178
Siodmak, Robert 258n.17
Sippy, Ramesh 284
Siu-Tung Ching 256n.4
Sivan, Pierre 13
Skelton, Red 111
Snyder, Gary 169
Sobchak, Thomas 123n.1
Soderbergh, Steven 5, 6, 17n.14
Solaris (2002) 6
Soni, Shantilal 265
Sontag, Susan 212
Sony Corporation 139, 140
Sophocles 101n.5
Sorcerer (1977) 5
Sothern, Ann 31, 36, 108–109, 111–112, 121, 123nn.5, 7, 9; 126n.25
The Sound of Music (1965) 132
Southey, Robert 62
Souvestre, Pierre *see* Allain, Marcel
spectators (and spectatorship) 34, 46, 52, 53, 75, 77, 81, 82, 85, 91, 92, 93, 95, 96, 97, 105, 114, 116, 117, 119, 120, 121; *see also* audience
Speed (1994) 134
"Speed Racer" series (television) (Japan) 212
Spider-Man series (film) 4, 5, 16n.9, 63; *Spider-Man* (2002) 4; *Spider-Man 3* (2007) 5
Spider-Man (hero and comics) 63
Spielberg, Steven 37n.20, 138, 144, 160, 161, 162, 170, 176n.7
Spinell, Joe 250
spin-offs 2, 64
Spottiswoode, Roger 145, 155n.1
Stage Door (1937) 111
Staiger, Janet 55n.10
Stalin-Ribbentrop Pact 186
star system 11, 31, 48, 49, 53
Star Trek series (film) 3, 133, 140
"Star Trek" series (television) 32–33
Star Wars series (film) 12, 16n.6, 60, 63, 132, 133, 140, 158–174, 175n.2, 176nn.3, 5; 243, 266, 267; *Star Wars* (1977) 132, 138, 143, 158, 159, 164, 175n.2 (see also *Star Wars: Episode IV—A New Hope*); *Star Wars: Episode I—The Phantom Menace* (1999) 155n.3, 158, 171, 173, 175n.2; *Star Wars: Episode II—Attack of the Clones* (2002) 170, 171, 172, 174, 176n.3; *Star Wars: Episode III—Revenge of the Sith* (2005) 158, 159, 168, 171, 174, 175, 175n.2; *Star Wars: Episode*

IV—A New Hope (reissue title of *Star Wars* 1994) 12, 158, 159, 162, 163, 172, 174, 175n.2, 176nn.2, 3 (see also *Star Wars*); *Star Wars: Episode V—The Empire Strikes Back* (1980) 159, 165, 176n.2; *Star Wars: Episode VI—The Return of the Jedi* (1983) 158, 159, 166, 172, 176n.3
Starship Troopers (1997) 140
Staver, Frank 125n.18
Steinhoff, Hans 181
Stella Dallas (1937) 118
Sternberg, Josef von 194
Stevens, George 122
Stoker, Bram 8
Storey, John 77
A Story in Arabesque (book) 178, 187
The Story of a Discharged Prisoner (1967) 242
subordination 107
subversion 24, 105
Sue, Eugène 258n.12
The Sum of All Fears (2002) 3
"Super Sentai" series (television) (Japan) *see* Mighty Morphin' Rangers series
superhero 11, 59, 60, 63, 64, 69, 75, 76, 78, 103n.26
"Superman" series (comic books) 22, 25, 27, 63
Superman series (film) 17n.18, 63, 285
Suzuki, D.T. 169
Switching Channels (1988) 124n.16
"symbolic blockage" 82, 93
syuzhet 45, 46, 47, 55n.13

A Tale of Two Cities (early silent film adaptation) 47
Talk to Her (2002) 16n.11
tamagotchi franchise 212
Tamahori, Lee 146, 155n.1
Tan Sor-hoon 247
Tanaka Tomoyuki 213, 214, 223, 227
Tarkovsky, Andrei 6, 17n.14
Tarzan series (Hindi cinema) 265; *Hurricane Tarzan/Toofani Tarzan* (1937) 265; *Rocket Tarzan* (1963) 288n.6; *Tarzan and Circus* (1965) 288n.6; *Tarzan and Cobra* (1988) 288n.6; *Tarzan and Delilah* (1964) 288n.6; *Tarzan and Gorilla* (1963) 288n.6; *Tarzan and Hercules* (1966) 288n.6; *Tarzan and King Kong* (1965) 265, 288n.6; *Tarzan and the Magic Lamp/Tarzan aur Jadui Chirag* (1966) 288n.6; *Tarzan Comes to Delhi* (1965) 265, 288n.6; *Tarzan in Fairyland/Tarzan Paristan Mein* (1968) 288n.6; *Tarzan Mera Saathi* (1962) 288n.6; *Tarzan 303* (1970) 288n.6; *Tarzan's Beloved/Tarzan ki Mehbooba* (1966) 288n.6; *Tarzan's Daughter/Tarzan ki Beti* (1938) 265
Tarzan series (Hollywood cinema) 11, 57–60, 64, 65, 68, 69, 72–78, 133, 285; *Tarzan and His Mate* (1934) 73, 74, 75; *Tarzan and the Amazons* (1945) 74; *Tarzan the Ape Man* (1932) 74; *Tarzan and the Huntress* (1947) 74; *Tarzan and the Lost Safari* (1957) 58, 74; *Tarzan and the Trappers* (1958) 59; *Tarzan Escapes* (1936) 73, 74, 75; *Tarzan Finds a Son* (1939) 73, 74; *Tarzan's Desert Mystery* (1943) 74; *Tarzan's Fight for Life* (1958) 58–59; *Tarzan's Greatest Adventure* (1959) 59; *Tarzan's Hidden Jungle* (1955) 58; *Tarzan's New York Adventure* (1942) 73, 74, 75; *Tarzan's Secret Treasure* (1941) 74
Tarzan series (novels) 11, 57–61, 63–72, 74–78; *The Return of Tarzan* 66, 67, 70, 71, 74; *Tarzan and the Ant Men* 71; *Tarzan and the City of Gold* 75; *Tarzan and the Foreign Legion* 71; *Tarzan and the Golden Lion* 71; *Tarzan and the Jewels of Opar* 71, 74; *Tarzan and the Lost Empire* 71; *Tarzan at the Earth's Core* 71; *Tarzan, Lord of the Jungle* 71; *Tarzan of the Apes* 57, 65, 67, 72; *Tarzan the Terrible* 71; *Tarzan the Untamed* 59, 70, 71, 74
Taves, Brian 126n.28
television 8, 25, 32, 63, 242
Ten Nights in a Bar-Room (film in episodes) 41; *Death of Little Mary* (1901) 41; *Death of Slade* (1901) 41; *The Fatal Blow* (1901) 41; *Murder of Willie* (1901) 41; *Vision of Mary* (1901) 41
Ten Nights in a Bar Room (play) 41
The Terror (Reign of) 203
Terror by Night (1946) 32
texts (open vs. closed) 25, 27, 36n.8
The Theogony (poem) 83, 101n.4
There's Always a Woman (1938) 108
Thiele, Wilhelm 74
Thin Man series (film) 7, 9, 16n.6, 108, 116, 123n.2, 133
Third Reich 178, 179, 185
Third World (culture, society, texts) 266, 267, 268, 288n.11; *see also* First World
This Gun for Hire (1942) 243
Thomas, Lowell 66–67
Thomas, William C. 128n.35
Thompson, Kristin 18n.25
Thorpe, Richard 73, 74, 124n.9
Three Colors trilogy 8; *Three Colors: Blue/Trois Couleurs: Bleu* (1993) 8; *Three Colors: Red/Trois Couleurs: Rouge* (1994) 8; *Three Colors: White/Trois Couleurs: Blanc* (1994) 8
Three Faces West (1940) 111
Three Hearts for Julia (1943) 123n.7
Thumin, Janet 152
Ti Lung 241, 242, 243, 244, 245, 256n.6, 257n.7
Tien Feng 243, 245
Tinling, James 111
Tirez sur le pianiste see *Shoot the Piano Player*
Titanic (1997) 155n.3
To, Johnnie 256n.4
Der Tod in Venedig see *Death in Venice*
Todorov, Tzvetan 17n.15
Toei Studios (Japan) 218

Tōhō Studios (Japan) 211, 212, 213, 215, 216, 218, 219, 220, 221, 227
Toler, Sidney 125n.19
Tolkien, J.R.R. 63, 176n.3
Tom Butler (1912) 52
Tom Jones (1963) 136
Tone, Franchot 108
Tora-san (*otoko wa tsurai yo*) series (film) (Japan) 12–14, 24, 210, 211, 227–39; *Tora-san, Our Lovable Tramp/Otoko wa tsurai yo* (1969) 228; *Tora-san, the Matchmaker/Otoko wa tsurai yo: Tonderu Torajirō* (1979) 229; *Tora-san's Easy Advice / Otoko wa tsurai yo: Haikei, Torajirō-sama* (1994) 234; *Tora-san's Love Call / Otoko wa tsurai yo: Torajirō koiuta* (1971) 233; *Tora-san's Tropical Fever / Otoko wa tsurai yo: Torajirō haibisukasu no hana* (1980) 229
"Tora-san" series (television) (Japan) 228
Tora-san trivia show (television) (Japan) 237
Torchy Blane series (film) 21–22, 24, 35, 36, 36n.3, 109, 110, 122, 123n.4, 124n.13, 128n.41; *The Adventurous Blonde* (1937) 36nn.1, 2; *Torchy Runs for Mayor* (1939) 21
Torgovnick, Marianna 67
Torrance, Richard 232, 234, 235, 236
Torrid Zone (1940) 110
Torry, Robert 12
Trade Winds (1938) 108, 110
Traffic (2000) 6
transvestism 89, 90, 102nn.13, 14, 15; 124n.13
The Treasure of the Sierra Madre (1948) 58
Tremaine, Jeff 4
Trenck, Franz 189, 190
Trenck, Friedrich von der 189, 190
Trenck, der Pandur see *Trenck the Pandour*
Trenck the Pandour (1940) 189
triads 14, 17n.17, 246, 247, 249, 253, 257nn.8, 10
Triumph des Willens see *Triumph of the Will*
Triumph of the Will (1935) 174, 182
Les Trois mousquetaires: La vengeance de Milady see *Vengeance of the Three Musketeers*
True Colors of the Hero/Ying hung boon sik (1986) 242
True Lies (1994) 134, 140
Truffaut, François 205
Tsang, Kenneth 247, 248, 258n.19
Tsivian, Yuri 43
Tsuburaya, Eiji 214
Tsui Hark 241, 242, 243, 244, 250, 251, 253, 256n.4, 257n.7
Tsutsui, William 13–14, 213
Turlupin 31
Twentieth Century–Fox 125n.19, 140, 155n.5
The Twenty-Four Eyes/Niju-shi no hitomi (1954) 217
Twin Pawns (1919) 47
2 Fast 2 Furious (2003) 7
Two Years Under the Ground/Do Gaz Zameen Ke Neeche (1972) 290n.24

Ucicky, Gustav 181, 182
Ufa (German film studios) 178
Umrao Jaan (1981, 2006) 284
Uncle Tom's Cabin (1903) 41, 55n.10
Uncle Tom's Cabin (novel) 41, 55n.10
United Artists 131, 135, 137, 138, 139, 154n.1
United International Pictures (UIP) 155n.5
United States v. Paramount Pictures, Inc. 135
Universal Studios 8, 32
upscaling 5, 6, 16n.13
d'Urfé, Honoré 30
Uricchio, William 42
Utz, Richard 77

Vaidya, R.N. 288n.2
The Vampire Bat (1933) 125n.18
Van Dyke, W.S. 74
Varan the Unbelievable/Daikaijū Baran (1958) 215
vaudeville 41, 42; *see also* popular entertainments
Vengeance (1970) 256n.6
Vengeance of the Three Musketeers (1961) 201
Venus series (novels) 60, 71
Verite Productions 290n.29
Verma, Ram Gopal 284
Verzea, Ileana 258n.12
Vichy Régime 203
Victorian era 61, 62, 63, 64, 65, 71
Vidor, King 118
La Vieille fille (novel) 28
Vietnam 160, 161, 162, 163, 164, 169, 170, 176n.4, 243
Virgil 60
Virilio, Paul 179
Vitagraph 47
Vitascope 39
Voltaire 181, 184
Vora, Neeraj 279
Vorhaus, Bernard 111

Wadia, Homi 264, 265, 288n.2
The Wages of Fear (1953) 5
Waise Lee 245
Walsh, Andrea 124n.15, 127nn.30, 33
Walz, Robin 55nn.12, 14
Wang, Wayne 9
Wang Yu, Jimmy 243, 244
The War of the Worlds (2005) 37n.20
Warner Bros. 16n.12, 101n.2, 140, 213
Warren, Joseph 170
Warsi, Arshad 285
Warwick Pictures 136
Washington, George 185
Watergate 160, 162, 163
Watts, Alan 169
Webber, Peter 3
Weimar era 181, 182
Weintraub, Sy 58
Weissmuller, Johnny 58, 59, 60, 74, 133
West, Mae 123n.5

Index

Westfahl, Gary 37n.17
Wetmore, Kevin, Jr. 176n.8
Whale, James 125n.18
White Oleander (2002) 4
White Paws (1949) 199
The Wild Bunch (1969) 249, 250, 253, 259n.25
Wilhelm II (emperor of Germany and king of Prussia) 183
Williams, Tony 256n.4, 260n.41
Wills, Gary 163
Wilson, Michael G. 140
Wilson, Woodrow 63
Win-chiat Lee 260n.45
Winthrop, John 160
Wiseman, Len 5
The Wizard of Oz (1939) 178, 188, 189, 195
woman (representation of) 71, 72, 73, 112, 113, 116, 119, 122, 149, 152–53, 205–206, 247, 288nn.2, 3
The Woman in Green (1945) 32
The Woman in White (novel) 47
Woman of the Year (1942) 122
The Women (1939) 111
Wong Feihong series (film) *see* Huang Feihong series
Woo, John 241, 242, 243, 244, 247, 249, 250, 251, 252, 253, 255, 256, 256nn.3, 5, 7; 258n.22, 260nn.34, 35, 36
Wood, Robin 147, 159
Woodfall Films 137
Woollacott, Janet 141, 148
Wooster, Arthur 145
Working Girl (1988) 4
World War I 181, 183
World War II 12, 108, 111, 112, 113, 119, 121, 122, 127n.32, 128n.40, 159, 162, 163, 164, 167, 169, 176n.4, 208n.11, 210, 214, 220, 222, 225, 226, 228, 233, 235

Wright, Will 147
Wunderbare Reisen zu Wasser und zu Lande see *Marvelous Travels on Water and Land*

X le mystérieux 52
X2: X-Men United (2003) 7

Y Tu Mamá También (2001) 16n.11
Yamada Yōji 228, 230, 233, 236, 238
Yates, David 5
Yoshikuni Igarashi 213
Young, Robert 114
Young, Terence 22, 145, 146, 154n.1, 155n.1
"Young general" (*wakadaisho*) series 210
You're Only Young Once (1937) 7
Yours, Angélique (book) 201

Zane, Billy 260n.39
Zanger, Jules 71
Zarak (1957) 136
Zatoichi series (film) 210
Zee Horror Show (television) (India) 290n.24
Zelnick, Friedrich 181
Zeman, Karel 187
Zeta-Jones, Catherine 241, 254, 258n.12, 260n.40
Zévaco, Michel 201, 208n.6
Zigomar series (silent film) 50, 51, 52
Zimmerman, Patricia 176n.7
Zinnemann, Fred 259n.29
Zizek, Slavoj 179
Zorro series (film) 14, 242, 245, 253, 254, 255, 256n.3, 260nn.38, 40; *The Legend of Zorro* (2005) 245, 254–55; *The Mark of Zorro* (1920) 253, 256n.3; *The Mark of Zorro* (1940) 245, 254, 256n.3; *The Mask of Zorro* (1998) 250, 254, 255

www.ingramcontent.com/pod-product-compliance
Ingram Content Group UK Ltd.
Pitfield, Milton Keynes, MK11 3LW, UK
UKHW041924140426
5217IPUK00014B/306